The Religion of

THE RELIGION OF PROTESTANTS

The Church in English Society 1559–1625

The Ford Lectures 1979

PATRICK COLLINSON

CLARENDON PRESS · OXFORD

Oxford University Press, Walton Street, Oxford OX2 6DP

Oxford New York Toronto
Delhi Bombay Calcutta Madras Karachi
Petaling Jaya Singapore Hong Kong Tokyo
Nairobi Dar es Salaam Cape Town
Melbourne Auckland
and associated companies in
Beirut Berlin Ibadan Nicosia

Published in the United States by
Oxford University Press, New York

First published 1982
First issued as a paperback 1984
Reprinted 1985, 1988

British Library Cataloguing in Publication Data
Collinson, Patrick
The religion of Protestants: the church in English society 1559–1625.
1. Protestantism—History   2. England—Church history—16th century
3. England—Church history—17th century
I. Title
280'.4'0942055 BR756
ISBN 0–19–820053–6 (pbk.)

Library of Congress Cataloging in Publication Data
Collinson, Patrick.
The religion of Protestants.
(The Ford lectures; 1979)
Includes bibliographical references and index.
1. Church of England—History.   2. England—Church history—17th century.
I. Title. II. Series.
BX5070.C58   283'.42   81–217110
ISBN 0–19–820053–6 (pbk)

Printed in Great Britain by
J. W. Arrowsmith Ltd., Bristol

For Liz, Helen, Andrew, Sarah, and Stephen

Preface

This book contains a modified and somewhat extended version of the Ford Lectures delivered in the University of Oxford in Hilary Term 1979. *The Religion of Protestants,* the title of these lectures, was not an original invention. The patent is held by the seventeenth-century controversialist William Chillingworth, author of a book which caused a stir when it was published at Oxford in 1638, *The Religion of Protestants a Safe Way to Salvation.*[1] In a dedicatory epistle to King Charles I, Chillingworth apologized for his insufficiency, 'not doubting but upon this Dedication I shall be censur'd for a double boldenesse, both for undertaking so great a Work, so far beyond my weak abilities, and againe, for presenting it to such a Patron, whose judgement I ought to fear more then any Adversary'. Substitute for Chillingworth's royal patron the University of Oxford and any historian elected on Mr Ford's foundation will share his worries. Chillingworth had the advantage of an Oxford birth and an Oxford degree. He was the godson of one of Oxford's greatest sons and benefactors, Archbishop William Laud. But I came to Oxford as an outsider whose formation and employment has been in other universities. I even had to ask the way to the Examination Schools where the lectures were given. But if I was a stranger, Oxford took me in, listened with courtesy to what I had to say, and entertained me generously. Even my ungracious strictures on Chillingworth's godfather were heard without visible signs

---

[1] Lord Edward Conway wrote to his brother-in-law Sir Robert Harley, 18 November 1637: 'Here is new comme out a booke mutch commended written by Mr Chillingworth against the Papists. That whitch I have read of him is very sharpe in gentle wordes, soe that it seemes we are not goeing to Rome, whither soever else we are goeing. It may be we shall make somme new discovery.' (BL Loan 29/172, fol. 172.)

of offence by Laud's biographer, Lord Dacre, who as Hugh Trevor-Roper and Regius professor introduced me to my audience and attended to my needs. Nor did they exclude me from the doors of Laud's own college, St. John's, where Sir Richard Southern saw to it that I had regular hospitality, although this obliged me to look with some misgivings from the windows of the President's Lodging at the crowns and mitres capping the very drain pipes of Canterbury Quad, Laud's creation. In short, the thanks which I owe to the University of Oxford for the signal honour of my election and for the warmth of the hospitality offered by the university and by several of its worthies are all the more heartfelt for the sense which came upon me of a certain antipathy between the matter of my discourse and all that Oxford used to stand for.

Chillingworth himself deserves an apology for the theft and misappropriation of the phrase immortalized in his famous aphorism: 'The Bible, the Bible only I say, is the religion of Protestants.' This dictum is profoundly true of the religion of the Elizabethan and Jacobean Church, but not quite in the sense which Chillingworth intended. This book does not offer safe ways to salvation. Theologically, it preserves what I take to be the historian's proper neutrality and even indifference. But confronting the climate of the early seventeenth century I feel bound to depict as almost peripheral both the High Church of Laud and the incipient Broad Church of Chillingworth and his friends of the Great Tew circle, who believed before its due time in the principle of free and rational biblical enquiry. The religion of protestants to be found in these studies is far from excluding what other historians, especially in America, would describe as the religion of puritans. In so far as this book is contentious, two perceptions are contended for. One concerns the unreservedly protestant character of the Elizabethan and Jacobean religious establishment. The other finds this in no way detrimental to the integrity and stability, especially of the Jacobean Church of England. The sometimes deceptive advantage of reading history backwards has made it difficult to appreciate that Church as it appeared to its contemporaries and defenders, and even as it evidently (Ranke's 'eigentlich') was. The immediate sequel of extreme instability and, in the 1640s, collapse has robbed the early seventeenth-century Church of its intrinsic merits, reducing it to an aspect of what Christopher Hill has called 'pre-revolutionary England'. The subsequent, post-revolutionary history of a Church of England erected on narrower and more exclusive principles has deceived historians into reading the ecclesiastical history of the Jacobean age against a standard of Anglicanism which is anachronistic. Moreover, the more recent, Victorian 'restoration' of all but a handful of church fabrics, a symbol of many other changes, has destroyed architectural and as it were archaeological evidence of the temper of the Church of the Elizabethan and Jacobean religious settlements. From these and other historically irrelevant circumstances has arisen the damaging mistake of writing the history of that Church in the anachronistically dichotomous terms of an Anglicanism not yet conceived and an alien puritanism not yet clearly disowned.

One path of escape from these false perspectives would be to focus on the concern of so many Jacobean Englishmen, perhaps their greatest concern, to defend the integrity of the protestant church and nation against what was perceived to be a fearful popish enemy, partly intestine, partly identified with the pope himself and the powers of catholic Europe. We must not forget the militancy of the religion of protestants, the spirit expressed by Sir John Eliot when he told the 1629 Parliament that the only novel ceremony he favoured was to recite the Creed standing erect, preferably with drawn sword in hand.[2] An account of the Elizabethan and Jacobean Church which dwells so much upon institutional equilibrium that it omits consideration of that seismic disequilibrium, the great religious divide of the age, may be thought to suffer from its own blind spots. But I have left it to other books which

---

[2] 'Some of these, Sir, you know are Masters of Ceremonies, and they labour to introduce new ceremonies into the Church. Some ceremonies are useful; give me leave to join in one that I hold both necessary and commendable, that at the repetition of the Creed we should stand up, to testify the resolution of our hearts, that we would defend the Religion we profess; and in some Churches it is added, that they did not only stand upright with their bodies, but with their swords drawn; and if cause were, to defend our Prince, Country, and Religion, I hope we should draw our swords against all opposers.' (*Commons Debates for 1629,* ed. Wallace Notestein and Frances Helen Relf (Minneapolis, 1921), p. 27.)

have already appeared or are likely to appear to explore the emerging tradition of anti-catholicism and the potent apocalyptic ideology which served to sustain it. And if I have not falsified the perspective, I have certainly artificially limited it by writing as if the English Church in this period was self-sufficient and self-contained, whereas its members, or many of them, were not only conscious of their wider participation in the multinational Reformed Church but also challenged and, increasingly scandalized by the implications for their own Church of persecution and war in France, the Netherlands, and, later, the Palatinate. I have not, I hope, altogether forgotten these important dimensions of my subject. However, six lectures are not enough to cover everything and I have chosen to limit myself to certain aspects of the domestic economy of *Ecclesia Anglicana,* its prelates, ministers, magistrates, and people.

Consequently there may be those who will complain that whatever these essays address themselves to it is not the *religion* of protestants, if by religion is meant the living content of belief, whether expressed in theological formulations, liturgical symbols, or the experience and language of piety. The mainspring, they will say, is missing, so that this account of the religion of protestants is but the casing of the watch. Among the working parts which have been removed, or at least not scrutinized, are the great affirmations of the Christian gospel as protestants apprehended it: *sola scriptura, sola gratia,* and, above all, *sola fide,* the religion which in principle rested upon but in reality wrestled with the mystery of predestination, and which explored the rich implications of the covenant relationship between God and the elect. Beyond question, that was the heart of the matter, unless indeed we look beyond faith to the many insecurities and uncertainties of life which some would see as the ultimate source of the religious obsessions of the age. However, this book understands 'religion' in the sense of *religio,* the fabric of institutions, obligations, and rites which a visitor from ancient Rome would have recognized as comprising the publicly endorsed religion of Englishmen in this period.

Above all, these lectures are offered as no more than one historian's perceptions. But if it would be rash to claim any

exclusive or absolute validity for my interpretation of this
chapter of ecclesiastical history, it would be arrogant to
represent it as simply my own invention or property. It is most
unlikely that I would have come to see things as I do without
the stimulus and enlightenment freely given by many friends,
including former and present pupils and colleagues. Among
the small army of professional historians who share some of
my interests, I hope that it will not seem invidious to single
out the names of Gina Alexander, Molly Barratt, John Bossy,
Susan Brigden, the late James Cargill Thompson, Claire
Cross, Andrew Foster, Christopher Haigh, Felicity Heal,
Ralph Houlbrooke, Martin Ingram, Sybil Jack, Peter Lake,
Willie Lamont, Geoffrey Nuttall, Rosemary O'Day, Bill
Sheils, and George Yule. For assistance in finding my bearings
in the religion and politics of the early seventeenth century I
must thank the alleged revisionists, Conrad Russell and
Nicholas Tyacke. And I am deeply indebted to Keith Thomas,
not only for inspiration and guidance on more matters than I
care to count, but for subjecting the work which follows to a
kind but critical examination. The entire text was also read by
Nicholas Tyacke who corrected me on several points. Kenneth
Fincham was equally helpful with Chapters Two and Three. I
have learned many things from the many unpublished
dissertations which are cited in these pages and I am grateful
for access to them and permission to cite them. It will be
apparent that the work of Martin Ingram, Peter Lake, and
Diarmaid MacCulloch, and the research at present in progress
of Kenneth Fincham have been especially useful for my
purpose.

I remain indebted to the many libraries and archives whose
doors have been open to me for some thirty years, and to the
friendly co-operation of librarians and archivists which I have
acknowledged on earlier occasions. For much research specific
to this undertaking, I am deeply in debt to the Dean and
Chapter of Canterbury and to Ann Oakley, who presides over
the Cathedral Archives and Library. I am grateful to the
Universities of Aberdeen, East Anglia, Kent, and London
(King's College and University College) for allowing me to try
out versions of some of these lectures on receptive and friendly
audiences. And to my own University of Kent at Canterbury I

owe additional thanks for the grant of study leave in Michaelmas Term 1978, which enabled me to write the lectures. The finishing touches were put to the book while enjoying a further period of study leave in Trinity Term 1981. Thanks to the singular honour which the Warden and Fellows of All Souls paid me in electing me to a visiting fellowship, this final lick of paint was applied in Oxford, where I was no longer such a stranger. It was a very great advantage at this late stage to be in close proximity to the Oxford University Press, where I have met not only with the expert guidance which one is entitled to take for granted, but with much kindness as well.

All Souls College, Oxford   Trinity Sunday 1981

Contents

Receive wholesome instruction, thou that readest: be desirous to walke in the strait way, but yet in the right way, keepe measure and thou shalt hold within the compasse of a holy and godly meane. Beware of Superstition in Religion to decline on the left hand, and take heede of rash zeale to runne on the right hand; endevour to bee what thou oughtest to bee, though thou canst not attaine to that thou shouldest be. Goe even: be no Atheistical Securitane, nor Anabaptisticall Puritane: bee no carelesse Conformitant, nor yet preposterous Reformitant: be no neuterall Lutheran, nor Hereticall popish Antichristian; be not a Schismatical Brownist, nor fond and foolish Familist: be not a new Novelist, nor yet any proud and arrogant Sectarie to draw disciples after thee: be no follower of any such, beware of them all carefully. But stand a constant Protestant, in the ancient, Catholike, Orthodoxall veritie and truth. Bee to God faithfull, and to lawfull authoritie not disloyall. To conclude, hold the truth after the word, and gainsay not laudable customes of the Church, not against the word ... Seeke the publike quiet of that established estate under a Christian Governour, whether it be *Politicall* or *Ecclesiasticall,* where thou art a member ...

> Richard Bernard, *Christian advertisements and counsels of peace* (1608).

For is it not worke enough to preach unles we dispute also? or, if we must dispute, were it not better to unite our forces against those who oppose us in Fundamentalls then to be divided amongst our selves about Ceremonialls? Who can, without sorrowe and fear observe how Atheisme, Libertinisme, papisme, and Arminianisme, both at home and abroad have stolne in, and taken possession of the house, whilest we are at strife about the hangings and paintings of it? and the enimye strikes at the hearte whilest we buisy our selves in washing the face of this body. How much better would it beseeme us to combine together in an holy League against the common Adversary ...

> John Davenport to Alexander Leighton, *c.* 1625(?): *Letters of John Davenport Puritan Divine,* ed. I. M. Calder (New Haven, 1937).

Oh! what comfortable Times had we (through Gods mercy) before the wars!

> Thomas Froysell, *The beloved disciple: A sermon preached at the funerall of the Honorable Sir Robert Harley* (1658).

Chapter One

Monarchy and Prelacy

I

Royal supremacy and monarchical episcopacy can be considered as abstract and static principles, in a manner corresponding to the classical exposition of political thought, or to the study of past institutions through their constitutional symbols: the divine right of kings and the divine institution of bishops. On the subject of episcopacy there have been special motives in the Church of England for fixation on what might appear to be arid questions of title and pedigree. For Anglican apologists the mere possession of episcopacy, almost regardless of the use to which bishops have been put, has been a critical matter of their Church's credentials.[1] As for the royal supremacy, the preoccupation of historians with that subject has been a response to ineluctable fact, and to the force of Tudor propaganda. Having pronounced that 'by the goodness of Almighty God and his servant Elizabeth we are', Richard Hooker proposed to make this the emblem, inscription, style, and title for the English Church.[2]

More recently, these royal and episcopal principles have been brought to life and made to move about the stage, as scholars have read their way into the dense literature of post-Reformation apologetics and apocalyptics.[3] Liveliness was inherent in the entire process of the Reformation itself, which was not a legislative and administrative transaction tidily concluded by a religious settlement in 1559 but a profound cultural revolution which persisted throughout the period

[1] See the symposia, *Episcopacy Ancient and Modern*, ed. Claude Jenkins and K. D. Mackenzie (1930), and *The Apostolic Ministry: Essays on the History and Doctrine of Episcopacy*, ed. Kenneth E. Kirk (Oxford, 1946). See also A. J. Mason, *The Church of England and Episcopacy* (1914).

[2] *The Works of Richard Hooker*, ed. J. Keble (Oxford, 1874), ii. 9.

[3] W. M. Lamont, *Godly Rule: Politics and Religion 1603–60* (1969), and *Richard Baxter and the Millennium* (1979). The indebtedness of this chapter to William Lamont will be apparent to readers who know his work.

with which these studies are concerned. In a climate congenial to 'further reformation', monarchy and episcopacy were regarded not only as the guarantors of order and stability but as instruments of energetic and creative reform. Or it could be said that order itself was an elusive quarry to be pursued, or a treasure to be jealously guarded. The martyrologist John Foxe and his modern commentators[4] have done most to familiarize us with these features of Elizabethan and Jacobean mentality. Encountered in the closing pages of 'The Book of Martyrs', the near-martyr Queen Elizabeth was modelled on the Emperor Constantine, whom, Foxe told his readers, God had so stirred up that 'all his care and study of mind was set upon nothing else, but only how to benefit and enlarge the commodities' of the Church of God. In the same way Elizabeth, in her very person the 'amends and recompense, now to be made to England for the cruel days that were before', was ceaselessly careful and active, a chosen instrument of divine clemency who 'helpeth neighbours, reformeth religion, quencheth persecution, redresseth the dross, frameth things out of joint'.[5] These panegyrics were to reverberate to the point of resonance long after the great queen's death. In 1627 Christopher Lever wrote that 'her hands were ever working for the defence of the Faith, defending it at home, defending it abroad, for her selfe defending it, and defending it for others; ever in travell for this holy businesse'.[6] That this paragon took the conservative motto 'Semper Eadem' and consistently preferred the policies of inspired inaction is not the least of the contradictions of the Elizabethan polity.

James I's prodigious labours as theologian and controversialist lent greater plausibility to the claim of his chaplain, John

---

[4] John Foxe, *Acts and Monuments*, ed. S. R. Cattley, 8 vols. (1837–41). The essential bibliography includes J. F. Mozley's biography, *John Foxe and His Book* (1940), William Haller's interpretative study, *Foxe's Book of Martyrs and the Elect Nation* (1963), and the more sophisticated appraisal of sixteenth- and seventeenth-century apocalyptic undertaken in three more recent studies: Richard Bauckham, *Tudor Apocalypse,* Courtenay Library of Reformation Classics viii (Appleford, 1978); Paul Christianson, *Reformers and Babylon: English Apocalyptic Visions from the Reformation to the Eve of the Civil War* (Toronto, 1978); and Katherine Firth, *The Apocalyptic Tradition in Reformation Britain 1530–1645* (Oxford, 1979).

[5] Foxe, *Acts and Monuments*, i. 296; viii. 600–1.

[6] Christopher Lever, *The history of the defenders of the catholique faith* (1627), p. 337.

White, that he had purchased 'that reputation in God's Church, and honour with strangers, and authority with adversaries, and admiration with all which few princes since Constantine have had before'. But White reminds us that we are still in a world of millenarian metaphor when he identifies his royal master as 'the Angell which God hath sent to raise up and to call his people out of Babylon'.[7] The mythological and dramatic figures of godly prince and godly bishop, calling the English people out of Babylon, have begun to supplant those immobile, late Victorian projections of royal supremacy and episcopacy which were false in so far as they were drained of the dynamism of the age. Animation of the scene prompts questions about the interaction of roles and functions which were active, even energetic.

The subject of this chapter is the interrelation of these two creative forces in a period of sustained ideological instability, seen from the standpoint of the bishops. What was the competence of a bishop under a monarchy held to be supreme in all causes, ecclesiastical no less than civil? Was it a distinct competence in any way, or merely an extension of omnicompetence, royal government through commissioners or superintendents bearing the courtesy titles of bishops?[8] The decision of the 1530s to retain the traditional function of bishops as ordinaries and visitors implied, in the words of Margaret Bowker, that they 'one and all became civil servants. They were the king's men, strengthened in their office by his power and impotent without it.'[9] There is little more to be said about a situation within which Henry VIII ruled as *supremum caput* and claimed the cure of his subjects' souls.

Only under Elizabeth, Supreme Governor rather than Supreme Head, could it be said that supremacy was one thing, jurisdiction another. And even in 1610 the distinction was sufficiently blurred for Bishop George Carleton to claim the

---

[7] John White, *A defence of the way to the true church* (1614), sig. * *.

[8] Claire Cross considers these questions in her essay which traverses some of the ground of this chapter, 'Churchmen and the Royal Supremacy', in *Church and Society in England Henry VIII to James I*, ed. Felicity Heal and Rosemary O'Day (1977) , pp. 15–34.

[9] Margaret Bowker, 'The Supremacy and the Episcopate: the Struggle for Control, 1534–1540', *Historical Journal*, xviii (1975), 227–43.

rights of a pioneer in writing the book he called *Jurisdiction: regall, episcopall, papall*:

> To distinguish this confused masse, and to give to each his own right, was a thing wherein I found the greater difficulty, because none of late yeeres had troden this path before me, whose footsteppes might have directed me. For the question of the supremacy is handled learnedly and worthily by others, who though they have given some light to this question of Jurisdiction, yet they doe it but in some passages, not handling the question fully and purposely, but by occasion sometimes falling into some parts thereof.[10]

In referring to these 'passages', Carleton may have recalled the limits which even Bishop Jewel in the Erastian 1560s had placed on the effective competence of the royal governor in matters of ecclesiastical jurisdiction. Insisting that 'we flatter not our prince with any new-imagined extraordinary power', Jewel included in the 'prerogative and chiefty' of the prince the authority to 'hear and take up cases and questions of the faith, *if he be able*;[11] or otherwise to commit them over by his authority unto the learned; to command the bishops and priests to do their duties'—and not, we may note, to do their duties for them.[12]

Carleton may not have known that in the then unpublished Eighth Book of his *Laws of ecclesiastical polity* Richard Hooker had pursued the implications of this argument. The king had supreme authority and power to uphold the received laws and liberties of the church, not to subvert them. And if it were asked who was competent to say what those laws and liberties were, Hooker answered that the definition of laws belonged naturally to specialists, 'the wisest in those things which they are to concern'. So 'in matters of God, to set downe a form of public prayer, a solemn confession of the articles of Christian faith, rites and ceremonies meet for the exercise of religion; it were unnatural not to think the pastors and bishops of our souls a great deal more fit, than men of secular trades and callings.'[13] Elizabeth herself would have found this more

[10] *Jurisdiction: regall, episcopall, papall* (1610), sig. ¶3.
[11] My italics.
[12] *The Works of John Jewel*, ed. J. Ayre, iii, Parker Society (Cambridge, 1848), 167.
[13] *Works of Hooker*, iii, 358, 410.

acceptable doctrine than Hooker's further opinion that, when wisdom had done its work of devising, it was the 'general consent of all', expressed in Parliament, which gave the law its authority and so determined the Church's affairs. She had repeated occasion to thwart parliamentary initiatives in matters of religion and to insist that spiritual matters belonged to spiritual persons.[14] Nothing made the queen less Erastian than the Erastianism of the House of Commons. It is thought that Elizabeth was personally responsible for the addition of a clause to the twentieth Article of Religion which asserts that 'the Church hath power to decree Rites or Ceremonies and authoritie in controversies of fayth'. That was to give rise to argument, as late as the Parliament of 1629.[15] But Article XX was a statement of what had historically occurred in 1563, when the whole schedule of the Articles of the Church of England had been defined by Convocation. Subsequently, and after an interval of eight years, Parliament was allowed a limited role in confirming the Articles for certain purposes by statute.[16] In 1576, Elizabeth diverted the demand of Parliament for new ecclesiastical legislation to the same quarter of Convocation, having first discussed with the bishops the measure and gist of the Canons to be enacted.[17] But when in 1595 Archbishop Whitgift presumed to under-write a further doctrinal statement, the Lambeth Articles, and that by his own primatial authority, he acted *ultra vires* and was threatened, only half in jest, with a praemunire.[18]

So long as there was substantial identity of purpose linking crown and episcopate, the positions stated by Jewel and elaborated by Hooker remained unexceptional constitutional

[14] J. E. Neale, *Elizabeth I and her Parliaments 1584–1601* (1957); Patrick Collinson, *The Elizabethan Puritan Movement* (1967).

[15] Edward Cardwell, *Synodalia* i (Oxford, 1842), 64, 97; C. Hardwick, *A History of the Articles of Religion* (Cambridge, 1851), p. 138; S. R. Gardiner, *History of England from the Accession of James I to the Outbreak of the Civil War 1603–1642*, vii (1894), 48.

[16] J. E. Neale, 'Parliament and the Articles of Religion, 1571', *English Historical Review*, lxvii (1952), 510–20.

[17] Patrick Collinson, *Archbishop Grindal 1519–1583: the Struggle for a Reformed Church* (1979), pp. 226–7.

[18] *Correspondence of John Cosin*, ed. G. Ormsby, i, Surtees Society lii (1869), 56; H. C. Porter, *Reformation and Reaction in Tudor Cambridge* (Cambridge, 1958), pp. 372–5; Peter Lake, 'Laurence Chaderton and the Cambridge Moderate Puritan Tradition, 1570–1604', Cambridge Ph.D. thesis, 1978, pp. 241–6.

doctrine, threatened only by the disruptive intervention of puritan parliamentarians and their clerical allies. This was how it was from 1583 to 1603, when Whitgift used his powers to pursue objectives which he shared with the royal governor. After Whitgift's death, his friend Archbishop Hutton of York referred to the queen as 'his late dear sister', and noted that she did 'allwaies beare and shew a spetiall good affection towards him'.[19] As Elizabeth lay on her own death-bed, she grasped Whitgift's hand as her father in his extremity had clung to Cranmer. When the archbishop, 'loth over long to trouble hir', made as if to depart, she 'by signes' called him back and, resuming her grip upon his hand, 'held fast'.[20] That personal as well as political bond was the sheet-anchor of the late Elizabethan Church.

But things were not always so harmonious, or so sure. Some religious questions remained contentious, or obscure. Under Elizabeth these were mainly matters of ritual and church polity. Under James attention shifted to those doctrines of grace and assurance of salvation which lay at the heart of protestant and especially Calvinist religious experience. The intention of the Crown with respect to disputed points could not always be divined, nor equally trusted by all parties, particularly at the beginning of a new reign. So the years after 1559 and 1603 and around 1625 were times of anxiety and vigilance for churchmen, and especially for partisan churchmen.

The atmosphere at such a moment of climacteric is captured in the account of a conversation which took place in 1623, but which was recorded many years later by the sole surviving participant, Bishop Matthew Wren.[21] When Wren as chaplain to Prince Charles returned from the fiasco of his master's Spanish adventure, he received an urgent summons

---

[19] Archbishop Matthew Hutton to Bishop Tobie Matthew of Durham, 7 March 1603/4, BL Add. MS 4274, fol. 237.

[20] Lambeth Palace Library, MS 3152, fols. 4–5. This newly acquired and previously unrecorded document is a form of letter sent, apparently, to London clergy on Archbishop Whitgift's behalf on 28 March 1603, providing details of the queen's last days and hours, for use in what was to be uttered in sermons and prayers on the Sunday following. I am grateful to the Librarian of Lambeth Palace Library, Geoffrey Bill, for bringing this letter to my attention.

[21] *Parentalia, or Memoirs of the Family of the Wrens,* ed. S. Wren (1760), pp. 45–7.

to attend upon his patron, Bishop Lancelot Andrewes of Winchester. With an air of secrecy, if not of conspiracy, he was admitted to Winchester House in Southwark by William Laud, at that time bishop of St. Davids. He found that Bishop Richard Neile, leader and co-ordinator of the anti-Calvinist faction, was also present. Speaking for all three prelates, Neile charged Wren to reveal what he knew of his master, the prince. '"We know you are no fool but can observe how Things are like to go."[22] "What Things my Lord" (quoth I). "In brief" said he "how the Prince's Heart stands to the Church of *England*, that when God brings him to the Crown we may know what to hope for."' Wren replied that while Charles was inferior to his father in learning, he was more likely to uphold the doctrine, discipline, and right estate of the Church than James, '"in whom they say . . . is so much inconstancy upon some particular cases"'. Such conversations were seldom recorded, and Wren composed his memoir only to preserve the remarkable prophecy which then fell from the lips of Lancelot Andrewes, that the time would come when Charles would support the Church at the expense of both head and crown. But we may well believe that in 1559, in Strasburg, Zurich, and Geneva, and in 1603 in Lambeth and Fulham, there were similar speculative discussions about 'how things are like to go', and that tactical dispositions were made. Underlying the unremitting chorus of conventional praise for divinely inspired monarchy there was an undertone of calculation and even opportunism to which the preacher Stephen Marshall would draw the attention of the House of Commons in 1643: 'And I suspect, in case the tables were turned and we had a king endeavouring to take down the bishops, . . . the world would hear another Divinity.'[23]

---

[22] Cf. Richard Montague to John Cosin, July 1626/7: 'I expected to have heard some more news from you, howe thinges are like to go, whether Puritans be like to prevale, if Prideaux, *quod Deus avertat,* be like to be a Bishop.' (*Correspondence of Cosin,* i. 98.) The moderate Calvinist, Bishop Arthur Lake of Bath and Wells, made a different assessment of 'things' at this juncture, in an undated letter to Dr Samuel Ward, master of Sidney Sussex College: 'I thank you for the comfortable advertisement touching the princes safe returne and so noble resolution in point of religion. God establish and increase it in him, it is none of the smalest hopes of God's Church, which is shrewdly shaken at this tyme.' (Bodleian Library, Tanner MS 73(2), no. 151, fol. 376.)

[23] Quoted, Lamont, *Godly Rule,* p. 57.

The possibility of an alternative divinity of radical episcopal claims and adventurous episcopal designs attracts little
attention until the historian reaches the Church of Archbishop Laud, and even then it is somewhat obscured by
Laud's apparent subservience to monarchical 'tyranny': so that
we depend upon the later Laudians and the Non-Jurors to
show us what stuff High Anglicanism was made of. The crude
and deceptive notion of Erastianism has also played some part
in obscuring the underlying resources of Anglicanism. A book
on Hooker tells us that the Elizabethan apologists were 'all
Erastians... They could hardly be anything else, for they
believed in the identity of Church and State'.[24] According to
D. H. Willson there was no change under James I, when 'the
English bishops of both schools [sc. Calvinist and Arminian]
were Erastian, accepting the supremacy of the state in
Ecclesiastical affairs'.[25] The rationale of Erastianism was in
one sense even plainer under James I than it had been under
Elizabeth. In the 1610 Parliament Archbishop Bancroft
volunteered the intriguing doctrine that 'though the Queen,
our late sovereign, had power to make canons ecclesiastical,
yet it is more proper to the King'.[26]

However, although it was Bancroft's intention on this
occasion to deny that an Act of Parliament was required to
give canons legal force, it is inconceivable that he can have
meant to say that James had a power which was lacking in
Elizabeth to declare canons out of his own mouth. His purpose
was not to assert nakedly 'Erastian' doctrine of this sort but to
defend the legal status of the Book of Canons of 1604 of which
he himself was the principal architect, and which had been
legislated in Convocation. As both Bishop Neile and Lord
Salisbury pointed out in the House of Lords debate of 1610, to
doubt the legality of these Canons was to call in question the
king's prerogative, and Salisbury even asked 'whether the
King hath not the power that the priest of Rome had?'
Bancroft later informed a conference of both Houses that the
Canons had 'no power in themselves unless they have the

---

[24] F. J. Shirley, *Richard Hooker and Contemporary Religious Ideas* (1949), p. 60.
[25] D. H. Willson, *James VI and I* (1956), p. 199.
[26] *Proceedings in Parliament 1610*, ed. E. R. Foster (New Haven, 1966), i. 101.

King's royal assent'.[27] But to say that the king had 'power' to make canons, an attribute of his supremacy and of his prerogative, was not to offer any comment on how canons were made.

Similarly, when Sir John Neale attempted a radical reinterpretation of the parliamentary settlement of the Church in 1559 he invited us to consider the possibility that the statutes which embodied the settlement, while enjoying the unchallengeable authority of the queen in Parliament, were not necessarily the product of the queen's intellect and will, nor simply the outcome of a collective decision of the queen's advisers, 'the government'. It was, in a sense, a mere accident of politics that an Act of Uniformity with an annexed Prayer Book became law in 1559.[28] Neale may have been wrong in his reading of the parliamentary record of 1559,[29] but he was not far from the truth in attributing the outcome to the relatively free play and interplay of political and ecclesiastical forces.

Episcopal appointments are another subject sometimes treated naîvely, as if they represented the royal choice as well as the royal commission. It would be absurd to suggest that either Elizabeth or James was a cipher when it came to ecclesiastical preferments. Royal preferences could be and were expressed, both positively and negatively. But the ways in which bishops emerged, in this as in all ages of the Church's history, were devious and complex and deserve more careful study than they have yet received, particularly in the correspondence of successive archbishops with the Cecils. Here the interests of the great courtly patrons will be found working a kind of counterpoint with sometimes devious ecclesiastical plots.[30]

[27] Ibid., i. 103, 124.

[28] J. E. Neale, 'The Elizabethan Acts of Supremacy and Uniformity', *English Historical Review*, lxv (1950), 304–32, and his *Elizabeth I and her Parliaments 1559–1581*, pp. 51–84.

[29] Norman L. Jones, 'Faith by Statute: the Politics of Religion in the Parliament of 1559', Cambridge Ph.D. thesis, 1977; Winthrop S. Hudson, *The Cambridge Connection and the Elizabethan Settlement of 1559* (Durham, North Carolina, 1980).

[30] Correspondence scattered through the Lansdowne MSS (BL), *Correspondence of Matthew Parker*, ed. J. Bruce, Parker Society (Cambridge, 1853), and successive volumes of the 'Hatfield Calendar', *HMC Reports, Salisbury MSS*, especially the

In short, we may turn Bishop Carleton's controversial point into a historical observation. Royal supremacy has been discussed, learnedly and worthily, but as if it were not only the ultimate basis and sanction for ecclesiastical government but the instrumentality by which ecclesiastical policy was made and the Church actively governed. This corresponds to primitive misconceptions about the nature and practice of systems of personal monarchy.

II

Stephen Marshall's alternative divinity is to be found, in embryonic form, in certain pronouncements of both Elizabethan and Jacobean churchmen. In the reign of James these grew into an overt, confident, and coherent body of episcopalian apologetics. In the Elizabethan Church similarly sturdy convictions were latent, and only occasionally a spur to action. Even in the 1560s the supposedly Erastian Bishop Jewel could assert the ultimate integrity of the Church as a spiritual society. 'We say to the prince as St. Ambrose sometime said to the Emperor Valentinian: . . . "Trouble not yourself, my lord, to think that you have any princely power over those things that pertain to God."'[31] But until the last decade of the reign the bishops were placed on the defensive by an unfriendly laity and a discouraging political and ideological climate.

The success of Archbishops Whitgift and Bancroft in restoring the morale of the episcopate depended paradoxically

---

volumes coinciding with the years of Archbishop Whitgift's ascendancy, ii–ix. See what Whitgift wrote to Burghley, 28 July 1586, apropos of the earl of Leicester's influence in bishop-making: 'From that fountaine are sprunge almost all the evle bishops and denes now living in England, and yet where is greater zeal pretended.' (*HMC Report, Salisbury MSS* iii. 153.) See also what Whitgift wrote to Sir Robert Cecil, 9 September 1595, as he anticipated Burghley's demise: 'That which I am able to do in such cases I am desirous to perfect whiles I have time and opportunity, knowing by experience the unfaithfulness of many such as are put in trust after a man's death.' (Ibid., v. 370.) For an example of devious ecclesiastical plotting, see a letter from Archbishop Sandys to Burghley, 28 December 1579, in which he attempts to get rid of the dean of York, Matthew Hutton, by the upstairs route: 'My good lord, stand my good frend in this matter. In nothing can youe more pleasure me, for I can not live with the man. The bushoprik of Litchfeld wold wel serve the turne . . .'. (BL Lansdowne MS 28, no. 80, fol. 175.)

[31] *The Works of John Jewel,* ed. J. Ayre, iv, Parker Society (Cambridge, 1850), 898.

on the puritan, and especially lay puritan, opposition which had done so much to depress it in the middle years of the reign. Episcopacy was able with some success to justify itself as an integral part of the social and political fabric which had a special role to play in the suppression of dangerous and subversive novelties. What a Scottish presbyterian later called 'that unkoth motto' 'No Bishop, no King'[32] has never been bettered as an encapsulation of the alignments maintained from 1583 to 1610, with only a momentary flutter in 1603–4. So it was in part as a blunt instrument with which to belabour English and Scottish anti-episcopalians that a new and confident episcopalian ideology assumed shape in the 1590s and early 1600s.[33] A path is traced from Bancroft's suggestive hints in his Paul's Cross sermon of 1589 through the pioneering *De diversis ministrorum evangeliis gradibus* of Adrianus Saravia (1590)[34] to Bishop Bilson's definitive *Perpetual government of Christes church* (1593). Bishop Barlow's 1606 sermon, *Concerning the antiquitie and superioritie of bishops,*[35] and Bishop Downame's 1608 sermon *Defending the honourable function of bishops,* were but echoes of Bilson.[36] Archbishop Bancroft, who probably inspired Saravia, was thought by some puritans to

---

[32] Patrick Collinson, 'Episcopacy and Reform in England in the Later Sixteenth Century', in *Studies in Church History,* iii, ed. G. J. Cuming (Leiden, 1966), 91–125.

[33] Norman Sykes, *Old Priest and New Presbyter* (Cambridge, 1956); W. D. J. Cargill Thompson, 'Anthony Marten and the Elizabethan Debate on Episcopacy', in *Essays in Modern English Church history in Memory of Norman Sykes,* ed. G. V. Bennett and J. D. Walsh (1966), pp. 44–75; W. D. J. Cargill Thompson, 'A Reconsideration of Richard Bancroft's Paul's Cross Sermon of 9 February 1588/9', *Journal of Ecclesiastical History,* xx (1969), 253–66; W. D. J. Cargill Thompson, 'Sir Francis Knollys's Campaign Against the *Jure Divino* Theory of Episcopacy', in *The Dissenting Tradition: Essays for Leland H. Carlson,* ed. C. Robert Cole and Michael E. Moody (Athens, Ohio, 1975), pp. 39–77, and reprinted in the author's posthumously published *Studies in the Reformation: Luther to Hooker,* ed. C. W. Dugmore (1980), pp. 94–130.

[34] An English edition followed in 1592, *Of the diverse degrees of the ministerie of the Gospel.* See the definitive study by Willem Nijenhuis, *Adrianus Saravia (c. 1532–1613): Dutch Calvinist, first Reformed defender of the English episcopal Church order on the basis of the ius divinum* (Leiden, 1980), esp. pp. 117–24, 222–43.

[35] *One of foure sermons preched before the kings majestie . . . concerning the antiquitie and superioritie of bishops* (1606).

[36] The author of a refutation of Downame's sermon wrote: 'If we compare this sermon with Dr Bilsons book of the *perpetual government of the Church* we may well say of the timber and stone thereof as the poore labourrer did of his axe when the head fell in the water 2 Kings 6.5 *Alas master, it is but borrowed.' (Mr Downames sermon . . . answered and refuted* (1609), p. 1).

have been at Downame's elbow as he composed his sermon,[37] and its publication led to a monumental controversy in the manner of the Elizabethan Admonition Controversy between Whitgift and Thomas Cartwright, to which logically it provided a kind of appendix.[38]

This terrain is not very fruitful for our purpose. To intimidate their presbyterian opponents, apologists for the ecclesiastical status quo erected a blank and uninviting wall bearing the single word Obedience: or rather the two terms which the royal chaplain William Wilkes made the title of a book written after the Hampton Court Conference: *Obedience or ecclesiastical union* (1605). It was only when late Elizabethan and Jacobean controversialists justified the constitution of their Church to Roman Catholic opponents that they demonstrated their skill in erecting more delicately balanced edifices. For the purposes of these polemics it was necessary on the one hand to deny that the will of the prince was the only rule of faith, and on the other to explain the nature and limits of ecclesiastical obedience. Consequently Barlow's book against the Jesuit Robert Parsons, *An answere to a catholike Englishman* (1609), is more interesting than his sermon on the *Antiquitie and superioritie of bishops*; and Bilson's *True difference between christian subiection and unchristian rebellion* (1585) a more rewarding book, for the present enquiry, than his *Perpetual government of Christes church*. Most fascinating of all are the relevant passages in two works published in 1610: Carleton's *Jurisdiction,* to which reference has already been made, and the fifth and final book of the once celebrated *magnum opus* of Richard Field, *Of the Church.*[39]

Carleton and Field, like Jewel before them, were concerned to repudiate what Carleton called 'a gross and impure' understanding of the royal supremacy, such as he attributed

---

[37] The writer of *Informations or a protestation and a treatise from Scotland* (1608) wrote (Epistle): 'But they [sc., 'many sound divines'] thinke that the sermon, especially the Epistle, was by the instruction of the Archbishop, whose chaplaine he is.'

[38] Bibliographical details will be found in Peter Milward, *Religious Controversies of the Jacobean Age* (1978), pp. 17–20. Downame's principal opponent wrote anonymously, but in 1621 the controversy drew into the lists a celebrated puritan divine, Paul Baynes, whose *The diocesans tryall* was published posthumously by the learned William Ames.

[39] Published in 4 vols., Ecclesiastical History Society (Cambridge, 1852).

to Bishop Stephen Gardiner, which made the will of the king
the Church's only law. This was to take 'the massie crown of
Jurisdiction' from the pope's head and to place it on the king's
head, 'gold, silver, coper, drosse and all'. We have seen that
Salisbury's concern for the royal prerogative offered to do no
less. In Carleton's view, Calvin and other reformed divines
had been justly offended with such doctrine. The king was 'a
Father and preserver of religion', 'a nourcing father', and 'a
keeper of Ecclesiastical discipline'. Carleton could say that it
was 'for the good of God's Church' that monarchy had been
ordained. For only the king had that power of coaction by
which laws were established and enforced.[40] (In Bilson's
phrase, 'only princes be governors'.)[41] But the Church also
existed, and it was not dependent upon princes for its
existence. Moreover it possessed an 'inward and spirituall
power', even 'Spirituall government by the lawes of God,
exerted within the court of Conscience'. This was sufficient for
the establishment of doctrine and for the maintenance of good
order in the Church.[42] It was equivalent to 'the power of
order', from which derived the authority to preach, minister
sacraments, and ordain, 'and this power', said Field, 'the
princes of the world have not at all'. 'It is proper to the
ministers of the Church.'[43] Even excommunication was a
spiritual weapon implying no power of coaction. It was by
means of this spiritual power 'without any coactive jurisdiction' that for the space of three hundred years the Church had
been called, faith planted, devils subdued, the world reduced
to the obedience of Christ, and the Church governed.[44] In
Barlow's estimation the Church was more flourishing in those
primitive times 'when the blood of *Martyred Bishops* was the
Seed of the Church' than in the days of papal ascendancy.[45]
No invidious comparison was attempted with its state under
Constantine and other Christian emperors. Yet Whitgift in his

[40] Carleton, *Jurisdiction*, sigs. ¶3ᵛ–4ʳ, pp. 6, 13, and Chapter III *passim*.
[41] Thomas Bilson, *The true difference betweene christian subiection and unchristian rebellion* (1585), p. 127.
[42] Carleton, *Jurisdiction*, p. 20.
[43] Field, *Of the Church*, iv. 93.
[44] Carleton, *Jurisdiction*, p. 39.
[45] William Barlow, *An answere to a catholike Englishman* (1609), p. 45.

controversy with Cartwright had conceded that the state of the Church 'under the cross' might in some sense be more flourishing and certainly purer than its condition under a godly prince.[46]

Richard Field insisted that before there were any Christian emperors the power of calling synods of the Church resided in the bishops themselves. For 'the state of the Christian Church . . . is such, that it may stand, though not only forsaken but grievously oppressed by the great men of the world; and doth not absolutely depend on the care of such as manage the great affairs of the world, and direct the outward course of things here below: and therefore it is by all resolved on, that the Church hath her guides and rulers distinct from them that bear the sword . . .'[47] Carleton said much the same, but with a ringing and memorable rhetoric: 'For the preservation of true doctrine in the Church, the Bishops are the great watchmen. Herein they are authorized by God. If Princes withstand them in these things, they have warrant not to obey Princes, because with these things Christ hath put them in trust.'[48] There was no difference between these sentiments and what the presbyterian James Melville was saying in Scotland: 'that diverse hunderith yeiris befoir thair wes ane Christiane Magistrat, thair wes maist flurisheing Churches'.[49]

Since these divines were writing with the doctrine of the Jesuits in their sights, it was the very nub of their argument to insist that resistance to the prince's will must assume passive, not actively rebellious forms. But whereas Carleton followed an ancient Christian tradition in teaching that the Church's only weapons were prayers and tears,[50] other writers were impressed with the force of utterance, not indeed to coerce princes but to convert and direct their consciences. Bilson thought that princes were to be 'directed unto truth the same

[45] William Barlow, *An answere to a catholike Englishman* (1609), p. 45.

[46] *The Works of John Whitgift*, ed. J. Ayre, i, Parker Society (Cambridge, 1851), 378–95.

[47] Field, *Of the Church*, iv. 62.

[48] Carleton, *Jurisdiction, p. 44.*

[49] *The Autobiography and Diary of Mr James Melville*, ed. R. Pitcairn, Wodrow Society (Edinburgh, 1842), p. 631.

[50] Carleton, *Jurisdiction*, p. 45.

way that al other Christians are, to wit, by perswasion and not by coaction'.[51] But were princes, like 'all other Christians', subject to the censure of excommunication? In the early Elizabethan Church, Jewel and Alexander Nowell were prepared to contemplate such a possibility. But after the papal excommunication of Elizabeth in 1570 Anglican apologists, and most notably Hooker, totally excluded it.[52] According to Barlow, the spiritual power of the keys was to be exercised in winning the souls of princes, not in disturbing their states, 'for preaching to them, not factioning against them; in exhorting, not threatning them'.[53] And no church-man was more skilled in the practice of this delicate art than Barlow himself.

Where the prince was Christian, he lent his coactive power to the service of the Church, so that the calling and policing of synods became his prerogative. All Anglican writers were at one with Jewel, that after Constantine's conversion there was no council properly called general which was not called by an emperor.[54] In 1610 no Anglican was likely to embrace the Scottish Presbyterian cause in denying that the king had power to summon ecclesiastical synods and assemblies. But while the coactive power of establishing ecclesiastical law pertained to the prince, the interpretative ability to define its content belonged to the Church: for 'the hearing and iudging of such things belong to such as are most skilfull in these affaires'.[55] In this respect it could be said that there was no difference between temporal and ecclesiastical affairs, or that temporal matters offered an apt analogy. In Bilson's view the issue turned on an elementary distinction between things and persons. Princes were not governors of things, for they could not be expected to compose music or prescribe medicine or draw up rules of grammar and logic. But they were governors of all persons, unreservedly.[56] This was consistent with an explanation in the Articles of Religion that the 'cheefe power'

[51] Bilson, *The true difference*, p. 124.
[52] *Works of Jewel*, iv. 991–2; Alexander Nowell, *A reproufe of a booke entituled A proufe of certayne articles by T. Dorman* (1566), fol. 51; *Works of Hooker*, iii, 444–55.
[53] Barlow, *An answere*, p. 45.
[54] *Works of Jewel*, iii, 98.
[55] Carleton, *Jurisdiction*, p. 20.
[56] Bilson, *The true Difference*, p. 126.

of the queen's majesty implied no power to minister God's word or sacraments, but the prerogative to rule 'all estates and degrees'; and with a similar statement made in 1569 in the *Declaration of the queen's proceedings.*[57]

From this spring-board Field launched into the claim that it was only with the advice and direction of his clergy that the prince could command things pertaining to God's worship and service, pointing out that the Act of Supremacy itself required 'the assent of the clergy in their convocation' for the definition of heresy. Touching errors in faith or aberrations in worship, 'there is no question but that bishops and pastors of the Church (to whom it pertaineth to teach the truth) are the ordinary and fittest judges: and that ordinarily and regularly princes are to leave the judgment thereof unto them'.[58] As J. W. Allen pointed out, this was as much as to say that it was the clergy in Convocation who made the Church's law. The king merely enforced it.[59] The Act for the Submission of the Clergy was very nearly placed on its head. Barlow speaks of synods as occasions when the clergy meet 'to cure the maladie, either by incision or infusion'.[60] Thus Convocation had set about its work of infusion, and codification, in 1604. It may be that the new episcopalian apologetics were intended primarily to justify the 1604 Canons, which came under fire in Parliament in 1610, the year in which Carleton and Field published their books.[61]

The ideology of these Jacobean divines has been called new, and there was certainly originality in the grandeur and confidence of its exposition. There was also apparent novelty in its logical backbone: the claim that episcopacy was of apostolic origin and rested on divine authority, that it possessed *jus divinum.* As Thomas Sparke wrote in 1607: 'For though in respect of that which they have from Princes they may be said to be theirs, and of human Constitution; yet in respect of their ministry and spiritual iurisdiction in the

---

[57] Cardwell, *Synodalia*, i. 71; E. T. Davies, *Episcopacy and the Royal Supremacy in the Church of England in the XVI Century* (Oxford, 1950), pp. 81–2.

[58] Field, *Of the Church*, iv. 94.

[59] J. W. Allen, *English Political Thought, 1603–1644* (1938), p. 129.

[60] Barlow, *One of foure sermons*, sig. B^v.

[61] *Proceedings in Parliament 1610*, i. 100–3, 124–7.

Church, they wel may be said to be of God's own ordinance.'[62]
There was a great difference between this doctrine and the
Erastian outlook of the ecclesiastical lawyer Dr John Hammond, who in 1590 had assured Sir Francis Knollys that
bishops were 'wholie her [Majesty's] creatures, and not the
immediate creatures of God at all'. Moreover Hammond
could take comfort from the fact that the bishops themselves
(or so he believed) claimed to derive their office from no other
source than the statute of the twenty-fifth year of Henry
VIII.[63] Richard Bancroft, who seems to have been the engineer
and promoter of the *jus divinum,* merely hinted at it in his
sermon of 1589. Within a year it was plainly stated by
Saravia, and elaborated in 1593 by Bilson. So the divine right
of bishops was a doctrine which advanced from its first
tentative formulations to its fullest statement in five years.
Under James I it was far from commanding a consensus of
support even among senior churchmen, but it ceased to be a
scandal. Bancroft had been challenged by a cousin of the
queen and a veteran of Henry VIII's Reformation Parliament,
Sir Francis Knollys, briefed by the most senior and respected
theologian in Oxford, Dr John Reynolds, and by a leading
civilian, Dr Hammond. Twenty years later, those who took up
the cudgels against Downame were anonymous, fugitive
puritans. There was no political, Erastian opposition to the
Jacobean divines, at least none which was publicly uttered.
Downame's sermon was preached at the consecration of that
most courtly of Jacobean bishops, James Montague, previously dean of the Chapel Royal, the king's friend and the
editor of his published works.

J. W. Allen wondered why this should have been so,[64] and
suggested that it was only when Richard Montague (no close
relation of James Montague, and a different species of
churchman) published the *New Gagg for an old goose* in 1624
that the House of Commons woke up to what ecclesiastics had
been saying for some time. Possibly. But we should not
overlook the great difference, *in modo* if not *in re,* between the

[62] Thomas Sparke, *A brotherly perswasion to unitie* (1607), p. 78.
[63] Cargill Thompson, *Studies,* pp. 111, 104.
[64] Allen, *English Political Thought,* pp. 135, 161–75.

Jacobean apologists for episcopacy and the so-called Arminians of the next generation, Richard Montague and his
friends. Downame, Carleton, and Field resembled Bilson
rather than Montague. They neither intended to provoke nor
were in fact provocative. As William Lamont has shown,[65]
Bilson's argument had been moderated with 'blandness, not
boldness', and even 'a certain inscrutability' which avoided
the gratuitously offensive clericalism of the later High Church
school. Not that Downame was inscrutable. The clergy in
general and the bishops in particular were advanced by
Downame above the conditions of other men to 'an honour
which might seem to become angels rather than men'.[66] But
rhetoric of this kind was proper to the occasion of an
ordination or consecration sermon, when only clergy were
present, and it was not apparently resented.

When Richard Montague's friend and constant correspondent John Cosin declared in Durham in 1628 that the
spiritual jurisdiction derived its power from Christ and only
the force of external coaction from the king, and that the king
himself made no claim to be Head of the Church, he said
nothing which the Jacobean divines had not already taught
without contradiction. But if witnesses are to be believed, he
made the point provocatively, and in lay company: 'King
Charles is not supreme head of the Church of England under
Christ, nor hath he any more power of excommunication than
my man that rubs my horse's heels.'[67] Even if these vivid words
were not spoken, Cosin was himself a provocation, shinning
up ladders in Durham Cathedral at Candlemas to light 220
candles and tapers, 60 of them on what he pleased to call the
high altar; personally schooling the bewildered congregation
on when to stand and when to kneel ('you must kneele, you
must kneele, it is a prayer'), 'crossing the cushions, kissing the
altar clothes and smacking them with his lippes'.[68]

---

[65] W. D. Lamont, 'The Rise and Fall of Bishop Bilson', *Journal of British Studies*, v
(1965), 22–32.
[66] George Downame, *Two sermons, The one commending the ministerie in generall: The other
defending the office of bishops in particular* (1608), p. 56 and *passim*.
[67] *Correspondence of Cosin*, i. 147–51.
[68] Peter Smart, *The vanitie and downe-fall of superstitious popish ceremonies* (Edinburgh,
1628), sigs. *2–5; *Correspondence of Cosin*, i. 161–99.

What mattered most was that Carleton and Downame, unlike Richard Montague and Cosin, were Calvinists. So was James Montague, at whose consecration Downame had preached in exaltation of episcopacy. Even Field, though more Lutheran than Calvinist, was a man of peace who chose to emphasize what all protestants held in common and deplored divisive debates about the matter of predestination.[69] Moreover, the Jacobean apologists to a man, unlike Richard Montague and Cosin, were sound in their denunciation of the Church of Rome, and some were seasoned controversialists against the Jesuits. These considerations guaranteed a measure of social and political acceptability, in the climate of opinion prevailing in Jacobean England.

That Calvinism and *de jure divino* episcopacy should have been bedmates disturbs conventional categories and classifications. Yet it was not a Calvinist but the anti-Calvinist and proto-Arminian Richard Neile who in his maiden speech in the House of Lords remarked of his episcopal office: 'When the king gave me this honor and laid his hands upon me.'[70] And it was Richard Montague who wrote *Appello Caesarem.* Conversely it was bishop Joseph Hall, whose roots were in the puritan and Calvinist tradition, whom Laud induced to write *Episcopacie by divine right asserted* (1640), and who did not shrink from the task. The new episcopalianism of the Jacobean Church, when its unexpected source has been noticed, has been considered an oddity, and special reasons have been sought for it. Was it a delayed response to the presbyterian movement, and did it reflect anxiety about the intentions of a Scottish king unaccustomed to Anglican ways, or the need to justify the promotion of episcopacy in Scotland itself? It was notorious that two of the apologists, Sparke and Downame, were themselves defectors from the puritan camp who publicly advertised the fact, perhaps at Bancroft's prompt-

---

[69] Nathaniel Field, *Some Short Memorials Concerning the Life of that Reverend Divine Doctor Richard Field*, ed. J. Le Neve (1716–17). The BL copy (C.14467) contains MS notes omitted from Field's text and inserted by Le Neve. See especially notes opposite p. 10 and on pp. 21–2.

[70] *Proceedings in Parliament 1610*, i. 101. In a later speech in the same Parliament, Neile said that 'the power we have is from the king'. (Ibid., i. 136.)

ing.[71] Yet the likelihood is that the Jacobean religious settlement did not so much provoke as permit and even encourage the free assertion of claims which had always been implicit in the office of a bishop. The new episcopalianism was not really new at all. But the bishops enjoyed a more secure and recognized place in society. The doctrine published in 1610 was an expression of security, not of undue anxiety; although, as the speeches of the bishops in the 1610 Parliament reveal, no little anxiety persisted when the laity in the House of Commons revived their good old cause.[72]

As for the *jus divinum,* which was relatively new, this was symbolical rather than practical. Even Knollys had been aroused, not by anything said by Bancroft at Paul's Cross, nor even by Saravia's scholarly treatise, but by the allegedly illegal proceedings of Whitgift against the preaching ministers, signifying 'a dangerous course against her Majesty's supreme government', even the perpetration of a praemunire. And for all that Knollys was an honest Erastian, he was obliged to mount a tactical offensive on this robustly Erastian front by the queen's warning to avoid interference in matters mere ecclesiastical.[73] The only circumstance in which the *jus divinum* could have had practical repercussions was one which had yet to arise, in which a bishop was threatened with dismissal at the hands of the secular power, the issue in 1643 and 1689. As Laud would later insist: 'Their calling, as far as it is *jure divino,* by divine right, cannot be taken away.'[74] Yet according to their careful distinctions, Bilson and Carleton would have allowed the Crown to deprive them not only of possessions and coercive jurisdiction but even of the right publicly to exercise the calling and spiritual functions which belonged to the *potestas ordinis*: in effect to denude the bishop

[71] Sparke, *Brotherly perswasion,* 'Epistle to the Christian Reader'; Downame, Dedicatory Epistle to *A sermon defending the honourable function of bishops,* in *Two sermons.*

[72] *Proceedings in Parliament 1610,* i. 71–9, 100–3, 124–7, 134–7, 219–27. Archbishop Bancroft detected in a bill against plurality and non-residence 'a great deal of spleen against the clergy'. Bishop Barlow was quoted as saying 'that the Lower House loved not the bishops'. (Ibid., i. 71, 102.) There was significant evidence of lack of affection, and of trust, in the promotion of the bill 'against canons ecclesiastical not confirmed by Parliament'. (Ibid, i. 100–4, 124–9.)

[73] Cargill Thompson, *Studies,* pp. 112, 98.

[74] *The Works of William Laud,* ed. W. Scott and J. Bliss, iv (Oxford, 1854), 311.

of everything which made him a bishop, in the eyes of the world. On the other hand, for all that the Elizabethan bishops, or some of them, occasionally expressed their willingness to be removed, or even to see their order abolished (Archbishop Parker once said that he left it to the queen and the Council whether they would have any bishops and how they would have them ordered)[75] yet no bishop ever was deprived, between 1559 and 1643. In the same breath Bishop Aylmer could express pleasure at the prospect of compulsory retirement ('I assure you I would thanke yow, for the charge being so importable'), but remind Lord Burghley that it was 'a rare cause yet in lawe to deprive a Bishop'.[76] In his famous letter to the queen, Archbishop Grindal offered to yield up his place, but then proved resolute and tenacious when Elizabeth did her best to unseat him.[77] Translation to a less profitable or more onerous see was a subtler mode of disparagement and there are examples of this muted punishment. Yet there are cases on record of churchmen who succeeded in rejecting offers which may have been hard to refuse.[78] The commissions issued for the appointment of the Elizabethan and Jacobean bishops no longer stated, as they had under Edward VI, that the office was to be held during pleasure.

III

The fact that the English Church retained a superior order of clergy and invested them with the title of bishop was consequently more significant than any theory of episcopal

[75] *Correspondence of Parker,* p. 454.

[76] Aylmer to Burghley, 26 May 1579; BL Lansdowne MS 28, no. 72, fol. 159. In 1579 Bishop Richard Cox of Ely was under pressure to resign and a draft exists of the terms of his resignation. But Cox died undisturbed. G. L. Blackman has suggested that the queen and Burghley may have been deterred by the lack of precedent and legal complications. (G. L. Blackman, 'The Career and Influence of Bishop Richard Cox, 1547–1581', Cambridge Ph.D. thesis, 1953, pp. 363–72). Marmaduke Middleton of St. Davids was deprived of his see in 1592 and so may be the exception to prove the rule. But it appears that Middleton's death in 1593 may have forestalled the completion of all the formalities of his deprivation. (R. E. Head, *Royal Supremacy and the Trials of Bishops 1558–1725* (1962), pp. 23–7.)

[77] Collinson, *Archbishop Grindal,* pp. 242–82.

[78] See, for example, Bishop Thomas Cooper of Lincoln to Burghley, 8 June 1579, resisting (successfully) translation to Norwich, and writing of 'the troblesomnes and the danger of The diocesse far greter then where I am now': BL Lansdowne MS 28, no. 73, fol. 161.

origins or titles. Knollys told Sir Francis Walsingham that 'my lorde archebyshopp and the reste' admitted that they received their bishoprics from the queen. But once they were made bishops they conducted themselves as if their superiority were 'knytte to theyre byshopryckes *jure divino* dyrectlye'. As Professor James Cargill Thompson argued, it was episcopal practice, not episcopal ideology, which prompted Knollys's anti-episcopal campaign.[79] With some reason, Archbishop Laud would appeal beyond less authoritative texts to the plain words of the Ordinal, asserting the historical fact that 'from the Apostles' time there have been three orders of ministers in the Church of Christ, bishops, priests and deacons'.[80] Once consecrating hands had been placed on their heads, even the first and apparently most Erastian cohort of Elizabethan bishops were free, and perhaps bound, to immerse themselves in that stream of precedent and example relating to the work of a bishop in the Church of Christ, springing from the New Testament ideal of the good shepherd and from the Pastoral Epistles, and filtering through rich deposits of patristic literature.

Nourished from these sources, which were readily accessible to the intelligentsia of sixteenth-century Europe, the ideal of the primitive and godly bishop was one of great power and, it has been said, 'almost tangible beauty'.[81] As a historical topic, the 'Bischofsideal' has been treated in the context of the continental Counter-Reformation. But there are no grounds for confining it to the world of Bishop Matteo Giberti and of Reginald Pole and the Council of Trent. When the two protestant reformers Peter Martyr Vermigli and Martin Bucer met in Strasburg, not long before both proceeded to this country to preside from university chairs over the English Reformation, Martyr expressed delight at discovering, in the person of Bucer, 'bishops upon the earth . . . which be truly

---

[79] Cargill Thompson, *Studies,* pp. 94–130.

[80] *Works of Laud,* iv. 311.

[81] Paul Broutin, SJ (adapting Hubert Jedin, 'Das Bischofsideal der katholischer Reformation'), *L'Évêque dans la tradition pastorale du XVIᵉ siècle* (Louvain, 1953). And see Oliver Logan, 'The Ideal of the Bishop and the Venetian Patriarchate: c. 1430–c. 1630', *Journal of Ecclesiastical History,* xxix (1978), 415–50. For the occurrence of these ideas and ideals in post-Reformation England, see my 'Episcopacy and Reform'.

holy'. 'This is the office of a pastor, this is that bishoplike dignity described by Paul in the Epistles unto Timothy and Titus. It delighteth me much to read this kind of description in these Epistles, but it pleaseth me a great deal more to see with the eyes the patterns themselves.'[82]

Among those who sat at Peter Martyr's feet, first at Oxford and later in Strasburg and Zurich, was John Jewel.[83] When in due course Jewel was made a bishop he boasted that 'those oily, shaven, portly hypocrites' had been sent back to Rome whence they were first imported. 'For we require our bishops to be pastors, labourers and watchmen.' He supposed that with the wealth and political influence of their order reduced, these new and utterly genuine bishops would be able 'with greater ease and diligence' to 'employ their leisure in attending to the flock of Christ', 'relieved from that royal pomp and courtly bustle'.[84] Bliss was it in that dawn to be alive. In the circumstances of 1559 these remarks were tinged with a kind of fantasy and few were better placed than Jewel and his colleagues to contrast fantasy with harsh reality in the years of arduous and ungrateful service which lay ahead.[85] When Aylmer of London was reminded of what he had said in 1559 in the *Harborowe for faithful and trewe subjects* ('Come off you bishops . . . yield up your thousands; be content with hundreds') he answered with the Apostle: 'Cum essem parvulus, loquebar ut parvulus, sapiebam ut parvulus . . .'—'When I was a child I spoke as child, I thought as a child, but now I have put away childish things.'[86] But it was

[82] *Martyrs divine epistles,* appended to Peter Martyr, *Common places,* tr. Anthony Marten (1583), pp. 62–3; whence printed by G. C. Gorham, *Gleanings of a Few Scattered Ears During the Reformation in England* (1857), pp. 19–27.

[83] W. M. Southgate, *John Jewel and the Problem of Doctrinal Authority,* Harvard Historical Monographs xlix (Cambridge, Mass., 1962), pp. 8–10, 20–2.

[84] *Zurich Letters,* i. ed. Hastings Robinson, Parker Society (Cambridge, 1842), 50–1. In 1588 Tobie Matthew remembered Jewel as 'episcopus episcoporum'. (Matthew to Francis Mills, 9 January 1587/8; BL MS Cotton Titus B VII, fol. 424ᵛ.)

[85] See the letter books of the two émigré bishops, Thomas Bentham and John Parkhurst, Jewel's old tutor: *The Letter-Book of Thomas Bentham, Bishop of Coventry and Lichfield,* ed. Rosemary O'Day and Joel Berlatsky, *Camden Miscellany* xxvii. Camden 4th ser. xxii (1979), 113–238; *The Letter Book of John Parkhurst Bishop of Norwich Compiled During the Years 1571–75,* ed. Ralph Houlbrooke, Norfolk Record Society 1974 and 1975 (Norwich, 1975).

[86] Sir John Harington, *A Supplie or Addicion to the Catalogue of Bishops to the Yeare 1608,* ed. R. H. Miller, Studia Humanitatis (Madrid, 1979), p. 46. See John Aylmer, *An harborowe for true and faithful subiects* ('Strasbourg', *recte* London, 1559), sig. O4.

significant that Jewel and his colleagues indulged in these perhaps ingenuous fantasies. They actually believed themselves to be bishops, not royal commissioners or mere superintendents.[87] And that conviction was fortified by the example of the episcopal martyrs whom the Marian persecution had made the most valuable possession of the English Church and the perfect antidote to Stephen Gardiner. Bilson asked: 'If we make Princes to bee iudges of faith, why were so many of us consumed not long since in *England* with fier and fagot for disliking that which the Prince and the Pope affirmed to be faith?'[88]

Among the patterns of bishoplike dignity available to students of primitive Christian literature, none was more exhilarating than St. Ambrose, bishop of Milan in the age of St. Augustine.[89] In a series of memorable encounters with the imperial Court, Ambrose had asserted the integrity of the Church and of his own office, in epistles and orations which were models of the form of address which a truly apostolic bishop might be bold to adopt towards unfriendly or misguided government, albeit Christian government. The demand by the young Emperor Valentinian II and his mother Justina that Ambrose should surrender a catholic basilica for the use of Arian heretics had prompted the dictum that palaces belong to the emperor, churches to the bishop.[90] A summons to contest the matter with his Arian rival before an imperial tribunal was countered with the rhetorical question: 'When did your gracious Majesty ever hear of laymen judging

[87] However, Bishop John Ponet had argued in *An apologie fully aunswering by scriptures and aunceant doctors, a blasphemous book gathered by D. Steph. Gardiner* (Zurich, 1555) that the word bishop was so abused by corrupt associations that it should be replaced by superintendent, 'another word out of the Scripture of the same signification': 'The word *superintendent* being a very Latin word, made English by us, should in time have taught the people, by the very etymology and proper signification, what thing was meant, when they heard that name, which by this term *bishop* could not so well be done; by reason that bishops, in time of Popery, were *overseers* in name, but not in deed.' (John Strype, *Ecclesiastical Memorials* (Oxford, 1822), II. ii. 141–3.)

[88] Bilson, *The true difference*, p. 173.

[89] See my article, 'If Constantine, then also Theodosius: St. Ambrose and the Integrity of the Elizabethan *Ecclesia Anglicana*', *Journal of Ecclesiastical History*, xxx (1979), 205–29.

[90] 'Sermo Contra Auxentium de Basilicis Tradendis', *Patrologia Latina* xvi, cols. 1007–18.

bishops in a matter of faith?' 'Si docendus est episcopus a laico, quid sequetur?'[91] When the Emperor Theodosius required a bishop in the East to make restitution for the wanton destruction of Jewish property, Ambrose not only protested but in the oration known as Epistle 40 defended his right to protest in a spirited justification of what English parliamentarians know as the liberty of free speech. An emperor ought not to deny this liberty and a bishop ought not to remain silent. The difference between good and bad princes was that the good loved liberty, the bad servitude. In a bishop nothing was more perilous before God or so dishonourable before men as not freely to declare his opinion. 'You are imperilled by my silence, you are benefited by my outspokenness. In God's cause [*in causa vera Dei*] whom will you listen to if not to the bishop?'[92] Two years later, when Theodosius perpetrated a hideous massacre in Thessalonica, Ambrose constrained him to undergo humiliating acts of penance before readmitting him to the sacrament.[93]

These episodes, and especially the last, have been seen as early steps along the road to Canossa. Their utility for an 'Erastian' Church rather than for its Romanist opponents may not be immediately apparent. But as glossed by Anglican divines, even the excommunication of Theodosius became a perfect example of the proper dispositions of spiritual authority under a Christian monarchy. For it was not excommunication at all in any punitive or coercive sense but a piece of fervent exhortation which had worked upon the emperor's own conscience. In the words of Archbishop Sandys, Ambrose had 'brought the Emperor Theodosius himself to unfeigned humility and hearty repentance'.[94] According to Bilson, to make more of the episode than this was to add to the historical record. 'The Jesuites helpe this storie with their admixtions.' 'You care not, to fit your purpose, though you make S. *Ambrose* a sturdie rebell.'[95] As for

---

[91] *Patrologia Latina* xvi, cols. 1005–6; *Early Latin Theology*, ed. S. L. Greenslade, Library of Christian Classics v (1956), 204.

[92] *Patrologia Latina*, xvi, cols. 1101–6; *Early Latin Theology*, 230.

[93] *Epistola LI*, *Patrologia Latina*, xvi, cols. 1159–64.

[94] *The Sermons of Edwin Sandys,* ed. J. Ayre, Parker Society (Cambridge, 1841), p. 72.

[95] Bilson, *The true difference*, pp. 173, 373.

Ambrose's defence of the basilicas, this was a splendid example of passive resistance *in causa Dei*. In Bilson's words: 'Hee refused to put his consent to the Prince's will: but hee resisted not the Princes power.'[96] Carleton's account of the same episode verged on the ecstatic:

This example of *Ambrose* his courage is worthily commended by all posterity, wherein this worthy man seemeth to direct a true rule of obedience . . . There appeared in him courage, godlinesse and exact obedience, all truly tempered. He denieth the Emperour to be a sufficient Iudge in a cause of faith and religion . . . And yet if the Emperour would by force doe any thing, he denieth that there is any power in him, or in the Church to resist by force.[97]

This was to make more of the episode than some other commentators made of it. Even Field followed Jewel and Hooker in emphasizing the exceptional nature of the circumstances, in which Valentinian, a juvenile, unbaptized, and a heretic to boot, proposed to reopen what had been decided at the Council of Nicea. How unlike ecclesiastical life under gentle Constantine! And for Constantine, read Elizabeth, or James.[98]

But the oration on free speech in Epistle 40 was perfectly tailored to the needs of the Church under Tudor and Stuart royal supremacy. 'Nam silentii mei periculo involveris, libertatis bono juvaris'—'If I remain silent it will be at your peril. You will benefit from my outspokenness.'[99] To persuade monarchy of the wisdom of these words would be to solve the problem of counsel, the most vexing political conundrum of the age. We are reminded of Peter Wentworth in the House of Commons, asserting that 'the libertye of free speech' was justified by 'the commodityes that grow to the prince and the whole state' by the use of it.[1] And also of Sir Francis Knollys,

---

[96] Ibid., p. 176.

[97] Carleton, *Jurisdiction*, p. 45.

[98] Field, *Of the Church*, iv. 96. Cf. *Works of Jewel*, iv. 1027–9, *Works of Hooker*, iii. 442–3.

[99] *Patrologia Latina*, xvi, cols. 1101–6; *Early Latin Theology*, 230.

[1] Wentworth's speech in the House of Commons, 8 February 1576, printed in *Proceedings in the Parliaments of Elizabeth, I*, i, *1558–1581*, ed. T. E. Hartley (Leicester, 1981), 425–34. See J. E. Neale, 'Peter Wentworth', *English Historical Review*, xxxix (1924), 36–54, 175–205, and his *Elizabeth I and her Parliaments, 1559–1581*, pp. 318–32.

ever conscious of his oath as a Privy Councillor: 'I had rather dye than to ympugne hir majesties safetye by anye pleasyng speache.'[2] The master card, which Ambrose had played with success in AD 388, was to represent the open ear as the most gracious of all princely attributes: 'Sed neque imperiale est libertatem dicendi negare'—'It is not the part of an emperor to deny liberty of speech.'[3]

IV

As a Roman patrician and trained rhetorician with a gift for 'passionate over-statement',[4] Ambrose conferred legitimation on tactics which English churchmen had learned for themselves, in the hard and perilous school of the Elizabethan Court. For the court divine, the problem of counsel arose when he was required to preach, as Sir John Harington tells us, *vis-à-vis* the queen in her closet in the Chapel Royal, eyeball to eyeball.[5] When Alexander Nowell, the dean of St. Paul's and a frequent court preacher, was accused of flattery in his sermons he replied that 'he had no other way to instruct the queen what she should be but by commending her':[6] an old rhetorical trick. But here was a knife-edge, for as Ambrose himself had insisted, the role of flatterer, *adulator*, was contrary to that of watchman, *speculator*.[7] The temptations to prefer the easy course of *adulator* were as numerous and strong as in Old Testament days of false prophecy. It would be naïve to suppose that many, and perhaps most, ecclesiastical careerists did not succumb. Of Bishop Richard Fletcher, the father of the dramatist, it was said that 'he knew what would please the Queene, and would adventure on that, though it offended others'.[8]

---

[2] Cargill Thompson, *Studies,* p. 126.

[3] *Patrologia Latina,* xvi, cols. 1101–6; *Early Latin Theology,* 229–31.

[4] Hans von Campenhausen, *The Fathers of the Latin Church,* tr. Manfred Hoffmann (1964), p. 90.

[5] Harington's observation applied particularly to the arrangements in the chapel at Richmond: Harington, *A Supplie,* p. 152.

[6] Ralph Churton, *The Life of Alexander Nowell* (Oxford, 1809), p. 92.

[7] The future Archbishop Whitgift cited this Ambrosian principle in a court sermon of 1574. (*Works of Whitgift,* iii (Cambridge, 1853), 578.) Cf. some late Elizabethan verses 'Against Flattering Preachers': copies in *HMC Report, Various Collections,* iii (T. B. Clarke-Thornhill), 117; BL Harl. MS 367, fol. 144 (in the hand of John Stow).

[8] Harington, *A Supplie,* p. 53.

But among those who trod this tightrope with some skill was William Barlow, one of the most favoured of court preachers in Elizabeth's declining years. A sermon preached in 1601 received its quaint and already very Jacobean title, *The eagle and the body,* from its text in Luke 17:37: 'Wheresoever the body is, thither will the eagles be gathered together.' In his entry to this text, Barlow toyed with its application to the corruptions of Church and State, beginning with the Court itself, 'a full *Bodie,* the fatnesse and marrow wherof hath fetcht many *Eagles* from all corners'. But then at once came a tactical and tactful withdrawal: 'Which I speke not out of envie of their desire, but with prayer for a blessing on the *Royal Foundresse.*' The preacher then turned to the Church. 'After that we might behold the *Church* in this land, that Bodye sometime plethoricall and goodly, though now (with the *Prophet*) it may truly cry, *My leannesse, my leannesse.* So long it has become a Prey to the Eagles of the Epicene gender, both Hees and Shees, that it is become . . . rather an Anatomie of Bones then a Bodie of Substance.' But a risky point having been scored, or almost scored, Barlow beat his retreat into a theological and spiritual exegesis of the text, in which the body became Christ and the eagles his elect. 'A true speach, but perhaps too bitter, and therefore I leave it.'[9] What consummate delicacy was later shown in Barlow's handling of James I in *An answer to a catholike Englishman*! The king 'knows what Princes *ought* to doe, not regarding what they *please* to doe, being desirous rather to governe by Christian *pietie* then *Irreligious Policie.*' In the same book we encounter a cameo of King James at his table, which was 'as *Constantine's* Court, *Ecclesiae instar,* a little *Universitie,* compassed with *Learned men* in all professions; and his Majesty in the middest of them . . . a *living Library,* furnished at all hands, to *reply, answer, obiect, resolve, discourse, explane*'.[10] It might be thought that such dainties were devoid of historical import, except for the advancement of Barlow's own career. But Barlow's masterpiece was his *Sum and substance* of the Hampton Court

---

[9] William Barlow, *The Eagle and the body: described in one sermon preched before Queene Elizabeth of precious memorie in Lent Anno 1601* (1609), sigs. B^v–B2^r.

[10] Barlow, *An answere,* pp. 122–3, 105.

Conference,[11] which persuaded all but the most canny of puritan critics, and most historians too, that Hampton Court was a triumph for the bishops and a rout for their opponents. The truth is that this journalistic *coup* was not so much an exercise in fair and objective reporting as 'a skilful piece of party propaganda'.[12] From the point of view of the hierarchy and its interests, Barlow had earned the reward of the bishopric which in due course followed.

If we now follow St. Ambrose back into the Elizabethan Church he will lead us to a churchman with none of Barlow's courtly finesse. In December 1576 Archbishop Edmund Grindal addressed Queen Elizabeth in an extraordinary letter which explained at gratuitous length why he was unable to comply with her royal command that he curtail the number of preachers and totally suppress the preaching festivals known as prophesyings.

I am forced with all humility, and yet plainly, to profess that I cannot with safe conscience, and without the offence of the majesty of God, give my assent to the suppressing of the said exercises: much less can I send out any injunction for the utter and universal subversion of the same . . . If it be your Majesty's pleasure, for this or any other cause, to remove me out of this place, I will with all humility yield thereunto, and render again to your Majesty that I received of the same . . . Bear with me, I beseech you, Madam, if I choose rather to offend your earthly majesty than to offend the heavenly majesty of God.[13]

What Bilson later said about the epistle of Ambrose to Valentinian might have been meant for Grindal's letter. It was 'stout but lawful, constant but Christian': 'He refused to put his consent to the Princes will: but hee resisted not the Princes power.'[14]

And this is hardly surprising, since Grindal's letter was replete with epigrams drawn from Ambrose. For example, the

---

[11] Edward Cardwell, *A History of Conferences and Other Proceedings Connected with the Revision of the Book of Common Prayer* (Oxford, 1849), pp. 167–212.

[12] Mark H. Curtis, 'The Hampton Court Conference and its Aftermath', *History*, xlvi (1961), 1–16.

[13] *The Remains of Archbishop Grindal*, ed. W. Nicholson, Parker Society (Cambridge, 1853), p. 387.

[14] Bilson, *The true difference*, pp. 174, 176.

sentence 'Bear with me, I beseech you, Madam...' is a concealed quotation from the sermon preached by Ambrose in the besieged basilica at the height of his battle with the Arians: 'Quia plus Dominum mundi, quam saeculi hujus imperatorem timerem.'[15] In particular, the requests which composed the final peroration of Grindal's letter and which generalized the point at issue were both specifically Ambrosian and an anticipation of the episcopalianism of the Jacobean divines. The queen was asked to follow the example of all godly emperors and princes in referring 'all these ecclesiastical matters which touch religion, or the doctrine and discipline of the Church' to the bishops and divines of her realm; and that in matters of faith and religion or touching the Church she 'would not use to pronounce so resolutely and peremptorily, *quasi ex auctoritate,* as ye may do in civil and extern matters... In God's matters all princes ought to bow their sceptres to the Son of God, and to ask counsel at his mouth, what they ought to do.' 'Si docendus episcopus a laico, quid sequetur?'[16] This Ambrosian influence amounted to more than a few well-chosen phrases to adorn an original composition of Grindal's own. Grindal's copy of the *Opera* of Ambrose survives in the Library of the Queen's College Oxford, to which he donated it, and its many significant underlinings and annotations underscore the fact that the 'book to the queen' was in form an oration in the manner of Ambrose, making of the prophesyings a *cause célèbre in* Church–State relations of equal magnitude with the disputed basilicas of the fourth century, and written 'with my own hand that you alone may read it', as Ambrose had written to Theodosius in Epistle 51. In his reading of Epistle 40, Grindal particularly noted the statement that 'sacerdotium est, libere denuntiare quod sentiunt', together with the rhetorical question: 'In causa vera Dei quem audies si sacerdotem non audies?' Grindal *was* Ambrose, and Elizabeth was Theodosius.[17]

But this was the sixteenth, not the fourth century. Grindal paid for the scholarly anachronism which his letter had

---

[15] 'Sermo Contra Auxentium', *Patrologia Latina*, xvi, col. 1007.

[16] *Remains of Grindal*, pp. 387–9.

[17] Collinson, 'If Constantine, then also Theodosius', 218–19; Collinson, *Archbishop Grindal*, pp. 243–4, 266.

perpetrated with suspension from office, which would have been followed by summary deprivation if the queen had not been otherwise advised and manipulated by councillors privately sympathetic to the archbishop and publicly dismayed by the scandalous and politically damaging consequences likely to follow from his dismissal.[18] A memorandum reflecting the queen's view of the matter is a reminder of Tudor realities. It was irrelevant that prophesying had been allowed by some bishops. For it was 'a thing not sufferable, that anie shall set up ani thinges in the Church without publick authorite, neither hath the bishop such poure'. Yet even this round condemnation of Grindal and his colleagues conceded that in a genuine matter of conscience the archbishop would have been justified in assuming a posture of passive disobedience. But since prophesying was an indifferent matter, part of the *adiaphora,* for Grindal to represent it as a conscientious issue was to impugn the queen's own conscience 'in dissenting from the archbishop'.[19]

With such a sequel it is not surprising that this was the last occasion on which the religious opinions and ecclesiastical policy of Queen Elizabeth were so directly challenged by one of her preferred divines. But it was not the first. In the early years of the reign, the bishops who had recently returned from exile had taken a number of initiatives which served to impart to the Church a character which was more protestant than the queen had evidently intended, especially in the externals of ceremony and worship. It appears that Elizabeth desired a celibate clergy, arrayed in eucharistic vestments, communicating the sacrament in the form of unleavened wafer bread from stone altars with the symbol of the cross in evidence, both on the altar and in its traditional place of prominence on the rood screen. The *émigré* clergy used their powers as royal visitors and presently as ordinaries to create a Church without crosses, copes, or altars, and they made bonfires of roods and rood statuary. On some issues, such as the type of bread to be used in the Communion, their success was only partial and led to a scandalous diversity of practice. On the matter of

[18] Collinson, *Archbishop Grindal,* pp. 246–82.
[19] Northamptonshire Record Office, F.(N).P.70.b.

vestments they achieved part of their objective by a generous interpretation of the royal injunctions which was made a sanction for the physical destruction of copes and chasubles. But the queen retaliated when she required the bishops to enforce the linen surplice and the outdoor apparel, with permanently divisive consequences.[20] On altars the bishops, or some of them, confronted the supreme governor with a reasoned case 'why it is not convenient that the communion shulde be mynystered at an altare'.[21] This memorandum contains some interesting phraseology. The queen was asked to 'tender the consent' of the survivors of the Marian persecution who 'if they were required to utter their mind or thought it necessarie to make petition' would certainly express their opposition to altars. This appeal seems to have won a significant victory in an injunction legalizing the *fait accompli* of the removal of altars 'in many and sundry parts of the realm', and which enabled the bishops in their 'Interpretations' of the Injunctions and in the Advertisements of 1566 to prescribe a Communion-table, set table-wise, as the norm for Anglican worship.[22]

So too with the still more emotive symbol of the cross. When in the autumn of 1559 Elizabeth restored a small silver cross or crucifix to her own chapel, this was interpreted as a signal for the replacement of the roods and rood statuary in all the thousands of parish churches from which the royal visitors had so recently removed them with much attendant labour and expense for local communities. The bishops, still technically bishops-elect, could not have survived such a blow to both conscience and credit. Some prepared themselves for resignation or dismissal.[23] In the midst of this grave ecclesiasti-

---

[20] Collinson, *Archbishop Grindal,* pp. 85–106.

[21] Copies in Inner Temple Library MS Petyt 538.38, no. 9, fols. 29–31 (whence printed, John Strype, *Annals of the Reformation* (Oxford, 1824), I.i.237–41), and Lambeth Palace Library MS 2002, no. 18, fols. 107–10.

[22] *Documentary Annals of the Reformed Church of England,* ed. Edward Cardwell (Oxford, 1844), i. 233–4, 326; *Visitation Articles and Injunctions of the Period of the Reformation,* ed. W. H. Frere, iii, Alcuin Club Collections xvi (1910), 59–73; W. P. M. Kennedy, *The Interpretations of the Bishops* (1908); W. P. M. Kennedy, 'The Early History of the Elizabethan Compromise in Ceremonial', in *Studies in Tudor History* (1916), pp. 143–64.

[23] The story is told in W. P. Haugaard, *Elizabeth and the English Reformation* (Cambridge, 1968), pp. 185–200.

cal crisis, a strongly-worded letter to the queen was drafted and attached to a treatise: 'Reasons against images in churches'.[24] This anonymous document bears a family resemblance to Grindal's letter of 1576. After rehearsing lengthy reasons and 'proofs' from the Bible and the Fathers, it too ends with a defiant peroration. 'We beseche your Highnes most humblie not to strean us any further...We pray your Majestie also not to be offended with this our plannesse and libertie, which all good and christiane princes have ever taken in good parte at the handes of godlie bishops. Saynt Ambrose writing to Theodosius the Emperor useth thies wordes.' And then follow the familiar phrases from Epistle 40: 'Sed neque imperiale est libertatem dicendi negare, neque sacerdotale, quod sentiat, non dicere.'

These and such like speeches of St Ambrose Theodosius and Valentinianus the emperors did always take in good parte; and we doubt not but your Grace will do the like, of whose not onlie clemencie but also beneficence we have largelie tasted. We beseche your Majestie also in thiese and such like controversies of religion to referr the discussement and deciding of them to a synode of your bishops, and other godlie learned men, according to the example of Constantinus Magnus and other christian emperors.

In 1563 the first Convocation of the new dispensation duly met, considered synodically many details of ecclesiastical practice, and adopted the articles of belief to which the Church of England remains in some measure committed, four centuries later. But in 1560, as if to illustrate the difference between the polities of the fourth century and of the sixteenth, the sensitive problem of images was referred not to a synod

---

[24] Copies in Corpus Christi College Cambridge MS 105, art. 11, pp. 201–15[r] (whence printed, *Correspondence of Parker*, pp. 79–95) and Foxe, *Acts and Monuments*, viii. 701–7 (having first appeared in the 1583 edition, pp. 2126–31), where it is assigned by Foxe to the reign of Edward VI and attributed to 'M. Nicolas Ridley'. Consequently the treatise was included in the *Works of Nicholas Ridley,* ed. H. Christmas, Parker Society (Cambridge, 1843), pp. 81–96. A further copy of the letter to the queen which accompanies the treatise in the Corpus Christi MS is in Lambeth Palace Library MS 2002, no. 5, fol. 29. The vexing problems posed by the treatise are discussed in my 'If Constantine, then also Theodosius', 220–5. Although the best text of the treatise occurs among Parker's papers in Corpus Christi College Library, there is no reason to identify the author as Parker but internal evidence to link it with Grindal, assuming, *pace* Foxe, that it did not originate with Ridley in 1548.

but to a lay committee, described by Jewel as 'persons selected
by the Council', who listened to the formal arguments
presented by select bishops. Jewel added: 'The decision rests
with the judges.'[25] Ambrose had refused to dispute God's cause
before a secular tribunal ('Si docendus est episcopus a laico,
quid sequetur?') but in the reformed Church of England this
was a recognized if occasional device for the clarification of
ecclesiastical policy. In 1584 a conference was held at
Lambeth, when prayer-book matters were disputed between
bishops and puritan divines, in the presence of the earl of
Leicester and other noblemen, and at their instigation.[26] In
1604 there was the more prestigious conference under royal
chairmanship at Hampton Court; and in 1626 the York
House Conference, when Calvinists and Arminians contended
in the presence of the duke of Buckingham and other
councillors, ostensibly over the contents of a book by Richard
Montague, in reality to determine the confessional bias of the
Church of England in the new reign of Charles I.[27]

The outcome of the 1560 disputation about images was
favourably construed by Bishop Sandys: 'God, in whose hands
are the hearts of kings, gave us tranquillity instead of a
tempest and delivered the Church of England from stumbling
blocks of this kind.'[28] But Sandys probably meant that there
was no longer a threat to restore the cross to the parish
churches, not that Elizabeth had allowed the bishops to
rearrange her private chapel. There the cross remained (and
for that matter the altar on which it stood also remained), and
when five years later the dean of St. Paul's launched a new
attack upon it in the context of an Ash Wednesday sermon at
Court he was loudly interrupted by the queen: a profoundly
disturbing experience, discussed as far away as Rome, which
still rang in the preacher's ears a year later and which may

---

[25] Haugaard, *Elizabeth and the English Reformation*, p. 190.

[26] Copies of Walter Travers's 'true reporte of the first conference at Lambeth' in BL
Add. MS 48064, fols 49–63 and *A Seconde Parte of a Register*, ed. Albert Peel
(Cambridge, 1915), i. 275–83. The date is supplied by George Paule, *Life of Whitgift*
(1612), p. 30.

[27] 'The Sum and Substance of the Conference Lately Had at York House
Concerning Mr Mountague's Books', in *The Works of John Cosin*, ii, Library of Anglo-
Catholic Theology (Oxford, 1845), 17–81.

[28] *Zurich Letters*, i. 74.

have had some permanent influence on the style and content of Elizabethan court preaching.[29]

On the day that Dean Alexander Nowell was shouted down, Archbishop Parker took him home to dinner 'for pure pity'. 'He was utterly dismayed.'[30] Parker himself knew what it was to confront his mistress on a matter of protestant principle. In 1561 she had revealed in his presence the depth of her hostility to a married clergy. Parker, himself a married man, was scandalized. 'I was in an horror to hear such words to come from her mild nature and christian learned conscience, as she spake concerning God's holy ordinance and institution of matrimony.' The queen had gone so far as to express 'a repentance that we were thus appointed in office, wishing it had been otherwise'—a clue, perhaps, to Elizabeth's less than total control of the processes of patronage which had brought the Elizabethan episcopate into being. Parker for his part, 'utterly discomforted and discouraged', regretted that he had consented to serve in a place where he was forced to receive complaints from other bishops and clergy 'daily and hourly'. And then came a veiled threat so radical as to seem quite out of character with Parker's public persona: 'I would be sorry that the clergy should have cause to shew disobedience, with *oportet Deo obedire magis quam hominibus*.'[31]

V

There is no need to multiply the Elizabethan instances of unreasonable and uncaring royal behaviour and of episcopal discomfiture. There would be many more before James I visited some at least of the bishops with favour and familiarity, advising his son that they were 'grave and wise men and best companions for princes'.[32] The Reverend F. O. White, having compiled short biographies of seventy-four

[29] *Calendar of State Papers, Spanish*, i. 405; Alexander Nowell to Sir William Cecil, 8 March 1564/5, John Strype, *Life of Parker* (Oxford, 1821), iii. 94; *Calendar of State Papers, Rome*, i. 171.

[30] *Correspondence of Parker*, p. 235.

[31] Ibid., pp. 156–60.

[32] Quoted, Arthur P. Kautz, 'The Selection of Jacobean Bishops', in *Early Stuart Studies: Essays in Honor of David Harris Willson*, ed. Harold S. Reinmuth (Minneapolis, 1970), p. 154.

Elizabethan bishops of the Church of England, carried away from his labours an extreme distaste for Elizabeth as a 'cruel despot tyrannizing over a helpless set of men'.[33]

The Elizabethan bishops, to be sure, were no Hildebrands or Beckets, still less Anglican ayatollahs. We cannot fault Lord Dacre's characterization of them as 'earnest, Protestant-minded, worried men, burdened with duties, uncertain of their position in a society which was both revolutionary and conservative'.[34] But we may notice what is not always observed: the capacity of these prelates to fight back, or to dig in their heels. When Burghley accused Aylmer of bad stewardship, the worm turned and the bishop confronted the lord treasurer with his constant undermining of episcopal discipline, particularly in the encouragement of puritan dissidents:

And to be plane with your lordship, you are the man that doth moste discorage me, . . . in that by your wordes and countenaunces my government is hindred. For when such wordes shall passe from yow, that such and such thinges be not of the substance of Religion, that the ecclesiasticall jurisdiction (which yow your selfe by statute have confirmede) is mere papall, that yow wolde such and such sholde preach which are disturbers etc.: yt cannot be my lord but three words from your mouth *huius generis* shall more imbolden them and hinder our labors then our toile and moile shall in manie yeres be able to helpe and salve. Theis are the thinges my lord that doth discourrage me and make me wearie . . .[35]

Aylmer suggested that to be rash enough to 'deal with your lordship as *Job* did with God' implied that he was desperate and ready to retire from such ungrateful toil into a private life, 'my old yeeres growing on'. When Parker wrote an equally despairing letter to Burghley he added: 'I am a fool to use this plainness with you in writing.'[36] Yet when Aylmer composed his own premature epitaph there were fifteen years of his episcopate still to run: singularly fruitful years, which worked a transformation in the quality of ecclesiastical life in his

[33] F. O. White, *Lives of the Elizabethan Bishops* (1898), p. vii.

[34] H. R. Trevor-Roper, *Historical Essays* (1957), p. 13.

[35] Aylmer to Burghley, 26 May 1579; BL Lansdowne MS 28, no. 72, fol. 159.

[36] Parker to Burghley, 18 February 1574/5; *Correspondence of Parker*, p. 473.

diocese, and especially in the city of London.[37] To be frank, his bold letter to Burghley cannot be read as a simple declaration of spiritual independence. In all probability it would not have been written if Aylmer had not been assured of the backing of his patron Sir Christopher Hatton, the rising star at Court.[38] And behind Hatton stood a queen who shared Aylmer's suspicions about covert support extended to puritans by some in high places.

Our argument is not that the bishops could survive in the glorious spiritual isolation of Carleton and Field's dreams, without the benefit of patronage. But they were not an utterly helpless set of men, and they were capable of deploying in their own defence such weapons and levers as lay to hand. If we accept the mildly anachronistic ascription of 'civil servants' proposed by Margaret Bowker for the 1530s and by Lord Dacre for the 1620s, it must be with recognition of the extensive opportunities available to the senior staff within any human organization to shape its public policy. The Elizabethan bishops were never required to conceal their wives in chests, or to send them packing to Germany. Instead they found safety in numbers. Of the seventy-six bishops consecrated in Elizabeth's reign, at least fifty-five were married men, and ten courted disaster by marrying for a second time. It has been well said that 'it was not the least of the achievements of the Elizabethan episcopate to establish the concept of a married clergy'.[39] (But not until the reign of William and Mary did another archbishop's wife take up residence at Lambeth.) Nor were the bishops totally dispossessed of their endowed wealth, a fate which befell them only on paper, in the abortive projects of mid-Tudor anticlericals. Numbers of anciently held manors with their concomitant political and social advantages were traded for less desirable sources of income. But much of this property was retained,

---

[37] H. G. Owen, 'The London Parish Clergy in the Reign of Elizabeth I', London Ph.D. thesis, 1957, pp. 540–76.

[38] Sir Harris Nicolas, *Life and Times of Sir Christopher Hatton* (1847), pp. 55–6, 58–9, 61–2.

[39] Joel Berlatsky, 'Marriage and Family in a Tudor Élite: Familial Patterns of Elizabethan Bishops', *Journal of Family History*, iii (1978), 6–22. One Elizabethan bishop was married three times.

and with it the symbolical and partly real independence of the
landed proprietor rather than the servile status of the salaried
state functionary, suffered by the Lutheran superintendents of
Scandinavia. In the long view, enjoyed from the sunny
uplands of restored episcopal prosperity in the late seventeenth century, the material fortunes of the lords spiritual
followed rather closely those of the secular peerage. And it is
only short-sighted historians who weep tears over the alleged
crisis of the aristocracy in the late sixteenth and early
seventeenth centuries.[40]

The first generation of protestant-minded bishops had as
much or more influence over what Jewel called 'the scenic
apparatus of divine worship' than the queen who had
appointed them. The second generation, admittedly with the
queen's enthusiastic support, successfully defended the
Church's constitution and scattered the forces of presbyterian
subversion. The third confirmed that victory by its tactics
before, during, and after Hampton Court. The Church which
emerged from its Elizabethan trials into its Jacobean heyday
had been shaped by the interplay of many forces. This chapter
has sketched the ideological framework within which the two
leading if unequal forces of monarchy and episcopacy
manoeuvred, sometimes together but often in subdued contention, for a controlling interest.

[40] On the economic fortunes and problems of the Tudor episcopate, all earlier
accounts are superseded by Felicity Heal, *Of Prelates and Princes: A Study of the Economic
and Social Position of the Tudor Episcopate* (Cambridge, 1980).

Chapter Two

Episcopal Roles and Reputations

I

How can justice be done to such a subject in a single essay? Seventy-six bishops were consecrated in the reign of Elizabeth and forty-one more under James, not to count the bishops of the Irish sees, of whom a few were men of distinction. Any general statement covering such a motley collection of ecclesiastics would be vacuous. To be sure, the subject could be Namierized and reduced to a factual bed-rock of social origins, educational formation, and patronage. From such a prosopographical enquiry significant regularities would emerge, but somewhat at the cost of those precious truths which reside in particulars. And such a method could only crudely depict the evolution of the episcopate and the changes in its fortunes, social setting, and social relations which occurred in the course of these sixty-six years. Somehow we must convey the transition from the threadbare years at the beginning, when Bishop Bentham of Coventry and Lichfield was preoccupied with the price of salt fish in Chester market and with the provision of cheap rugs to keep his servants warm,[1] to the late 1620s, when Bishop Williams of Lincoln 'wither'd away in a happy Retirement' at Buckden, creating 'Arbors, Orchards, Pools for Water-fowls, and for Fish of all variety', and ransacking 'all the nurseries about *London* for fair Flowers and choice Fruits'.[2] The alteration from early Elizabethan impecuniosity to Jacobean affluence can, to be sure, be expressed statistically. Of the first Elizabethan cohort, only 5 per cent of bishops died rich, 45 per cent poor. With James's original stock of bishops the position was exactly

---

[1] *The Letter-Book of Thomas Bentham, Bishop of Coventry and Lichfield,* ed. Rosemary O'Day and Joel Berlatsky, *Camden Miscellany* xxvii, Camden 4th ser. xxii (1979), 165, 170; and for further evidence of threadbareness, 129–31, 134–9, 143.

[2] John Hacket, *Scrinia Reserata: A Memoriall Offer'd to the Great Deservings of John Williams, D.D.* (1693), ii. 88, 29.

reversed, 5 per cent dying in poverty or debt, 32 per cent in some prosperity.[3]

At the beginning of our period, bishops travelled on horseback, with a train of attendants to proclaim their status. When John Whitgift came to the Parliament of 1581 as bishop of Worcester, he was 'very well attended' with 'an orderly troope of Tawny coats'. The puritans of Ashby-de-la-Zouche wondered why the bishops could never undertake a journey without 'some great troupe of horses', and begged their own diocesan to 'come amongest us sometymes in christian humilitie, layeng asyde all popishe lordlynes'.[4] By 1625 bishops moved from place to place by coach.[5] What was the significance of the change from late medieval stateliness to early modern privacy? Was the coach more or less an instrument of isolation and alienation? Some bishops had books read to them in their coaches as they travelled. One historian imagines them as 'perhaps too preoccupied to observe how they had made themselves the gazing-stock of the envious and the vulgar'.[6] An arresting image, somewhat beyond our period, is of the mobs out in Palace Yard Westminster in December 1641, peering into the windows of the coaches by torchlight in search of bishops to intimidate.[7]

In 1573 a puritan preacher thought it his duty to alert the Privy Council to a sermon preached in St. Paul's which had proposed returning the great offices of state to the bishops. The preacher had said: 'I would five or six of the Counsell

---

[3] Felicity Heal, *Of Prelates and Princes: A Study of the Economic and Social Position of the Tudor Episcopate* (Cambridge, 1980), pp. 316–18.

[4] Sir John Harington, *A Supplie or Addicion to the Catalogue of Bishops to the Yeare 1608*, ed. R. H. Miller, Studia Humanitatis (Madrid, 1979), pp. 38–9; BL Add. MS 27632, fols. 47–8.

[5] When did the change occur? In 1608 Harington recorded (*A Supplie*, p. 181) that 'not long since' Archbishop Tobie Matthew had made a journey to Bristol on horseback, 'accompanied with a troope fit for his calling', a 'troope of his retinew'. In later years (see pp. 48–9 below) Matthew used a coach.

[6] Geoffrey I. Soden, *Godfrey Goodman Bishop of Gloucester 1583–1656* (1953), p. 117. When Bishop Thomas Morton travelled by coach, which he did 'after that he had obtained greater preferments', he 'had always some choice and useful book, which he either read himself, or else caused a Chaplaine as his *Amanuensis* to reade unto him, who attended on his Journeying'. (J[oseph] N[elson], *The Life of Dr Thomas Morton Late Bishop of Duresme* (1669), pp. 86–7.)

[7] *The Works of Joseph Hall*, ed. Philip Wynter (Oxford, 1843), i. lvii.

weare Aarons; I would the Lord Keeper weare a bishop . . .; I would a bishop were Master of the Rolls.' 'It greveth me', wrote Edward Dering, 'to see one pretend the person of Christ and to speak woordes of so great vanitie.'[8] By the 1620s, for bishops to be Privy Councillors was no longer unthinkable, and for the first time in ninety years the great seal had been held by an ecclesiastic, Bishop Williams. From the 1570s and 1580s, when virulent anticlericalism was still an 'automatic reflex' of the landowning class,[9] it would be hard to find a kind word said for the episcopate by a councillor or in Parliament. Job Throgmorton compared them to 'a northern wind that seldom bloweth good to the Church of God'.[10] That was the remark of an incorrigible puritan. But Lord Burghley, who so often mirrored the typical mental attitudes of his generation, said that he found such worldliness in those that were otherwise affected before they came to cathedral chairs that he feared the places altered the men. And he wrote of their 'evill examples in covetousness, looseness of lyff and manny other defaultes'.[11] The lay protestant imagination could hardly be restrained when invited to discourse on the theme of episcopal 'worldliness'. The author of a 'plot for reformation' complained that the bishops maintained 'a grete rowte of people aboute them lieke princes, appareling them in chaines of golde, silckes and other costly apparel, feasting, banqueting and entertayning'.[12] Edwin Sandys as bishop of London found that the bishops' estimation was little, their authority less. They were *excrementum mundi*.[13]

But from the 1620s it is not difficult to collect evidence of the good estimation enjoyed by the episcopate, even among those whom it is usual to call puritans. Sir John Eliot told the House of Commons in 1629 that 'there are amongst our

[8] Edward Dering to the Privy Council, 26/27 November 1573; copies in BL Lansdowne MS 17, no. 92, fols. 203–4, and *HMC Report, Salisbury MSS,* ii. 63.

[9] Heal, *Of Prelates and Princes,* p. 215.

[10] Quoted, J. E. Neale, *Elizabeth I and her Parliaments 1584–1601* (1957), p. 151.

[11] Burghley to Archbishop Whitgift, 17 September 1584, BL Add. MS 22473, fol. 12 (another copy, BL Lansdowne MS 396, fols. 16–17); 'A memoryall of thynges to be reported to hir Majesty', PRO, S.P. 12/4/40 (misplaced in this volume of the Domestic State Papers since internal evidence dates the memorandum after 1580).

[12] 'Plot for Reformation', BL Add. MS 48066, fol 8[r].

[13] Sandys to Burghley, 5 August 1573, BL Lansdowne MS 17, fol. 96.

Bishops such as are fit to be made examples for all ages, who shine in virtue'. Admittedly Eliot's purpose in this speech was to pillory those bishops of whom he did not approve, particularly the enemy of the hour, the Arminian controversialist Richard Montague. For the purpose of an argument based conventionally on antithesis good bishops were necessary. Yet there is no reason to doubt his sincerity when he said of Montague: 'I reverence the order, I honour not the man.' It appears that John Pym and his half-brother Francis Rous were two other members of this Parliament whose view was that Montague's promotion brought a worthy order into disrepute.[14] When Sir Edward Dering spoke in the Long Parliament of 'the ancient, lawful and just episcopacy' and Lord George Digby said 'let us not destroy bishops but make them such as they were in primitive times', it is likely that they drew less upon scholarly acquaintance with the primitive Church than on personal experience of the merits of some of the bishops of their own century.[15] 'Primitive' was no more remote than the days of James I.

By such tokens one can measure an upward movement in the fortunes and reputation of the bishops. But we cannot isolate this trend from the disaster which followed, in the 1640s. The question which lies near the centre of this chapter is whether, by the 1620s, the episcopate had reached a plateau of social and political acceptability and some effectiveness, in a Church enjoying equilibrium, which Archbishop Laud's divisive and unpopular policies destroyed in the following fifteen years; or whether on the contrary the Church which Laud inherited and strove to redeem had already been betrayed by an effete episcopate, the puppets of a corrupt and corrupting Court, as Lord Dacre has suggested.[16] Was the

---

[14] *The Commons' Debates for 1629*, ed. W. Notestein and F. Relf (Minneapolis, 1921), pp. 12–16, 27. See N. R. N. Tyacke, 'Puritanism, Arminianism and Counter-Revolution', in *The Origins of the English Civil War*, ed. Conrad Russell (1973), p. 135; and Conrad Russell, 'The Parliamentary Career of John Pym, 1621–9', in *The English Commonwealth 1547–1640: Essays in Politics and Society Presented to Joel Hurstfield*, ed. Peter Clark, Alan G. R. Smith, and Nicholas Tyacke (Leicester, 1979), pp. 159–61, 164–5.

[15] William A. Shaw, *A History of the English Church During the Civil Wars and under the Commonwealth* (1900), i. 79, 32.

[16] The account given by Lord Dacre (H. R. Trevor-Roper) of 'James I and his Bishops' (*Historical Essays* (1957)) may be compared with J. Rogan, 'King James's

homely advice of Archbishop Abbot and of Bishop Williams the counsel of wise men who understood the needs and capacities of the Church, or did it express the treason of clerks and the cynicism of world-weary prelates whom Dacre has condemned as 'indifferent, negligent, secular'? Abbot's proverb was 'Play for no more, lest you lose your Stake.' Williams said: 'It is an Epitaph for the Grave-stone of a Fool, I was well, and would be better; I took Physick, and dyed.'[17] When towards the end of James's reign Bishop Hall professed to discern the sky thickening for a coming storm, and to hear the winds whistling afar off, what did he have in mind?[18]

Such questions remain open to discussion because the Civil War and the downfall of the Church have made them prejudicial. They almost oblige us to declare our preference for one of two alternative episcopal strategies and, among historians, to choose one of two opposed diagnoses of the religious origins of the English Revolution. We must line up either with Richard Baxter, who wrote of the Elizabethan Archbishop Grindal, the soul of protestant moderation: 'Such bishops would have prevented our contentions and wars'; or with Clarendon, for whom the 'never enough lamented' death of the Anglican disciplinarian Archbishop Bancroft in 1610 was one of the earliest events to which it was profitable to refer in accounting for the Great Rebellion—'with whom died', wrote Heylyn of Bancroft, 'the *Uniformity* of the Church of *England*'.[19]

II

But the uncertainty of judgement surrounding the Jacobean Church is also a reflection of the unsatisfactory state of our knowledge. This chapter of English church history remains largely unwritten, the middle ground lost between books on

Bishops', *University of Durham Journal,* xlviii (1956), 93–9, D. E. Kennedy, 'The Jacobean Episcopate', *Historical Journal,* v (1962), 175–84, Arthur P. Kautz, 'The Selection of Jacobean Bishops', in *Early Stuart Studies: Essays in Honor of David Harris Willson,* ed. Howard S. Reinmuth (Minneapolis, 1970), pp. 152–79.

[17] Hacket, *Scrinia Reserata,* ii, 103.

[18] Hall quoted by Herbert Hensley Henson, *Disestablishment* (1929), p. 80.

[19] Richard Baxter, Preface to *Gildas salvianus: the reformed pastor (1656)* (a reference I owe to William Lamont); Clarendon, *History of the Great Rebellion,* ed. W. D. Macray (Oxford, 1888), i. 118; Peter Heylyn, *Cyprianus Anglicus* (1668), p. 62.

the English Reformation and the Elizabethan Church on the one side, and studies of religion in the English Revolution on the other. Lancelot Andrewes and John Donne are subjects: literature has seen to that. And so is puritanism: America has seen to that. But not the ordinary mainstream history of the Jacobean Church. It was not a subject for Gilbert Burnet or for John Strype and no one has chosen to make it a subject since.

Sometimes the evidence exists and has not been exploited: much of it in print, in the substantial theological and controversial tomes which so many bishops and bishops-to-be published. In 1606 William Barlow thought that the English bishops outshone both English and Scottish presbyterians by their learned and laborious writing and sound disputing against Papistry. By the time the Long Parliament met, and Ussher and Morton and Davenant and Downame and Hall were added to the tally of episcopal champions, this proud comparison had become a commonplace.[20] But who is prepared to engage seriously with this mountain of extinct divinity?—to penetrate, for example, the ten volumes of the *Works* of Bishop Joseph Hall, which contain at least a million words of theology, greatly outweighing Hall's juvenilia, the satires and characters for which he remains famous?[21] And who is able to discuss such works in a comparative context, setting them alongside the scholarly productions of other reformed churches? In these respects we are not better than our fathers, less and not better able to pass judgement on the early seventeenth century than our great grandfathers, for whom this theology was alive and well.

On the other hand, much of the surviving manuscript evidence for episcopal activity is scarce or even non-existent. And here there are two problems rather than one for the reputations of the bishops: the obvious problem of missing sources, and the less obvious problem which concerns the historian who fails to notice that his sources are deficient and

---

[20] William Barlow, *One of foure sermons* (1606), sigs. A3–4ʳ; Robert Ashton, *The English Civil War, 1603–1649* (1978), p. 100.

[21] See the recent and mainly literary study, F. L. Huntley, *Bishop Joseph Hall 1574–1656: A Biographical and Critical Study* (Cambridge, 1979).

who proceeds as if the surviving evidence, and even the most readily accessible evidence, contains the essential truth about the subject. So we have brick-making without straw and brick-makers who seem unaware that the straw is in short supply.

Let us take the case of Tobie (or Tobias) Matthew, a figure of some consequence in the University of Oxford for twenty years, public orator, president of St. John's, then dean of Christ Church and vice-chancellor.[22] Matthew left Oxford for Durham in 1583, where he was successively dean and bishop. Archbishop Hutton of York thought him likely to succeed his brother Whitgift of Canterbury. Instead, Matthew succeeded Hutton himself and remained archbishop of York for twenty years. His long career, running from the mid-1560s to the late 1620s, almost exactly covers the time-span of these studies. (The Elizabethans were still alive and influential in the early seventeenth century, like the Victorians in our own century.) By virtue of his marriage, Matthew became one of the more quintessential Anglican churchmen of his time. For his wife Frances was a daughter of William Barlow, the Henrician bishop whose consecrating hands preserved the episcopal succession through Archbishop Parker. All five of Barlow's daughters married future bishops. And since Frances was previously matched to Parker's son, it could be said of Mrs Matthew on her memorial in York Minster that 'a Bishop was her Father, an Archbishop her Father-in-Law; she had Four Bishops her brethren, and an Archbishop her husband'.[23] The

[22] What follows draws on 'Memorials of the Life of Toby Matthew, Archbishop of York', appended to the surviving transcript of his diary (see p. 48 below), pp. 136–53); supplemented by F. O. White, *Lives of the Elizabethan Bishops* (1898), pp. 335–42, Harington, *A Supplie*, pp. 175–82, and *DNB*, art. Matthew.

[23] Frances Matthew's epitaph in York Minster is printed in full in A. H. Mathew and A. Calthorp, *The Life of Sir Tobie Mathew Bacon's Alter Ego* (1907), pp. 285–6. See also *A History of York Minster,* ed. G. E. Aylmer and Reginald Cant (Oxford, 1977), pp. 210–11, 437, 441; Joel Berlatsky, 'Marriage and Family in a Tudor Élite: Familial Patterns of Elizabethan Bishops', *Journal of Family History,* iii (1978), 11. Barlow's daughters were matched as follows, in order of age: Anne m. Herbert Westphaling, bishop of Hereford (having been previously married to Augustin Bradbridge, brother of Bishop William Bradbridge of Exeter), Margaret m. William Overton, bishop of Coventry and Lichfield, Elizabeth m. William Day, bishop of Winchester, Frances m. Tobie Matthew (having been previously married to Matthew Parker, second son of the archbishop), Antonia m. William Wickham, bishop of Winchester. BL Add. MS 4274 fol. 178 is a letter from Bishop Wickham to Tobie Matthew, endorsed by Mrs Matthew 'my Brother Wickhams letter to my husband May 16 1592'. In it Wickham thanks Matthew 'for my wyfes great entertainmente'.

admirable Mrs Matthew was to outlive the archbishop by one year, dying in 1629 at the age of seventy-eight. In earlier days, when the Matthews were not sure that they were happy in the north country, her husband had described her as that 'night crowe that ever croked in myne eare, "For God's sake gett us goen hence, Why came we hither? Who but us would any longer tarry here"' But of the 'night crow' he also wrote: 'which voyce you wott well hath halfe the force of an inchantment somtymes'.[24]

There were two Tobie Matthews and some historians have only known the one whom a later age accused of having 'a great inclination to church jobbing'.[25] Queen Elizabeth's own suspicions on this account led to a tart rejoinder when Matthew complained from the pulpit of her failure to reward those who most deserved it. 'Well: whosoever have missed their rewards thou hast not lost thy labour.'[26] Matthew himself wrote of his 'verie hard passage as it were through the pykes for everie suite that ever I obteined in Courte'.[27] His pursuit of a bishopric was sedulous and sustained. In 1587 there was some hope that he would obtain the extremely wealthy see of Durham, through the good offices of Sir Francis Walsingham, backed by the earls of Huntingdon, Essex, and Leicester. But Leicester intervened to indicate that his intention was that Piers of Salisbury should be translated to Durham and that Matthew should replace Piers at Salisbury. Matthew knew that in and around Durham this would be counted a 'disadvantage with a disgrace', and he implored his patrons that 'if this bushopric maie not conveniently be obtained, yet I maie rest upon my deanerie without offence'.[28] Piers was not

---

[24] Matthew to Francis Mills, 23 November 1587; BL MS Cotton Titus B II, fol. 284. Harington commended Frances Matthew as 'the best reported and reputed of her sort I thinke in England', adding: 'They live together by Saint Paules rule.' (*A Supplie*, p. 181.)

[25] The insinuation is attributed by the author of 'Memorials' (p. 146) to Peter Heylyn and John Le Neve.

[26] White, *Lives*, p. 337.

[27] Matthew to Francis Mills, 23 November 1587; BL MS Cotton Titus B II, fol. 284.

[28] Tobie Matthew to Francis Mills, 23 November 1587, 23 December 1587, 9 January 1587/8, 26 February 1587(/8), 11 April 1588, Tobie Matthew to Sir Francis Walsingham, 23 December 1587, 26 February 1587/8; BL MS Cotton Titus B II, fols. 284, 314, Titus B VII, fols. 424–7, Vespasian F XII, fol. 198, Titus B II, fols. 314, 316. Cf. *Calendar of Border Papers, 1560–94*, pp. 275 ff. In his letter to Mills of 23 November

translated, Matthew Hutton the dean of York was preferred, and Matthew stayed where he was. Subsequently, Matthew hunted with the Cecils. When London fell vacant in 1594, Burghley's secretary wrote to assure Matthew of his master's goodwill. 'For my selfe, I am but as one that giveth ayme, and can but wishe well, and hope well where preferrment is so well deserved'.[29] Richard Fletcher's translation from Worcester to London was yet another disappointment. But the death at about the same time of the archbishop of York, the same John Piers who had threatened to spike Matthew's guns in 1587, now saved him from Worcester, a fate worse than Salisbury.[30] With Hutton translated to York, he at last came into his inheritance at Durham and settled his debts with his patrons. To Burghley he sent 'a slender token' in the shape of £100 in gold, and to Burghley's secretary Michael Hicks and to his son Robert Cecil other and perhaps larger rewards. These transactions have been described as a 'dubious intrigue', and it is undeniable that they provide one of the more patently documented cases of simony in the Elizabethan Church.[31] More gold and rich church lands were later employed to advance the career of Matthew's eldest son: money ill-spent if it was the father's ambition to found a dynasty, since Tobie Matthew the younger turned papist and Jesuit.[32] But gold may have counted for less in Archbishop Matthew's rise than his talents as a witty court preacher and even as a famous punster.[33] From all these circumstances it would not be

1587 Matthew asked for advice on how the matter should be 'solicited', and wrote darkly of the 'many agentes and instrumentes' of 'the rest that be suitors'.

[29] Michael Hicks (?) to Matthew (draft), 1 September 1594; BL Lansdowne MS 77, no. 57, fol. 153. For Matthew's earlier indebtedness to Burghley for the deanery of Durham, see John Strype, *Annals of the Reformation* (Oxford, 1824), II. i. 514–15, III. i. 257–9.

[30] White, *Lives*, pp. 338–9.

[31] Strype, *Annals*, III, i. 257–9; A. G. R. Smith, *Servant of the Cecils: the Life of Sir Michael Hicks* (1977), pp. 75–7, 161.

[32] Mathew and Calthorp, *Life of Sir Tobie Matthew*; David Matthew, *Sir Tobie Matthew* (1950); Berlatsky, 'Marriage and Family', p. 14; Heal, *Of Prelates and Princes*, p. 230. BL Lansdowne MS 89, no. 107, fol. 207 contains 'An abstract out of sondry letters from my sonne Tobie Matthew (the originalls whereof remayne in my custodie) testifying his constancie in Religion since his departure out of England'. The letters are dated May 1605–December 1606.

[33] The author of 'Memorials' (p. 142), noting, as Harington had done, Matthew's 'facetiousness in the Art of Punning which about that time began [to] grow very fashionable', reports that it became a Yorkshire saying 'to a bold merry or jocose fellow': 'Thou are a Toby.'

difficult to compose an unflattering portrait of a light-weight and self-interested careerist, 'indifferent, negligent, secular'.

The other Matthew remains hidden in his diary, which is preserved in an eighteenth-century transcript in the Minster Library at York.[34] In form, this journal is a tally of the sermons preached over a period of forty years, from the time of Matthew's appointment as dean of Durham up to 1622. It records a total of 1,992 sermons: 721 preached as dean,[35] 550 as bishop of Durham, and a symmetrical 721 as archbishop of York. Some were delivered at or around Court but most were preached in the country: and not so much in Durham Cathedral or York Minster as at Grinton in Swaledale and Middleton in Teesdale, and at Bradford, Halifax, Leeds, and Wakefield. There were visitation sermons, assize sermons, wedding and funeral sermons, and many occasions when this high dignitary humbly took his turn at 'exercises' and fasts. But a good proportion were associated with no special occasion and some were preached to very thin country congregations. On one occasion Matthew arrived to find an empty church. Entries in the diary relating to the weather, health, and sundry 'providences' convey some of the difficulties with which this indefatigable prelate contended: 'so deep in snow that I could not pass to any church'—'I came to Southwell through higher waters and foul ways'—'a wonderful great distillation of rheum'—'sore vexed with a flux'—'an intollerable pain by a corne in the upper part of my middle toe of my left foot'—'a sore blow on my head in the

---

[34] Matthew's Diary survives in the Minster Library in a transcript made by the eighteenth-century Leeds schoolmaster Thomas Wilson. References in this paragraph are to pp. 47, 82, 132, 86, 100, 105, 98, 112, 103, 91, 127. A scrap of paper in BL Add. MS 4274 fol. 18 additionally lists the sermons which Matthew preached before the king in 1603–6. I owe this latter reference to Kenneth Fincham of University College, London.

[35] On Matthew's preferment to the bishopric, Sir Robert Cecil was petitioned for the deanery by the civilian and diplomat Dr Charles Parkins, who referred to Matthew's reputation when he argued that the place should not be thought 'rather too good for her Majesty's service than for any one whose principal gifts may be to forge a speech fit for the capacity of the simple common people'; and that his service to the queen would do more good 'for the benefit of the people than some good number of eloquent sermons by the year may come unto'. (Parkins to Cecil, 9 September 1595; *HMC Report, Salisbury MSS*, v. 369.) Matthew had been preceded in the deanery of Durham by the civilian and diplomat Thomas Wilson.

coach'—'I began to have a pain in my ancles divers daies, yet I preach'd as soon as I could'. As early as 1608 Harington thought that for preaching Matthew could say with St. Paul: 'I have labored more then ye all.'[36] As with John Wesley, these truly Methodist itineraries continued into great old age, beyond the conclusion of the journal. In 1625, when he was thought to be 'almost eightie years old', and was in fact eighty-one,[37] the vicar of Leeds reported that 'the most reverend archbishop of *York'* still preached more sermons in a single year than all the popes in history, from the time of Gregory the Great.[38] When Matthew found his final rest he left behind what is said to have been the largest private library of its time in England: 3,000 volumes valued at £600, which his widow bequeathed to the cathedral to become the nucleus of the modern Minster Library. A motto appears on the flyleaf of many of Matthew's books: 'Vita Christus Mors Lucrum'—'Christ is life, riches are death'.[39]

The moral to be drawn is not that Matthew won his place in the Jacobean edition of the *Guiness Book of Records,* but that since his preaching diary has survived more or less by accident and is unique we cannot tell how exceptional his track record may have been. The country parson William Harrison, writing in Elizabethan times, believed that the bishops would all be found preaching somewhere in their dioceses, Sunday by Sunday or even oftener.[40] This was sanguine but not beyond credibility. Most bishops were continuously resident in the country and available for preaching, having lost the London inns once attached to their sees and the major functions of state which would have detained them at Court or elsewhere on the king's service.[41] A substantial catalogue

---

[36] *A Supplie,* p. 176.

[37] Matthew's age: The *DNB* states that he was born in 1546 and his memorial in York Minster gives his age as eighty-two at the time of his death in March 1628. However, Matthew himself stated in January 1588 that his mother, who was with him at the time, would testify that he was three years of age 'lacking a fortnight' when Henry VIII died. So he was born in February 1544 and died aged eighty-four. (BL MS Cotton Titus B IV, fol. 424ᵛ.)

[38] Alexander Cooke, *The abatement of popish braggs* (1625), p. 49.

[39] *History of York Minster,* pp. 500–4.

[40] *Harrison's Description of England in Shakspere's Youth,* ed. F. J. Furnivall (1881), p. 16.

[41] It may be demonstrable that both the will and the leisure which were the conditions of diocesan residence declined in the reign of James I with the greater

could in fact be compiled of bishops who are said to have preached in season and out of season, or whose principal activity before they became bishops was as preachers. Here are only a few examples. One of the most celebrated of early Elizabethan preaching bishops was the witty William Alley of Exeter. At the time of his elevation a correspondent wrote: 'Mr Alley a joly preacher hathe Exeter.'[42] Whitgift as bishop of Worcester was said to have 'never failed to preach upon every Sabbath-day; many times riding five or six miles to a Parish Church' and preaching so early in the morning that there was time to ride back to the sermon in the cathedral. These habits persisted after his elevation to Canterbury. 'No *Sunday* escaped him in *Kent,* as the Gentlemen there can well witness, who would exceedingly resort unto him.'[43] Of Richard Curteys, bishop of Chichester in the 1570s, it was said that 'over and above his ordinary preaching upon Sondayes and holidays' he had undertaken three apostolic tours through Sussex, 'preaching himself at the greatest townes and many learned preachers with him in other places'.[44] Many Jacobean and Caroline bishops had a lifetime's experience of preaching before their elevation. Two years after he became bishop of Peterborough in 1634 Francis Dee wrote: 'I have been long versed in preaching, now 33 yeares.'[45] Barnaby Potter of Carlisle had begun his career as a lecturer at Abingdon and Totnes. 'When he was a Bishop he was a constant Preacher' and 'a great

---

social esteem enjoyed by some bishops, and with the concomitant growth in the courtly and political responsibilities of, for example, Lancelot Andrewes. John Chamberlain wrote in 1621: 'As for my lord of Winchester, he is so much employed at Court . . .'. (PRO S.P. 14/122/31. I owe this reference to Kenneth Fincham.) Bishop Williams's attention to his diocese was made possible by his political rustication, an echo of the experience of Fox and of Wolsey in the early sixteenth century.

[42] William Honning to the earl of Sussex, 25 July 1560; BL MS Cotton Titus B II, fol. 434.

[43] George Paule, *The Life of John Whitgift* (1699), p. 87. However, by Paule's own testimony, Whitgift allowed six years of his archiepiscopate to elapse before he visited his diocese for the first time, and subsequently visited it only every third year. (Ibid., pp. 104–5.)

[44] Richard Curteys, *An exposition of certayne words of S. Paul to the Romaynes* (1577), Preface.

[45] Bishop Dee to Lord Montague, 2 June 1636; *HMC Report, MSS of Duke of Buccleugh at Montague House,* i. 275.

favourer of Zealous Professors and Lecturers'.[46] Bishop Williams, in the years of his political rustication, was credited with directing his clergy to their duties by his own 'often preaching'. "Many a Sabbath-days Journey he took to the adjacent Towns, to let them see and hear their Diocesan.'[47]

But almost all these country sermons went unrecorded. Only two of Matthew's two thousand survive.[48] So it is not possible to measure their impact on country and market town congregations. Are we to trust Williams's biographer Bishop Hacket when he tell us that up to 'the brink of our great changes', 'high and low of all sorts and degrees came with their greatest attention to hear the sermon of a bishop', receiving the message of God with most reverence 'when it was deliver'd by one that look'd like an extraordinary Embassadour'?[49] Or did the popular attitudes of the 1620s already anticipate the response to the restored episcopate which Pepys observed in London in 1660? 'But Lord, at their going out, how people did most of them look upon them as strange Creatures, and few with any kind of love or respect.' 'And indeed, the bishops are so high, that very few do love them.'[50] We cannot say.

Archbishop Matthew's diary contains additional and rare evidence of his practice in confirming children, a function to which modern bishops devote much time and travel but which is so seldom mentioned in our documents that we cannot be sure that it was part of the settled economy of the Elizabethan Church. From 1591, when Archbishop Whitgift complained of the neglect of the rite, there are signs of a revival, enshrined in Canon 60 of 1604 which required bishops

---

[46] Life of Potter in Samuel Clarke, *Lives of Thirty-Two English Divines* (1677), p. 156.

[47] Hacket, *Scrinia Reserata*, ii. 38.

[48] Two of Matthew's sermons (from a source which cannot now be traced) were printed in *The Christian Remembrancer*, xlvii (1847). I owe this reference to Nicholas Tyacke.

[49] Hacket, *Scrinia Reserata*, ii. 39. Cf. what Bishop Richard Fletcher of London reported to Sir Robert Cecil in the first year of his episcopate. On his primary visitation he had preached at 'eight several places' in Hertfordshire and Essex, 'the confluence of the people and particular occasions requiring it'. (*HMC Report, Salisbury MSS*, v. 394.)

[50] *The Diary of Samuel Pepys*, ed. R. Latham and W. Matthews, i (1970), 259; ii (1970), 57.

to confirm children in the course of their visitations.[51] This was
no doubt symbolical of advancing episcopal claims, for the
bishop's confirming touch was a kind of charisma, analogous
to touching for the king's evil. Whenever Matthew confirmed
it was *en masse*, laying hands on 'multos' or 'plurimos'. In
Hartlepool in 1600 he confirmed three to four hundred in the
churchyard; in Hull in 1607 at least a thousand, 'impositione
manuum'; in Stillingfleet in 1614 he laid hands on 'many,
both young and old, in my way to Bishopthorp'. This tallies
with Richard Baxter's recollection of running out of school to
the churchyard and of kneeling on the path to receive a
blessing from Bishop Thomas Morton, and of Bishop Williams's casual practice as he moved about the country, stirring
up the gift of God that was in him by the putting on of
hands.[52] When Bishop Babington of Exeter came to Barnstaple in August 1595, he confirmed 'divers children' at the
Castle Green. The next day such a multitude came in from the
country that he retreated to his lodgings and slipped quietly
out of town, whereupon 'the people lamented that they had
lost a fine harvest day'.[53] But of Arthur Lake, bishop of Bath
and Wells in the 1620s, it was said that his confirmations were
never performed tumultuously, 'hand over head', but with
deliberation, on evidence of sufficient instruction in the
principles of religion.[54] The moral, once again, is of the
considerable obscurity of an important subject.[55]

[51] *Documentary Annals of the Reformed Church of England,* ed. Edward Cardwell (Oxford,
1844), ii. 42–4; *Synodalia,* ed. Edward Cardwell (Oxford, 1842), i. 281. A document in
Foxe's papers speaks of Bishop Bird of Chester, who after his deprivation for marriage
acted as suffragan to Bishop Bonner of London, 'attending upon the Bishope in his
visitation to confirme children, after the manner of that office'. (BL Harleian MS 421,
fol. 1.) This prompts the suggestion that the neglect of confirmation was not unrelated
to the growing rarity of suffragan bishops. On the topic of confirmation, and also on
episcopal preaching, see Ralph Houlbrooke, 'The Protestant Episcopate 1547–1603:
The Pastoral Contribution', in *Church and Society in England: Henry VIII to James I,* ed.
Felicity Heal and Rosemary O'Day (1977), pp. 78–98.

[52] Archbishop Matthew's Diary *passim* and especially pp. 60, 85, 109; Richard
Baxter, *The English Nonconformity* (1689), p. 101 (a reference I owe to Geoffrey Nuttall);
Hacket, *Scrinia Reserata,* i. 86.

[53] *Sketches of the Literary History of Barnstaple,* ed. J. R. Chanter (Barnstaple, 1866), pp.
129–30. I owe this reference to John Roberts.

[54] [John Harris], 'A Short View of the Life and Vertues of the Author', prefacing
Arthur Lake, *Sermons with some religious and divine meditations* (1629).

[55] Compare this Jacobean evidence with the revived enthusiasm for confirmation
upon the restoration of episcopacy after 1660. When Bishop Morley visited the Isle of

Tobie Matthew has led us to only two of the many aspects of episcopal activity which are usually hidden from us. There are many others. The loss of most of the records of Convocation makes it all but impossible to observe the bishops in action where, according to the apologists for their order, they should have been most at home, *in synodo.*[56] This gap in our knowledge has enhanced the Erastian image of the post-Reformation Church. On the other hand, the inadequate documentation of debates in the House of Lords, until Robert Bowyer's diary lifts the veil in 1610,[57] has left us uninformed about much of the political activity of the bishops at a national level.

Sitting in the House of Lords was only an occasional part of onerous political obligations still laid upon the bishops as servants of the Crown. The patterns and rhythms of their labours for the state can be inferred from Privy Council registers, state papers, and from their own correspondence. C. G. Cruickshank estimated that the invasion scare of 1599 involved Archbishop Whitgift and his secretaries in the writing and dispatch of between one and two hundred letters.[58] A study of the letters and reports regularly passing between Burghley and the more reliable of the bishops placed in sensitive areas, such as Lancashire, might suggest that, with assize judges and lords lieutenant, the bishops provided the intendancy of the Elizabethan and Jacobean state. They lent themselves to this role not so much by outstanding political and administrative talent as by their dependence on the Crown, retrospectively and prospectively, for advancement, and their relative local independence from the networks of kinship and faction.[59] In the early years of the Elizabethan regime, when it could be assumed that the bishops had

Wight he confirmed 'neere a 1000 of all sortes and amongst them all the gentry male and female young and old of the whole iland'. (I. M. Green, *The Re-Establishment of the Church of England 1660–1663* (Oxford, 1978), pp. 141–2.)

[56] There is a rare record of a debate in the Upper House, 23 May 1604; All Souls College MS 155, fols. 49–52ᵛ.

[57] *Proceedings in Parliament 1610,* ed. E. R. Foster (New Haven, 1966), i, *The House of Lords.*

[58] C. G. Cruickshank, *Elizabeth's Army* (2nd edn., Oxford, 1966), pp. 71–3.

[59] M. E. James, *Family, Lineage and Civil Society: A Study of Society, Politics and Mentality in the Durham Region, 1500–1640* (Oxford, 1974), pp. 150–60.

informed themselves about local politics but had not yet become utterly entangled in its toils, they were required by the Privy Council to report on the loyalty of JPs with respect to the religious settlement. Their returns were subsequently used to remodel the Commission of the Peace.[60]

But bishops were themselves parts of the local administration as well as occasional rapporteurs on its loyalty and effectiveness. If the early Tudor episcopate was often to be found in the great offices of state or in diplomacy, their Elizabethan and Jacobean successors were confined to a lowlier sphere of service on the local bench. But it is not easy to assess the extent and value of their participation as magistrates and as magnates whose presence contributed, in ways not always tangible, to the quality of provincial life. Since the bishops had forfeited many of their houses and were often limited to a single country residence, their influence was likely to be exerted in pockets rather than evenly throughout their dioceses.[61] The otherwise ineffective and financially hamstrung Bishop Parkhurst of Norwich joined his neighbours in the little market town of Acle in dispensing useful justice in an early form of divisional or petty sessions. For Acle was hard by the bishop's manor of Ludham where Parkhurst lived quietly and frugally.[62] Bishop Aylmer of London blamed ecclesiastical disorders around Maldon on his lack of any residence in that part of Essex. 'My being at my other house at Hadham some small time in the year hath made all the country of Hertford ... now to be most quiet and orderly.'[63] Yet the episcopal presence, if localized, was far from insignificant, even in military terms. According to his secretary and biographer, Whitgift as bishop of Worcester maintained 'a good Armory and fair Stable of great Horses', and from time to time he was able to muster as many as fifty horse and one hundred foot from his own household.[64] The armoury

[60] *A Collection of Original Letters from the Bishops to the Privy Council, 1564,* ed. M. Bateson, *Camden Miscellany* ix (1893).

[61] Heal, *Of Prelates and Princes,* pp. 39–42.

[62] A. H. Smith, *County and Court: Government and Politics in Norfolk, 1558–1603* (Oxford, 1974), pp. 104–5.

[63] Quoted, Heal, *Of Prelates and Princes,* p. 260.

[64] Paule, *Life of Whitgift,* pp. 97–8.

of Bishop Thomas Cooper, his contemporary at Lincoln, contained among other 'furniture' seven petronels, eight muskets, sixteen calivers, twenty-seven corslets, thirty-three swords, seventy-two pikes, sixteen staves for lances and seventeen for light horse.[65]

Bishops contributed to the stabilization of the commonwealth in a variety of other ways which cannot be so readily quantified. In pressing the claims of the people of the north to an archbishop, Parker told Cecil: 'You would not believe me to tell how often it is required of divers men's hands, and how the people there is offended that they be nothing cared for.' At about the same time the justices of Gloucestershire were asking for the speedy supply of a bishop, 'by whose meanes they hope muche the better to governe the countie'. Yorkshire was to be well served for the purposes of secular government by Archbishop Young, a lawyer whom Parker described as 'both witty, prudent and temperate, and man-like', and who performed effectively as president of the Council in the North, the most responsible secular office held by any Elizabethan prelate. But the men of Gloucester had to be content with the incompetent and theologically eccentric Richard Cheyney. Within ten years Parker was reporting that Cheyney was so decrepit that 'he would bring his people to his contemplations'.[66] Yet by the end of the reign, or so it was said, nothing did more to encourage the sagging fortunes of Gloucester than the return of a later bishop to reside in the vicinity of the town. The townsmen were stimulated to rebuild their marketplace, and to erect 'a fair hall for justice'.[67] By contrast, the bishop of Worcester in the same period was only an occasional visitor to his cathedral city, 'a distant, primarily political figure, a force for the city to beware of rather than a very positive element in its life'.[68] So various was the experience of the Elizabethan provinces in their pastors and governors.

The Elizabethan bishops knew that their coercive power

---

[65] Lindsay Boynton, *The Elizabethan Militia* (1967), p. 35.

[66] Parker to Cecil, 16 October 1560, *Correspondence of Matthew Parker,* ed. J. Bruce, Parker Society (Cambridge, 1853), pp. 123–4, 332; 'Considerations for a bishoppe to be placed in the see of Gloucester now vacant', PRO S.P. 12/20/53.

[67] Harington, *A Supplie,* p. 58.

[68] Alan D. Dyer, *The City of Worcester in the Sixteenth Century* (Leicester, 1973), p. 235.

was insufficient to reduce potent and recalcitrant elements in their dioceses to ecclesiastical obedience. Excommunication, wrote Bilson of Winchester, was a penalty utterly despised by the recusant gentry. One promising remedy was to seek an augmentation of episcopal authority by a commission under the Great Seal which secured the co-operation of lay magistrates in a joint tribunal, empowered to employ the more credible sanctions of fine and imprisonment unavailable to the bishop in his ordinary capacity.[69] These local diocesan commissions are another obscure subject, only a little better documented than the central Court of High Commission for the southern province.[70] However, it would appear from the nearly continuous series of act books for the York Ecclesiastical Commission,[71] that this experiment in the enforcement of the religious settlement through a hybrid jurisdiction was ultimately a failure, after some passing success in the major objective of discouraging catholic recusancy.

In the late 1570s, ecclesiastical commissions represented the most effective instrument available for this purpose. But the penal laws of 1581 transferred the major role in policing recusancy to purely secular tribunals, leaving the ecclesiastical commissions with a diminished function not easily distinguishable from ordinary ecclesiastical justice. Moreover, with the worsening of relations between many bishops and the more active and reliable of the gentry, which was the result of Archbishop Whitgift's campaign of the 1580s against nonconformist preaching ministers, some of the basis was lost for the lay–clerical co-operation on which the institution depended.

[69] R. B. Manning, 'The Crisis of Episcopal Authority During the Reign of Elizabeth I', *Journal of British Studies,* xi (1971), 1–25.

[70] For the deficiencies both of the documentation of the Canterbury Ecclesiastical Commission and of the standard historical account of it, see Philip Tyler's introduction to the 1969 edition of R. G. Usher, *The Rise and Fall of the High Commission.* An act book for a single year of a diocesan commission has been published: *The Commission for Ecclesiastical Causes Within the Dioceses of Bristol and Gloucester,* ed. F. D. Price, Records Section of the Bristol and Gloucestershire Archaeological Society, x (1972). See also Dr Price's article, 'The Commission for Causes Ecclesiastical for the Dioceses of Bristol and Gloucester, 1574', *Transactions of the Bristol and Gloucestershire Archaeological Society,* lix (1937), 61–84.

[71] Philip Tyler, 'The Ecclesiastical Commission for the Province of York, 1561–1641', Oxford D.Phil. thesis, 1965; and his article, 'The Significance of the Ecclesiastical Commission at York', *Northern History,* ii (1967), 27–44.

The diocesan commissions consequently tended to become episcopal courts under another name, and with enhanced powers. Roger Manning has suggested that the *jure divino* claims of the late Elizabethan episcopate were a direct consequence of this failure in co-operation with the lay magistracy, and that both the *jure divino* principle and the earlier experiment with commissions provide evidence of a profound 'crisis of episcopal authority'.[72] This is very plausible, although it must be said that, with the exception of the York Commission, the records of government by ecclesiastical commission are too scanty for confident judgement to be possible.

Much episcopal influence in the social domain was exerted by informal means which were not a matter for record. The clergy had an acknowledged out-of-court role as peacemakers, arbitrating and composing quarrels: inferior clergy at an inferior level, bishops at the level of county and Court. Bishop Matthew's diary for 1600 has the cryptic entry: 'The gentlemen of Cumberland and Westmorland to be reconciled.'[73] We can only speculate about the usefulness in such a connection of episcopal hospitality, to which so much importance is attached by both biographers and accountants.[74] And in this respect were the bachelor prelates at an advantage or a disadvantage, presiding over such all-male establishments as Bishop Williams's Buckden, where it was said to be 'better to endure a little Dust in the Rooms' than the Company even of female servants?[75] It is no easier to form a mental picture of how the bishops conducted themselves at Court, and especially at the Elizabethan Court, where they enjoyed little apparent honour. Church jobbing can hardly have occupied all their waking hours. Perhaps they sometimes did a little disinterested good. When Archbishop Grindal was under suspension in the later 1570s attention was drawn to certain informal primatial functions which his disgrace had placed in temporary abeyance:

[72] Manning, 'The Crisis of Episcopal Authority'.
[73] Archbishop Tobie Matthew's Diary, p. 61.
[74] Heal, *Of Prelates and Princes,* pp. 76–8, 221, 257–62. Felicity Heal has further work in progress on the subject of hospitality.
[75] Hacket, *Scrinia Reserata,* ii. 35.

Where aswell the Bishops and others of the clergy as also of the Layety throughout the whole province were wont to resorte to the Archbishop to consult with him and have his direction in matters of greate weight, wherby many controversies and occasions of strife and slander within their dioces were cut of, although there do arise many like occasions dayly, yet their lacketh the authority of the same Archbishop for the appeasing thereof.[76]

There are glimpses to be had of many of these matters in episcopal correspondence. But this is widely and thinly scattered. From the whole period under survey only two sizeable and compact collections of letters survive, to reveal the bishop in his political and social relations and administration, from day to day. These are the letter books of Bishop John Parkhurst of Norwich, covering the years 1571–5, and of Bishop Thomas Bentham of Coventry and Lichfield, belonging to 1560–1. It is unfortunate that both collections illuminate administratively inexperienced bishops coping with the disarray of the early Elizabethan years, so that they give an excessively unfavourable impression.[77]

III

On either side of the gap which we have now defined, where the historian clutches eagerly at straws and fragments of evidence, there are two unequal and disparate classes of material, both for very different reasons inadequate as the basis for a study of episcopal roles and reputations, but which tend to loom large in the literature of the subject. On the one hand there is a body of contemporary characterization and anecdote, much of it reflecting the peculiar and perennial vulnerability of prelates to personal ridicule. Some of this discourse originated in the Marprelate Tracts in which the late Elizabethan establishment was mercilessly pilloried, and

[76] Bodleian Library Tanner MS 280, fol. 330ᵛ; another copy in Inner Temple Library Petyt MS 538.54, fol. 278.

[77] *The Letter Book of John Parkhurst Bishop of Norwich Compiled During the Years 1571–75*, ed. Ralph Houlbrooke, Norfolk Record Society 1974 and 1975, xlii (Norwich, 1975); *Letter-Book of Thomas Bentham*, 113–238. See also M. R. O'Day, 'Thomas Bentham: A Case Study of the Problems of the Early Elizabethan Episcopate', *Journal of Ecclesiastical History*, xxiii (1972), 137–59, and J. A. Berlatsky, 'Thomas Bentham and the Plight of the Early Elizabethan Bishops', *Historical Magazine of the Protestant Episcopal Church*, xliii (1974).

in a continuing Martinist tradition which was soon reinforced by a new taste for character literature, what Bishop Barlow called *'escritures picquants'*, *'satyricall inventions'*.[78] To this genre belong the episcopal cameos composed by Sir John Harington for the edification of Prince Henry, and variously known as *A supplie or addicion to the catalogue of bishops* and *A briefe view of the state of the Church of England*.[79] Harington intended this offering for a defence of the Church and its hierarchy, but he served it with liberal helpings of sauce. From this and similar collections come the good stories which enliven an otherwise dull subject, but which tend to corrupt judgement. Was it Bancroft ('Dr Bankrupt') or Aylmer ('Don John of London') who when playing bowls rubbed his bowl and sent it on its way with 'the Devil go with thee', and then trotted after it himself?[80] It scarcely matters. One good story concerns the bizarre death of Bancroft's predecessor, Bishop Fletcher, taking tobacco with his new and fancy wife, looking upon his man servant, and saying 'Oh boy, I die';[81] another, Bishop Anthony Rudd's ill-

---

[78] William Barlow, *The eagle and the body* (1609), sig. B2ᵛ. As an example of the continuing Martinist tradition, see the scurrilous verses on Bishop Richard Fletcher in All Souls College MS 155, fols. 107ᵛ–8ʳ, of which this is the second stanza:

John London was condemnede for spoiling wood
And nowe Dick London commons doth inclose.
He sought his private, this the publique good
And both ther credit by their getting loose.
Nowe tell me Martin whethers gaine is more.
He sould the woode, and this hath bought an whore.

Another version in Corpus Christi College Oxford MS 327, fol. 29 has:

None but a Lady fits his lordlike eyes
None but a whore his wanton lusts suffice.

[79] R. H. Miller collates the various texts of this work in his edition in Studia Humanitatis, op. cit. See also his 'Sir John Harington's *A Supplie or Addicion to the Catalogue of Bishops, to the yeare 1608*: Composition and Text', *Studies in Bibliography*, xxx (1977). The *Catalogue* for which Harington composed this semi-apologetical, semi-satyrical appendix was Bishop Francis Godwin's *A catalogue of the bishops of England* (1601).

[80] Harington followed Martin Marprelate in attaching the story to Aylmer: 'The bishop would cry rub, rub, rub to his bowle, and when it was gone too far, say the Devill goe with yt, and then (sayeth he) the bishop would follow.' (*A Supplie*, p. 47.) John Manningham did not trouble to link the jest to Aylmer when he retailed it in 1602–3, when Bancroft was bishop of London: 'Ha! the Divel goe with thee! said the Bishop of London to his bowle when himselfe ran after it.' (*The Diary of John Manningham of the Middle Temple 1602–1603*, ed. R. P. Sorlien (Hanover, New Hampshire, 1976), p. 124.)

[81] Harington, *A Supplie*, p. 54.

judged sermon on old age preached to the elderly queen,
which brought the retort: 'I see . . . the greatest clerks are not
the wisest men.'[82]

In particular, the efforts of churchmen to gain preferment
encourage the satirist by exposing them as the victims of all-
too-human weakness. Moreover, their schemes and ploys have
left behind plentiful traces in the muniment rooms of their
great patrons, so that a disproportionate quantity of surviving
episcopal correspondence has to do with place-hunting.
Bishop Aylmer may be allowed to speak for all in a letter of
1559 to the future earl of Leicester on which many variants
would be worked in the remainder of our period: 'Good my
lord, if the deanery of Winchester be not already swallowed
up, lett me among the rest of the small fisshes have a snatche
at the baite: if yt be gone, I besech your good lordship cast a
hooke for the deanerie of Durham.'[83]

But in an age when death came suddenly and unan-
nounced, ecclesiastical office, like marriage, was an institution
lacking in permanence. And in a society which functioned by
patronage at every level, what John Chamberlain called
'posting and suing' was only to be expected. Some good men
who were not so pressing may have lost in this frantic rat race.
After the ineffably learned Richard Field was dead, James I
was heard to remark 'I should have don more for that Man'.[84]
But Field was comfortably provided for as dean of Gloucester
and canon of Windsor. Nor can we assume that such an
incorrigible scholar would have made a suitable bishop. And
as we have seen in the case of Archbishop Matthew, the often
unseemly manœuvres of preferment did not of necessity lead
to bad appointments. While patronage was indispensable for
preferment to the episcopal bench, and not simply and only
royal patronage, its operations were not arbitrary but almost
predictable. Many bishops, almost a majority, were recruited
from the headship of Oxford and Cambridge colleges where

[82] Ibid., pp. 151–3. The story was also known to Manningham. (*Diary of
Manningham*, p. 194.)

[83] John Aylmer to Lord Robert Dudley, 12 August 1559; BL Add. MS 32091, fol.
172.

[84] Nathaniel Field, *Some Short Memorials Concerning the Life of that Reverend Divine
Doctor Richard Field*, ed. J. Le Neve (1716–17), p. 17.

they had acquired valuable and relevant administrative experience[85] In 1597 Whitgift recommended Dr Robert Some of Peterhouse for the bishopric of Exeter as 'a very honest man, well learned, an ancient Doctor of Divinity, and one that governeth the College whereof he is master with good commendation'.[86] Bishop Williams's biographer notes that Bancroft, Abbot, Matthew, King, Bilson, Andrewes, Morton, Overall, Lake, Felton, and Davenant all 'gave great content and received great content from the Colleges and Bishopricks which they govern'd respectively, by keeping them in that Obedience, wherein they found them'.[87] So the topic of bishop-making belongs as closely to the history of the universities, in both their internal power-structure and external relations, as it does to court patronage. But the study of how bishops came to be bishops, while important and of consuming interest to the John Chamberlains of this world, is not to be confused with the study of what bishops did, once they were in.

IV

For this we must cross to the other side of our gap to contend with the mountainous and still only partially explored records of spiritual administration and justice. Surely here, if anywhere, the role of the bishops must be adequately documented, in bishops' registers, the copious information amassed in visitation, and the act books, bulky deposition books, and thick bundles of cause papers which have been left behind by the ecclesiastical courts. The exploitation of a mere tithe of this material has been the most impressive recent development in sixteenth- and seventeenth-century ecclesiastical studies, reversing the retreat from administrative history observable in some other fields, but also yielding rich rewards

---

[85] David Mathew, *The Social Structure of Caroline England* (Oxford, 1947), pp. 71–2; and his *King James I* (1967), p. 127.

[86] Whitgift to Sir Robert Cecil, 20 August 1597; *HMC Report, Salisbury MSS,* vii. 359.

[87] Hacket, *Scrinia Reserata,* ii. 45. When John Davenant, master of Queens' College, Cambridge, and Lady Margaret professor, was made bishop of Salisbury in 1621 he told Samuel Ward, master of Sidney Sussex: 'My body may be tossed up and down to other places, but Cambridge will alwaies have my heart.' (Bodleian Library, Tanner MS 73, no. 9, fol. 25.)

for the social historian.[88] But episcopal administration and justice were the preserve not so much of the bishops themselves as of their officers, the professional civil lawyers and administrators. At least this is the impression created by the formal records, which were compiled by the professionals themselves. The system was one of advanced bureaucratization, symbolized by the automatic and administrative imposition of the ultimate spiritual weapon of excommunication as the penalty for contumacious absence from the court's proceedings. There is no reason to suppose that even the extended vacancy of a see, such as Ely suffered from 1581 to 1593, had any marked influence on its effectiveness. Moreover, in the eye of the social historian even this bureaucratic image is an optical illusion. The courts were embedded in society, not imposed upon it, and they satisfied public demand by their response both to the parochial authorities in their detection of offences, and especially sexual offences, and to private individuals who were concerned to make good their claims to property or to an unsullied reputation. Only to a limited extent did the church courts determine their own agenda.[89]

Nevertheless, modern students of ecclesiastical justice are favourably impressed with its relative efficiency and with the volume and velocity of the business which the courts transacted.[90] The credit for these modest achievements belongs to the senior functionaries within the system: the vicar-general and official principal, often one and the same individual, bearing the title of chancellor; the registrar, who

[88] An excellent prospect of the work of a recent generation of historical researchers is offered by the two symposia *Continuity and Change: Personnel and Administration of the Church in England, 1500–1642,* ed. Rosemary O'Day and Felicity Heal (Leicester, 1976), *Church and Society in England: Henry VIII to James I,* ed. Felicity Heal and Rosemary O'Day, (1977).

[89] M. J. Ingram, 'Ecclesiastical Justice in Wiltshire 1600–1640, With Special Reference to Cases Concerning Sex and Marriage', Oxford D.Phil. thesis, 1976.

[90] Ronald A. Marchant, *The Church Under the Law: Justice, Administration and Discipline in the Diocese of York 1560–1640* (Cambridge, 1969); Ralph Houlbrooke, *Church Courts and the People During the English Reformation 1520–1570* (Oxford, 1979); M. J. Ingram, 'Ecclesiastical Justice'. These authors all dissent, explicitly or by implication, from the verdict passed on the church courts by Christopher Hill in *Society and Puritanism in Pre-Revolutionary England* (1966).

was steadily tightening his grip on the machine;[91] the episcopal secretary, palely reflecting in the small world of the episcopal household the signal role of secretaries of state in larger affairs; and the steward and comptroller, whose competence in economic management was as indispensable as the skill of accountants in a modern company. By the end of the sixteenth century, men of distinction and stature were emerging in these roles: among them Sir John Boys, servant to three archbishops of Canterbury, and Whitgift's steward; Sir George Paule, comptroller of Whitgift's household and registrar to the High Commission, who wrote his master's biography; and Sir Edward Stanhope, chancellor to four successive bishops of London and vicar-general for the province of Canterbury.

Delegation did not necessarily mean dereliction. A bishop ought, in principle, to have exercised his maximum influence over the quality of the government operated in his name through his power of patronage in appointing and directing officers such as these. Stanhope was a notable discovery of Bishop Aylmer, and so in some sense a product of Aylmer's own considerable administrative talent.[92] Bishop Williams's biographer remarks that it is a foolish magistrate who fails to 'research his Deputies' and who places 'an indefinite confidence in their Honesties'. Williams himself was said to have looked upon his officers 'with a new Probation in every great Cause, as if he had never known them'.[93] Perhaps so. The ineffectiveness of Bishop Parkhurst of Norwich had much to do with his inability to appoint reliable officers and to hold them in check, while the indifference of dreamy Bishop Cheyney was one reason for the advanced corruption of the church courts in early Elizabethan Gloucester.[94] Conversely,

[91] Rosemary O'Day, 'The Role of the Registrar in Diocesan Administration', in *Continuity and Change*, pp. 77–94.

[92] H. G. Owen, 'The London Parish Clergy in the Reign of Elizabeth I', London Ph.D. thesis, 1957, pp. 542–3; B. P. Levack, *The Civil Lawyers in England, 1603–42* (Oxford, 1973), pp. 270–1.

[93] Hacket, *Scrinia Reserata*, ii. 44.

[94] *Letter Book of John Parkhurst*; F. D. Price, 'An Elizabethan Church Official—Thomas Powell, Chancellor of Gloucester Diocese', *Church Quarterly Review*, cxxviii (1939), 94–112; F. D. Price, 'Elizabethan Apparitors in the Diocese of Gloucester', *Church Quarterly Review*, cxxxiv (1942), 37–55.

the achievement of Richard Neile as he advanced through no less than five bishoprics in the first three decades of the seventeenth century was equally the achievement of the able lawyer William Easdall with whom he worked closely for twenty-five years, and who served him as secretary in three dioceses and as chancellor of Durham and then of York.[95]

But with the consolidation of the machinery of ecclesiastical government and the growing practice of granting office by life patent, judges and officials tended to form a self-perpetuating officialdom and a self-contained profession.[96] It took a bishop like Neile (and as Richard Montague told his friend John Cosin, 'every man is not my Lord of Durham'),[97] who was himself at home in the world of Doctors Commons, to ensure that the expertise of the profession was effectively mobilized to serve his particular interests and objectives. Some officials, like Sir John Boys or the episcopal secretary of Norwich, Anthony Harison,[98] were primarily attached to the see, and served successive bishops with indifferent loyalty. Easdall, whose loyalty was to his master, represents a different pattern. Either way, it was desirable for the achievement of sound administration that the bishop and his officers should enjoy the confidence of each other, and that both should prefer the interest of the see to self-interest or family interest. Such unselfish and efficient harmony was no doubt hard to achieve.[99]

It would be a mistake to suppose that the direct interest of a bishop in the government of his diocese ended with the appointment of his officers. Sometimes the formal act books themselves reveal the bishop conducting his personal court of audience, or taking the place of the official principal in presiding over some case of special interest in the consistory

---

[95] Andrew Foster, 'The Function of a Bishop: The Career of Richard Neile, 1562–1640', in *Continuity and Change*, pp. 47–8.

[96] Levack, *The Civil Lawyers in England*.

[97] Quoted, Foster, 'The Function of a Bishop', p. 45.

[98] Harison's monument is the miscellany of documents from Norwich diocesan administration collected in *Registrum Vagum*, ed. T. F. Barton, 2 vols., Norfolk Record Society xxxii, xxxiii (Norwich, 1963–4).

[99] Heal, *Of Prelates and Princes*, pp. 310–11.

court.[1] Bishop Aylmer once offended puritan susceptibilities by boasting that his consistory was wheresoever his person was.[2] The implications of this perfectly sound doctrine could be pastorally beneficial and not merely arbitrary, as the puritans suspected.

If episcopal correspondence and other ephemeral documentation had survived in the same volume as the formal acts of the courts, we might enjoy a more impressive view of active episcopal oversight of the administrative and judicial system. When these loose papers do survive, as they have done for the archdeaconry of St. Albans,[3] they are a revelation. In principle there existed a tight chain of command, from the crown and its agencies, through the archbishop of Canterbury and the bishop of London as dean of the province, to the diocesan bishops, and on to the archdeacons and ultimately the parishes. The St. Albans papers show that this chain could and sometimes did function effectively. When Richard Fletcher became bishop of London in 1594 he wrote to the archdeacon of St. Albans, and presumably to his four other archdeacons, requiring detailed reports on the state of their jurisdictions. They were to supply lists of benefices, with career details of the incumbents and other clergy, the names of patrons, the reputed values of livings, and the numbers of communicants, mentioning by name any 'men of worth'

[1] See, for example, the Vicar General Book 'Huicke', covering the years 1561–74, in the Greater London Record Office. This contains a number of cases heard by Bishop Grindal of London in person: discussed in Patrick Collinson, *Archbishop Grindal 1519–1583: The Struggle for a Reformed Church* (1979), p. 119. See also the office of the bishop of Lincoln (Thomas Cooper) against the rector of Congerston, Leicestershire, which he conducted in person at Buckden in July 1576. (*Lincoln Episcopal Records in the Time of Thomas Cooper*, ed. C. W. Foster, Lincoln Record Society ii (1912), reissued, Canterbury and York Society, xi (1913), 135.)

[2] Robert Beale to Sir Christopher Hatton, 25 November 1589; BL Add. MS 48039, fol. 69[r].

[3] This material is now concentrated in the Hertfordshire Record Office, Hertford. There are four bound volumes of papers which were collected by H. R. Wilton Hall and calendared by him in *Records of the Old Archdeaconry of St. Albans. A Calendar of Papers A.D. 1575 to A.D. 1637*, St. Albans and Hertfordshire Archaeological and Architectural Society (St. Albans, 1908); two bundles of papers collected by Wilton Hall (Shelf 192, Box X, Bundles A and B); and further loose and miscellaneous papers transferred from Somerset House to Hertford (Box I, Bundle i). See a study based on these records: Robert Peters, *Oculus Episcopi: Administration in the Archdeaconry of St. Albans 1580–1625* (Manchester, 1963).

within each parish. The archdeacons were asked to report the names of any 'speciall men' who were fit to preach at Paul's Cross. 'Further my desire is that you repaire unto me at London the first daie of the next term, that I maie further advise with you concerning the state and government of your Archdeaconrye.'[4]

The file copy of the St. Albans certificate survives.[5] It would have been compiled not by the archdeacon but by his own administrative staff, which means the omnicompetent Thomas Rokett, who saw many archdeacons and bishops come and go in his half-century of continuous service as registrar.[6] But what was said on both sides when the bishop met with his archdeacons in London was not a matter for record and we have no knowledge of it. Both bishops and archdeacons held regular chapters or synods of their clergy,[7] but what transpired on these occasions is almost entirely hidden from view. We can only hope that it was normally more harmonious and constructive than a meeting of Bishop Overton of Coventry and Lichfield with his clergy in 1581, held to share out responsibility for a military subsidy. There was resentment that the richest incumbent in the diocese had got off scot-free and had openly boasted of his good fortune. 'Ever since that time there hathe beene muche grudging and murmuring amongst the clergie and every one hathe sought to flype his head out of the coler, so that I have had verye muche adoo with them and have been fayne even to use the ecclesiastical censures upon some.'[8] Overton's episcopal reputation is not unsullied. Yet it appears that he should not be charged with undue remoteness from his clergy.

Further occasions for face-to-face encounter occurred in the course of the periodic tours of inspection known as visitations, although not all bishops found it convenient on all occasions to conduct their primary and subsequent triennial visitations in person. The records of an episcopal visitation most likely to survive consist of *comperta*, mere lists of the clergy and

[4] Hertfordshire County Record Office, MS ASA 5/5/201.
[5] Ibid., MS ASA 5/5/202.
[6] Peters, *Oculus Episcopi*, pp. 16–20.
[7] See pp. 122–7 below.
[8] Overton to Sir Francis Walsingham, 11 June 1581; PRO S.P. 12/149/37.

churchwardens making their appearance, and *detecta,* the criminal matters of presentment from the parishes. These are evidence of the machine in action, and reveal little of the quality of the pastoral care bestowed by a particular bishop. On this subject, the published visitation articles and injunctions—containing as it were the agenda: the articles for the visitation itself and the injunctions for its sequel—are more informative, although it cannot be presumed that all bishops devoted an equal and personal diligence to the construction of their articles, or that they always resisted the temptation to supplement their own inventiveness with borrowings from the questionnaires prepared for other dioceses by other bishops.[9] But the most significant part of a visitation, seen as an occasion for taking the pulse of a diocese or for strengthening its morale, must have been the exchange of civilities between bishop and clergy, the sermons preached *ad clerum,* sometimes by the bishops themselves, the 'charges' which these bishops, like their eighteenth- and nineteenth-century successors, may have delivered, and the matters discussed over dinner.[10] These courtesies and amenities were of marginal interest to the registrar, and for the historian they are so much water poured into the sand. Most episcopal visitation sermons and charges, and *a fortiori* most table talk, formal but ephemeral, went unrecorded, or the record has been lost.

In the absence of the more intimate and revealing of the

[9] The visitation articles and injunctions surviving from the Elizabethan Church will be found in W. H. Frere and W. M. Kennedy, eds., *Visitation Articles and Injunctions of the Period of the Reformation,* 3 vols., Alcuin Club Collections xiv–xvi (Oxford, 1910), and W. P. M. Kennedy, ed., *Elizabethan Episcopal Administration. An Essay in Sociology and Politics,* 3 vols., Alcuin Club Collections xxv–xxvii (Oxford, 1924–5). Kennedy's introductory essay in the first volume of *Elizabethan Episcopal Administration* is the authority for the cautious remarks made here about the use of articles and injunctions as historical evidence. The Jacobean articles and injunctions have not been systematically reprinted and are widely scattered in their original printed editions.

[10] We possess a bare account of the sermons preached in the course of Grindal's primary visitation as bishop of London, 1561, and of the episcopal 'beneplacitus' or 'voluntatis' extended to the clergy at each session of the visitation. (Guildhall Library London, MS 9537/2.) There are recorded details of the table-talk at the various sessions of Bishop Neile's primary visitation of the diocese of Lincoln, 1614, in Cambridge University Library, Baumgartner MS 8, fols. 220–2, being Ralph Thoresby's transcript, communicated to John Strype, of Lincoln Dean and Chapter MS A 4/3/43, whence printed, *Associated Architectural Societies Reports and Papers,* xvi (1881), 31–54. See below pp. 123–4 for some discussion of this evidence.

relevant evidence, it is difficult to reconstruct the experience of an episcopal visitation from the point of view of the visited. Bishop Neile's officers reported on his visitation of 1614 as if it had been a not disagreeable social occasion.[11] But in Elizabethan times it had been a commonplace of lay prejudice that the real, if veiled, purpose of visitation was to fleece the meagre incomes of the clergy by means of 'procurations', the visitation fees. A letter from Bishop Scambler of Norwich to his clergy tends to confirm these suspicions. In requesting from his 'well beloved frends, brethren and fellowe laborers in the Lord' a 'benevolence' towards the payment of his first-fruits, Scambler acknowledged that an alternative means to 'ease' himself would be a visitation, the 'ordinary and to to comon' means. But visitations were grievous, chargeable, and vexatious. What remained of the proceeds after overhead expenses had been met tended to enrich the officials rather than the bishops themselves. Accordingly, he preferred to solicit their voluntary charity. Scambler alleged that his brethren of Lincoln, Coventry and Lichfield (Overton again!), St. Davids, 'and divers other places' had done the same, so encouraging among the clergy what he called a 'certeyne reverent familiarity with theire diocessans and to expecte such pleasure at their handes as in requitall of there curteses'.[12]

We might expect the bishops to have had their most direct influence on the state of the Church through the power which was peculiarly theirs to renew the clergy by the conferring of orders. But in this respect modern studies[13] have emphasized

[11] Cambridge University Library, Baumgartner MS 8, fols. 220–2.

[12] As an example of lay suspicions about the motivation of visitations and other aspects of ecclesiastical jurisdiction, see Lord Burghley's letter to Archbishop Grindal, holograph, 25 November 1575, in which he expressed the desire that there might be 'more caution and circumspection in all their canonical jurisdictions and consistories, that the exercise thereof might be directly *ad edificationem*, and not to make gain of that which was meant to punish or prevent sin'. (Quoted, Collinson, *Archbishop Grindal*, p. 233.) Scambler's letter was copied in the commonplace-book of a Suffolk gentleman, where it is followed with some lines of doggerel verse which it inspired, beginning: 'O Father ffeade the fflocke of Christe and ffleeze it not by might./The one is creditt to yor name, the other shames it quite.' (Bodleian Library, MS Gough Norfolk 43, fols. 1–2.)

[13] Particularly the work of Rosemary O'Day. See her *The English Clergy: the Emergence and Consolidation of a Profession 1558–1642* (Leicester, 1979), and her articles, 'The Law of Patronage in Early Modern England', *Journal of Ecclesiastical History*, xxvi

their relative impotence. Many bishops subjected candidates for ordination to an oral examination of their fitness, or required their archdeacons to do so. It is unusual to find a full record of these tests but where they exist, as for the diocese of Ely in the time of Bishop Cox, they suggest that the failure rate could be as high as a quarter of all those presenting themselves.[14] But the bishop was not responsible for the quality of the human material which presented itself and he usually exercised his veto only to turn away the illiterate or otherwise flagrantly unsuitable. When the academic qualifications of ordinands improved dramatically, in the early seventeenth century, this was not the simple achievement of the bishops but the product of a number of social factors, and especially of a growth in numbers at the universities.[15] The bishop's control over entry to livings was also severely limited. Where he was both patron and ordinary he could collate ministers of his own choice, subject only to the supply of suitable men. (But how those hand-picked, well-qualified ministers were found and recruited bishops' registers will not tell us.)[16] However, a majority of benefices were subject to lay patronage, and here the bishop's role was restricted to granting institution. This too was no formality and institution was from time to time refused, most commonly on grounds of insufficient learning. But rejection of a candidate for institution always ran the risk of the expense and inconvenience of a civil suit brought by the patron against the bishop.[17] The endemic poverty of thousands of livings was another formidable obstacle in the path of a general rehabilitation of the ministry. And so was the everlasting backlog of unsatisfactory

(1975), 247–60, and 'The Reformation of the Ministry, 1558–1642', in *Continuity and Change*, pp. 55–75. See also much information in the seminal study by D. M. Barratt, 'Conditions of the Parish Clergy from the Reformation to 1660 within the Dioceses of Oxford, Worcester and Gloucester', Oxford D.Phil. thesis, 1950.

[14] O'Day *The English Clergy*, pp. 49–54.

[15] Ibid., pp. 126–43; O'Day, 'The Reformation of the Ministry'.

[16] For example, it is easy to cite Archbishop Grindal's oft-quoted statement that he 'procured above forty learned preachers and graduates, within less than six years, to be placed within the diocese of York', harder to name all these forty, and nearly impossible to determine how they were recruited in each case. (*The Remains of Edmund Grindal*, ed. W. Nicholson, Parker Society (Cambridge, 1843), p. 380.)

[17] O'Day, *The English Clergy*, pp. 75–85; O'Day, 'The Law of Patronage'.

clerics, enjoying the nearly total security of the parson's freehold.

From this compressed survey of episcopal government it appears that the impact of the bishops on ecclesiastical and social life is a subject which lies beyond administrative history and which cannot be judged from the administrative record alone. We conclude that the role of a bishop in the Elizabethan Church, while by no means irretrievable, is elusive. So elusive in fact that it is possible that some of the judgements which historians have expressed about particular bishops or groups of bishops may be insecurely founded and even wrong.[18] Before we are finished we shall test this possibility. But first it is necessary to look more closely at the status of bishops in post-Reformation society.[19]

V

For this the episcopal palace at Lincoln can serve as a symbol. After describing this building as a monument to the power and privilege of the pre-Reformation Church, Bishop Williams's biographer remarked that it was 'fit for the Pomp of those great Potentates', but 'formidable to their poor Successors, that could not keep it warm, with the Rents that remain'd'.[20] If anyone could have afforded to keep Lincoln Palace warm it was Williams—who like most bishops of Lincoln preferred the comfort of the Huntingdonshire seat of Buckden. But Bishop Hacket's observation conveys the general truth that the Elizabethan and Jacobean bishops were the poor relations of their predecessors, inhabiting the shell of the late Medieval Church. In assessing the revenues of the early Henrician bishops, Felicity Heal has suggested that by 'right of wealth' as well as by formal right they were indeed peers of the realm, in power and physical resources commensurate with the secular nobility.[21] But their successors were both really and relatively worse off and socially at a very distinct disadvantage. As married or marriageable men, and

---

[18] As I argue in my *Archbishop Grindal*, Grindal is one prelate who has been persistently mistaken and misrepresented by posterity and in the historical literature.

[19] Heal, *Of Prelates and Princes*, is definitive for the Tudor period.

[20] Hacket, *Scrinia Reserata*, ii. 34.

[21] Heal, *Of Prelates and Princes*, pp. 72–3, 177.

fathers of marriageable daughters, they found their level among the lesser gentry, the urban bourgeoisie and other ecclesiastics. Not one Elizabethan bishop achieved a marriage alliance with the lay nobility.[22]

Yet the economically and socially diminished episcopal order was required to perform functions which had not been radically redefined and which the enhanced demands of the Tudor state had rendered in many ways more onerous. It was political necessity, not personal vanity, which dictated that their housekeeping should still be consistent with the life-style of magnates. In the early seventeenth century the household of the bishop of Norwich contained upwards of forty persons, including a dwarf and a trumpeter.[23] This seems to have been typical of bishoprics of the middle rank.[24] When a new bishop of Norwich arrived in 1603 many gentlemen flew in 'like butterflies in the Springe' but moved on when they found 'little hope of benefitt'.[25] Most bishops now had wives to support and children to advance, who were competitors with the household staff and ultimately with society at large for limited resources. Joel Berlatsky has found that of the money specified in the wills of fifty-one Elizabethan bishops, only £6,255 or 22 per cent was devoted to charitable bequests, compared with £22,000 bestowed on kindred.[26] Edmund Grindal as bishop of London, a bachelor, spent more than his entire nominal income on what was broadly defined as 'hospitality'. His successor and boyhood friend Edwin Sandys managed to spend rather less on this item, perhaps with the aid of Mrs Sandys, and he went on as archbishop of York to establish several of his sons in the ranks of the gentry.[27] Before

---

[22] Berlatsky, 'Marriage and Family'.

[23] Harison, *Registrum Vagum*, ii. 238–42. To 'personal vanity' and 'political necessity' we should perhaps add the motive of charity of Arthur Lake, bishop of Bath and Wells from 1616 to 1626. Thomas Fuller (following Robert Harris's 'Short View' of his life, see pp. 87–8 below) reported that he kept fifty servants 'not so much for state or attendance on his Person but pure charity in regard of their private need'. (*The History of the Worthies of England* (1662) ii. 7–8.)

[24] Heal, *Of Prelates and Princes*, pp. 258–9.

[25] Harison, *Registrum Vagum*, ii, 238–42.

[26] Berlatsky, 'Marriage and Family'.

[27] Collinson, *Archbishop Grindal*, pp. 299–300; Heal, *Of Prelates and Princes*, pp. 241–2; Berlatsky, 'Marriage and Family', 13.

the Reformation it was a fine and not unrealistic principle that a bishop should not spend more than a third of his revenues on food and drink.[28]

There is no need to dwell on the predicament into which insupportable financial pressures thrust the more feckless or unlucky bishops. In 1956 Christopher Hill alerted historians of the period to the economic problems of the Church and their repercussions and study of the subject is now reaching its maturity.[29] Thanks to Felicity Heal we understand the invidious rather than disastrous effects of the Act of Exchange of 1559, which replaced rents from anciently held manors with impropriate tithes and fiscal revenues as the economic basis of some bishoprics.[30] We also appreciate the severe embarrassment in which some bishops were placed by their responsibilities as collectors of clerical taxation as well as by their own fiscal obligations.[31] The Elizabethan Exchequer, especially in the lord-treasurership of the marquess of Winchester, was impersonal and merciless in pursuing its episcopal debtors with distraint of goods, both in life and beyond the grave. Bishop Godwin of Bath and Wells wrote of these procedures: 'Process is so terrible to me, and so disgraceful to my place . . .'. When Bishop Chaderton of Chester asked to be excused his first-fruits he was told that the queen was 'very loath . . . to hearken to any suit of this kind'.[32] In practice, the rare

---

[28] Heal, *Of Prelates and Princes,* p. 86.

[29] Christopher Hill, *Economic Problems of the Church from Whitgift to the Long Parliament* (Oxford, 1956). And, most recently *Princes and Paupers in the English Church,* ed. Rosemary O'Day and Felicity Heal (Leicester, 1981).

[30] Heal, *Of Prelates and Princes,* pp. 204–8, 222–31, 267–71, following her articles, 'The Bishops and the Act of Exchange of 1559', *Historical Journal,* xvii (1974), 227–46 and 'The Tudors and Church Lands: Economic Problems of the Bishopric of Ely During the Sixteenth Century', *Economic History Review,* xxvi (1973), 198–217. See also Claire Cross, 'The Economic Problems of the See of York: Decline and Recovery in the Sixteenth Century', in *Land, Church, and People,* ed. J. Thirsk, *Agricultural History Review Supplement* (1970), pp. 64–83; Gina Alexander, 'Victim or Spendthrift? The Bishop of London and his Income in the Sixteenth Century', in *Wealth and Power in Tudor England: Essays Presented to S. T. Bindoff,* ed. E. W. Ives, R. J. Knecht, and J. J. Scarisbrick (1978), pp. 128–45; and W. J. Sheils, 'Profit, Patronage, or Pastoral Care: the Rectory Estates of the Archbishopric of York, 1540–1640', in *Princes and Paupers in the English Church,* pp. 91–109.

[31] Heal, *Of Prelates and Princes,* pp. 89–96, 233–6, following her essay 'Clerical Tax Collection under the Tudors: the Influence of the Reformation', in *Continuity and Change,* pp. 97–122.

[32] Heal, *Of Prelates and Princes,* pp. 233–6, 249.

privilege of relief from first-fruits was reserved to bishops who had held the office of royal almoner, or who had rendered other notable service to the Crown, or to bishops who had been thoroughly fleeced in other ways as the price of their promotion.[33] Poor management or unwise litigation or large families often compounded these difficulties and visited disaster on some bishops, or wiped out any estates which they might have hoped to leave behind them. Among other cases of episcopal shipwreck, four Elizabethan bishops stand out: Parkhurst of Norwich, Horne of Winchester, Overton of Coventry and Lichfield, and Bradbridge of Exeter, who died owing the crown £1,235 and whose executors could find no money to bury him decently.[34] Both Parkhurst and Bradbridge were the partly innocent victims of the villainy of their collectors of clerical taxation.

Our concern is not directly with these details of profit and loss, which have been dealt with definitively by Felicity Heal, with many warnings that for the episcopal order as a whole we

[33] Ibid., pp. 248–54. In addition to the evidence cited by Felicity Heal, the Exchequer rolls contain evidence of two cases of debts excused. The executors of Archbishop John Piers of York (*ob.* 28 September 1594) were authorized to appropriate certain rents due to be paid at Michaelmas, and technically owing to the Crown, for the payment of the archbishop's funeral expenses, legacies, and debts, the queen being moved by the damage to the estate occasioned by his 'hospitality at home and liberality abroad', and 'for that he was a man of great note to us and in respect of his great learning, virtue and good lief greatly favored of us'. Piers had been royal almoner. (PRO, E 159/468, Easter 37 Eliz.) In Michaelmas Term 1568 Bishop Hugh Curwen of Oxford was excused and indemnified from the payment of one tenth, payable at Christmas, and from the first and second payments of the 1567 clerical subsidy, on the grounds of his faithful service as lord chancellor of Ireland. (PRO, E 159/356.) But the bishopric of Oxford was evidently regarded as Curwen's Irish pension. After his brief tenure of the see for one year it remained vacant for twenty-one years. I owe both these references to Sybil Jack.

[34] To Ralph Houlbrooke's account of Parkhurst's financial and legal distress at the time of his death (*Letter Book of John Parkhurst*, 28–30, 53–5) may be added evidence from the Exchequer rolls that as late as 1591, sixteen years after his death, there was litigation between the bishop's executors and certain 'approved men' of Guildford concerning Parkhurst's legacy to the poor of the town. (PRO, E 112/Bundle 63/134. I owe this reference to Sybil Jack.) Horne died heavily in debt, mainly to the Crown, but may have already provided generously for his four daughters. (John Darrell (Horne's son-in-law and executor) to Burghley, 12 June 1579, PRO, S.P. 12/131/23; Heal, *Of Prelates and Princes*, pp. 241, 314, 317.) For Overton, see M. R. O'Day, 'Cumulative Debt: the Bishops of Coventry and Lichfield and their Economic Problems', *Midland History*, iii (1975), 85–6; for Bradbridge, see Heal, 'Clerical Tax Collection' p. 116, *Of Prelates and Princes*, p. 251.

are dealing not with wholesale calamity nor even with a major
crisis in their affairs but with relative hardship. For the
present purpose what matters is the effect of financial
exigency on relations between the bishops and the governing
and landowning classes. Bishops, and especially married
bishops, were strongly tempted to make good their losses by
means which were contrary to custom and the principles of
good husbandry, if not actually illegal. Like all landlords in a
period of inflationary pressure, they faced the choice between
winning hearts and minds and the maximization of profits.
Felicity Heal has shown how the aggressively modern estate
management practised by Bishop Cox of Ely, especially in the
resumption and selling of leases, poisoned relations with his
tenantry and to some extent with the entire laity of the see.[35]
Another source of instant gain was timber, a resource to be
either conserved for the continuing profit of the see or wasted
for its capital value to the sitting incumbent and his
dependants. In 1580 the scandalous entrepreneurship of
Bishop Aylmer of London as forester and timber merchant
provoked a full-scale government inquiry into the episcopal
exploitation of trees and woodland, from which some bishops
emerged with tarnished reputations. Yet Aylmer alleged that
it was his debts to the queen which had forced him to sell
many hundreds of pounds worth of timber.[36]

To have used these trees for constructive purposes on the
bishop's own estate would have been legitimate. But understandably the episcopate failed to participate in the famous
'great rebuilding' which transformed the face of large sectors
of Elizabethan and Jacobean England.[37] The Church had
known its own 'great rebuilding' a century earlier, when the
princely Cardinal Morton and his emulators had pioneered
the use of brick on a spectacular scale. But the legacy of this
ambitious past was a running sore of repairs and maintenance
which absorbed scarce resources and threatened any claim the
Elizabethan hierarchy might have had, not to sanctity but to

---

[35] Felicity Heal, 'The Bishops of Ely and their Diocese during the Reformation',
Cambridge Ph.D. thesis, 1972, Chapter 7; Heal, *Of Prelates and Princes*, pp. 296–7.

[36] Heal, *Of Prelates and Princes*, pp. 286–9; Collinson, *Archbishop Grindal*, pp. 306–8.

[37] Heal, *Of Prelates and Princes*, p. 320.

simple honesty. For nothing was more calculated to sour good relations among the bishops themselves than the need at each new translation to settle with previous tenants of the see or their executors the contentious matter of dilapidations. And nothing so damaged the bishops in the eyes of the laity, since such cases were sometimes heard by courts of delegates appointed by the Crown.[38] In 1579 it was Sir Francis Walsingham, principally, who was obliged to hear the bitter recriminations which Archbishop Sandys visited on the head of his brother and successor of London, Aylmer, whom he had helped to consecrate. 'So soon as the bishop of York had holpen him on with his rochet he was transformed and showed himself in his own nature.' 'Coloured covetousness, an envious heart covered with the cloak of dissimulation will, when opportunity serveth, shew itself forth.'[39] Once again it was the necessity of paying the Exchequer its pound of flesh which turned these men of God into squabbling fishwives. But no wonder Walsingham's secretary wrote about 'that crew' and their 'offensive conversations', whereof, he said, the Court was 'too much and often a witness'.[40]

The bishops could respond in one of two ways to the relative material disadvantage which they shared with the entire Church of which they were representatives. Either they could accommodate themselves to things as they were, working with the grain of an emancipated protestant lay society. Or they could seek to change things for the better and to strengthen the Church as an ecclesiastical corporation, financially and politically. The latter was the policy of Whitgift and Bancroft and, more audaciously, of Laud. I must confess that my reading of the church history of the period has tended to persuade me of the merits of the first strategy, the policy of bishops whom some in the seventeenth century praised and some condemned as 'moderate', 'less formal', and

[38] Ibid., pp. 39–42, 87–9, 299–303; Phyllis Hembry, 'Episcopal Palaces, 1535 to 1660', in *Wealth and Power*, pp. 146–66; Collinson, *Archbishop Grindal*, pp. 302–6.

[39] Sandys to Walsingham, 20 April, 3 June 1579, PRO, S.P. 12/130/39, 131/21; Nicholas Faunt to Anthony Bacon, 6 May, 6 August 1583, Lambeth Palace Library, MS 647, nos. 72, 74, fols. 150–2, 157ᵛ.

[40] Nicholas Faunt to Anthony Bacon, 6 May, 6 August 1583; Lambeth Palace Library, MS 647, nos. 72, 74, fols. 150–2, 157ᵛ.

even 'popular', and whose prototype in many respects was Archbishop Grindal.

Archbishop Whitgift was charged by some Kentish gentle-men with 'setting himself against the gentry'. That was unpopular. Archbishop Abbot was accused by Heylyn of 'compliance with the gentry against the clergy', the policy of 'popularity'.[41] At the county level this was where episcopal strategies differed and even divided: a matter of more or less affability, social civilities, and entertainment, of policies towards preaching ministers (Whitgift's major offence), and of the preferences exercised in the leasing of episcopal land and disposing of other forms of patronage with which friendship could be purchased and cemented. No bishop could dispense with allies among the ruling gentry. Bishop Bentham as a total stranger in early Elizabethan Staffordshire was without credit in the most literal sense: no one would lend him any money.[42] Bishops who were natives enjoyed certain advan-tages, especially in the clannish north country.[43] The lack of local roots was doubtless the cause of Mrs Matthew's unhappiness, of which she complained to her husband in bed.[44] But when Bernard Gilpin, in refusing the see of Carlisle, pleaded 'the inconvenience of the place' he meant that as a member of a prominent Westmorland family he would be unable to retain the neutrality in local politics which he considered appropriate for a bishop, and which enabled him as a kind of unofficial bishop to pacify the warring tribes of the Northumberland dales.[45] Sometimes the 'church interest' itself became a focus and a distinct force in local politics. Mervyn James has shown that in the north it assumed the form of one of the 'gentry affiliations' by which regional affairs in County Durham were structured.[46]

The history of the Elizabethan Church contains more than

---

[41] Dr Williams's Library, MS Morrice L, no. V, pp. 8–11; Peter Clark, *English Provincial Society from the Reformation to the Revolution: Religion, Politics and Society in Kent, 1500–1640* (Hassocks, 1977), pp. 305–6.

[42] *Letter-Book of Bishop Bentham*, p. 196.

[43] Heal, *Of Prelates and Princes*, p. 172.

[44] See above, p. 46.

[45] D. Marcombe, 'Bernard Gilpin: Anatomy of an Elizabethan Legend', *Northern History*, xvi (1980), 30–1.

[46] James, *Family, Lineage and Civil Society*, pp. 150 ff.

one example of the unwisdom of bishops who attempted trials of strength with dominant factions while lacking an effective 'affiliation' of their own. In the late 1570s Bishop Richard Curteys of Chichester was a new broom who made a vigorous onslaught on the notorious backwardness of Sussex, organizing and himself leading an enthusiastic team of preaching ministers. Forty-two of his brethren were prepared to testify that 'whereas it was a rare thing before his time to heare a learned sermon in Sussex, now the pulpittes in moste places sounde contynuously with the voyce of learned and godly preachers, he him selfe as *dux gregis* geving good example unto the rest'.[47] But if Curteys was a success as an apostle he was a disastrous failure as ecclesiastical judge and magistrate. When he challenged the recusants and church papists among the Sussex gentry by citing them in a body to appear in his consistory court, the Privy Council, for all its advanced protestant sympathies, was forced to agree with local opinion that it was 'a great oversight of the said lord bishop to appoint so great a number of gentlemen of such worship and calling to appear in such an open place, all at one day, time and instant'. Curteys was repudiated and removed from all positions of local influence.[48] Simultaneously, in East Anglia, Bishop Edmund Freke's efforts to reduce the puritan clergy to conformity and to make himself independent of their powerful patrons brought him into confrontation with ruling groups of staunchly protestant gentry. His power base was both narrow and scarcely respectable, and he fared little better than Curteys. To one Privy Councillor he was 'the foolish bishop' whose complaints against 'dyvers most zealous and loyall gentlemen' were beneath contempt. Some of the local gossip insinuates that Bishop Freke's greatest handicap was Mrs Freke. When people came about their business but without an appropriate gift, this formidable lady looked over them 'as the Devil looks over Lincoln'. 'This ys vox populi, a principall well known throughout all Norfolke, sprede by his household, that

---

[47] Curteys, *An exposition*, Epistle, signed 'in Sussex 16 December 1576' by forty-two ministers.

[48] Roger B. Manning, *Religion and Society in Elizabethan Sussex* (Leicester, 1969), pp. 91–125.

whatsoever Mrs Freake will have done, the Bishop must and will accomplishe.'[49]

Freke's unpopular conduct may be usefully compared with the episcopal style of John Jegon, bishop of Norwich from 1603 to 1618, and as representative a Jacobean bishop as one could hope to meet: a Calvinist and promoted from the headship of a Cambridge college. Jegon's letters to his clergy are models of tact and civility. Some of them relate to the market-day lectures provided by combinations of the neighbouring ministers.[50] They reveal the bishop co-operating amicably with 'knights and worthy gentlemen', the townspeople, and the clergy, in the promotion of preaching in neglected places like Swaffham, where, Jegon was assured, the inhabitants were 'more rude than easilie will bee believed to be of those that have been brought up in more civill places, the greater part of them utterlie destitute of teaching ministers'. In putting this to rights, Jegon said that he was 'presuming upon his credit' with the preaching clergy: 'Wherin if I may prevail, as the woorke shall growe to Gods glory, the good example of other like places in my dioces, the comfort of my hart and the testimonie of your worth, so it shall give good occasion to me to solicite your better preferment, aunswerable to your guiftes, to the uttermost of my power. And so I recommend myselfe to your good love and prayers.'[51] This is the quality of bishop–clergy relations which Bishop Joseph Hall later claimed to have promoted in his diocese of Exeter: 'the happy sense of that general unanimity and loving correspondence of my clergy'.[52] One of the most puritanical of the Suffolk preachers, Nicholas Bownd, who wrote the most famous work of sabbatarian divinity, assured Bishop Jegon 'how readie we are, and shall be, to yeild obedience to all your lordship's godly proceedings', blessing God 'not only for your

---

[49] Extensive documentation in PRO S.P. 12/26, S.P. 15/25. See Smith, *County and Court*, pp. 210–25; D. N. J. MacCulloch, 'Power, Privilege and the County Community: County Politics in Elizabethan Suffolk', Cambridge Ph.D. thesis, 1977, pp. 144–7.

[50] Patrick Collinson, 'Lectures by Combination: Structures and Characteristics of Church Life in 17th-Century England', *Bulletin of the Institute of Historical Research*, xlviii (1975), 182–213. See pp. 136–40 below.

[51] Harison, *Registrum Vagum*, i. 96–103.

[52] *Works of Hall*, i. xlvii.

comming among us, but much more for your continuance with us, and over us'.[53]

VI

No one has ever doubted that the type of Jacobean bishop represented by Jegon knew the value of good relations with the county and how to cultivate them. Williams, thanks to his voluminous biographer, provides the most familiar example of these affable qualities. Even before the days of his greatness, but when he already lived in his Northamptonshire parsonage 'like a *Magnifico*', Williams had 'mightily won the Friendship of all the Gentry in the whole District', not least by the use of his musical talents, as well as 'favour and countenance from the Nobility'. Later, at Buckden, the entertainment and the music continued on a more lavish scale.[54] When Oliver St. John in due course rose in the Long Parliament to denounce Williams—his own diocesan—he nevertheless conceded that he was 'the best affected of any in these times in that function', a man 'well reputed and thought of by most in this kingdom'.[55]

Such a reputation has sometimes served to discredit and diminish the bishops who earned it. This suggests excessive deference to the party of Neile and Laud and to their contrary ideology. There is much talk of the Church in the letters to John Cosin of that seminal high churchman Richard Montague, which Montague asked Cosin to burn, but which have survived to impart the most private of insights into the rise of the Arminian faction.[56] 'I am ready not only to be bound but . . . to dye for the Church', wrote Montague, at the time of the initial agitation over his book the *New gagg*.[57] But, as Lord

---

[53] Nicholas Bownd, *The holy exercise of fasting* (Cambridge, 1604), Epistle, sigs. ¶ 5–6. The second edition of Bownd's *Doctrine of the Sabbath* was also dedicated to Jegon.

[54] Hacket, *Scrinia Reserata*, i. 35; ii. 31. Did Williams have a castrato voice? Hacket (i. 8) reports that he was made a eunuch by a boyhood accident when he jumped from the walls of Conway town on to the beach.

[55] *Mr St John his speech in Parliament on Monday January the 17 An. Dom. 1641* (1642), sig. A2ᵛ. I owe this reference to Robert Ashton.

[56] *Correspondence of John Cosin*, ed. G. Ormsby, i. Surtees Society lii (1869). The request to burn the letters is mentioned in a letter from Montague to Bishop Neile, 10 July 1625. (Ibid., i. 78–9.)

[57] Ibid., i. 9.

Dacre asked in his biography of Laud, what, or rather who, was the Church in the late 1620s? An interesting development of the early seventeenth century is the growth and expression of effusive reverence for the English Church as Mother. This sentiment is most familiar from George Herbert's poem 'The British Church': 'I joy, deare Mother, when I view Thy perfect lineaments and hue'.[58] But it was not an image confined to some élitist High Anglican revival but widely invoked, especially in the course of defending the Church against her enemies.[59] However, Montague's letters seem to speak of an almost imaginary Church, or they reduce the Church to a remnant, little more than the talented group of Arminian scholars and activists who in the early twenties frequented Bishop Neile's company at Durham House. In 1625 Montague wrote: 'The visible Church I do not greatly care to look upon. I have beheld such enough heretofore.'[60] By the visible Church he meant the hierarchy, then on public display in Convocation, whom he regarded more in sorrow and distaste than anger. 'I feare I shall live to see their rochetts pul'd over their eares.'[61] There were five bishops of whom Montague had reason to approve when his parliamentary ordeal began: Andrewes of Winchester, Neile of Durham, Buckeridge of Rochester, Laud of St. Davids, and Cary of Exeter. But he wrote as if he had only one friend on the entire bench. Sometimes it was Laud: 'For our Bishops I never expected assistance from any but my lord of Bath.' 'God send him health and strength to stand in the gap.' At other times it was Neile, 'the only man that standeth up to purpose in the gapp'. When Cosin went north to Durham Montague wrote: 'Well God kepe his Church and you. If I dy you will write my *Martyrologe* I knowe.'[62]

[58] *The Works of George Herbert,* ed. F. E. Hutchinson (Oxford, 1941), p. 109.

[59] In 1610 Joseph Hall dedicated his *Common apologie of the Church of England against the . . . Brownists* to 'our gratious and blessed Mother, the Church of England'. In 1639 Robert Abbot, vicar and 'preacher of God's word' at Cranbrook in Kent, a parson in the moderate puritan tradition and a client of his namesake, Archbishop Abbot, followed suit in dedicating *A triall of our church-forsakers* to 'my dear mother, the much honored, holy and blessed Church of England'.

[60] *Correspondence of Cosin,* i. 42.

[61] Ibid., i. 75.

[62] Ibid., i. 97; BL Add. MS 4274, fols. 98, 102, 103.

The author of the *New gagg* was entitled to a dose of persecution mania, and we may admire the humour with which he bore it. But the paranoiac mentality was by no means confined to Montague. That other secret document, Archbishop Laud's diary, breathes the same atmosphere, which seems to have arisen from the coercion of anti-Calvinists by Calvinists in the universities: in Cambridge in the 1590s, in Oxford somewhat later.[63] This fratricidal conflict accounted for the fatal instability of the Jacobean Church in its superstructure, and for the strident sense of insecurity as a remnant and an anti-movement which the Arminians carried into their era of power in the 1630s. In his Star Chamber speech against Henry Sherfield, the Recorder of Salisbury,[64] Laud spoke of a time still to come when such puritan laymen as he was would be laid 'as low as the Church is now'.[65] That was in 1633, when Laud's triumph was complete.

By identifying their own cause with that of the Church, as Laud did in marking off churchmen with 'O' for Orthodox and 'P' for Puritan,[66] the Arminians inverted what the religious majority believed to be the true order of things. As Nicholas Tyacke has convincingly argued,[67] that majority, 'a society steeped in Calvinist theology', believed Calvinism and the religious practice associated with Calvinist belief to be the true orthodoxy: what one writer calls 'the good old Doctrine of the Church of *England,* even that which in the University was taught and maintained by Famous *Whitaker, Perkins, Davenant, Ward* and many others in their times'.[68] Such an understanding of 'orthodox protestant religion', with a suspicious fear of 'innovation', was shared by a majority of the bishops whom

---

[63] N. R. N. Tyacke, 'Arminianism in England in Religion and Politics from 1604 to 1640', Oxford D.Phil. thesis, 1969, pp. 104 ff.; Peter Lake, 'Laurence Chaderton and the Cambridge Moderate Puritan Tradition, 1570–1604', Cambridge Ph.D. thesis, 1978, chapter 6, 7.

[64] See pp. 147–9 below.

[65] Quoted, Paul Slack, 'Religious Protest and Urban Authority: The Case of Henry Sherfield, Iconoclast, 1633', in *Schism, Heresy and Religious Protest, Studies in Church History,* ix, ed. Derek Baker (Cambridge, 1972), 297.

[66] *The Works of William Laud,* ed. W. Scott and J. Bliss, iii (Oxford, 1853), 159.

[67] Tyacke, 'Puritanism, Arminianism and Counter-Revolution'.

[68] 'The Life and Times of Doctor [Thomas] Hill who died Anno Christi 1653', in Clarke, *Lives of Thirty-Two English Divines,* p. 232.

Montague so despised: in Tyacke's phrase 'the mainstream of Calvinist episcopalianism'. A list of the more notable members of this mainstream might include John King of London, James Montague of Bath and Wells and Winchester, Arthur Lake, his successor at Wells, the two Abbots, George and Robert, of Canterbury and Salisbury respectively, Tobie Matthew of Durham and York, George Carleton of Chichester, Thomas Morton of Chester, Coventry and Lichfield, and Durham, John Davenant of Salisbury, Miles Smith of Gloucester, Joseph Hall of Exeter and Norwich, John Bridgeman of Chester, Henry Robinson of Carlisle, and a later bishop of Carlisle, Barnaby Potter; and, among the Irish bishops, James Ussher of Armagh, William Bedell of Kilmore, and George Downame of Derry. When Archbishop Abbot died in 1633 the earl of Clare, the father of Denzil Holles, wrote that he was 'a timorous weak man, yet he was orthodox and hindered much ill'.[69]

'Orthodox' meant Calvinist. Calvinism can be regarded as the theological cement of the Jacobean Church, in Tyacke's phrase 'a common and ameliorating bond' uniting conformists and moderate puritans. It interlocked with the prevalent anti-Catholic ideology, and it had broad implications for the sustenance of the existing political and social order, with which it was assumed to be entirely coherent.[70] But to emphasize only the Calvinism may divert attention from the distinctiveness of the churchmanship exhibited by those representing 'Calvinist episcopalianism', as well as somewhat falsifying the principles of some, like Joseph Hall, who believed in theological reconciliation and strove to mediate between the Calvinist and Arminian positions. In his youth John Williams was a constant auditor of William Perkins, but he was also an admirer of John Overall, theologically an opponent of Perkins' Calvinism, but himself seen by many as a centrist and a reconciling figure. Williams's biographer remarks: 'He that is discreet will make his Profit out of every side, or every Faction, if you like to call it so.' Hacket alleged

---

[69] Patricia Crawford, *Denzil Holles 1598–1680: A Study of his Political Career* (1979), p. 9.

[70] See pp. 149–53 below.

that in exercising his patronage Williams followed Whitgift, Bancroft, Harsnet, Andrewes, Barlow, and Overall in making 'no discrimination' with respect to differences in the doctrine of grace. Everything changed in this respect with the accession of Charles I, when 'the Fathers of our Tribe' began 'to prefer them only who were of the same Judgment with themselves'.[71] Not the least of the posthumous triumphs of these 'fathers' has been the total neglect of the merits of mainstream Jacobean episcopacy from the point of view of churchmanship and church order, and the consequent downgrading of the Jacobean Church.

The character of this churchmanship is well captured in the biographies and biographical memoirs of its principal exponents, of which Bishop Hacket's ambitious political biography of John Williams, *Scrinia Reserata,* is the longest and most famous.[72] Allowance must of course be made for hagiographical literary convention, some of it post-Civil War and retrospectively apologetic. As Gilbert Burnet was to write in the preface to his life of Bishop Bedell: 'There is nothing that can have a stronger operation to overcome all prejudices against Episcopacy than the proposing eminent Patterns, whose lives continue to speak still, though they are dead.'[73]

---

[71] Hacket, *Scrinia Reserata,* i. 9–10; ii. 42. The allegation of indifference in these hotly disputed matters was, of course, a valuable polemical weapon and therefore suspect. See Richard Montague to John Cosin, 2 July 1627: 'I shall not Calvinise it, not yet Arminianise it, but with the Church of England, Augustine and Prosper, go the middle way.' (*Correspondence of Cosin,* i. 125.)

[72] The paragraphs which follow draw upon the following biographies and biographical and autobiographical memoirs: Gervase Babington of Llandaff Exeter and Worcester: biographical memoir by Bishop Miles Smith prefacing the 1637 edition of his *Works*; William Bedell of Kilmore: two lives, by the bishop's son William Bedell and by Alexander Clogie, the latter the basis of Gilbert Burnet's *Life of William Bedell* (1685), gathered in *Two Biographies of William Bedell,* ed. E. S. Shuckburgh (Cambridge, 1902); Joseph Hall of Exeter and Norwich: the autobiographical 'Observations of some specialities of Divine Providence in the Life of Joseph Hall', included in Philip Wynter's edition of the *Works*; Arthur Lake of Bath and Wells; John Harris's 'Short View of the Life and Vertues', prefacing the 1629 edition of Lake's *Sermons*; Thomas Morton of Chester, Coventry and Lichfield, and Durham: John Nelson's *The Life of Dr Thomas Morton* (1669); Miles Smith of Gloucester: biographical memoir prefacing the 1632 edition of his *Sermons*; Richard Vaughan of Bangor, Chester, and London: Archbishop Williams's life, 'Vaughanus redivivus, sive amplissimi viri Domini Richardi Vaughani . . . vita atque obius', BL Harl. MS 6495, art. 6, fols. 51–114; John Williams of Lincoln and York: Bishop John Hacket's life, *Scrinia Reserata.*

[73] Preface to Gilbert Burnet's *Life of Bedell.*

These narratives contain many familiar components of the sixteenth-century 'Bischofsideal'. The bishop presides over an orderly and exemplary household. His own diet is frugal, but he offers plentiful hospitality to 'the better sort' and is equally generous to the poor. Good books are read aloud, at table and while travelling. The bishop is an indefatigable student. Williams's lamp burned many nights until morning as he laboured at an immense and apparently abortive Latin commentary on the Scriptures. 'Neither Colick, nor Catarrhs, nor the Stone, the sharpest of Pains, could stay him from his main purpose.'[74] In the bishop's public life, preaching takes priority, as it had done for the fathers of Trent. The bishop ordains 'carefully', laying hands only on graduates of whose worth he is personally satisfied. He is an exemplary visitor and a stern disciplinarian. These are the ritual components of 'primitive' or 'apostolic' episcopacy, as advertised in the title of another biography of Bedell: *Speculum Episcoporum: or, The Apostolicall Bishop.*

This churchmanship often had its source in Elizabethan puritanism. When James I asked his Council why so many of the bishops should favour puritans Lionel Cranfield told him that it was because his Majesty made so many puritans bishops.[75] But it was Charles I who elevated Joseph Hall, grown from sanctified stock at Ashby-de-la-Zouch; and Charles who preferred to Carlisle his chaplain Barnaby Potter, who 'was accounted by many a *Puritanical* Bishop'.[76] How often, wrote Hall, had he 'blessed the memory of those divine passages of experimental divinity' which he heard from his puritan mother's mouth.[77] Hall became a fellow of Emmanuel, like Bishop Bedell and Bedell's friend Samuel Ward who succeeded James Montague as Master of Sidney Sussex. Montague sprang from puritan gentry in Northamptonshire.

---

[74] Hacket, *Scrinia Reserata*, ii. 40.
[75] *The Court of King James the First, by Godfrey Goodman*, ed. J. S. Brewer (1839), i. 313–14.
[76] Clarke, *Lives of Thirty-Two English Divines*, p. 156.
[77] *Works of Hall*, i. xxi. However, Hall retained no affectionate memory of Anthony Gilby, the puritan patriarch of the Ashby of his youth, whom he called 'one of the godfathers of [this discipline—sc., Presbyterianism] . . . the author of that bitter dialogue [sc., the *Soldier of Barwicke*] . . . one of the hottest and busiest sticklers in these quarrels at Frankfort'. (Ibid., ix. 272–3.)

He preached William Perkins's funeral sermon, and Bedell purchased Perkins's library.[78] Bishop Thomas Morton, called by Williams's biographer *'simpliciter optimus'* and 'the Darling of Divines', was a protégé of the puritan oracle of late Elizabethan Cambridge, William Whitaker.[79] With Bedell, Hall, and Morton the initial puritanism seems to have been broadened and mollified through the effect of patristic learning and the combined influences of aristocratic patrons, foreign travel including controversial contacts with Roman Catholics, and, of course, preferment.[80]

The biographical and autobiographical memoirs are also pointers to the internal connections of this group and provide evidence of a circle as distinctive as the more celebrated Arminian/Laudian connection which succeeded and displaced it.[81] The identifiable members were James Montague, bishop of Bath and Wells and then of Winchester; Montague's successor first as dean of Worcester and then as bishop of Bath and Wells from 1616 to 1626, Arthur Lake; Samuel Ward, who besides following Montague at Sidney Sussex was also archdeacon of Taunton; and John Young, dean of Winchester but also chancellor and prebendary of Wells. There were other minor members or dependants of this circle among the dignitaries of the cathedral churches of Winchester and Wells, and in the ranks of the parish clergy: men like the prolific and popular religious author Richard Bernard, whose 'planting' at Batcombe in Somerset was contrived by Bishop Montague, 'not by sollicitation of friends but onely out of his former remembrance of me in *Cambridge*', and by another archdeacon of Taunton, Philip Bisse, who purchased the advowson of Batcombe for one turn in order to bring Bernard over from Nottinghamshire. Bernard described Montague's successor Bishop Lake as *'a blessed Bishop, a very man of God'*: so far had the

---

[78] Tyacke, 'Puritanism, Arminianism and Counter-Revolution', p. 123; *Two Biographies of William Bedell*, p. 6.

[79] Hacket, *Scrinia Reserata*, i. 22; *Life of Morton*, p. 7.

[80] This process of transmogrification can be best observed in the long series of letters from Bedell to Samuel Ward among the Tanner MSS in the Bodleian Library. A selection of these is printed with *Two Biographies of William Bedell*.

[81] Tyacke, 'Arminianism in England', pp. 141–3. I am grateful to Nicholas Tyacke for alerting me to the connections between these figures.

radical puritan tradition travelled in reconciliation to the hierarchical Church by the 1620s.[82] We may call this the Somerset, or more specifically the Wells connection, or, since Lake had begun his career as warden of New College, the Wells–Winchester connection. William Bedell lived in some obscurity in Suffolk until 1627, when he crossed the Irish Sea to become provost of Trinity College, but he was connected to the circle through his lifelong correspondence with his old contemporary Samuel Ward. In 1613 he wrote: 'I pray remember my service to my Lord of Bath [Montague] and commendations to our Emmanuel College freends.'[83] Thomas Morton may also be counted a member. As Young's predecessor as dean of Winchester he was 'most intimate and beloved' of Arthur Lake, at that time master of St. Cross in Winchester.[84] Dean Young, a Scot and close to the king, may be described as the Neile of this contrary faction, that is to say, its organizer and animator. When Neile was bishop of Winchester and Young dean, the two men fell out with more than the ordinary Trollopian rancour of cathedral closes. Young recorded the climax of this quarrel in his diary: 'And will ye thus, my lord, forget al the good offices I have doune for you? . . . His lordship went chubbedly away from me, saying that he had doune me a manie good offices, and more then ever I dide for him, and so we parted abruptly.'[85]

The principal monument to this group, dedicated to Dean Young, was a posthumous edition in folio of the sermons of Bishop Arthur Lake, which included an account of Lake's life composed by John Harris, a prebendary in turn of Wells and

[82] Richard Bernard, *The ready way to good works, or, a treatise of charitie* (1635), sig. A4, p. 316; Richard Bernard, *The faithfull shepherd: wholy in a manner transposed and made anew and very much inlarged* (1621), Epistle.

[83] *Two Biographies of William Bedell*, p. 253. Samuel Ward's incoming correspondence, preserved in the Tanner MSS (Bodleian Library), also includes nine letters from Bishop Lake, and letters from Dean Young, Bishop Morton, Archbishop Matthew, and another Calvinist bishop, John Davenant of Salisbury. It appears from the letters that survive that Lake, Davenant, and Archbishop Ussher of Armagh were very regular correspondents, as well as Bedell.

[84] *Life of Morton*, p. 48.

[85] *The Diary of John Young S.T.P. Dean of Winchester 1616 to the Commonwealth*, ed. F. R. Goodman (1928), p. 90. The original diary, from which Goodman prints only extracts, is preserved in Winchester Cathedral Library.

Winchester.[86] It is significant that churchmen as unlike in their sympathies as Thomas Fuller and Peter Heylyn should both testify to Lake's exemplary piety, Fuller perpetuating what is probably a legend: that Lake's elevation owed more to his own deserts than to the fact that his brother was Secretary of State.[87] Since Lake's successor at Wells was none other than William Laud, the elaborate publicizing of his virtues may have had a polemical intention.[88] So perhaps was Fuller's report that Lake (unlike Laud) seldom if ever dreamed: a fact attributed not to 'the dulness of his fancy, in which faculty he had no defect, but to the staidness of his judgment, wherin he did much excel, as by his learned sermons doth appear'.[89] Be that as it may, in his memorial volume Lake appears as a typical mirror of primitive episcopacy: an assiduous preacher, making 'frequent excursions into the parishes adjoining' (but careful not to devote an inordinate portion of time to sermon preparation), a scrupulous ordainer, 'tender and fatherlike' to his clergy, careful to instruct the weaker sort, a model visitor. Izaak Walton records that 'he sate usually with his chancellor in his Consistory and at least advis'd if not assisted in most sentences for the punishing of such offenders as deserved church censures'. Walton also notes that he rarely condoned the commutation of penance.[90] Lake was sometimes present in person when penance was performed in the churches of Wells,

---

[86] Arthur Lake, *Sermons with some religious and divine meditations . . . whereunto is prefixed by way of preface a short view of the life and vertues of the author* (1629). The volume contains ninety-nine sermons. In 1641 further sermons were published in *Ten sermons upon several occasions preched at Saint Pauls Crosse and elsewhere*. I have benefited from discussing Bishop Lake with Kenneth Fincham of University College, London, who is including Lake in a study of some members of the Jacobean episcopate.

[87] Thomas Fuller, *Church History of Britain* (Oxford, 1845), vi. 38; Fuller, *Worthies*, ii. 7–8; Heylyn, *Cyprianus Anglicus*, p. 159. Godfrey Goodman reported that Lake's first preferment, the rich mastership of St. Cross, Winchester, came to him when his brother obtained it from the king's agent, James Hudson, for a 'consideration'. (*The Court of King James the First*, i. 14–15, 63.)

[88] Yet Lake himself had stipulated in his will (P.C.C. 99 Skynner) that the sermons should be published for a non-controversial purpose, 'the good of younge students'. I owe this information to Kenneth Fincham.

[89] Fuller, *Church History*, vi. 38.

[90] Izaak Walton, *Life of Dr Robert Sanderson* (1681), p. 7. Kenneth Fincham has found more evidence of direct episcopal intervention in the processes of ecclesiastical justice in Lake's time than in the episcopates of James Montague (1608–16) and Walter Curll (1629–32). Laud's episcopate was little more than an interregnum.

preaching and pronouncing absolution when notorious and exotic offenders were involved: bigamists, incestuous persons, schismatics, women preachers.[91] At the end of his sermons in the cathedral, 'the psalm done', Lake would rise in his seat to give the benediction. This practice was enjoying a revival in the Jacobean Church, another outward symbol of the *jus divinum*.[92]

For Lake was a high churchman, for all his Calvinism. Preaching at Paul's Cross before he was a bishop he told the laity: 'Remember you have your Spiritual Birth from us, and your Spiritual Life is maintained by us. Our hands wash you from your sinnes, our mouthes instil into you God's grace. You owe more unto us than to all Professions besides ours.'[93] His biographer thought that if he had been a Roman Catholic he would have been a strong candidate for canonization. Fuller wrote that since the Calendar knew no St. Arthur, Lake might 'pass for the first saint of his name'. He 'lived a real comment upon Saint Paul's character of a Bishop'.[94] But let us call him St. Charles Borromeo of the Mendips.

In 1625, Lake preached a fast sermon before Parliament in which he identified the last of the plagues threatening the earth as 'the great diminution of the Orthodox Church'. Sharing the mood of the hour, he expressed approval for responding to this challenge by 'politicke unions of States' and 'warlike preparations', but suggested that the truest remedy lay in making much of God's truth. 'Neither is it enough for us to make much of it for our own good, but also wee should propagate it to others.'[95] By 'others' Lake meant the American Indians. This was the very first occasion on which an Anglican bishop used the word 'propagate' in this special sense, later familiar from the Society for the Propagation of the Gospel. The regicide Hugh Peter reported that Lake was much

[91] The sermons preached on some of these occasions are included in the 1629 collection.

[92] Bishop Lancelot Andrewes advocated the episcopal benediction and complained of its neglect. (*Works*, ed. J. Bliss (Oxford, 1841–54), iii. 81.) I owe this reference to Kenneth Fincham.

[93] Lake, *Ten Sermons*, p. 10.

[94] Fuller, *Church History*, vi. 38; Fuller, *Worthies*, ii. 7–8.

[95] Arthur Lake, *Sundrie sermons de tempora* (bound with the 1629 *Sermons* but separately paginated), pp. 207, 217–18.

involved in the formation of the Massachusetts Bay Company and even told John White of Dorchester, his contemporary at New College, that if he were a younger man he would himself have gone to New England.[96] Yet it was the same Lake who walked beside Neile under the canopy of state when Charles I was crowned, and it was Bishop Nicholas Felton of Ely who heard his last confession.[97] Felton was a friend and protégé of Lancelot Andrewes, but like Lake a moderate Calvinist.

For the historian who turns over in his mind the question posed at the beginning of this chapter, the most challenging element in these episcopal careers is the emphasis on the reconciliation of puritans and other opponents, as a preferred alternative to forceful suppression: a pointedly anti-Laudian message. Lake was said to be 'apter to reconcile differences than to make them'.[98] Morton engaged the puritans of the north-west in a famous controversy over the disputed ceremonies, but with the intention of winning their hearts and minds. When he ordained Richard Mather, the grandfather of Cotton Mather, he detained him for some private talk. Mather was afraid in case the bishop had been informed of his nonconformity. But Morton's purpose was to ask for his prayers.[99] Miles Smith of Gloucester used 'instruction and

[96] Hugh Peter, *A dying fathers last legacy to an onely child* (1660), pp. 101–2. I owe this reference to Susan M. Hardman of the University of Durham.

[97] This may be why Geoffrey Soden mistook Lake for a Laudian and a member of the Durham House circle. (*Godfrey Goodman*, p. 159.) Kenneth Fincham helped me with this point. Lake's moderate Calvinism is established by his letters to Samuel Ward at the time of the Synod of Dort. On 12 October 1619 he wrote: 'All that I canne saie is, that I wish it remembered, that such divinity must be concluded in a synode as is least doubtfull and most usefull'; and he went on to draw a clear distinction between points of contention and the kind of doctrine which should appear in catechisms and popular sermons: 'that the people maie knowe what must be beleeved . . .'. On 12 December he advised Ward that 'if the orthodox propositions were fairly opened and the distasteful accessoryes which either ignorance or malice have fastened to them iudiciously removed, they [sc., the Remonstrants] would be brought to think better of them and happily perceive that the distance is not great between them and those whom they oppose.' On 28 January he congratulated Ward and his colleagues for their 'charitable course' in presenting their case with disarming moderation. (Bodleian Library, Tanner MS 74, nos. 60, 73, 81, fols. 134–6, 174, 190.)

[98] Harris, 'A Short View of the Life and Vertues'.

[99] Samuel Clarke, *The Lives of Sundry Eminent Persons* (1683), p. 128. In 1618 Morton published *A defence of the innocencie of the three ceremonies of the Church of England, viz the surplice, crosse after baptisme and kneeling at the receiving of the blessed sacrament*. For the

rebuke to the contrary minded', but with 'sweet and soft words of meekness', not 'the voyce of thunder', 'the byas of his good inclination still hanging in matter of doubt . . . toward the better sense.[1] Joseph Hall of Exeter employed 'all faire and gentle means' to win factious spirits to good order, 'and therein so happily prevailed that saving two . . . they were all perfectly reclaimed. So as I had not one minister professedly opposite to the anciently received orders . . . of the Church in that large diocese. Thus we went on comfortably together.'[2]

Was this largely fantasy and make-believe, like Jewel's 1559 boast about 'pastors, labourers and watchmen'? Arthur Lake's moving sermons preached over the bowed heads of penitents were edifying, but perhaps no more than marginally relevant to the ordinary stuff of ecclesiastical justice in Somerset. Before the death of James it was already possible to discern a troubled, even catastrophic future. In 1622, Hall declared that 'there needs no prophetical spirit to discern by a small cloud there is a storm coming towards our Church'.[3] By 1643, when 'moderate' and 'popular' bishops were suffering the general fate of their order and Bishop Hall himself had known his share of 'hard measure',[4] the tempest was raging in full fury. But if these accounts of the Jacobean bishops were only half true, then Archbishop Laud was indeed the greatest calamity ever visited upon the English Church. Let us end where we began, with the homespun reflections of John Williams, another bishop by whom puritans were 'not imperiously commanded to be silent' but dealt with humanely and reasonably: 'He that seeks a thing in the wrong way goes so far backward . . . Besides, he must have more than Power, he must have the Hearts of Men that will form them to a new Model;

---

extensive controversy to which this gave rise, see Peter Milward, *Religious Controversies of the Jacobean Age* (1978), pp. 24–9. The puritan divine John Paget remembered that Bishop Morton had told him that 'his remisse course with us had beene prejudiciall to his preferment to Lincolne Bishoprick, vacant about that time'. (*A defence of Church-government* (1641), sig. * *1ᵛ.*)

[1] *Sermons of Smith,* Preface.
[2] *Works of Hall,* i. xlvi.
[3] Henson, *Disestablishment,* p. 80.
[4] See the autobiographical 'Bishop Hall's Hard Measure', in *Works of Hall,* i. lvi–lxix.

this the Metropolitan wants . . . And it is well known, how he that will bring a People from custom in God's Worship with which they have been inured, to a Change, must be more than wise: that is, he must be thought to be wise: Look you to that.'[5]

[5] Hacket, *Scrinia Reserata,* ii. 103.

Chapter Three

Clerus Britannicus Stupor Mundi

I

In 1624 Joseph Hall, the future bishop of Exeter and of Norwich, preached the sermon *ad clerum* at the opening of Convocation in St. Paul's Cathedral. Addressing 'the flower of our English clergy'—'flos cleri Anglicani, cultissima capita'—he said: 'It is a great word that I shall speak; and yet I must and will say it, without all either arrogance or flattery, *Stupor mundi clerus Britannicus,* "The wonder of the world is the clergy of Britain".'[1] This was to set in an apophthegm an authentic note of the post-Reformation Church of England in its Jacobean heyday, patriotic and somewhat complacent. Bishop Jegon of Norwich was fond of saying that no bishop in the realm, 'nay in Europe', had 'so grave, learned and judicious a ministry as hee had'. This was quoted by a Suffolk man, Robert Reyce, who put first among the 'commodities' of his native county 'the great number of religious, grave, reverend and learned ministers of God's word which are planted in this shire'.[2]

---

[1] Joseph Hall's *concio synodica* was printed in 1624 as *Columba Noae olivam adferens jactatissimae Christi arcae.* It is reprinted, together with a later translation, in *The Works of Joseph Hall,* ed. Philip Wynter (Oxford, 1843), x. 1–44. The passage in question runs (p. 14 in the 1624 edn.): 'Magnum est, quod dicturus sum: dicam tamen, procul omni fastu et assentatione; ringantur, rumpantur invidi; Stupor mundi Clerus Britannicus. Tot doctos theologos, tot disertos concionatores frustra uspiam alibi hodie sub coelo quesieris. Quid memorem magna illa Ecclesiae lumina, jam nuper occidua; Juellos, Humfredos, Foxios, Whitgiftos, Fulcones, Whitakeros, Rainoldos, Bilsonios, Greenamios, Babingtonios, Eedios, Hollandos, Playferos, Abbotios, Perkinsios, Fieldios, Hookeros, Overallios, Willettos, Whitos, Massonios?' It will be noticed that Hall's list makes no distinction between such 'puritans' as Greenham and Perkins and such 'Anglicans' as Bilson and Overall. His slogan was subsequently quoted in the life of Andrew Willett, one of these 'great lights'. (Samuel Clarke, *The Lives and Deaths of Eminent Persons* (1675), p. 449.)

[2] *Suffolk in the XVIIth Century: the Breviary of Suffolk by Robert Reyce 1618,* ed. Lord Francis Hervey (1902), p. 21. And cf. Dr Googe, an ecclesiastical publicist accused of 'speaking for his penny' in the 1621 Parliament, who pronounced: 'I speak it confidently, there were never better ministers since this kingdom stood.' (*Commons Debates, 1621,* ed. W. Notestein, F. H. Relf, and H. Simpson (New Haven, 1935), ii.

When Hall spoke of the English clergy as the wonder of the world he meant the scholar princes of the Anglican Church. Where else under Heaven, he asked, would one find such learned theologians and preachers, naming twenty 'great lights' of the Church, from Jewel, Foxe, and Whitgift to Greenham and Perkins, Field, Hooker, and Overall. But applied to the generality of the parish clergy his slogan may sound like a joke in poor taste. Richard Baxter's indictment of the ministers whom he knew in rural Shropshire in the 1620s has been so often quoted as to turn these low-grade clerics into old friends: 'These were the Schoolmasters of my Youth . . . who read Common Prayer on Sundays and Holy-Days and taught School and tipled on the Week-days, and whipt the Boys, when they were drunk, so that we changed them very oft. Within a few miles about us were near a dozen more Ministers that were near Eighty years old apiece, and never preached; poor ignorant Readers, and most of them of Scandalous Lives.' There was Mr Cope, who read but never preached; and Mr Yale, a Bachelor of Divinity who preached once a month but drank himself, wife, and children to be stark beggars. Baxter's own parson was William Rogers, 'above fourscore, had two livings and never preached in his life as was said; when his eyesight failed him he said Common Prayer by memory'. Rogers engaged as curates first his son, an actor who played for cheap laughs by appearing on the stage with his private parts exposed, and then a grandson who was unlearned and never preached. These were followed by one Richard Bathoe, a lawyer's clerk broken by drinking, 'who was wont to our smart to let us know when he was drunk and never preached there but once, which was in my hearing, when he was drunk'. The longevity and secure tenure of such unsatisfactory clergy was the curse of the Church of England. In 1681 Baxter thought that Bathoe might still be alive 'and yet a minister'.[3]

440.) And Sir Dudley Digges who said in 1626: 'No clergy in Christendom is clearer from badness than the body of the Church of England.' (Cambridge University Library MS Dd.12.20, fol. 9.)

[3] *Reliquiae Baxterianae*, ed. Matthew Sylvester (1696), p. 2; Richard Baxter, *A Third Defence of the Cause of Peace* (1681), pp. 17 f. (I owe the latter reference to Geoffrey Nuttall.) Cf. Adam Martindale's childhood experience in Lancashire (*c.* 1630) of 'an

Suffolk and Shropshire, the hinterlands of Bury St. Edmunds and Shrewsbury, were two nearly extreme cases, the one of a kind of excellence, the other of dereliction. Bishop Hall's slogan has become ironical in the context of Baxter's memories. But I use it in recognition of the magnitude of the secular change which the clergy underwent in the course of our period. For it was between 1559 and 1625 that the ministry of the Church of England became what it would remain until far into the twentieth century: a graduate ministry, recruited from the colleges of Oxford and Cambridge.

The facts have been established by Molly Barratt, Rosemary O'Day, and other students of clerical recruitment. Except in such favourable locations as the city of London and the diocese of Oxford, graduate ordinands were rare birds in the early years of the Elizabethan Settlement. In the diocese of Chester, only one candidate for orders out of 282 was so identified in the decade 1560–70. But whereas only 19 percent of beneficed clergy in the diocese of Worcester were graduates in 1560, the proportion had risen to 52 percent by 1620 and to 84 percent by 1640. In the relatively well-favoured see of Oxford, 38 percent of incumbents had university degrees in 1560, 50 percent by 1580, 80 percent by 1620 and 96 percent in 1640. Recruitment in the diocese of London was already almost exclusively graduate by the turn of the century, and in 1601 nearly a third of the incumbents in London itself held degrees in divinity. Even in the backwoods of Coventry and Lichfield, a see described in 1582 as 'the very sinke of the whole realme, both for corrupt religion and lyfe', graduate recruitment was the norm by the second quarter of the seventeenth century. In 1570 none of the thirty-six candidates for orders at Gloucester had a degree. In the second decade of the seventeenth century very few Gloucester ordinands were without any university experience.[4] Oxford conferred more

---

old humdrum curate, that had almost no scholars, nor deserved any, for he was both a simpleton and a tipler'. (*The Life of Adam Martindale,* ed. Richard Parkinson, Chetham Society iv (Manchester, 1845), 12.)

[4] Statistics derived from Rosemary O'Day, *The English Clergy: the Emergence and Consolidation of a Profession 1558-1642* (Leicester, 1979), especially Chapter 4

bachelors' degrees in divinity between 1610 and 1639 than in any other twenty years of its history, the nineteenth century not excepted.[5] This was very far from solving all the Church's difficulties. Indeed, by improving the quality of its recruits without achieving any balancing reform of its finances these were in some ways compounded. In 1584 Archbishop Whitgift estimated that scarcely 600 livings out of almost 9,000 were capable of supporting a learned man.[6] So there can be no intention on this occasion of opening a court of appeal against the damning verdict of Christopher Hill's *Economic Problems of the Church*. Nevertheless, it is a fact of some importance that towards the end of our period the Church proved its capacity to attract a clergy which was sufficiently qualified by the only objective standards which bishops' examiners chose to apply. So it was that a Restoration writer could recall that 'about this time of King Charles the First's reign it was justly said, *Stupor mundi Clerus Anglicanus*'. At the beginning of Elizabeth's reign if a man understood Greek 'there was a deanery for him', if Latin, a good living. 'But in the long reign of Queen *Elizabeth* and King *James,* the Clergy of the *Reformed Church of England* grew the most learned of the World.'[7]

Hall's apophthegm may consequently be invoked to correct the fashionable stress on what Claire Cross has called 'the triumph of the laity in the English Church'.[8] That the Reformation was a time of assertive lay-mindedness is not in

'Recruitment' and Chapter 10 'The Reformation of the Ministry'; Christopher Hill, *Economic Problems of the Church from Archbishop Whitgift to the Long Parliament* (Oxford, 1956), p. 207, following D. M. Barratt, 'The Condition of the Parochial Clergy from the Reformation to 1660, with Special Reference to the Dioceses of Oxford, Worcester and Gloucester', Oxford D.Phil. thesis, 1950; H. G. Owen, 'The London Parish Clergy in the Reign of Elizabeth I', London Ph.D. thesis, 1957, Chapter 3 'Education and Learning'. See also J. I. Daeley, 'The Episcopal Administration of Matthew Parker, Archbishop of Canterbury, 1559–75', London Ph.D. thesis, 1967. The reference to the state of the diocese of Coventry and Lichfield occurs in a letter from Bishop Overton to Lord Burghley, 20 May 1582, BL Lansdowne MS 36, no. 16, fol. 45.

[5] Lawrence Stone, 'The Size and Composition of the Oxford Student Body 1580–1910', in *The University in Society*, i, *Oxford and Cambridge from the 14th to the Early 19th Century*, ed. Lawrence Stone (Princeton, 1974), 21–2.

[6] John Strype, *The Life and Acts of John Whitgift* (Oxford, 1822), i. 380–1.

[7] *A Century of Sermons . . . Preached by John Hacket,* published with a life of Hacket by Thomas Plume (1675), p. xii.

[8] The phrase is used as the subtitle of Claire Cross's *Church and People 1450–1660* (1976).

question. But the clerical mind was also reasserting itself. It was a significant novelty of the later sixteenth century to concede to virtually all clergymen the honorific style of 'Master', whereas pre-Reformation priests were known distinctively, but by the sixteenth century almost disparagingly, by their Christian names, prefixed with 'Sir', as in the general and even pejorative 'Sir Johns'. The clergy were now ranked as honorary or pseudo-gentry, far above any status which would have been theirs by right of wealth.[9] At clerical gatherings it was now the usual thing to serve wine. These are significant pointers to a trend observed by Lawrence Stone: 'The rise of the parish clergy was as much a feature of the age as the rise of the gentry'[10]—and perhaps a less disputable feature! The two social facts, of lay emancipation and neo-clericalism, may seem to have been in conflict but were in some measure complementary. One way in which lay-mindedness asserted itself, from the Elizabethan Settlement to the days of the Long Parliament, was in the incessant demand of so many Members of Parliament for 'a godly, learned, resident preaching ministry'.

However, learning was one thing, professional competence another. The studies leading to degrees in the liberal arts were never a vocational training for the parish ministry, and no such training was institutionalized in the Church of England before the nineteenth century. The case of Baxter's drunken Mr Yale, BD, is a reminder that not even a theological degree was any guarantee of pastoral excellence, whereas Baxter himself, the Reformed Pastor *par excellence,* was never at a university. To be sure, a training in the schools was some preparation for the pulpit, and prevalent religious values virtually reduced the ministry to a pulpit function.[11] But the

[9] A recent investigation of wealth differentials in early modern England, employing the evidence of probate inventories, rates the clergy in general a little below the yeomen and somewhat above husbandmen, while noting their courtesy rank among the gentry. (David Cressy, *Literacy and the Social Order: Reading and Writing in Tudor and Stuart England* (Cambridge, 1980), pp. 139, 122.)

[10] Lawrence Stone, *The Causes of the English Revolution 1529–1642* (1972), p. 81.

[11] Of the puritan divine Jeremiah Whitaker, it was said that 'in the pulpit he stil was like a fish in the water'. (Simeon Ashe, *Living loves betwixt Christ and dying Christians* (1654), p. 54.) Richard Bernard's *The faithfull shepherd,* which was two or three times reprinted and enlarged, was not, as its title might suggest, a general pastoral treatise but a handbook on preaching and catechizing.

truly godly preacher knew that the pulpit was not to be turned into a 'philosopher's chair'.[12] To communicate with the simple and unlettered it was necessary to unlearn, or at least to conceal academic learning.[13] As for the other pastoral arts, the power to correct and to comfort, the ministry of reconciliation, these were not taught or learned in universities but, if at all, in the practical school of life.

So we may well ask how 'professional' were the English clergy of the seventeenth century. Did 'the rise of the parish clergy' imply the 'emergence and consolidation' of one of the professional groups diversifying modern English society?[14] The notion has some appeal, when the facts of improved academic standards and enhanced clerical status are considered in the light of the sociological theory of professionalization. What can be said for the suggestion will appear in the course of this chapter. Much of the evidence amounts to the fact that the post-Reformation clergy, in common with their counterparts in other national churches, acquired, or had attributed to them, a single-minded devotion to the parochial ministry. The ideal Christian of the entire epoch separating the Reformation and the Counter-Reformation from modern times was a model parish priest, a type which achieved its apotheosis in the nineteenth century in the cult of the curé d'Ars.[15] 'His lyfe', wrote John Earle in eulogizing the character of 'a grave divine', is 'our Religions best Apology'.[16] In the Medieval Church, to be a beneficed parish priest was only one of several options available to 'clerks', and it was a career beyond the reach and expectations of almost a majority. Now it could be

---

[12] Patrick Collinson, *A Mirror of Elizabethan Puritanism: The Life and Letters of 'Godly Master Dering'*, Friends of Dr Williams's Library 17th Lecture 1963 (1964), p. 5.

[13] William Perkins wrote: 'If any man thinke that by this meanes barbarism should be brought into pulpits; he must understand that the Minister may, yea and must privately use at his libertie the artes, philosophy, and varietie of reading, whilest he is framing his sermon: but he ought in publike to conceale all these from the people, and not to make the least ostentation. *Artis etiam est celare artem: it is also a point of Art to conceale Art.*' (Quoted, Owen C. Watkins, *The Puritan Experience* (1972), p. 7.)

[14] As Rosemary O'Day argues in *The English Clergy*. I am glad to acknowledge my considerable dependence on this valuable monograph.

[15] J. Delumeau, *Catholicism Between Luther and Voltaire: A New View of the Counter-Reformation* (1977), Chapter 4(b) 'The Typology of the New Priest', pp. 179–89.

[16] John Earle, *Microcosmographie* (facsimile of the autograph manuscript) (Leeds, 1966), p. 12.

assumed that the minister would seek and usually find a benefice. Some desirable occupations once appropriated by the clergy were no longer open to the seventeenth-century cleric. Others, including schoolmastering, were commonly regarded as a stopgap or *pis aller*. Moreover, if the seventeenth-century clergy were without a properly professional training, many of them readily adopted an exactingly professional code of practice once they were in post, a kind of ecclesiastical 'work ethic'. John Earle's 'grave divine' was 'one that knowes the burden of his calling, and hath studied to make his shoulders sufficient'. George Herbert was a failed courtier before he was a parson. Yet the country clergyman whom he described was a true professional and an entrepreneur, setting to work on a Sunday like a market man on market-day, or a shopkeeper when customers come into his shop. 'His thoughts are full of making the best of the day, and contriving it to his best gaines.'[17] This parson was an industrious sort of person.

Yet there are grave difficulties in the way of attaching to the seventeenth-century clergy the concept of professionalization. A parson secure in the enjoyment of his freehold was not so much a salaried functionary as a man of property, only marginally dependent upon fees for his livelihood. In this respect he differed not at all from his pre-Reformation ancestor. As late as the mid-nineteenth century, Trollope's Miss Dunstable complained of the pride of the clergy in their proprietorial splendour. 'You must be paid from land and endowments, from tithe and church property. You can't bring yourself to work for what you earn, as lawyers and doctors do.' For Trollope himself it was still a fantasy to imagine ecclesiastical work 'bought and paid for according to its quantity and quality'.[18]

It would also be absurd to suggest that the pre-Reformation clergy were utterly lacking in 'professional' qualities. To claim that the clergy constituted a profession in the seventeenth century and not in the fourteenth century is like discovering

[17] Ibid., p. 8; George Herbert, *A Priest to the Temple, Or, The Parson, his Character, and Rule of Holy Life* (1652), pp. 28–9.
[18] Anthony Trollope, *Framley Parsonage* (1859–60), World's Classics (Oxford, 1980), pp. 32, 169.

the phenomenon of bureaucracy for the first time in the age of Thomas Cromwell, or in the eighteenth century, and the distinction has been not unjustly called 'spurious'.[19] The fourteenth century, after all, provides plentiful examples of a form of literature which was much rarer in the seventeenth: the treatise informing the parish priest in the technicalities of his trade—or profession. Some of these manuals reflect a sincere commitment to the parochial ministry on the part of their authors. Others seem to have been written by armchair experts for the instruction not so much of the privileged clergy who were beneficed as for the small army of stipendiary priests upon whom the performance of pastoral duties so often depended.[20] In some important respects, the 'parish priest' in this typical, late medieval sense, who was paid a salary by an employer in respect of specified functions, was more of a 'professional' than the seventeenth-century parson, let alone the eighteenth-century 'squarson' whom Dean Church defined as 'the patriarch of his parish, its ruler, its doctor, its lawyer, its magistrate, as well as its teacher'. In Bishop Hensley Henson's opinion, it was the Oxford Movement of the nineteenth century which for the first time (and regrettably) 'made the English Clergy professional'.[21] Nevertheless, provided the term is not used presumptuously and absolutely, the concept of 'professionalization' is not unhelpful in understanding the transformation which occurred in the century following the Elizabethan Settlement. Certainly it is quite erroneous to suggest that the effect of the Reformation was actually to 'deprofessionalize' the clerical role.[22] In what

[19] By Peter Heath in *Journal of Ecclesiastical History*, xxxii (1981), 101. On the dating of bureaucracy, see the articles in *Transactions of the Royal Historical Society*, 5th ser. xxx (1980).

[20] W. A. Pantin, *The English Church in the Fourteenth Century* (Cambridge, 1955), especially Chapter 9 'Manuals of Instruction for Parish Priests' and Chapter 10 'Religious and Moral Treatises in the Vernacular'. See also Bernard Lord Manning, *The People's Faith in the Time of Wyclif* (Cambridge, 1919).

[21] R. W. Church, *The Oxford Movement: Twelve Years 1833–1845* (1891 edn.), p. 3; Herbert Hensley Henson, *Disestablishment* (1929), p. 66. Anthony Russell agrees that it was in the nineteenth century that the clergy came to regard themselves and to be regarded as a professional body with specific functions and duties, while still not approximating entirely to a professional role, since this remained very diffuse. (Anthony Russell, *The Clerical Profession* (1980), p. 6.)

[22] Russell, *The Clerical Profession*, p. 28.

follows we shall distinguish broadly between 'professional' and 'sub-professional' clerical types.

II

Richard Baxter's catalogue of scandalous Shropshire clerics is a late example of a genre invented by the Elizabethan puritans and deployed as background propaganda in the parliamentary campaigns for further reformation in the 1580s.[23] In form, the puritan 'surveys of the ministry' combined elements of the official returns called for from time to time by ecclesiastical authority with the detailing of grievances which had its origin in litigation and petitioning.[24] And sometimes there was an extra, bonus element: the gift for satirical invention which runs like an undercurrent in sixteenth- and seventeenth-century culture, the voice of the mute inglorious Skelton who captured for ever the Warwick-shire parson who 'could not one daie reade the commande-ments for want of his spectacles'.[25]

The surveys suggest two general observations about the thoroughgoing unprofessional standing of those clergy who were ordained in the early years of Elizabeth, if not earlier,

[23] Patrick Collinson, *The Elizabethan Puritan Movement* (1967), pp. 273–316.

[24] The puritan surveys of 1584–6 are printed from the MS copies in the Morrice MSS in Dr William's Library in *The Seconde Parte of a Register,* ed. Albert Peel (Cambridge, 1915), ii. 88–184. There are several examples of nearly contemporaneous certificates or 'states' of the clergy in Lambeth Palace Library, MSS Carte Miscellanee XII and XIII. Those relating to the diocese of Lincoln are printed in *The State of the Church in the Reigns of Elizabeth and James I as illustrated by Documents Relating to the Diocese of Lincoln,* i, ed. C. W. Foster, Lincoln Record Society, xxiii (Horncastle, 1926), 33–114. The best comparative discussion of these two sources is by Canon Foster, ibid., xxxi–xxxviii. See also D. M. Barratt's edition of *Ecclesiastical Terriers of Warwickshire Parishes,* ii, Dugdale Society, xxvii (Oxford, 1971).

[25] *Seconde Parte of a Register,* ii. 169. The historical value of these undisguisedly partisan reports has often been doubted. Yet detailed comparison of the surveys with other data has suggested to C. W. Foster that they were compiled 'with great care' and to D. M. Barratt that they are 'surprisingly trustworthy' and were based on detailed local knowledge. In the case of the Warwickshire clergy, the puritan verdict can be compared with the self-assessment of the same clerics in response to the visitation articles of 1585. Of one incumbent the puritans reported: 'No precher, nor learned, yet honest and zealous, and sometime expounding to his flocks according to his talent.' This man reported of himself: 'A prechor lycensed I am not, but in myne owne Cure and not elsewhere I do accordinge to my function and the poore talent that god hathe given me.' (*Ecclesiastical Terriers,* ii. xxx, 104; *Seconde Parte of a Register,* ii, 168.)

and who were the butts of puritan complaint. First we may note how many were 'men of occupation', late entrants to the ministry out of some other trade or calling, of which the surveys specify thirty-four, including those of girthmaker, harper, and sow-gelder, as well as any number of tailors and weavers. A survey of the same parishes fifty years later would have revealed a clergy with a more respectable and homogeneous background. But the surveys provide additional evidence that after ordination the clergy continued to be men of a variety of aptitudes, frequently involved in agriculture, more rarely in industry, and sometimes pursuing interests of a specialized nature. The chief trade of the aged and barely literate vicar of Grafton in Warwickshire was 'to cure hawks that are hurt or diseased, for which purpose manie do usuallie repair to him'.[26] As for the vicar of Lanteglos, he was simply 'the best Wrastler in Cornewall'.[27] Elsewhere in these documents we meet working physicians, surveyors, dealers in livestock, and money-lenders, as well as several 'jesters'. For a proportion of the Elizabethan clergy seem to have been, to all intents and purposes, professional entertainers, like William Glibery, vicar of Halstead, described as a 'verie ridiculous preacher', whose witty but gross performance in the pulpit was lovingly recorded by his scandalized neighbours.[28] Others, like their eighteenth-century descendants, made a living out of clandestine marriages. But the vicar of Warwick was a mere scholar, 'learned in the tongues, yet the people profit not'.[29]

In these respects there was to be no absolute transformation within our period. To this day, the parson's freehold continues to accommodate a variety of pursuits, something either more or less but certainly other than a simple profession. John Favour, the Jacobean vicar of Halifax, described his life as consisting of 'preaching every Sabbath day, lecturing every day in the week, exercising justice in the commonwealth, practising of physic and chirurgery in the great penury and necessity thereof in the country where I live'. He was also the

---

[26] *Seconde Parte of a Register,* ii. 167. It has been suggested that this was the minister who married Shakespeare. *(Ecclesiastical Terriers,* ii. xxix.)

[27] *Seconde Parte of a Register,* ii. 109.

[28] Ibid., ii. 163; PRO S.P. 12/159/27.

[29] *Seconde Parte of a Register,* ii. 165.

author of a book of poetry.[30] This was a foretaste of the future, not some relic of old ways. If we knew only a little about Ralph Josselin, vicar of Earls Colne in Essex from 1641 until 1683, we might consider him as a true professional, engaged exclusively in preaching, pastoral care, and study. But Josselin's diary[31] reveals him as a farmer who rented and leased land, worked ten to twenty acres of it himself, and bought and sold at markets and fairs. Josselin was also a lifelong schoolmaster. Alan Macfarlane can show that about half his income was derived from sources other than his ecclesiastical living.[32] Yet none of this detracts from Josselin's professional dedication, which had deep roots. He wrote: 'I confesse my childhood was taken with ministers and I heard with delight and admiracion and desire to imitate them from my youth, and would be acting in corners.'[33]

The second aspect of clerical professionalization for which the puritan surveys provide a convenient baseline concerns the standing and posture of the parson in relation to his flock, a matter of relative distance in an almost physical sense. It has often been remarked that the late medieval rural priest lived as a peasant among peasants. In nearly every parish, wrote W. G. Hoskins of the sixteenth-century Leicestershire country parson, he was 'a practical farmer', and usually a poor one.[34] M. W. Barley has concluded from architectural evidence, perhaps a little too readily, that the country parson of this period was a member of the village community, not a poor

---

[30] A. L. Rowse, *The England of Elizabeth: the Structure of Society* (1951), p. 483; A. G. Dickens, 'The Writers of Tudor Yorkshire', *Transactions of the Royal Historical Society*, 5th ser. xiii (1963). 67, Cf. Herbert, *Priest to the Temple* (p. 94): 'The Country Parson desires to be all to his Parish, and not onely a Pastour, but a Lawyer also, and a Phisician.'

[31] *The Diary of Ralph Josselin 1616–1683*, ed. Alan Macfarlane, Records of Social and Economic History NS iii (Oxford, 1976). Mildred Campbell commented: 'There was always much of the yeoman in Ralph Josselyn.' (*The English Yeoman under Elizabeth and the Early Stuarts* (New Haven, 1940), p. 293.)

[32] Alan MacFarlane, *The Family Life of Ralph Josselin A Seventeenth-Century Clergyman: An Essay in Historical Anthropology* (Cambridge, 1970), p. 39.

[33] *Diary of Ralph Josselin*, p. 1. Cf. Henry Newcome who as a child (in the 1630s and early 1640s) 'was attempting making English discourses sermonwise at vacant times', and whose 'fancy ran much after preaching, it being my ordinary play and office to act the minister amongst my playfellows'. (*The Autobiography of Henry Newcome, M.A.*, ed. Richard Parkinson, Chetham Society, xxvi (Manchester, 1852), 7.)

[34] W. G. Hoskins, 'The Leicestershire Country Parson in the Sixteenth Century', *Transactions of the Leicestershire Archaeological Society*, xxi (1940–1), 89–114.

member of the gentry class elevated above it.[35] The evidence of clerical wills and inventories suggests that our period saw no sudden change in this way of life. Rosemary O'Day has found that the seventeenth-century Staffordshire parsonage was first and foremost a farmhouse, set in a farmyard. 'A great barn was a constant feature', and often bigger than the house itself. The 'backside' with its vegetables and fowls was the preserve of the parson's wife, as it was of the farmer's wife. Similarly, Molly Barratt found that in Warwickshire 'a majority of the parsonages were small farmhouses'.[36]

But the puritan surveys have more to say about the alehouse than the plough, making the leisure of the parson rather than his labours the measure of an undesirable submergence in the values and habits of unredeemed, mundane existence. The charge is stereotyped and repetitive: 'a common alehouse haunter' (a phrase still in use in accusations against 'scandalous ministers' in the 1640s),[37] 'a common gamester and pot companion', 'subject to the vice of good fellowship'; with sometimes a hint of how time spent in this idle fashion could be justified: 'useth to plaie after a sorte the reconciler amongest the simple'.[38] George Gifford, the puritan vicar and preacher of Maldon whose acute social observations have reaped from Alan Macfarlane the accolade

[35] M. W. Barley, 'Rural Housing in England', in *The Agrarian History of England and Wales*, iv, *1500–1640*, ed. J. Thirsk (Cambridge, 1967), 726.

[36] M. R. O'Day, 'Clerical Patronage and Recruitment in England in the Elizabethan and Early Stuart Periods, with Special Reference to the Diocese of Coventry and Lichfield', London Ph.D. thesis, 1972, pp. 326–55; *Ecclesiastical Terriers of Warwickshire Parishes,* i, ed. D. M. Barratt, Dugdale Society xxii (Oxford, 1955), xxxiii.

[37] *The Suffolk Committees for Scandalous Ministers 1644–1646*, ed. Clive Holmes, Suffolk Records Society, xiii (Ipswich, 1970), 28, 40, 42, 49, 57, 62, 66, 73. One Suffolk cleric was described in 1644 as 'a frequent company keeper'. (Ibid., 56.) Cf. two presentments in the archdeaconry of Canterbury eighty years earlier. In 1560 the churchwardens of Elmstead reported: 'Our vicar dothe haunte to ale houses.' In 1566 it was reported from Marden: 'We present that Mr Barnes our vycar hath haunted the alehouse contrary to the viith Injunction.' (Cathedral Archives and Library Canterbury, X.1.2, fols. 22ᵛ–3ʳ; X.1.8, fol. 14.)

[38] A phrase from the puritan survey for Warwickshire (*Seconde Parte of a Register*, ii. 166) applied to Geffrie Heath, rector of Oldbarrow, who, invited to assess himself by the ecclesiastical authorities, reported: 'Item I have taken no Degre of scole in Either of the universities nether doe I preache.' (*Ecclesiastical Terriers*, ii. 22.)

of 'Tudor anthropologist',[39] supplies us with a rounded version of this stereotype, placed in the mouth of an Essex parishioner: 'Hee is as gentle a person as ever I see; a verye good fellow, hee will not sticke when good Fellowes and honest men meete together too spende his groate at the Alehouse. I cannot tell, they preache and preache, but hee doeth live as well as the best of them all.' Instead of reproving naughtiness from the pulpit, this man preferred to reconcile enemies over a game of bowls or cards, or a drink. 'I thinke it a godlye waye to make Charitie: hee is none of these busie Controulers.' To which the voice of Gifford himself retorts: 'I doe not mislike true friendship, whiche is in the Lorde, knitte in true Godliness, but I mislike this vice, which overfloweth everie where, the Drunkardes meete togeather and sitte quaffing, and the minister whiche shoulde reproove them, to bee one of the chiefe; when he shoulde bee at his studie, to bee upon the Alebench at Cardes or dice'.[40] When Gifford was deprived of his living for nonconformity he was replaced by a vicar who ran his own bowling alley and regularly played at tables in the New Inn in Maldon.[41] We call Gifford's censorious attitude puritan. Yet it was consistent with the Royal Injunctions of 1559 and with the Canons of 1604, which forbade ecclesiastical persons to resort to alehouses and taverns and insisted that they should not 'give themselves to any base or servile labour, or to drinking or riot, spending their time idly by day or by night, playing at dice, cards, or tables, or any other unlawful game . . . Having always in mind, that they ought to excel all others in purity of life, and should be examples to the people to live well and christianly.'[42]

George Gifford encourages us in the construction of two ideal types. The less than professional parson identified with the community of which he was a part, shared its round of work and leisure, talked its language, and made little attempt

---

[39] Alan Macfarlane, 'A Tudor Anthropologist: George Gifford's *Discourse* and *Dialogue*', in *The Damned Art: Essays in the Literature of Witchcraft*, ed. Sydney Anglo (1977), pp. 140–55.

[40] George Gifford, *A briefe discourse of certaine points of the religion which is among the common sort of christians which may bee termed the Countrie Divinitie* (1581), fols. 1ᵛ–3ʳ.

[41] Essex Record Office, D/B/3/3/178.

[42] *Documentary Annals of the Reformed Church of England*, ed. Edward Cardwell (Oxford, 1844), i. 214–15; Edward Cardwell, *Synodalia*, (Oxford, 1842), i 290.

to impose upon it an exacting and alien moral code. He read the Prayer Book services, which in themselves neither transcended nor challenged rustic existence, and which was an office which many laymen could perform equally well and sometimes did. His ministry lacked both the quasi-magical aura of the catholic priesthood and the prophetic charisma of the preacher. Pastoral care was reduced to playing, after a sort, the reconciler. Like any other villager this parson had his personal feuds, which often concerned the modalities of tithe collection, but which in this litigious society might arise from almost any circumstance. One Elizabethan Chancery case concerned whether or not a certain incumbent was bound to serve a free breakfast to the choir on Easter and Christmas mornings.[43] But there was nothing in the way of life of this humdrum specimen to arouse general, communal resentment, still less rejection. Robert Spenser, rector of Haseley and of Bilsley in the Warwickshire of Shakespeare's youth, came close to the ideal type. He was not a preacher, nor learned, but a 'companion and goodfellow, in all companies well liked, and commended of his parishioners for an honest quiet felow as ever came amonge them'.[44]

The professional and godly minister was a strongly contrasted type. In dress, speech, and domestic life-style he drew apart from his flock, castigated their sins, and denounced them to the bawdy court. He was conscious, in George Herbert's words, of standing 'in Gods stead to his Parish'.[45] Above all he was a preacher. This was the criterion invariably used to distinguish the worthy, fully professional clergyman; as if, complained one critic (but his criticism was made in a sermon), his parishioners had turned all their members into ears 'for nothing else but *Hearing* of *Sermons*'.[46] In Edward Dering's exalted estimation, he was 'the minister by whom the people doe beleeve'.[47]

Reality was naturally more diverse than these ideal types. The behaviour of some subprofessional, companionable par-

[43] W. J. Jones, *The Elizabethan Court of Chancery* (Oxford, 1967), p. 391, n. 2.

[44] *Seconde Parte of a Register*, ii. 167.

[45] Herbert, *Priest to the Temple*, p. 79.

[46] Richard Tedder, *A sermon preached at Wimondham* (in Bishop Wren's primary visitation of the diocese of Norwich, 1636), (1637), p. 12.

[47] Collinson, *A Mirror of Elizabethan Puritanism*, pp. 10–11.

sons was so unseemly as to repel the entire parish, godly or not. Few inhabitants of the Wealden village of Sandherst can have approved of their curate Mr Olton, who going through the woods with certain honest women told them: 'If I were as lusty as ever I was I would gett you all with childe before I wente out of this woodd.'[48] Not all parsons went to the alehouse as peacemakers. In 1571 William Russell, vicar of Preston next Faversham, made it the place of assignation for a fight with a gentleman of the parish, and this was the fifth affray perpetrated in his time as vicar by this 'common fyghter and quarreler'. It was said that he made house with a woman who had been carted as a whore in Shoreditch and who had robbed him of his household stuff, only to be welcomed back with open arms when the magistrate had finished with her. Mr Russell was preoccupied with animal husbandry, 'a common cowe keper'. He kept his cattle and their fodder in the churchyard and church porch, to the annoyance of his parishioners, and he drove the beasts through Faversham, a 'town of worship', dressed in a jerkin, 'not like a prelate but rather like a common roge'.[49] For many Elizabethans a respectable marriage made the parson an honest man, and more tolerable than Mr Olton or Mr Russell. The sexual misadventures of John Wood, a late Jacobean vicar of Marden in Kent, seem to have been squeezed into the interval between the death of his wife and his incongruous remarriage to a maidservant.[50] But for those with conservative prejudices, a respectable clerical marriage was a contradiction in terms. In 1574 a troublesome Kentish parishioner quarrelled with his vicar in the churchyard after Morning Prayer and was heard to say that 'there is never newe tryck but ministers wyfes bring them first of all upp'.[51] Two years later in Old Romney a young couple composed a slanderous rhyme with the refrain 'all priestes wyves are drabbles or quenes'.[52]

Among the subprofessionals there were many points on the

---

[48] Cathedral Archives and Library Canterbury, X.1.13, fol. 4ᵛ.

[49] Ibid., X.1.11, fol. 133ᵛ.

[50] Ibid., X.11.16, fols. 259ᵛ–68ᵛ; PRC 39/39, fols. 66ʳ–73ᵛ, 74ᵛ–6ᵛ. I owe these references to Susan Callaway of the University of Kent.

[51] Ibid., X.1.12, fol. 01ᵛ. The parishioner, William Harmon, was given to saying: 'I care not', 'I have nothing to loose', and 'I am lawles'.

[52] Ibid., X.1.13, fol. 44ᵛ.

scale between behaviour which was agreeable to all but the most censorious of puritans, and the outrageous conduct of Martin Marprelate's 'vicar of Hell',[53] just as there was a great variety of livings, from the pitifully meagre which were scarcely compatible with respectability, to the generously endowed. Our ideal types and the values they represent were liable to coalesce in curious mixtures. John Wood of Marden was an alehouse haunter. It was 'an ordinary and usuall thing with him'. His drinking companions were a motley crew, including, on one occasion, 'a tooth drawer, a wanderer'. A respectable parishioner declined to drink his health. He 'cared not for pledging of drunken preists'. A local clothier was a victim of the parson's skill at the pub game of shufflecap, 'his usuall game', which cost him a tongue pie worth ten groats. Two other villagers were forced to sell their lands to pay their gambling debts to Mr Wood. Yet Wood was also a preacher, and one of his adulterous paramours affirmed that she was no 'swearer, saboath breaker, contemner of God's holy word and sacraments', while the wife of the parish clerk who procured another of his mistresses assured the woman that it was no sin, 'for were it a thing sinfull . . . Mr Wood being her pastor and having care and charge of her soule would not excite her thereunto'.[54] Richard Parker, vicar of Dedham in the 1580s, was minutes secretary of a select conference of preaching ministers.[55] Yet a common fame in the Vale of Dedham linked him suspiciously with various married women, including the wife of the tailor whose shop occupied the other half of his semi-detached vicarage. When the tailor discovered what was going on he said: 'Yf Mr Parker be of that sorte what shall one saye to ytt?'[56] Shades of Le Roy Ladurie's *Montaillou*!

Among the more professional and impeccable clergy,

[53] The original was Jefferie Jones of Corlie, Warwickshire, described by the puritan surveyors as 'dumbe, drunkard, gamster, quarreler, swearer, pilferer, adulterer', (*Seconde Parte of a Register,* ii. 171.)
[54] Cathedral Archives and Library Canterbury, X.11.16, fols. 259ᵛ–68ᵛ; PRC 39/39, fols. 66ʳ–73ᵛ, 74ᵛ–6ᵛ.
[55] John Rylands Library, Rylands English MS 874, published in an incomplete and imperfect edition, *The Presbyterian Movement in the Reign of Queen Elizabeth as Illustrated by the Minute Book of the Dedham Classis, 1582–1589,* ed. R. G. Usher, Camden 3rd ser. viii (1905).
[56] Greater London Record Office, Consistory Court of London Records, DL/C/213, depositions of 10, 14 May, 4 July 1590.

historians are accustomed to make a further distinction between 'puritans' and 'Anglicans' (or less anachronistically, 'formalists'). The difference had implications for the relations between parson and parish. Puritans who complained of 'the vice of good fellowship' were themselves accused of disrupting communities previously at peace. Reginald Scot, who wrote humanely on witchcraft and usefully on the husbandry of hops,[57] attacked the 'preachers of Kent' for basing their ministry on the text that Christ came to bring not peace but a sword. 'Hath not Minge brought Ashford from being the quietest towne of Kent to be at deadly hatred and bitter division? . . . What broile and contention hath Fenner made in Cranbrooke, and all the rest likewise in their severall Cures?'[58] Calvinist preaching was limited in its intellectual and spiritual appeal and divisive in its psychological and social consequences. 'Busy controlling' made enemies: 'malignant spirits', as one puritan biographer puts it, 'who were haters of a plain, powerfull and searching Ministry'.[59] George Gifford's response to the charge that preaching divided towns 'one part against another' was to ask: 'Can yee put fire and water together but they will rumble? . . . Light is come into the worlde and men love darkenesse more then light, because their workes be evill.'[60] When the anti-puritan spoke of unity and concord the puritan replied caustically: 'You speake of that which was never seene in this world, nor never shall.'[61] Modern students of the social history of religion are inclined to agree.[62]

George Herbert's country parson, a formalist who spent his Sunday afternoons 'reconciling neighbours that are at variance', had a different understanding of the minister's role. He 'condescended' to old and harmless customs, and particularly to the traditional perambulation of the parish at Rogation-

---

[57] Sydney Anglo, 'Reginald Scot's *Discoverie of Witchcraft:* Scepticism and Sadduceeism', in *The Damned Art*, pp. 106–39.

[58] *Seconde Parte of a Register*, i. 238.

[59] Samuel Clarke, *A Collection of the Lives of Ten Eminent Divines* (1662), p. 5.

[60] Gifford, *Countrie divinitie*, fols. 46ᵛ–7ᵛ.

[61] *A dialogue concerning the strife of our Church* (1584), p. 131.

[62] John Bossy, 'Blood and Baptism: Kinship, Community and Christianity in Western Europe from the Fourteenth to the Sixteenth Centuries', in *Sanctity and Secularity: the Church and the World, Studies in Church History*, x, ed. Derek Baker (1973), 129–43.

tide, with its opportunity for 'charity in loving walking, and neighbourly accompanying one another, with reconciling of differences at that time, if there be any'.[63] But 'beating the bounds', which had a truly Durkheimian significance as a symbolic affirmation of the community of the parish, was denounced by many puritans as an archaic superstition. Yet it would be a mistake to represent this difference as absolute. Puritans could be as responsive to the need to promote a general social harmony as any of the clergy. As ministers of the Communion it was a responsibility they could not ignore. The quintessentially puritanical Richard Greenham was said by his biographer to have been a 'promoter of Peace and Concord amongst his Neighbours and Acquaintance', and William Whateley, one of the founders of Banbury's puritan reputation, was described as 'a great Peace-maker amongst any of his flocke that were at variance'.[64]

Nor was the formalist Herbert as remote from the prevalent Calvinist churchmanship of his age as Izaak Walton and others who subscribed to his posthumous hagiography.[65] The author of *The Country Parson* required the church to be adorned with 'fit and proper texts of Scripture', the painting 'grave and reverend, not with light colours or foolish anticks'. The pulpit was the parson's 'joy' and 'throne', which he occupied in the knowledge that country people were 'thick and heavy', needing 'a mountaine of fire to kindle them'. And in conversing with his people, says Herbert, 'one way or other, he ever reproves them, that he may keep himself pure, and not be intangled in others sinnes'—which sounds sufficiently puritanical. Herbert ruled that it was not for the servant of Christ to frequent inns, taverns, and alehouses. 'The parson doth not so.'[66] And when he recommended the parson to spend his afternoons in visiting his flock, 'wallowing in the midst of their affaires',[67] Herbert was speaking of the common practice of

---

[63] Herbert, *Priest to the Temple*, pp. 30, 157–8.
[64] Samuel Clarke, *The Lives of Thirty-Two English Divines* (1677), p. 13; Clarke, *Lives and Deaths of Eminent Persons*, p. 461.
[65] Izaak Walton, *The Life of Mr George Herbert* (1670).
[66] Herbert, *Priest to the Temple*, pp. 58, 21, 23, 63–4, 8.
[67] Ibid., p. 60.

many puritan ministers.[68] When the Suffolk preacher John Carter came across one of his flock, a tanner, busily tanning a hide, he stole up behind him and gave him a little clap on the back. The man started and blushed and said: 'Sir, I am ashamed that you should find me thus.' Carter told him that for himself he hoped that when Christ returned he would find him similarly engaged, 'faithfully performing the Duties of my Calling'.[69] Almost identical stories are told about Herbert and about Carter. Each was secretly observed inside his church by someone peering through a window. Herbert was seen to lie prostrate before what Izaak Walton calls the altar but which Herbert still knew as the Communion-table. Carter was seen to read a chapter and to pray 'largely and very heavenly'. This was the difference between holiness and godliness, and it was not an immense difference.[70]

John Bossy suggests that throughout the rural parishes of Europe, from the fourteenth to the seventeenth centuries, the primary social task entrusted to the parish priest or his equivalent was that of a settler of conflicts.[71] It seems likely that the seventeenth-century English clergy, whether inclining towards puritanism or formalism, found that task complicated by alterations in their status, role, and parochial relationships, and even more by their perception of these things. The godly puritan minister achieved full familiarity only with fellow saints, the groups of notable 'private christians' with whom he would hold voluntary house meetings on Sunday evenings.[72] 'His loves were most enlarged to the people of God', 'his love flowed forth to the saints'.[73] But love so intense was exclusive, and between the saints and the community at large there was

---

[68] See, for example, the practice of Richard Rothwell: 'His manner was to spend the forenoon at his Studies, and the afternoon in going through his Parish, and conferring with his people.' (Clarke, *Lives of Thirty-Two English Divines*, p. 70.)

[69] Clarke, *Lives of Ten Eminent Divines*, pp. 11–12.

[70] Walton, *Life of Herbert*, p. 42; Clarke, *Lives of Ten Eminent Divines*, p. 16.

[71] John Bossy, 'Blood and Baptism', 139. For an extreme, indeed heroic, example of this role played in the wilds of Northumberland, see George Carleton, *The Life of Bernard Gilpin* (1727 edn.), pp. 41–3, Cf. the reputation of Henry Copinger, rector for forty-five years of Laneham, Nottinghamshire, a market town of 900 communicants, 'amongst whom, all his time, no difference did arise which he did not compound'. (Thomas Fuller, *Church History of Britain* (Oxford, 1845), v. 537.)

[72] See pp. 264–7 below.

[73] Said of Jeremiah Whitaker; Clarke, *Lives of Ten Eminent Divines*, pp. 174–5.

likely to be some degree of estrangement.[74] John Dod, whom Thomas Cartwright called 'the fittest man in England for a pastoral office',[75] was credited with success in peace-making between desperate and almost implacable adversaries. But his method was to 'mightily convince them with gospel arguments', which must sometimes have proved counter-productive.[76] By contrast, Herbert's celibate parson had no special bond attaching him to any section of his parish. Yet the singular holiness and dedication of his life set him generally apart, at a distance which could only be narrowed with the practice of studied pastoral arts, and what Herbert calls 'the parson's condescending'. Herbert represented him as 'standing on a hill, and considering his flock'. He described country people with objectivity and curiosity, almost as if they were inhabitants of another continent. In prayer the parson made 'many apostrophes to God' on their behalf: 'Oh Lord blesse my people.'[77]

Both species of churchmanship breathed a neo-clerical ideology. The model Elizabethan puritan divine Edward Dering told Burghley that the minister was 'the mouth of God, in whose person Christ himself is either refused or receyved'.[78] Some preachers were credited with a charisma which was physically perceptible. John Rogers of Dedham, himself an electrifying figure, could never come into the presence of his fellow divine Richard Blackerby 'without some kind of trembling upon him; because of the Divine Majesty and Holinesse' which seemed to shine in him.[79] The diarist John Manningham repeated a tale about a 'good, honest,

---

[74] See, for example, the extreme case of East Hanningfield, Essex, in the 1580s, discussed in my *Elizabethan Puritan Movement*, pp. 349–50.

[75] Cartwright's opinion cited in the Life of Robert Harris, Clarke, *Lives of Thirty-Two English Divines*, p. 319.

[76] Ibid., p. 177.

[77] Herbert, *Priest to the Temple*, pp. 157, 105, 2, 23, 24. A more obscure cleric, Richard Kilby, wrote: 'It is a true saying, that too much familiaritie breeds contempt; and so I have alwaies found it. Therefore use to retire your selfe, and be no common companie keeper: for howsoever you may preserve your personall reputation, yet the power of your office, which is much grounded upon a reverent estimation, will be by companie keeping manie waies diminished.' (*The burthen of a loaden conscience* (Cambridge, 1608), pp. 94–5.)

[78] Collinson, *Mirror of Elizabethan Puritanism*, p. 11.

[79] Clarke, *Lives and Deaths of Eminent Persons*, p. 65.

poor, silly puritan of Cranbrook' who 'goes to the ground
when he talks in Divinitie with a preacher'.[80] Discoursing at a
clerical synod in Durham Cathedral in 1608, when Calvinism
still reigned supreme in the north-east, Thomas Oxley spoke
of 'the Minister and Messenger of God' as 'the eye of the world
and as it were a Sunne in the Firmament of the Church, to
disperse the clouds of ignorance, and give light unto such as sit
in darkenesse'.[81] But when George Downame declared in a
sermon of the same year that God had advanced the ministry
'above the condition of other men, calling them, as to a
charge, so also to an honour, which might seeme to become
Angels, rather then men', he was in transition from the
Calvinist emphasis on the minister as God's instrument of
salvation to the stress later associated with Arminianism on
the uniquely exalted status and privilege of the priesthood.[82]
By the 1630s an Oxford preacher could address himself to the
'duty' of the laity, who maintained 'an humble distance from
God', while extolling the 'privilege' of the priesthood which
enjoyed 'immediateness of accesse'.[83] 'It is most necessary to
reflect upon our selves,' said a Kentish Divine, preaching at a
visitation in Canterbury in 1635, 'upon us that are *Parsons* and
Vicars, upon us the dispensers of God's Word and Sacraments,
upon us that have the cure of soules; since in us mainely
consists *Salus Ecclesiae et pax Reipublicae,* the well-fare of the
Church, and peace of the Common-weale.'[84]

The recognition that such high claims would conflict with
what Downame called 'the carnal conceits of profane men'
was a required convention of the rhetoric offered in defence of
the clergy. 'The Countrey Parson knows well', wrote Herbert,
'that both for the generall ignominy which is cast upon the
profession, and much more for those rules, which out of his
choysest judgment hee hath resolved to observe, and which
are described in this Book, he must be despised.'[85] When the

[80] *The Diary of John Manningham of the Middle Temple,* ed. R. P. Sorlien (Hanover, New
Hampshire, 1976), p. 44.
[81] Thomas Oxley, *The shepheard. Or, a sermon preached at a synode in Durisme Minster*
(1609), sig. B4ᵛ.
[82] George Downame, *Two sermons* (1608), p. 56.
[83] Thomas Laurence, *Two sermons* (1635), p. 20.
[84] Edward Boughen, *Two sermons* (1635), pp. 1–2.
[85] Herbert, *Priest to the Temple,* p. 116.

Kentish divine Herbert Palmer was asked as a child 'what course of life he best liked to follow, whether to be a Lawyer, a Courtier, a Countrey Gentleman etc.', he always answered that he would be a minister of Jesus Christ, whereupon his friends, 'for triall sake', would seem to dissuade him, telling him that ministers were 'hated, despised, and accounted as the offscouring of the world'; to which the five-year-old paragon would reply: 'It was no matter for that; for if the world hated him, yet God would love him.'[86]

Some clergy already in harness found it harder to resign themselves to the ingratitude of an uncaring world. Robert Abbot was a singularly devoted pastor of the populous Wealden parish of Cranbrook, a preacher twice on Sundays, a sensitive physician of the soul, and a total professional who made confident claims on behalf of his office and to the tithe income which was his due. When, after nearly a quarter of a century, his ministrations were rejected by part of the godly inner core of his congregation he found the experience incomprehensible and unacceptable.[87] 'It is a wonder to think (notwithstanding all my paynes) what disaffections, discouragements and misreports I undergo.'[88] In the past he had proudly addressed his flock as 'my brethren beloved and longed for, my joy and my crowne'.[89] Now, in equally Pauline language, he wrote with bitterness: 'I have loved and desired to spend and to be spent, though the more I love, the lesse I am loved of some few.'[90] On the eve of the Long Parliament there were many reasons for Abbot's discomfiture, few of them under his own control. Yet within Abbot's professional success were the seeds of an ultimate failure. Anticlericalism, which

---

[86] Clarke, *Lives of Thirty-Two English Divines*, p. 184.

[87] Patrick Collinson, 'Cranbrook and the Fletchers: Popular and Unpopular Religion in the Kentish Weald', in *Reformation Principle and Practice: Essays in Honour of A. G. Dickens*, ed. P. N. Brooks (1980), pp. 201–2.

[88] Robert Abbot to Sir Edward Dering, 15 March 1640; BL Stowe MS 184, fols. 27–30.

[89] Robert Abbot, *Davids desires* (1623), sig. A6. Cf. Edmund Staunton, vicar of Kingston upon Thames and subsequently president of Corpus Christi College, Oxford, who 'would to the last call the People of Kingston (as Saint *Paul* did the Philippians, Phil. 4.1) *His Joy and his Crowne.*' (Clarke, *Lives and Deaths of Eminent Persons*, p. 162.)

[90] Robert Abbot, *A triall of our church-forsakers* (1639), sig. A6ᵛ.

historians have made a principal cause of the English Reformation, was also one of its consequences.[91]

If the claims made on behalf of the reformed ministry were intolerable to many laymen, the moral and spiritual athletic-ism on which such claims depended for their credibility was no doubt too much of a strain for the tender consciences of many of the ministers themselves. We cannot tell how often the failure of the preacher to reach the exalted standard set for his profession and to live by and even to believe for himself the doctrine which he himself preached may have been a source of much inner misery. 'This hath been the inside of my life', wrote Richard Kilby, an obscure Derby curate, whose entire career, according to his own testimony, was one long tale of sinful lapses, and of a kind of infidelity, compounded by wretched health. 'Yet I have no power to turne unto God.' Kilby supposed that of all counterfeits, the most incurable was a counterfeit preacher. 'My soul can hardly think how such a one should have the grace of repentance.'[92]

III

The unhappy Richard Kilby thought much upon himself. But when the preacher of the Canterbury visitation sermon said 'it is most necessary to reflect upon ourselves' he had in mind not the inside of one man's life but the common concerns of a professional group. If one aspect of the newly professionalized status and mentality of the clergy was their distance from lay society, a matter of external relations, another, the aspect of consolidation, consisted in the intensification of internal connections among the clergy as a social group, a matter of collective self-consciousness. So far we have discussed the clergyman as an individual within his own parochial environ-

---

[91] I owe this perception to Christopher Haigh.

[92] Richard Kilby made his scandalous confession in a book published anonymously in Cambridge in 1608, *The burthen of a loaden conscience,* which had reached its 12th edition by 1635 (see especially Epistle and pp. 1, 5, and 94 of the first edition). He promised to reveal his identity if and when he attained repentance. *Hallelu-iah. Praise ye the Lord for the unburthening of a loaden conscience* (Cambridge, 1618) (see especially p. 28) was the promised sequel. Yet the triumphant title of this book is not altogether consistent with its mostly doleful contents. Cf. the private thoughts of Richard Rogers, lecturer of Wethersfield, Essex, in *Two Elizabethan Puritan Diaries,* ed. M. M. Knappen, American Society of Church History (Chicago, 1933).

ment, and even within the innerness of his own experience, exemplifying a type but not professionally involved with others of his own kind. But a profession is a social institution, and a professional *esprit de corps* finds shape and expression as members of the profession come together for any purpose. The occasions for much of the high rhetoric uttered on behalf of the clergy were provided by convocations, visitations, synods, and ordinations, when sermons were delivered to audiences predominantly or entirely composed of clergy.

The social experience of the Elizabethan and Jacobean clergy, as distinct from their qualifications, livelihood, and status, is a still neglected subject. One of its dimensions, following hard on the heels of the legitimation of clerical marriage, was endogamy, a kind of priestly tribalism. The dynastic propensities of famous puritan divines has been often observed, for example by William Haller in a celebrated chapter of his *Rise of Puritanism*.[93] And we have already seen that the Elizabethan bishops threatened to compose a small tribe on their own.[94] But current demographic studies are likely to reveal further ramifications of this phenomenon. Already we know that in the first half of the seventeenth century, one-third of the Kentish clergy married the daughters of other clergymen.[95] In a most suggestive phrase an early seventeenth-century vicar of Chebsey, Staffordshire, recorded his desire that his daughter should be 'married to the vicaridge of Chebsey'—that is, that she should wed his successor.[96] In the diocese of Exeter, a quarter of the Jacobean

[93] William Haller, *The Rise of Puritanism* (New York, 1938), especially Chapter 2 'The Spiritual Brotherhood'. Most celebrated of all was the Culverwell connection. Nicholas Culverwell was a London merchant and brother of Richard Culverwell, a member of the Mercers, and a generous patron of godly causes. His sons Ezekiel and Samuel were notable preachers. Two of his daughters married famous Cambridge divines, while a third was the mother of the Jacobean curate and preacher of St. Ann's, Blackfriars, William Gouge. Nathaniel Culverwell, a London preacher of the 1640s and prolific writer, was presumably a member of the same family. (Patrick Collinson, 'The Puritan Classical Movement in the Reign of Elizabeth I', London Ph.D. thesis, 1957, pp. 379–79b.)

[94] See pp. 45–6 above, and Joel Berlatsky, 'Marriage and Family in a Tudor Elite: Familial Patterns of Elizabethan Bishops', *Journal of Family History*, iii (1978), 6–22.

[95] Lawrence Stone, *The Family, Sex and Marriage in England, 1500–1800* (1977), p. 61.

[96] O'Day, 'Clerical Patronage and Recruitment', p. 323. J. J. Goring has drawn attention to a parallel case in the Sussex parish of Warbleton. Persis, daughter of

incumbents had, in effect, inherited their livings from their fathers.[97] There is no need to look beyond the *Dictionary of National Biography* to be impressed by the numbers of divines who were the sons of divines and in their turn the fathers of divines.[98] By the 1630s the sons of clergy accounted for 15 percent of all Oxford matriculants.[99]

Demographic research is also likely to reveal the remarkable philoprogenitive powers of the early generations of married clergy. When the wife of the famous divine William Gouge died in childbirth it was said that she died like a soldier on the

---

William Hopkinson, rector from 1571 to 1604, married her father's successor, Thomas Lord, rector from 1605 to 1640. Their daughter Anne married her father's curate, Joseph Bennet. (Jeremy Goring, *Church and Dissent in Warbleton c. 1500–1900*, Warbleton and District History Group Publications no. 5 (Eastbourne, 1980).) It could be said that the retention of livings within the kindred of a married clergy was a 'natural' state of affairs, observable at the present day in, for example, the Ethiopian Orthodox Church, and one which had been altered with great difficulty in the Western Church, at the time of the Gregorian reforms. See Brian R. Kemp, 'Hereditary Benefices in the Medieval English Church: A Herefordshire Example', *Bulletin of the Institute of Historical Research,* xliii (1970), 1–15.

[97] I. Cassidy, 'The Episcopate of William Cotton, Bishop of Exeter, 1598–1621', Oxford B.Litt. thesis, pp. 53, 55. An early example of ecclesiastical inheritance from this diocese is recorded in William Carnsewe's diary for 1576: 'Our vycar Sir Robert Goldsmythe dyed 28 April of a putrefactyon of hys longis. I sawe hym openyd. His sonne John Goldsmythe roed for the benyfyce obtayned hit of my Lord Keper retorned by Oxforde and Brystowe in eche of which he abode 3 dayes and came home the 20 daye of Maye with the brodd sele for it.' (PRO S.P. 46/16, fol. 35ᵛ.)

[98] See, for example, the generational connections of Henry Newcome (1627–95). Newcome's grandfather was a schoolmaster at Ely who married the sister of a Mr Cropley who was rector of Girton. After her husband's death, Mrs Newcome married Mr Noble, rector of Ampton, near Bury St. Edmunds. Her daughter, Henry Newcome's aunt, married Richard Wigmore, an incumbent in the Isle of Ely and brother to Daniel Wigmore, archdeacon of Ely. Newcome's father, Stephen Newcome, was rector of Caldecote, Huntingdonshire. He married Rose, the eldest child of Henry Williamson, BD, rector of Connington, Cambridgeshire. Rose Williamson's mother was the daughter of Thomas Sparke, one of the puritan spokesmen at the Hampton Court Conference. Another of Sparke's daughters, Grace, was married to Henry Williamson's brother Robert Williamson, DD, rector of Tichmarsh. After her husband's death, Newcome's Williamson grandmother married his successor as rector of Connington, Mr Watts. Henry Newcome and two of his brothers became ministers, his elder brother Robert succeeding his father as rector of Caldecote. Henry Newcome's eldest son Henry became a minister, as did his third son Peter (1656–1738) and in his turn Peter's son Peter Newcome (1684–1744). (*The Autobiography of Henry Newcome; DNB,* art. Henry Newcome.)

[99] Stone, 'The Size and Composition of the Oxford Student Body', 19.

battlefield or a preacher in the pulpit: performing her office.[1] When Richard Rogers of Wethersfield listed 'inconveniences if my wife should chance to die' he put first 'necessity of marrying again'. There was no question of sharing the celibacy of John Knewstub, the doyen of the Suffolk ministers, whom Rogers could only admire from afar for his 'contentation in a sol life'.[2] Among Knewstub's brethren in Suffolk was one minister with fourteen children and others with eleven, ten, and nine.[3] W. G. Hoskins discovered several clerical families of more than ten children in early seventeenth-century Leicestershire, living in circumstances indicative of the extreme poverty of some married parsons. The vicar of Cosby was another Mr Quiverfull, and supported thirteen children on a living worth officially no more than £10; another, ten on twenty marks.[4] Yet in other parishes the 'magnificent' parsonical bed of which so many wills and inventories speak symbolized a more secure and hopeful fecundity. The prophets and the sons of the prophets, often distinguished by some of the more resounding and colourful of biblical names, were an expanding and self-renewing tribe. But later, or so Lawrence Stone has suggested, shortage of livings tended to limit the fertility of the clergy by enforcing Oxbridgian collegiate celibacy on the abler men until well into middle life.[5] By the late seventeenth century, a puritan divine could write nostalgically of 'this old stock of preachers, worn or wearing out'.[6]

---

[1] Nicholas Guy, *Pieties pillar: or, a sermon preached at the funerall of Elizabeth Gouge* (1625).

[2] *Two Elizabethan Puritan Diaries*, p. 95.

[3] Patrick Collinson, 'Magistracy and Ministry: A Suffolk Miniature', in *Reformation Conformity and Dissent: Essays in Honour of Geoffrey Nuttall,* ed. R. Buick Knox (1977), p. 76.

[4] Hoskins, 'The Leicestershire Country Parson', 109.

[5] Stone, *Family, Sex and Marriage,* pp. 48–50.

[6] *Oliver Heywood's Life of John Angier of Denton,* ed. E. Axon, Chetham Society, NS xcvii (1937), 43–7. A Suffolk clergyman wrote of Sir Nathaniel Barnardiston: 'He was a Benefactor to our Tribe.' (*Suffolks tears: or elegies on that renowned knight Sir Nathaniel Barnardiston* (1653), p. 15.) Samuel Crook, son of Thomas Crook, rector of Great Waldingfield, Suffolk, was described as 'a Prophet and the Son of a Prophet'. He married the eldest daughter of Robert Walsh, rector of the neighbouring parish of Little Waldingfield, 'a wife of his own tribe'. (Clarke, *Lives of Thirty-Two English Divines*, pp. 202, 205.)

The educational formation of the clergy marks the second stage of their socialization and professional consolidation. This topic concentrates our attention not only on the internal affairs of the universities, and especially of those colleges like Emmanuel which were primarily devoted to the production of a learned preaching ministry, but on the network of connections between colleges and their tutors and parents, schoolmasters, patrons, and alumni. The annual return migration to the universities for the formalities and festivities of the Act and the Commencement, part of 'the rhythm of a provincial year', the contacts renewed and the bargains struck on these occasions, were of particular significance. At one Cambridge Commencement the carnival figure of the *praevaricator* alarmed the authorities with a whimsical proposal that they should provide roast beef for all the country clergy who were present.[7] It tells us much about the corporate identity of those 'religious, grave, reverend and learned ministers' of Robert Reyce's Suffolk to know that most of the mid-Elizabethan preachers of this county belonged to the same Cambridge generation, and that no less than thirty had been bred in one college, St. John's; and that the next generation was recruited out of Emmanuel.[8]

The postgraduate seminary experience which the Victorian Church would institutionalize in the theological college was not entirely neglected in the Elizabethan and Jacobean Church, but it was furnished privately, as a domestic enterprise. Bernard Gilpin, the 'Apostle of the North', grafted onto the grammar school which he helped to found at Kepier a kind of seminary for up to twenty scholars, who were boarded in his rambling rectory at Houghton-le-Spring. The students included Gilpin's biographer, the future Bishop George Carleton.[9] In the 1580s a representative conference of puritan clergy took a formal resolution that as a general rule

[7] Victor Morgan, 'Cambridge University and "The Country" 1560–1640', in *The University in Society*, i. 227. For Oxford, see J. K. McConica, 'The Social Relations of Tudor Oxford', *Transactions of the Royal Historical Society*, 5th ser. xxvii (1977), 115–34. See also relevant material and fruitful suggestions in C. M. Dent, 'Protestants in Elizabethan Oxford', Oxford D.Phil. thesis, 1980.

[8] Collinson, 'Magistracy and Ministry', p. 76.

[9] Carleton, *Life of Gilpin*, pp. 31–2, 91–2; D. Marcombe, 'Bernard Gilpin: Anatomy of an Elizabethan Legend', *Northern History*, xvi (1980), 20–39.

every minister should entertain a student of divinity, 'being well grounded in other knowledge of Artes and tongues', and should train him for the ministry so 'that there may be alwaies sufficient and able men in the Church for that Callinge'.[10] In this way John Angier was brought up under John Cotton at Boston and 'many goodly and learned young men' under Richard Greenham at Dry Drayton, including the famous Arthur Hildersham, who recorded Greenham's casuistical table-talk as visitors came from far afield for resolution of their conscientious difficulties.[11] In Jacobean Essex Richard Blackerby, excluded from the parish ministry by his extreme nonconformity, made the training of ministers a career which he pursued for twenty-three years. 'Divers young students (after they came from the university) betook themselves to him to prepare them for the Ministry, whom he taught the Hebrew Tongue, to whom he opened the Scriptures, and read Divinity and gave them excellent advice for Learning, Doctrine and Life.' Among 'many eminent persons' who proceeded from Blackerby's seminary was Samuel Fairclough, a commanding preacher of fast sermons to the Long Parliament.[12]

Such were the roots of the fraternal spirit which found expression in the books published by the Suffolk ministers, which reverberate in their prefaces with such phrases as 'brethren and fellow ministers', 'the reverend, wise and godly learned fathers and brethren'. These clerical circles fomented persistent habits of theological learning and stimulated the publication of substantial works of divinity by their members. At least fifteen of the clergy 'planted' in Suffolk at the turn of the sixteenth and seventeenth centuries were authors, and some of their books advertise their origin in sermons originally heard by fellow ministers.[13] One work of a thousand pages on

---

[10] *The Presbyterian Movement in the Reign of Queen Elizabeth*, 93.

[11] *Heywood's Life of Angier*, p. 52; Clarke, *Lives of Thirty-Two English Divines*, p. 17; John Rylands Library Manchester English MS 524.

[12] Clarke, *Lives and Deaths of Eminent Persons*, p. 58.

[13] The following is a list of late Elizabethan and Jacobean Suffolk clerical authors, with the dates of their first and last publications: Robert Allen 1596/1612; Bartimaeus Andrewes 1583/1595; Samuel Bird 1580/1621; Nicholas Bownd 1595/1608; Bezaleel Carter 1615/1621; Alexander Chapman 1606/1610; George Estey 1601/1603; John Knewstub 1577/1579; Miles Mosse 1595/1614; Timothy

The doctrine of the gospel, which the author, Robert Allen, published so that the world should know 'what these things are which the faithfull Ministers of Jesus Christ doe beate their wittes about', professed to contain the coherent body of divinity taught by the ministers to whom it was dedicated. 'I have beene a hearer of many of your owne selves, who are yet living, and also of some of those who have died most blessedly in the Lord.' Allen believed that his book would demonstrate 'in how many truthes, that is in particulers above number, we do agree, teaching the same things from one and the same word, by one and the same Spirit, with a sweete consent, in comparison of those fewe things wherein the iudgements of some doe differ'.[14] Clerical funerals and funeral sermons were occasions of special importance and of a kind of triumphalism.[15]

This experience, more real and persuasive than academic argument or ecclesiological dogma, was the mainspring of presbyterianism as a force in Elizabethan clerical life, and as a continuing tendency which came to fruition in the 1640s. The dozen or more Suffolk and Essex ministers who held their monthly conferences in and around Dedham in the 1580s were responding to an intensely felt and practical desire to share their theological and pastoral problems, and even to

---

Oldmayne alias Pricke 1619/1636; Oliver Pigge 1582/1589; Robert Pricke 1608; Thomas Rogers 1584/1608; Thomas Settle 1587; Samuel Ward 1615/1628. In 1590 there was a literary controversy between two of these authors, Miles Mosse and Thomas Rogers, Rogers responding to what he interpreted as a personal attack in Mosse's allegation that there was an excess of publication, the 'multitude of writings' having 'overflowed all the bankes of modestie and discretion in this present age'. (Thomas Rogers, *Miles Christianus or a iust apologie of all necessarie writings and writers* (1590). The BL copy (4103.bbb.26) contains much additional matter in MS. by the author.)

[14] Robert Allen, *The doctrine of the gospel by a plaine and familiar interpretation of the particular points or articles thereof* (1606), sig. *4–5. In the next generation Samuel Fairclough preached a Thursday lecture at Ketton in Suffolk which was virtually a sermon *ad clerum*. 'They were actually preached to so great a number of the Clergy, all the Ministers (for many miles compasse) coming constantly to heare them; and there were frequently not less than ten or twenty scholars (both Fellows of colledges and others) from Cambridge,' (Clarke, *Lives and Deaths of Eminent Persons,* p. 164.)

[15] Patrick Collinson, '"A Magazine of Religious Patterns": An Erasmian Topic Transposed in English Protestantism', in *Renaissance and Renewal in Christian History, Studies in Church History,* xiv, ed. Derek Baker (Oxford, 1977), 223–49.

submit themselves and their congregations to the discipline of a group of equals. When that discipline seemed unreasonable in its bearing on the affairs of any of the members it was the occasion of real pain. When Richard Crick, a Doctor of Divinity, broke fellowship after a difference of opinion, he wrote with passion, the passion of a biblical topos, that his fellow ministers were men 'whose faces I have seen as if I had seen the face of God, whose backs I have beholden with far greater joy than ever I have done almost the eyes of any other company'.[16]

But the presbyterianism of this clandestine *classis* and of similar experiments in Northamptonshire and elsewhere[17] was only a particular expression of a more generalized and pervasive sense of clerical collegiality which was as much a characteristic of the Church as it was an index of alienation from it or of a desire for radical change. This collegiality supplied the texture of the Church as an ecclesiastical society. It did so at regular but widely spaced intervals on a diocesan or archidiaconal scale, and more persistently at a level intermediate between the microcosm of the parish and the macrocosm of the diocese or archdeaconry. This level corresponded to the localized world of the market town and its satellite villages, which circumscribed the bounds of experience and activity for most secular purposes. It would be strange indeed if ecclesiastical life uniquely failed to conform to localized patterns of social existence which were determined by geography and the distance it was possible to travel to and fro in a day and to transact one's business. It is implausible to confine the clergy, as by implication historians often do, to the parish, and not to attribute to a significant proportion of them local as well as parochial interests and responsibilities. Whether a minister was willing or able to play such an extended role would depend upon a multitude of circumstances. Possession of a university degree would have been an advantage; but equally, if not more so, possession of a horse.

[16] Collinson, *Elizabethan Puritan Movement*, pp. 230–1.

[17] Ibid., Parts 6 and 7; W. J. Sheils, *The Puritans in the Diocese of Peterborough 1558–1610*, Publications of the Northamptonshire Record Society, xxx (Northampton, 1979), 51–66.

At its loosest and most extended, the fabric of ecclesiastical society was held together by episcopal and archidiaconal visitations, and by clerical synods and chapters, which were distinguished from visitations by the absence of the church-wardens. In the records of one archdeaconry we read on the one hand of the 'synodus sive congregacio cleri', and on the other of the 'visitacio necnon synodus sive congregacio tam cleri quam populi'.[18] In plain English, George Herbert wrote that the country parson should attend and make due use of visitations, 'as of Clergy councels'.[19] Not much is known in our period about 'clergy councels', although a search would probably reveal that they were a regular institution in most parts of England, at either the diocesan or archidiaconal level.[20] In the archdeaconry of Canterbury, in the 1570s, meetings of the clergy described as 'capitula' took place in May, alternating with the annual visitations in October.[21] In the diocese of Ely, Whitsuntide was the season for the annual diocesan synods, and here a long series of 'libri sinodorum' establishes that the institution went back as far as the first decade of the sixteenth century and indeed much further. The synods still held in our period were but the fag-end of the vigorous tradition of synodal activity in the late medieval Church.[22] From the same diocese there are records of an annual 'convocacio sive congregatio generalis' for the deaneries of Ely and Wisbech which was usually held in the autumn and where, in Bishop Cox's time, the bishop occasionally presided in person. These 'convocations' were

[18] Hertfordshire Record Office, Act Books of the Archdeaconry Court of St. Albans, ASA/7. See, for example, entries relating to a synod held on 14 October 1583 and a visitation held on 24 March 1584: ASA/7/11, fols. 36, 46.

[19] Herbert, *Priest to the Temple*, p. 76.

[20] When the puritan preacher John Ward wrote to the magistrates of Ipswich in 1589 'I thinke not to come over, till the Synode, which is (as I take it) a moneth after Michaelmas', Richard Bancroft chose to interpret this as a reference to an illicit puritan synod. But Ward doubtless referred to the archidiaconal synod. (Richard Bancroft, *Daungerous positions and proceedings* (1593), p. 89.) For details of the twice-yearly synods at Ipswich and Norwich, see Ralph Houlbrooke, *Church Courts and the People During the English Reformation 1520–1570* (Oxford, 1979), p. 30.

[21] See two call books for chapters and visitations, running in sequence from 1576 to 1582: Cathedral Archives and Library Canterbury, Z.7.1, X.2.3.

[22] D. M. Owen, 'Synods in the Diocese of Ely in the Latter Middle Ages and the Sixteenth Century', *Studies in Church History*, iii, ed. G. J. Cuming (Leiden, 1966), 217–22.

attended by churchwardens and questmen as well as clergy, and resembled visitations more than synods.[23]

Visitations themselves had a significance for the clergy which was tangential to their corrective function and had much to do with the exchange of civilities, the discussion of matters of common professional interest, and the principal amenity of such an occasion: the dinner. This extra-judicial business was recorded sparingly, if at all, so that it tends to be overlooked by historians.[24] But when Bishop Richard Neile's officers reported on his primary visitation of the diocese of Lincoln in 1614, they commented on these aspects of the tour to the exclusion of other matters.[25] Neile was informed that at each session 'according to your lordship's special direction' his love and commendation was tendered to the clergy. 'And they reciprocally with remembrance of their humble duties acknowledge themselves much bound to your lordship for your honourable favour'—more especially since the bishop had waived his right to the fees known as procurations. On the other hand Neile had followed normal practice in requesting a 'benevolence' to help pay his first-fruits. He was told that 'the abler and discreator sort of clergie' were inclined to be cooperative in this matter, observing that Neile had tactfully excused the poorer ministers and had not pressed the richer sort 'as they thinke by your place might be done', but had made the contribution a voluntary matter. If we are to give credence to the visitors' report, other topics of current concern were discussed in an atmosphere of equal cordiality and reciprocity. 'The country' was 'glad to hear' of a certain proposal for administrative reorganization. The particular reports relating to each session of the visitation were concerned exclusively with the content of the sermon and with the matters discussed over dinner. At Stony Stratford the table-talk was whether children dying before baptism might

[23] Cambridge University Library, Ely Diocesan Records, B 2/8, fol. 59 ff.

[24] But the Lincoln *Liber Cleri* of 1603 begins with the summary of a sermon, apparently preached at one of the sessions of the visitation. (*State of the Church*, 253–5.) See an episode recorded in Carleton's *Life of Gilpin* (p. 88) when Gilpin preached at a visitation at Chester-le-Street: 'After the Sermon, they met altogether at Dinner . . .'.

[25] Copies of the report in Cambridge University Library Baumgartner MS 8, fol. 220–2 and in Lincoln Cathedral Library Dean and Chapter MS A 4/3/43, whence printed in *Associated Architectural Societies Reports and Papers*, xvi (1881), 31–54.

be saved. At Bedford one of the clergy spoke strongly against the visitation sermon, which had maintained episcopacy *jure divino*. Over dinner at Luton non-residence was 'much spoken against, without limit or distinction'. At Leicester, the question was whether laymen might tie the knot of matrimony, at Grantham the talk was about the power of excommunication. But at Louth 'we had many grave and learned ministers, but al silent', while at Horncastle 'our table conference was to no greate purpose'.

These are rare insights into Jacobean ecclesiastical society. When records of synods survive at all, they are likely to take the form of simple call books, or *libri cleri,* containing lists of parishes with names of incumbents and other bare details. But at Ely in 1557 discussion in synod led to the drafting of a memorandum to the diocesan chancellor on the subject of plays, dancing, and maygames in churches and churchyards. And in 1566 the synod, 'episcopus ac universus clerus', formally received Archbishop Parker's injunctions known as the *Advertisements,* giving their assent and consent and approving and confirming them 'quantum in nobis est'.[26]

From the archdeaconry of St. Albans there survives a unique collection of loose papers of a kind which most ecclesiastical officials in the course of time threw away, but which Thomas Rokett, the registrar of this small jurisdiction, carefully filed.[27] They illustrate the sociability associated with 'clergy councels' and the variety of business which they transacted. In 1583, the archdeacon's official, 'with the consent of the rest of the ministers', ordered that in future clergy absent from synods should pay a shilling 'towards the charges of the dyner the same dayes'.[28] In November 1584, with a Parliament approaching, it was necessary for the St. Albans clergy to meet for the purpose of electing their representatives for the Lower House of Convocation. On the day before this event, the rector of Barnet, Edward Underne, wrote to the registrar to excuse his absence. He was obliged to preach at a Communion on the same day, and again three

---

[26] Cambridge University Library, Ely Diocesan Records, B 2/1, fol. 256, F 5/35, fols. 78ᵛ–9.

[27] See above, p. 65.

[28] Hertfordshire Record Office, ASA/7/11, fol. 21.

days later, which was 17 November, the Queen's Day. 'I lack a horse and am not verye well.' But he appointed a proxy, Roger Williams, the rector of St. Albans, and sent four shillings and threepence, the benevolence of the parish and himself, 'with commendacions to Mr Williams, to both your wyves and all the companye, praying yow to speake a good word for me.'[29] Mr Williams to whom Underne had awarded his proxy was himself one of three candidates for the two seats in Convocation. All seventeen electors cast their first vote for Dr Edward Stanhope, chancellor of the diocese, vicar-general of the province, and soon to be pilloried by Martin Marprelate as 'Tarquinius Superbus'.[30] They then divided their second votes between Williams and a certain John Sterne, who like Stanhope was a carpet-bagger and may have enjoyed official backing. Williams cast his own voice and that of his proxy in favour of Sterne and lost by one vote. But there must have been a misunderstanding, because later he alleged that he had been duly elected but that 'other ded take upon them that offyce'.[31] This record of a genuinely open election for Convocation is unique. Not so, perhaps, the event itself.

From other St. Albans papers it appears that meetings of the clergy of the division were held periodically for the collection of money or for the equitable distribution of the many financial burdens laid on the hard-pressed Church. These included the benevolences requested by the bishops, and the charitable collections recommended by ecclesiastical authority or by the Privy Council for such miscellaneous causes as the repair of St. Paul's, the endowment of a school,

---

[29] Ibid., ASA 5/5/94.

[30] See above, p. 63.

[31] Hertfordshire Record Office, ASA 5/5/95, ASA/7/11, fol. 110. See an account of a highly political election of the proctor for the Suffolk clergy for the Convocation of 1623, recorded in William Bedell's *Life and Death of William Bedell:* 'But, as it often falls out, there was much packing and plotting and making of friends by the more ambitious of the clergy, to be chosen for that honour, as they accounted it; insomuch that Mr Bedell himself was dealt withall by letter and otherwise, touching the disposal of his voice at the election. But those indirect proceedings did make such an impression upon his spirit, that he wholly declined the meeting appointed for the election. The ministers being met upon the day, there was great stickling and much opposition of some against others, till at last Mr Bedell himself, that was absent and never made any means for the employment, was the man they pitch'd upon.' (*Two Biographies of William Bedell*, ed. E. S. Shuckburgh (Cambridge, 1902), p. 22.)

or the relief of distressed individuals and communities. [32] Most oppressive and contentious of all were the contributions required from the clergy towards the provision of 'armour' or 'warlike furniture', a liability which, unlike clerical subsidies, was supposedly adjusted to the real capacity of the clergy to pay. Whether a particular incumbent should furnish a light horse, or a lance, or a musket, was a matter determined partly in the First-Fruits Office of the Exchequer, partly by the ecclesiastical authorities themselves on the basis of local knowledge. [33] The matter was sufficiently invidious to require the clergy to assemble, and sometimes to engage in unseemly wrangling. [34] At St. Albans such problems were confronted in a civilized manner, but not without disagreement. In 1585 the entire clergy rejected the bishop's novel demand that they should pay the expenses of their proctors in Convocation, asking that their refusal be taken in good part until they were persuaded that this was indeed a duty which they were bound to pay. [35]

In 1582 there was a national collection for the relief of the besieged city of Geneva, a cause strongly backed by authority. [36] The St. Albans clergy met in synod and committed themselves to contributions ranging from a quarter of a mark to a pound. Among the ministers who were unable to attend, one asked the official to communicate to the assembled company his willingness to be put down for two shillings: 'you partlie knowe the state of my living, what it is'. Another, pleading his great charges and debts, 'I fare full sadde',

[32] *Records of the Old Archdeaconry of St. Albans, A Calendar of Papers A.D. 1575 to A.D. 1637.* ed. H. R. Wilton Hall, St. Albans and Hertfordshire Archaeological and Architectural Society (St. Albans, 1908), *passim.*

[33] C. G. Cruickshank, *Elizabeth's Army* (2nd edn., Oxford, 1966), pp. 30–2, 71–3; Lindsay Boynton, *The Elizabethan Militia* (1967), pp. 33–6, 222 ff. See the list of 'The armor and warlike furnitur provided by the clergie within the diocese of Lincoln' in 1590; *State of the Church,* 145–68.

[34] See a reference in a Lincolnshire letter of 1596 to 'a great nomber of the ministers, being that daie in Lincoln about provision of their armor.' (BL Lansdowne MS 82, no. 53, fol. 112ᵛ.) For evidence of unseemly wrangling, see the letter of Bishop Overton of Coventry and Lichfield to Sir Francis Walsingham, 11 June 1581; PRO S.P. 12/149/37.

[35] *Records of the Old Archdeaconry of St. Albans,* pp. 79–80; Hertfordshire Record Office, ASA/7/11, fols. 109–10.

[36] Patrick Collinson, *Archbishop Grindal 1519–1583: The Struggle for a Reformed Church* (1979), p. 270.

nevertheless contrived to send ten shillings 'to helpe these godlie people, trobled for the gospel of Jesus Christ', and he contributed a further two shillings to purchase wine for the dinner. 'Thus with my veri harti commendations to Mr Archdeacon Cotton and you and all other frends there . . . '.[37]

This was a tiny archdeaconry, containing only twenty-six parishes. Elsewhere, some of the business transacted at St. Albans in synod was dealt with at the rural deanery level. For example, in 1585 the archbishop of Canterbury 'in her Majesty's name' wrote to his suffragans to commit the raising of funds for the endowment of a grammar school at Kingston upon Thames to the 'carefull endeavour of three or iiij preachers or other discreate ministers in everie deanerie of your diocesse'. The ministers were to assemble the remaining clergy and to exhort them and their parishioners to contribute to 'so necessarie a worke'. But so far as St. Albans was concerned, this was a matter for the archdeaconry and its human machinery.[38]

The rural deanery corresponded in scale to the most natural unit of social existence: a cluster of a dozen or twenty parishes, often grouped around a market town or other centre. Sir Nicholas Bacon, the lord keeper, was one of several Elizabethan publicists who thought that the remedy for ineffective ecclesiastical discipline lay to hand in 'the devideinge of everye of the dioceses accordeinge to their greatenes into deaneryes (as I knowe commonlye they be) and the committeinge of thease deaneryes to men well chosen (as I thinke commonly they be not) . . . '.[39] Historical opinion used to agree with Bacon that rural deaneries survived into the sixteenth century only as convenient subdivisions of larger units of ecclesiastical government, and that the rural dean was a nearly extinct species, whose ancient responsibilities had been usurped by the archdeacon.[40] Modern research has shown that

---

[37] *Records of the Old Archdeaconry of St. Albans*, pp. 22–3.

[38] Ibid., pp. 46–7.

[39] *Proceedings in the Parliaments of Elizabeth I*, i, *1558–1581*, ed. T. E. Hartley (Leicester, 1981), 82. See my 'Sir Nicholas Bacon and the Elizabethan *Via Media*', *Historical Journal*, xxiii (1980), 268–9.

[40] William Dansey, *Horae Decanicae Rurales*, 2 vols. (2nd edn., 1844); A. Hamilton Thompson, *Diocesan Organization in the Middle Ages: Archdeacons and Rural Deans* (1943); A. Hamilton Thompson, *The English Clergy and their Organization in the Later Middle Ages* (Oxford, 1947), pp. 63–70.

this was not the whole truth. The appointment of rural deans was an annual item of business at the Ely diocesan synods, and in other areas rural deans have been positively identified in the field.[41]   Paper projects for ecclesiastical reorganization showed a persistent interest in formal reinvigoration of the office of rural dean as a superintendent minister, mediating the authority of the bishop in a humane and truly pastoral fashion and enabling him to enjoy 'a special knowledge of every particular man of his diocese as near as possibly he may'. For some, such a reform was a preferred alternative to more radical schemes for the multiplication of bishoprics and a drastic reduction in their size, or even to the more revolutionary platform of presbyterianism, which involved the abolition of bishoprics and hierarchy.[42] But while Parliament and Convocation did little or nothing to satisfy these aspirations, the talents of 'discreet' ministers, as individuals or in small groups, were extensively employed in relatively informal ways, both within the rural deaneries and on a wider scale. In 1572 the vicar of Norborne in Kent was presented in the archdeacon's court for persistently carting and ploughing although he had been 'both publykely and pryvately admonysshed by the ministers of the deanrye'.[43] An Essex clergyman who had confessed the crime of incest and was thought to be of unsound mind was bound by the archdeacon's court 'to take good instruction of Leper the minister as also of other good preachers thereby for his amendment of lyef'.[44] A rustic heretic in the same county was prescribed conference with three named preachers of the deanery, 'sondrie tymes meetinge in Lee church, whereby he may be perswaded of the immortalitie of the sowle and to recant'.[45]

It was principally the inadequacy of the incompetent majority of the Elizabethan clergy which provided the

[41] Cambridge University Library, Ely Diocesan Records, B 2/7. See my 'Episcopacy and Reform in England in the Later Sixteenth Century', *Studies in Church History*, iii. 105–11. See also R. W. Dunning, 'Rural Deans in England in the XVth Century', *Bulletin of the Institute of Historical Research*, xl (1967), 207–13.

[42] Collinson, 'Episcopacy and Reform', 91–125; Collinson, *Elizabethan Puritan Movement*, pp. 177–90.

[43] Cathedral Archives and Library Canterbury, X.1.11.A, fol. 158.

[44] Essex Record Office, D/AEA/12, court held on 7 April 1584.

[45] Ibid., D/AEA/13, court held on 8 December 1587.

professional minority with an extended role beyond their own cures. One of their functions, and a source of additional income, was to provide the quarter sermons to which all parishes were entitled and which non-preaching incumbents were bound to procure and to pay for. In 1587 Convocation assigned this duty to 'six or seven public preachers' in each jurisdiction, 'to preach by course every Sunday, in the parishes within a convenient limit, near adjoyning to their habitation'.[46] Above all, the graduate, preaching ministers were the backbone of the Elizabethan programmes for what would nowadays be called the 'further education' of the unlearned and substandard clergy. These 'exercises' derived from the sixteenth Royal Injunction of 1559 which required all clergy serving parishes and below the degree of Master of Arts to obtain the New Testament in Latin and English and the Paraphrases of Erasmus, and to undertake regular and supervised study. Parker's *Advertisements* of 1566 and the Canons of 1571 laid the responsibility for setting and examining these tasks on archdeacons in their visitations.[47] In London, the diocese of Winchester, and subsequently in most parts of the northern province, provision was made for regular inspection of the academic progress of the unlearned clergy in quarterly or half-yearly synods.[48]

But with the growing popularity of the public preaching conferences known as 'prophesyings', several bishops and archdeacons found this the most convenient and efficient means of sending the ignorant clergy to school.[49] In most of the more important and populous dioceses, including Canterbury, London, Lincoln, and Norwich, the 'gravest, best learned and discreetest' of the clergy were recognized by the bishops as moderators of the prophesying, with delegated powers to convene those ministers who were 'tied to the exercise'. Having heard the two or three sermons preached in the public

[46] Strype, *Life of Whitgift*, iii. 196.
[47] *Documentary Annals of the Reformed Church of England*, i. 218; *Visitation Articles and Injunctions of the Period of the Reformation*, iii, Alcuin Club Collections xvi (Oxford, 1910), 178; Cardwell, *Synodalia*, i. 117. For the further history of these orders, see Patrick Collinson, 'The Puritan Classical Movement in the Reign of Elizabeth I', London Ph.D. thesis, 1957, pp. 244–59.
[48] Ibid., pp. 246–7, 265–9; Houlbrooke, *Church Courts and the People*, p. 30.
[49] Collinson, *Elizabeth Puritan Movement*, pp. 168–76.

prophesying, the unlearned exhibited their written tasks to the moderators or, the practice in Sussex, 'four of the best learned ministers or more of that deanery'. Such at least were the arrangements on paper. It was hoped that regular attendance and examination, which in practice extended beyond matters academic to investigation of lives and conduct, would equip the unlearned to take their turns in the public proceedings. These, in the words of a Leicestershire preacher, were the 'universities of the pore ministers'.[50]

After Queen Elizabeth's direct intervention to suppress the prophesyings, the role of the learned clergy as monitors of the unlearned was salvaged in a revised form, especially by Bishop Cooper of Lincoln, and later recommended to the Church at large in the orders 'for the better increase of learning in the inferior ministers' which were drawn up by Convocation in 1587. These orders envisaged the appointment of 'certain grave and learned preachers' as supervisors, with six or seven of the unlearned assigned to each. In the diocese of Norwich 'commissioners of the exercise' were appointed by formal patent, and at Colchester lists of preachers and of those who were 'no preachers but tied to the exercises' were entered in the act book of the archdeacon's court and regularly revised. In the Jacobean Church the abler clergy continued to be appointed as academic supervisors and examiners of their feebler brethren and consequently to exercise effective control over the granting of preaching licences and the admission to their own privileged circle of 'sufficient' ministers.[51]

IV

It is time to look back over the ground which has been covered and to assess its significance for the progressive professionalization of the clergy. Given the poor quality of those ordained in the early Elizabethan Church and the extreme poverty of thousands of parochial livings, any effort made to realize the ideal of a godly, preaching, professional ministry tended to

[50] John Ireton to Anthony Gilby, May 1576; Cambridge University Library, MS Mm.1.43, p. 452.

[51] Collinson, 'Puritan Classical Movement', pp. 249–59. For the Jacobean continuation of these arrangements I am dependent upon information communicated by Kenneth Fincham of University College, London.

divide the Church into two unequal tiers. This stratification was implicit in the ordination policy of some bishops, particularly of Edmund Grindal.[52] Both as bishop of London and as archbishop of York, Grindal conducted general ordinations, which in the early days in London were mass ordinations, a necessity if the parishes were to be served. But on special and even somewhat private occasions Grindal ordained and subsequently took pains to place better-qualified men. In Yorkshire in 1570 this was a small leaven in a very large lump. The efforts of conscientious patrons (according to Rosemary O'Day never more than a minority of patrons)[53] to attract competent clergy and to top up inadequate livings had a similar effect, creating oases of pastoral excellence. A learned clergy was created here and there, and the pastoral ministry acquired a professionalized upper tier.

Some of the continuing efforts to reform the ministry accentuated the gap between the professional and subprofessional strata. Among other things the so-called 'classical movement' of the Elizabethan presbyterians was an élitist response to a situation of widespread dereliction. In such circles the doctrine gained ground that the non-preaching ministry was no ministry at all and that the godly should reject it.[54] Yet in opposition to such semi-separatist tendencies, the enterprise of prophesyings and exercises together with many practical necessities of ecclesiastical administration invested the professionalized upper tier of the clergy with many responsibilities towards their less qualified brethren. With the passage of time there was hope of bridging the gulf and homogenizing the ministry on a common basis of professional competence.

Nevertheless much of the manpower brought into the Church in the lean years was as irredeemable as the clergy and schoolmasters of Baxter's youth. In the event, the transformation came not from within but by the infusion of a new kind of recruit, a graduate or at least a product of the country grammar schools with some experience of higher education.

---

[52] Collinson, *Archbishop Grindal*, pp. 112–15, 205–12.
[53] O'Day, *The English Clergy*, p. 86; O'Day, 'Clerical Patronage and Recruitment', p. 164.
[54] Collinson, *Elizabethan Puritan Movement*, p. 390.

Rosemary O'Day has shown that this revolution in recruitment was brought about almost suddenly, within a generation, but with a time-lag between the more or less developed localities. By the end of the sixteenth century, the city of London already pointed to the future. Three-quarters of its incumbents and half of its parochial curates were graduates.[55]

In London, the lateral split between professionals and subprofessionals may have all but disappeared. This was not to be looked for in the country, even in the favourable situation which obtained in what a preacher called 'that fruitfull and rich shire of Suffolk'.[56] In the 1640s the Suffolk Committee for Scandalous Ministers was bombarded with complaints against clerical alehouse-haunters, and it was still an unfulfilled ambition of Sir Simonds D'Ewes, a Suffolk MP, to change the 'greater part of the clergy from brazen, leaden–yea, and blockish persons–to a golden and primitive condition'.[57]

In Jacobean Herefordshire and Shropshire, the situation was much more unfavourable, resembling that of more 'civil' counties fifty years earlier. Learning was still at a premium and preaching a scarce commodity: the pastoral desert described by Baxter. In these circumstances, the minority of preaching ministers, clients of the godly Harley family of Brampton Bryan, assumed a relation to the common run of clergy reminiscent of the days of the Elizabethan prophesyings. On his arrival in Herefordshire, the Harleys' own minister, Thomas Pierson, organized the other public preachers, eight in all, to form a combination lecture[58] at Leintwardine which was licensed by the bishop, perhaps at Sir Robert Harley's prompting. Like the old prophesyings and unlike most Jacobean combinations, this lecture was under the authority of four moderators, of whom Pierson was one, who

---

[55] H. G. Owen, 'Parochial Curates in Elizabethan London', *Journal of Ecclesiastical History,* x (1959), 66–73.

[56] The phrase occurs in a sermon preached in Constantinople at the funeral of the wife of the ambassador, Lady Anne Glover, a native of Suffolk, *ob.* 1608. (William Forde, *A sermon preached at Constantinople in the vines of Perah* (1616), p. 74.)

[57] *Suffolk Committees for Scandalous Ministers,* 9.

[58] For combination lectures, see my 'Lectures by Combination: Structures and Characteristics of Church Life in 17th-Century England', *Bulletin of the Institute of Historical Research,* xlviii (1975), 182–213.

had power to call before them the non-preaching ministers of the deanery, 'such as they thought fit', and to set them exercises on the articles of the Creed or the Lord's Prayer or the Decalogue. Not surprisingly, some of the clergy resented these arrangements, thinking it beneath their dignity 'to be dealt with like schooleboys'. They were told that they must graduate in this school and show some readiness to preach in their own cures before being admitted to preach in the public congregation. Lectures on the same pattern are said to have been set up in many other parts of Herefordshire, Shropshire, and Radnorshire, mainly through Pierson's 'encouragement'.[59]

Slightly more favourable conditions may have prevailed in Somerset, where Richard Bernard, a veteran preacher and controversialist who was rector of Batcombe, was said to have been 'a *leader* and *patterne*' in the weekly lectures. 'Divers painfull and profitable labourers in the Lords Vineyard had their first *initiation* and *direction* from and under him.' At the turn of the century there was still an acute shortage of preaching ministers in parts of Somerset. In 1608 the vicar of Pitminster, preaching in London at Paul's Cross, thought that scarcely one in five congregations enjoyed 'ordinary preaching', which in consequence was enough 'to bring upon any man the crime of puritanisme', though never so conformable to the discipline established. In 1617 the vicar of Aller told James Ussher that he was 'seated in a barren place' where there was little incentive to share his learning with his neighbour ministers. Yet in 1621 Bernard could dedicate a textbook on homiletics to no less than twenty-eight preachers among the incumbents of Bath and Wells (including these two complainers) and in these terms: 'Preaching is, as you well know (right worshipfull and brethren beloved) . . . '.[60]

---

[59] BL Harleian MS 7517, fols. 20–3. I owe this reference to Jonathan Harris of the University of Sydney. The monthly combination lecture founded at Bishop's Castle, Shropshire, by Walter Stephens, which continued until 1660, was said to have begun when Mr Stephens lit his candle from Mr Pierson. (Ibid., fol. 35ᵛ.) Sir Robert Harley included among 'matters of petition', at a fast the following note: 'For . . . Brampton, Wigmore, Leyntwardine, Ayltones etc. exercises, Lemister, Webley, Sallop etc.' (BL Loan 29/202, Harley Papers i, 1582–1629, fol. 238ʳ.) 'Ayltones' is Elton.

[60] Preface by John Conant to Richard Bernard, *Thesaurus Biblicus seu premptuarium sacrum* (1644); Clarke, *Lives of Ten Eminent Divines* (1662), p. 30; William Sclater, vicar

Lincolnshire provides another and perhaps more typical and central example. In 1614 it was said that the preachers of the market town lectures in the county despised the clergy 'not of their company' as at best 'good moral men' and dumb dogs.[61] These were the sort described in 1603, more charitably and officially, as 'honest ministers, well hable to catechize, and privately to exhorte, though they have not the guifte of utterance and audacitie to preche in the pulpit'. At that date 646 out of 1,184 clergy in the diocese of Lincoln were graduates and a somewhat larger number, 712, were licensed preachers.[62] So above the lateral division there was now a large and even dominant body of more or less competent clergy who set the tone for the Church as a whole. This thick upper crust must have corresponded approximately to that economically privileged section of the beneficed clergy, chiefly the rectors, which through rising incomes derived from the collection of tithe in kind and the exploitation of glebe land had greatly improved its living standards in a period of buoyant agricultural prices.[63]

In measure as professional competence, particularly preaching ability, ceased to be the mark of an exclusive minority and began to characterize a moral majority of the ministry we should expect the professional and social interaction of the clergy to move towards what George Herbert called 'good correspondence with all the neighbouring pastors',[64] a state of settled professional parity. Puritan conferences and *classes* had

---

of Pitminster, *A threefold preservative against three dangerous diseases of these latter times* (1610), p. 30; Ralph Cudworth, vicar of Aller, to James Ussher, 1617, Bodleian Library, Rawlinson MS Letters 89, fol. 25; Richard Bernard, *The faithfull shepherd: wholy in a manner transposed and made anew, and very much inlarged* (1621), Epistle. I owe the references to Conant, Sclater, and Cudworth to Kenneth Fincham.

[61] Cambridge University Library, Baumgartner MS 8, fol. 201.

[62] *State of the Church*, lii–lix. Canon Foster argues convincingly for preferring these figures from the *Libri Cleri* to the more optimistic figures returned to the archbishop and presented to the king in 1603.

[63] F. W. Brooks, 'The Social Position of the Parson in the Sixteenth Century', *Journal of British Archaeological Society*, 3rd ser. x (1945–7), 23–37; Barratt, 'The Condition of the Parochial Clergy', p. 197; Philip Tyler, 'The Status of the Elizabethan Parochial Clergy', *Studies in Church History*, iv, ed. G. J. Cuming (Leiden, 1967), 90–1; Hoskins, 'The Leicestershire Country Parson', 89–114.

[64] Herbert, *Priest to the Temple*, p. 76.

reflected a grossly unequal situation. The prophesyings had entrusted a small élite with the task of redeeming the profession, or rather of creating a profession out of unpromising materials. But Jacobean 'clergy councels' were devoted to the support and advancement of individuals within a profession which was tending to be an accomplished and secure fact.

As a model of this kind of 'correspondence' we may refer to the way of life of 'that famous Grecian' John Bois, himself a good example of solid academic learning applied to a rustic ministry.[65] Bois was the son of a Suffolk parsonage and a product of a country grammar school, at Hadleigh. He was a fellow of St. John's College, Cambridge, for fifteen years and a lecturer in Greek for ten, one of the translators of the Authorized Version and a contributor to Sir Henry Savile's great edition of Chrysostom. It was Bois's habit to give lectures in Greek from his bed to pupils who 'preferred their nightly studies before their rest and ease'.[66] He ended his days as a canon of Ely. But first came thirty-three long years as a country parson at Boxworth near Cambridge. And here, says his biographer, 'when he began to be acquainted in the Country with his Neighbour-Ministers he agreed with, I think, twelve of them to meet every Friday at one of their Houses at Dinner, by Course: and there to give an Account of their Study; and by Joynt Help to discuss and resolve Doubts and Questions propounded by any of them, to the publique Benefit of them all.' This circle makes a nice contrast with Baxter's Shropshire dozen, while its tactful appearance of informality and parity contrasts with the heavy magisterial hand of Thomas Pierson in contemporary Herefordshire. How pleased a certain Emmanuel man exiled to deepest Somerset would have been to have found himself a member of Bois's study circle. In 1617 Ralph Cudworth, vicar of Aller and father of a more famous son of the same name, the Cambridge

---

[65] Anthony Walker, 'The Life of that famous Grecian Mr John Bois, S.T.B., one of the translators of the Bible', in *Desiderata Curiosa,* ed. Francis Peck (1735), ii. VIII. 36–58; supplemented by *DNB,* art. Bois.

[66] The London preacher Thomas Gataker was one of those who attended these lectures. He kept the notes 'as a treasure' and showed them to Bois many years later, 'to the no small joy of the good old man, who professed that he was made some years younger by that grateful entertainment.' (Clarke, *Lives of Thirty-Two English Divines,* p. 249.)

Platonist, told Archbishop Ussher: 'I should desire noe greater earthly blessing, then to live in that or such like societie, where I might have the continuall companie of learned men, to conferre together about Controversies and Antiquitie: and if I might have their good company either there or elsewhere, I should think myselfe happy.' The statutes of Emmanuel forbade the indefinite enjoyment of such amenities in Cambridge, and Cudworth had been forced out into what he called 'a barren place, where my neighbour ministers either want skill and cannot, or have some skill and will not conferre together about matters of learning.'[67]

At the risk of harping on a tedious refrain, it must be said that Jacobean clerical societies are an obscure as well as a neglected subject. But they are retrievable through the 'lecture by combination', an enterprise to which many such circles were devoted and which, as I have argued elsewhere, was the most characteristic institution of the Jacobean Church.[68] Information which can be gathered from almost every part of the country suggests that it was a nearly universal practice of the more capable clergy to take their turns in preaching a lecture in the local market town, usually on market-day. Such exercises were attended by the remainder of 'the company' and were followed by dinner, with table-talk about matters of common and professional concern. At Leintwardine, for example, the setting up of the lecture led naturally to the provision of an 'ordinary' 'where the ministers might dine together by themselves without any other company', and after dinner debate some question in controversy, or a case of conscience, or some difficult place of Scripture.[69]

Such arrangements had obtained in many market towns since the time of the prophesyings. At Bury St. Edmunds the weekly market-day lecture was a continuous tradition for more than sixty years. In the early days of this institution a Suffolk preacher remarked that 'your townsmen of Burie are such diligent hearers of the Word on the Monday exercises

[67] Ralph Cudworth, vicar of Aller, to James Ussher, 1617; Bodleian Library, Rawlinson MS Letters 89, fol. 25. I owe this reference to Kenneth Fincham.

[68] Collinson, 'Lectures by Combination'.

[69] BL Harleian MS 7517. fols. 20–3.

that they may easily be singled out from other men'.[70] Richard Carew's *Survey of Cornwall* describes the arrangements at the other end of England, at Saltash, in late Elizabethan days.[71] The 'neighbourhood ministers successively bestowed their pains in the preaching there on the market days, and the bordering gentlemen yielded their presence.' These 'bordering gentlemen' included Carew himself and Sir Anthony Rous, father of Francis Rous and stepfather of John Pym. 'Sermon ended', continues Carew's account, 'the preachers resorted to one ordinary and the gentlemen to another. This afforded commendable effects to many works of love and charity.' By the time Carew wrote, this exercise had been 'wholly given over', as one would expect in the diocese of Exeter under the unsympathetic Bishop Cotton.[72] But in all probability, like the lecture at Leicester, it was later 'restored again'.[73] A generation later Bishop Hall spoke of 'willingly giving way to orthodox and peaceable lecturers'.[74] John Ley described how the clergy made their way to dinner after the exercise at Winwick in Lancashire, in the days of Charles I: 'Our sermon ended, and some of us invited to a place of convenient repose, the rest of our Tribe . . . resorted unto us, every man accompanying his acquaintance and so making as it were a whole chaine of many linkes'—a precious clue to the structure of these clerical circles.[75]

The prevalence of combination lecturing by the second and third decades of the seventeenth century is conveyed in an account of the Cheshire exercises, written in 1641: 'The

---

[70] Rogers, *Miles Christianus*, p. 17.

[71] Richard Carew, *Survey of Cornwall* (1602), pp. 112–13. I owe this reference to Jonathan Vage of St. Catherine's College, Cambridge. For the involvement of Carew and Rous see the testimonials signed at Saltash in 1585 for the Scottish minister John Cowper, by seven 'brethren of the exercise' and six Cornish JPs. (*The Warrender Papers*, ed. A. L. Cameron and R. S. Rait, i, Scottish Historical Society xviii (Edinburgh, 1931), 203–4.)

[72] Cassidy, 'The Episcopate of William Cotton'.

[73] Cambridge University Library, Baumgartner MS 8, fol. 200ᵛ.

[74] *Works of Hall,* i, xlvi.

[75] John Ley, *Defensive doubts and reasons for refusall of the oath* (1641), sig. a4. And see the defence offered by a curate of Aldeburgh to a charge of drunkenness: 'He goinge to the Lecture [at Saxmundham] (as he constantly did yf he were at whome) on foote, which is five myles from Aldeburgh, where dyninge with the Ministers, it beeing very late, he stayed there . . .'. (*Suffolk Committees for Scandalous Ministers,* 118.)

ministers had their spiritually glorious monthly exercises at Northwich, Namptwich, Knutsford, Macclesfield, Bowden, Frodsham, Budworth, Torpolley [Tarporley], Tarvin, Ince, Motteram etc.' Within the 'etc.' we may include the little market town of Congleton.[76] As the language of this account suggests, combination lectures were a feature of the Calvinist ascendancy in the early seventeenth-century Church. But they were not a cave of Adullam for disaffected puritans. When Bishop Williams of Lincoln delivered his judgement in the Grantham altar dispute he communicated it to 'the Divines of the Lecture of *Grantham,* to be examined by them upon their next meeting-day'. This was so that the formalist vicar who had occasioned the dispute by positioning the Communion- table altar-wise 'being one of their company, might read the Contents'.[77]

It is a grave distortion of early seventeenth-century ecclesi- astical history which has largely overlooked this important and typical institution and has associated 'lecturing' almost exclusively with the activities of unbeneficed, stipendiary preachers, called by Christopher Hill 'a free-lance clergy' and by a contemporary writer an 'anti-clergy'.[78] Stipendiary lecturers, to be sure, were no figment of an overwrought historical imagination. They existed in some strength, a 'popular' and sometimes disruptive element. It is possible that these 'ambitious' men and their aiders and abetters did some of the harm with which they were credited by the Laudian divines, and later by Thomas Hobbes. But the seventy 'lecturers' named in a report submitted to Bishop Neile of Lincoln in 1614 were, almost without exception, beneficed country clergy who came into the market towns of Lincoln- shire to take their turns in the combination, to dine together, and to confer on clergy matters, conducting themselves within

---

[76] Thomas Paget, brother of the more celebrated John Paget, incumbent of Blackley, Lancashire, and author of the preface attached to his brother's *Defence of church government* (1641). I owe this reference to Geoffrey Nuttall.

[77] John Hacket, *Scrinia Reserata: A Memoriall Offer'd to the Great Deservings of John Williams D.D.* (1693), ii. 101. See also copies of Williams's letter to the vicar, Mr Tittley, BL Add. MS 29584, fols. 1–2, Harleian MS 1219, fols. 41–7.

[78] Christopher Hill, *Society and Puritanism in Pre-Revolutionary England* (1966), pp. 80, 79. See also Paul S. Seaver, *The Puritan Lectureships: The Politics of Religious Dissent 1560–1662* (Stanford, 1970).

arrangements which the bishops of the diocese had approved.[79] It was a serious error for Mark Curtis, in an influential essay, to mistake these 'lecturers' for lecturers in the stipendiary sense and then, observing that virtually all of them were graduates, to cite them as examples of 'surplus clergymen', some of the 'alienated intellectuals of early Stuart England'.[80]

Combination lecturing was not a symptom of alienation from a Church incapable of employing its sons or of satisfying the religious aspirations of society. On the contrary, it was typical and symbolic of a satisfactory adjustment of the clergy to social realities, and to religious and social needs as these were perceived by those exercising dominance in provincial affairs. By providing this service, over and above their parochial duties, and usually for the price of their dinner and a cup of wine, the Jacobean clergy helped themselves. It was observed in Norfolk that among the 'utilities' of preaching in market towns was 'advauncement to the clergie men, when their guiftes shalbe knowne'. But market-town preaching benefited society equally, not only by what our Norfolk observer called 'the propagation of the ghospell and edefieng of the Church' but also materially: 'Benefit also to the inhabitauntes for their markett, by concurse of people.'[81] An account of the market-day combination at Cranbrook in Kent illustrates the mutually profitable coexistence of preaching and commerce. Cranbrook, Mr Secretary Walsingham was informed, was a town 'where the use or trade of good clothing doth alwayes nouryshe a great nomber of yong people, and where the conveniencye and necessitie of the market dothe once a weeke of all sortes and of all quarters moche encrease that nomber of people'. Set preaching in this ready market for religion and 'very likely yt ys that towardes thamendment of

---

[79] Cambridge University Library, Baumgartner MS 8, fols. 220–2.

[80] Mark Curtis, 'The Alienated Intellectuals of Early Stuart England', *Past and Present*, xxiii (1962), reprinted in *Crisis in Europe, 1550–1660*, ed. T. Aston (1965), pp. 295–316. Since this chapter was completed, an important critique of Curtis's scenario of academic over-production and ecclesiastical unemployment has appeared in print: Ian Green, 'Career Prospects and Clerical Conformity in the Early Stuart Church', *Past and Present*, xc (1981), 71–115.

[81] *Registrum Vagum of Anthony Harison*, i, ed. T. F. Barton, Norfolk Record Society xxxii (Norwich, 1963), 97.

men's maners yt wolde be a matter of moche moment'.[82] It matters little whether trade drew a market for religion or religion attracted customers for the traders. It was a case of true symbiosis.

This glimpse of what (in a sense) was 'popular religion' leads us away from the clerical themes which have occupied us in these first three chapters, and towards the more expansive and challenging subject of the religion of protestants in its social setting, to which the remainder of this book is devoted.

---

[82] Thomas Wotton to Sir Francis Walsingham, 3 May 1579; *Thomas Wotton's Letter-Book 1574–1586*, ed. G. Eland (1960), pp. 24–5.

Chapter Four

Magistracy and Ministry

I

In 1607 the churchwardens of the Norwich parish of St. Andrew's were required by the diocesan chancellor to remove from their church what the parish in an appeal to the bishop described as 'divers convenient seates', only recently erected. Disputes over seating were endemic in parish life and they normally reflected contests for social precedence. But this was an unusual case, its nature public rather than private. For the seats in question were not family pews but stalls for publicly notable figures: 'in which seates', the parishioners explained, 'the ministers of the citty were placed in one roumthe, and in another, next them, the aldermen.'[1]

The scandal of these seats leads us at once to a paradox. St. Andrew's was one of those rare churches where the parishioners had possession of the tithe income, together with a privilege which the puritans everywhere so ardently desired: the legal right to choose their own pastor. Indeed, these Norwich parishioners supported as many as three preaching ministers from an augmented income.[2] For twenty years, until his death in 1592, the church was dominated by one of the most celebrated preachers of his time, John More, known as 'the apostle of Norwich'. His successors included the future pastor to the Pilgrim Fathers, John Robinson, and the Suffolk sabbatarian writer Nicholas Bownd, who was More's literary executor and married his widow.[3] So St. Andrew's, like the

---

[1] *The Registrum Vagum of Anthony Harison*, ed. T. F. Barton, ii, Norfolk Record Society, xxxiii (Norwich, 1964), 279–80. Archbishop Neile of York recalled that in his time as bishop of Winchester 'noe causes perteyninge to the ecclesiasticall jurisdiction under him were more frequent then broyles about seates'. (*Reports of Cases in the Courts of Star Chamber and High Commission*, ed. S. R. Gardiner, Camden NS xxxix (1886), 140.)

[2] Francis Blomefield, *A Topographical History of Norfolk*, iv (1806), 301.

[3] Champlin Burrage, *New Facts Concerning John Robinson, Pastor of the Pilgrim Fathers* (Oxford, 1910), pp. 5–17, 32–3. In dedicating More's *A table from the beginning of the world to this day* (Cambridge, 1593) to Bishop Scambler of Norwich, Bownd said that

London parishes of Holy Trinity Minories, St. Ann's, Blackfriars, and St. Stephen's, Coleman Street, was virtually a gathered puritan congregation and the refuge of a religious remnant, or élite. Their early morning devotion to preaching, psalm-singing, and prayer earned them a local nickname: 'Saint *Andrewes* birds'. In 1589 it was said that to be a member of this flock was 'a riote of a Brownist, a Puritane and a disobedient person'.[4] When the churchwardens resisted the order relating to the seating in their church, they were summarily excommunicated and the whole parish was reviled in the ecclesiastical court as schismatics, factious persons, and 'contemners of authoritie'. Yet as these 'contemners of authoritie' were quick to protest, some of them had borne the highest offices in the government of their great and wealthy city.[5] Herein was the paradox. The presence of the disputed seating was itself proof that St. Andrew's was no back-street conventicle but a civic church. In August 1603, when John Robinson preached the thanksgiving sermon for the Gowrie Conspiracy, his auditory at St. Andrew's included the mayor and his brethren. Some of the leading gentry of the county were willing to testify that his sermon on this occasion had not been 'factious'. 'I would not wryte for eny that I knewe factious', wrote Sir Henry Gaudy to the bishop.[6]

Although the seats were new, the tradition of civic godliness at St. Andrew's had been established thirty years earlier, by John More. The stigma of 'factious person' sits uneasily on Mr More. He was said to have grown the longest and largest beard of his time so that no act of his life should be unworthy the gravity of his appearance.[7] Nicholas Bownd recalled his

---

the work had come into his hands 'by a certaine hereditarie right'. Bownd's mother married as her second husband Richard Greenham, and his sister married John Dod. This was sabbatarian as well as clerical tribalism.

[4] William Burton, *A sermon preached in the cathedrall church in Norwich, the xxi day of December 1589* (n.d.), sig. G4ᵛ.

[5] *The Registrum Vagum of Anthony Harison*, ed. T. F. Barton, i, Norfolk Record Society, xxxii (Norwich, 1963), 279–80.

[6] *Registrum Vagum*, i. 34–6, 156–7, 158–9; ii. 344.

[7] *DNB*, art. More. Cf. what was said of the preacher William Gouge: that 'toward his latter end', in visage he did 'much resemble the Picture that is usually made for *Moses*. Certainly he was the exact *Effigies* of *Moses* his spirit.' (Samuel Clarke, *A*

'continuall grave carriage of himselfe in the whole course of his life, which worthily did purchase him great reverence amongst all'. In twenty years this John Knox of East Anglia preached 'many hundred Sermons, or rather certaine thousandes'.[8] He was the author of a catechism which remained in print for sixty years, and which seems to have served as a standard of sound doctrine for the sermon-goers of Norfolk.[9] He was the adviser on religious affairs of leading Norfolk families.[10] In the words of William Burton's idealized description of life in John More's Norwich, 'heavenly harmony and sweete amitie' prevailed, 'the magistrates and the ministers imbracing and seconding one another, and the common people affording due reverence and obedience to them both'. The magistrates concluded no matters of weight for the good of their city without first consulting with the grave and godly preachers. These 'worthy senatours and governors' graced the daily sermons with their presence and took the preachers back to their houses: 'whither some went, all went . . . all were imbraced alike'.[11] In their public appearance and performance, the ministers were careful to preserve parity and

Collection of the Lives of Ten Eminent Divines (1662), pp. 114–15.) Compare also John Earle's character of an alderman: 'He is venerable in his Gowne, more in his Beard, wherein he setts not forth his owne so much as the Face of a City.' (*The Autograph Manuscript of Microcosmographie* (Leeds, 1966), p. 17.)

[8] John More, *Three godly and fruitfull sermons* (1594), Epistle.

[9] Patrick Collinson, *A Mirror of Elizabethan Puritanism: The Life and Letters of 'Godly Master Dering'*, Friends of Dr Williams's Library 17th Lecture 1963 (1964), pp. 9–10. In 1592 John Trendle of Overington was presented at the archdeacon's visitation for catechizing 'but not the Catechisme articulate but with Mr Mores'. (R. G. Usher, *The Reconstruction of the English Church* (1910), i. 263.)

[10] There is a letter from More to Nathaniel Bacon, 27 November 1575, ending: 'Let every one praye for an other. Yours in the Lorde, John More.' (BL Add. MS 41140, fol. 9.) See another letter from More to Lady Knyvett, 8 December 1587 which ends: 'My wyfe doth send her humble commendacions to yow with most harty thanks for all yor kyndnes and for your last token sent by Mr Portman. Yor loving brother in the Lord Jesus, J. Moore.' (BL Egerton MS 2713, fols. 210–11ʳ.) More's mental world is neatly defined in this entry for 1564 in his *Table from the beginning of the world* (p. 223): 'CALVIN dyed Maii. THAMES frozen. OWSE bridge down.' The road from Cambridge to Norwich passed over the Little Ouse.

[11] William Burton, *Seven dialogues both pithie and profitable* (1606), sig. A2. Cf. what was said of Walter Stephens, minister at Bishop's Castle in Shropshire for more than fifty years up to his death in 1629: 'He was so grave and discreet, that the grave Religious Aldermen of his Towne would not act any thing of importance without him.' It was said that the town was 'famoused from him'. (BL Harleian MS 7517, fols. 35ʳ, 36ʳ.)

decorum, never publicly contradicting or confuting one another.[12] If there was any 'contemning of authority' and disobedience in this self-contained East Anglian Geneva it arose from the scorn and contempt of 'the multitude', those godless and covetous inhabitants who 'for a fashion' heard the preacher but went home to jest at him 'their bellyesfull'. Or so Burton alleged in a sensational sermon preached in the cathedral for which he was deemed 'an enemy to Caesar' by the ecclesiastical authorities, deprived of his living and driven out of the city. Burton asked why he had suffered this fate while 'rebellious and obstinate disobeyers both of God and man' were allowed to hurl accusations of disobedience at the most religious and law-abiding element in the community. 'They crie obedience to the law, when no man doe more disobey it then they doe.'[13]

Burton was an outspoken presbyterian and nonconformist.[14] By 1607 the vestrymen of St. Andrew's were careful to avoid such provocations, insisting that they had no quarrel with 'the good order of the Church government established by the lawes of this realme'. But this could not save them from a humiliation which was all the more scandalous for its occurrence in open court, with 'advantage geven to the meaner sorte and some of evill disposition to breake forthe to contemne us and our government'.[15] A generation later, the high Laudian Bishop Wren constrained an unwilling mayor, sheriff, and aldermen to attend a sermon in the cathedral and seated them inconveniently, in a draughty position under a public gallery. From this gallery a Bible dropped on the mayor's head, shattering his spectacles, while worse indignities

---

[12] 'The Order of the Prophesie at Norwich in Anno 1575, Began *Sede Vacante*', Dr Williams's Library, MS 'Seconde Parte of a Register', i. 268–70; printed, J. Browne, *History of Congregationalism and Memorials of the Churches in Norfolk and Suffolk* (1877), pp. 18–20.

[13] Burton, *Sermon preached in the cathedrall church in Norwich*, sig. D4ᵛ, Epistle, sig. Hᵛ.

[14] It is doubtful whether the same could be said of John More in his later years. His *Table from the beginning of the world* was published posthumously by Nicholas Bownd, who dedicated it to Bishop Scambler 'under whose governement hee [sc., More] happelie enjoyed great libertie in his ministerie'. (Epistle dated from Norton, Suffolk, 24 August 1593.)

[15] *Registrum Vagum*, ii, 279–80.

were visited on the aldermen when a sailor defecated on the gown of one and a man spat on the head of another.[16]

The spectre of inverted or confused values which haunted the 'Saint Andrewes birds' of Norwich had its parallels in many places in Elizabethan and Jacobean England. In 1589 there were demonstrations and counter-demonstrations in and around Banbury, when one party took direct action to pull down the traditional maypoles and to suppress the seasonal festivities of maygames and Whitsun ales, which the contrary faction defended. Each side accused the other of provoking riot and disobedience and each claimed to have the law on its side. The opponents of carnival included a Banbury mercer who was high constable of the hundred, Richard Whateley, and the JP and parliament man Sir Anthony Cope. They also claimed the support of a deputy lieutenant, Lord Norris. Their opponents were headed by the sheriff of the county, John Danvers, a suspected church papist. The Privy Council upheld the Banbury maypoles as a harmless tradition, but required that they be enjoyed in 'due and peaceable manner', without 'disorder, riotts and unlawful actes'.[17] A few years later Whateley and other members of a puritan group which by then had gained control of the town demolished famous Banbury Cross, or rather the two great market crosses, and they defaced the toppled carvings with the cry: 'God be thancked, Dagon the deluder of the people is fallen downe.' This was iconoclasm, arbitrary and tyrannical in the eyes of those who were excluded from this godly oligarchy and valued the amenity of the crosses. Nevertheless, it was not the work of a mob but the orderly iconoclasm of aldermen, bailiffs, and constables.[18]

---

[16] John T. Evans, *Seventeenth-Century Norwich: Politics, Religion and Government 1620–1690* (Oxford, 1979), p. 113.

[17] PRO S.P. 12/223/47, 224/54, 55, 57, 58, 61, 65, 66. There is an extensive account of this affair in Elliot Rose, *Cases of Conscience: Alternatives Open to Recusants and Puritans under Elizabeth I and James I* (Cambridge, 1975), pp. 169–76.

[18] PRO St. Ch. 5 B 31/4. (I possess among papers of Edna Bibby which were made available to me by Sir John Neale an undated note of *c.* 1930 to Miss Bibby from Lady Neale, then Miss Elfreda Skelton, passing on this reference. I should like to record my indebtedness to Lady Neale and, as so often before, to the late Miss Bibby.) George Blincoe, gentleman, who brought the bill of complaint against the iconoclasts in Star chamber, alleged that the defendants, some of whom were allied by marriage, had

Preaching outside Cambridge at the annual Stourbridge Fair to an audience drawn from 'the most populous cities and townes of England', William Perkins complained that 'contempt of the christian religion' was the English disease. It was bad enough to suffer the scorn of 'the simplest fellow in a countrie towne' that 'knowes not one point of religion'. But even among 'the better sort', 'such as live civilly', it was not profanity and wickedness but religion which was made 'a mocking stock and matter of reproach'. Perkins urged his congregation of merchants to 'carry home this message to your great towns and cities where you dwell, for in these populous places are the great mockers'. This sermon went into seven editions between 1604 and 1609.[19]

If it was worse to be mocked by the 'better sort' than by the 'meane sort', it was worst of all to be repudiated by the best of all. That was the ultimate scandal of the royal Book of Sports, endorsing with the highest authority Sunday recreations which the godly considered sacrilegious and unlawful.[20] The godly London turner Nehemiah Wallington recorded no less

---

'plotted and combyned betweene them selves' to retain the offices of bailiff and justice. Their government was said to have been hostile to sociable drinking and gaming. Three of the defendants, including Richard Whateley and his brother Thomas, had signed a petition on behalf of the vicar, Thomas Brasbridge, who was deprived for nonconformity in 1590. (BL Lansdowne MS 64, no. 13, fols. 43ᵛ–4ʳ.) Thomas Whateley, twice mayor of the town, was the father of the famous Banbury preacher William Whateley, the 'Roaring Boy of Banbury'. (*DNB,* art. Whateley.) The future Bishop Corbet who came out of Oxford with other wits to hear Whateley wrote verses on the headless crosses of Banbury. (*The Poems of Richard Corbett,* ed. J. A. W. Bennett and H. R. Trevor-Roper (Oxford, 1955), pp. 47–8.) For a further account of the destruction of the crosses, see *Records of the English Province of the Society of Jesus,* ed. Henry Foley, SJ, i (1872), 5–8.

[19] William Perkins, *A faithfull and plaine exposition upon the two first verses of the second chapter of Zephaniah* (1606), p. 15. Perkins's editor, William Crashawe, a preacher of Beverley, Yorkshire, specifies the towns represented in Perkins's auditory as London, York, Cambridge, Oxford, Norwich, Bristol, Ipswich, Colchester, Worcester, Hull, King's Lynn, Manchester, Kendal, Coventry, Nottingham, Northampton, Bath, Lincoln, Derby, Leicester, Chester, and Newcastle. (See J. A. Newton, 'Puritanism in the Diocese of York, Excluding Nottinghamshire, 1603–1640', London Ph.D. thesis, 1956, p. 212.)

[20] L. A. Govett, *The King's Book of Sports. A History of the Declarations of King James I and King Charles I as to the Use of Lawful Sports on Sundays* (1890). On the background to the reissue of the Declaration, see Thomas G. Barnes, 'County Politics and a Puritan Cause Célèbre: Somerset Churchales, 1633', *Transactions of the Royal Historical Society,* 5th ser. ix (1959), 103–22.

than thirteen acts of sudden divine judgement visited within the year 1634 upon those who identified themselves with 'the book of liberty' on its promulgation or who rejoiced at it. In one Sussex parish an 'honest man' was overtaken in the way by a neighbour who told him the news about the book 'and fell to scoffing and deriding . . . and asked him if he would go dance with him the next sunne day': to whom the honest man said 'Take heede that you be not dancing in Hell before that daye.' Within a week his neighbour and two more of his family were dead.[21] As late as 1740, a Cambridgeshire farmer preserved as a piece of oral tradition the horror with which the reading of the royal proclamation from the pulpits had seized the generation of his father. 'Now, thought I, iniquity is established by a law.' Defoe recorded the same tradition. Charles I was the first king in history to have 'established wickedness by a law'. When awaiting execution as a regicide, Hugh Peter remembered that it was the publication of the Book of Sports which had prompted many to leave for America. If it was disaffection, it was disaffection of a very special kind to refuse, as many did, to read the Book of Sports from the pulpit.[22]

In Salisbury, a little beyond our period, there was the *cause célèbre* of Henry Sherfield, the recorder of the city whose physical onslaught on a stained glass window in St. Edmund's church won him a £500 fine in Star Chamber, where Archbishop Laud was among his judges.[23] Here was the very situation which William Burton had envisaged at Norwich: 'When we speake against idolatrous and blasphemous pictures in churchewindowes and elsewhere . . . these men which have their mouthes full of obedience call us disobedient.'[24] Paul

---

[21] BL Sloane MS 1457, fols. 12–13. Two quaker writers told Oliver Cromwell in 1654 that God had raised him up 'and throwest down the mountains and powers of the earth before thee, which had established wickedness by a Law . . .' (*This was the word of the Lord which John Camm and Francis Howgill was moved to declare and write to Oliver Cromwell* (1654).)

[22] Margaret Spufford, *Contrasting Communities: English Villagers in the Sixteenth and Seventeenth Centuries* (Cambridge, 1974), p. 231; Christopher Hill, *Society and Puritanism in Pre-Revolutionary England* (1966), pp. 194, 202; Hugh Peter, *A dying fathers last legacy to an onely child* (1660), pp. 101–2. I owe the last reference to Susan M. Hardman.

[23] S. R. Gardiner, *History of England from the Accession of James I to the Outbreak of the Civil War* (1883–4), vii. 254–8.

[24] Burton, *Sermon preched in the cathedrall church in Norwich*, sig. Hᵛ.

Slack has explained what lay behind this episode.[25] St. Edmund's, Salisbury, like St. Andrew's, Norwich, was a church harbouring a puritan élite which, in the 1620s, assumed control of local government in a time of acute social distress. Motivated by their common religious convictions, Sherfield and his brethren devised original and ambitious remedies for the problem of poverty, which involved an onslaught on the familiar syndrome of 'drunkenness, idleness, running to the alehouse'. (In Salisbury there was one alehouse for every sixty-five inhabitants.) The most radical part of this policy was the municipalization of brewing and the appropriation of the profits to the maintenance of the workhouse.[26] These measures amounted to an imaginative attempt to abolish poverty and to erect a godly commonwealth in Salisbury, by direction from above. But they aroused resentment among what one of Sherfield's colleagues called 'the great unjust rude rabble', and the ruling group, isolated both by religion and by its adventurous social policies, was ground between upper and nether millstones. In words which echoed the complaint of the Norwich vestrymen, the earl of Dorset, one of the judges, vainly opposed a harsh sentence for Sherfield's act of inspired iconoclasm, arguing that it would provoke 'the tumult of the rude ignorant People in the Countries where this Gentleman dwelleth, and where he hath been a good Governour'. Such persons would rejoice and triumph, saying: 'This you have for your severe Government.' Salisbury under puritan rule was accused of 'inconformitie to the state governors', and Sherfield was called 'factious'. Paul Slack draws our attention to the irony of this situation. 'But in his own local community, it was Sherfield who was the representative of authority and the guardian, so it seemed, of social order. In that context, the

---

[25] Paul Slack, 'Religious Protest and Urban Authority: The Case of Henry Sherfield, Iconoclast, 1633', in *Schism, Heresy and Religious Protest, Studies in Church History*, ix, ed. Derek Baker (Cambridge, 1972), 295–302; Paul Slack, 'Poverty and Politics in Salisbury 1597–1666', in *Crisis and Order in English Towns*, ed. P. Clark and P. Slack (1972), pp. 164–203.

[26] See Frances Rose-Troup, *John White The Patriarch of Dorchester (Dorset) and the Founder of Massachusetts 1575–1645* (1930), p. 31, for details of a similar enterprise at Dorchester, Dorset, inspired by the same ideals. A hospital and workhouse having been built, a civic brewhouse was established, 'the profit thereof being wholly set apart for the maintenance of the said hospital and workhouse'.

charge that "he is an Encourager and Maintainer of all such as are ill affected Persons to their Government, and Contemners of their Authority" was completely misplaced.[27]

That this irony has sometimes been lost on historians is a tribute to Laudian and royalist controversialists whose allegations that puritanism was the root of schism and sauciness, and market towns an environment naturally disposed to faction and innovation, has enjoyed a remarkable posthumous success, among historians of more than one ideological persuasion and of none. Much depends upon what is meant by faction and innovation. Henry Sherfield and his friends were a faction, and their novel approach to the endemic social problems of their city was an innovation. But Sherfield, or John White, the 'patriarch' of Dorchester, or that most austere of urban magistrates, Ignatius Jordan of Exeter,[28] would have been astonished to learn from Paul Seaver that by taking religion and its consequences seriously these towns under such a government had already 'turned their backs on the Established Church, and by implication the Crown'.[29] In Jordan's Exeter, Wallace MacCaffrey found 'an earnest, sober and purposeful religious spirit', but 'very little evidence of overt discontent with the religion established by law'.[30] Similarly, in Norwich John Evans found that the puritans 'did not constitute a socially, religiously, or politically radical movement and the breakdown of harmony between the customary authorities of Crown, Church and Corporation which occurred in the city between 1620 and 1640 was not precipitated by them ... By the 1620s, Puritanism was a socially respectable movement with deep roots and its leaders were among the town's élite.'[31]

At another level, we have begun to appreciate that the fervently religious members of the Elizabethan and Jacobean

[27] Slack, 'Religious Protest', 301–2.

[28] Ferdinand Nicholls, *The life and death of Mr Ignatius Jurdaine* (1655): Frances Rose-Troup, 'An Exeter Worthy and his Biographer', *Transactions of the Devon Association*, xxix (1897), 350–77.

[29] Paul S. Seaver, *The Puritan Lectureships: The Politics of Religious Dissent 1560–1662* (Stanford, 1970), p. 90.

[30] Wallace T. MacCaffrey, *Exeter, 1540–1650: the Growth of an English Country Town* (Cambridge, Mass., 1958), pp. 199–200.

[31] Evans, *Seventeenth-Century Norwich*, p. 102.

Parliaments are equally miscast as 'rebels' and as an opposition, whether in the sense that parliamentary historians speak of an opposition[32] or in the psycho-sociological sense intended by Michael Walzer when he calls these political activists 'oppositional men'.[33] The political methodology of godly parliamentarians.was indeed as precocious as the social engineering of the Salisbury magistrates. And Bishop Godfrey Goodman tells us almost as much about it as Neale or Notestein when he reports that 'always the first bill that was proposed was either against papists or the Church, or for the keeping of the Sabbath, only to feel men's pulses, to see how they stood affected'.[34] Such MPs were in varying degrees hostile to the ecclesiastical hierarchy and ready to overstep what Elizabeth I and James I regarded as legitimate bounds in giving expression to their hostility and desire for ecclesiastical change. To this extent they too could be represented as 'contemners of authority'. Yet they conducted themselves not as 'oppositional men' but out of a high sense of public obligation as the representative of other 'gentlemen of greatest worship' in their countries, expressing what was alleged to be 'the grief of the whole realm'.[35] Like Sherfield of Salisbury, in their own localities such men were not 'contemners of authority' but authority itself. Their desire for religious reform was not part of a wider interest in political reform, it was not an expression of social anomy, and it was not in any proper sense of the term revolutionary. On the contrary, it was consistent with an intensely conservative world view. It would be crassly reductionist to dismiss gentry puritanism as no more than the ideological expression of the material interests of landowners and urban oligarchs. But it is apparent that urban magistrates, gentlemen, and noblemen too, perceived no conflict between evangelical protestantism and the social status and public responsibilities of magnates and notables.

Within these mental perspectives, the institutional Church, in so far as it was deficient in its proper role of proclaiming the

[32] J. E. Neale, *Elizabeth I and her Parliaments, 1584-1601* (1957), pp. 77, 436-7.

[33] Michael Walzer, *The Revolution of the Saints: A Study in the Origins of Radical Politics* (1966), p. 3.

[34] *The Court of King James the First, by Godfrey Goodman*, ed. J. S. Brewer (1839), i. 86.

[35] Neale, *Elizabeth I and her Parliaments, 1584-1601*, pp. 61, 64.

Gospel and exerting a religious and moral discipline, was worse than unsatisfactory. It was actively subversive of order and good government, in the same way that popery, false religion on a global scale, was seen as an intelligent and malevolent principle of subversion. In a famous sermon of the 1580s,[36] the first master of Emmanuel, Laurence Chaderton, asked how it was that in a supposedly Christian country there should be 'such a huge masse of olde and stinkinge workes, of conjuringe, witchcraft, sorcerie, charming, of blaspheming the holie name of God, swearing and foreswearing, prophaning of the Lord's Sabbothes, disobedience to superiores, contempt to inferioures, murther, manslaughter, robberies, adulterye, fornication, covenauntbreakers, falsewitnesse bearing, liars, with all kindes of unmercifull dealing with one another?' He found the answer in the lack of ecclesiastical discipline. 'Wee lacke Elders and Governoures of everye congregation.' In the view of this presbyterian, the disorder of society was due to a profound and structural disorder in the Church, whereby its proper assets were misappropriated by archbishops and bishops and the rest of the hierarchy—'all such as be rather members and parts of the whore and strumpet of Rome'. Yet even in the terms of this extreme diagnosis, which for most Jacobean divines in the puritan tradition would have been too radical in its pessimism, there was no suggestion of equivalent structural faults in the secular order of society. The social hierarchy of degrees and the distinction of callings was exactly as it ought to be, requiring only that order should be preserved by each member respecting his proper place. In a somewhat

---

[36] *A fruitfull sermon upon the 3.4.5.6.7. and 8. verses of the 12 Chapiter of the Epistle of S. Paul to the Romanes* (1584). This sermon was anonymously published but widely attributed to Chaderton. See, for example, *Mr Henry Barrowes platform* (1593): 'Mr Chaderton of Emmanuel College in Cambridge hath truely taught and confidently affirmed in his Sermon in Rom. 12.' See also the dialogue by the reformed separatist Henoch Clapham, *Errour on the right 'hand* (1608), where the character of *Mal-content*, intended for a non-separating puritan, claimed credit for the sermon and *Flyer*, perhaps intended for the separatist leader Francis Johnson, responded: 'And if you remember, I was one of your Classis, when in Cambridge you (in secret) chattred out that Sermon upon Rom. 12 which afterwards was published without name: because (it seemeth) you were not minded for it publiquely to take up Christ's crosse and to follow him.' (pp.3–4.) I am indebted to Peter Lake's discussion of the sermon in 'Laurence Chaderton and the Cambridge Moderate Puritan Tradition, 1570–1604', Cambridge, Ph.D. thesis, 1978, pp. 43 ff.

tautological diagnosis, Chaderton attributed the cause of all
disorder, at home and abroad, in public and private persons,
in commonwealth and Church, in towns, universities, and
cities, to neglect and transgression of 'this general lawe and
commaundement of God' in respect of order. And the essence
of that transgression was ambition, 'proud and high lookes'. It
is significant that the preacher gave a central place in his
catalogue of disorders to 'disobedience to superiores' and
'contempt to inferiores'.

Above all other callings, Chaderton valued the magistrate.
For it was the task of 'the Lord's servauntes in magistracie' to
establish all those within their charge and jurisdiction in their
proper stations. 'For none in the Church and house of God
must wante his office: none must walk inordinately: none
must be idle in his calling and unprofitable.' 'For God is not
the author of confusion, but of good order, and necessary
distinction.' Chaderton imagined a perfect congruence between the Church as it ought to be and the commonwealth as
it already in principle was. Puritan magistrates knew that they
were already performing their proper functions in offices
which enjoyed divine as well as political sanction. Where the
preaching ministry was locally an established fact, as for
example in Elizabethan Norwich, they were already 'sec-
onded' by the most essential part of what the Church had to
contribute to the maintenance of order. And for what was still
lacking, the corrupt structure and government of the hierarchical Church bore the blame. This was the scenario acted out
in Norwich Cathedral in 1640, when Bishop Wren ushered the
mayor and his brethren into seats where they were exposed to
the gross insults of the rabble in the gallery.[37]

So the protestant governing class progressed from the
Elizabethan demand for a new religious order to the Jacobean
enjoyment of such an order, already partly achieved. And
when in the reign of Charles I that order appeared in danger
of overthrow by a new conjunction of the forces which had
never ceased to threaten it, the reaction was defensive and
conservative. But whether in assertion or defence, the animat-
ing spirit was not one of disobedience or ill-affection but of a

---

[37] Evans, *Seventeenth-Century Norwich*, p. 113.

profound veneration for order and a strong disposition towards obedience: the double need to obey God and his earthly representatives, and in turn to exact the obedience due from inferiors.

II

I hope that it is something more relevant than mere loyalty to my native county which suggests the model of Elizabethan and Jacobean Suffolk as the closest approximation to such a godly and conservative commonwealth as Chaderton had envisaged.[38] Certainly the doctrine of the mutuality of magistracy and ministry and its authoritarian, even repressive, implications received its most eloquent expression in two Suffolk sermons preached and published in the reign of James I: one by Samuel Ward, the locally celebrated preacher of Ipswich, the other by Robert Prick, the more obscure minister of the tiny parish of Denham, near Bury St. Edmunds.

Samuel Ward's *Jethros Iustice of Peace* was an assize sermon, dedicated to a lord chancellor of Suffolk stock, Sir Francis Bacon, and several times reprinted.[39] The biblical figure of Jethro, father-in-law of Moses, was both priest and prince, the archetype for what Ward called 'the principal lights' of magistracy and ministry, 'these two opticke peeces'. On these 'guardians and tutors' the health of the body politic utterly depended.[40] The office of ministers 'as God's Trumpeters and

---

[38] This may serve as a bibliography for what follows: Patrick Collinson, 'The Puritan Classical Movement in the Reign of Elizabeth I', London Ph.D. thesis, 1957, chapter 9, 'Puritanism and the Gentry in Suffolk, 1575–1585: A Case-Study', pp. 860–930; J. S. Cockburn, *A History of English Assizes, 1558–1714* (1972), pp. 199–206; Rose, *Cases of Conscience*, pp. 158–68; Patrick Collinson, 'Magistracy and Ministry: A Suffolk Miniature', in *Reformation, Conformity and Dissent: Essays in Honour of Geoffrey Nuttall*, ed. R. Buick Knox (1977), pp. 70–91; D. N. J. MacCulloch, 'Power, Privilege and the County Community: County Politics in Elizabethan Suffolk', Cambridge Ph.D. thesis, 1977. Of these writers, Diarmaid MacCulloch has the most authority. I am grateful for permission to refer to his thesis.

[39] Samuel Ward, *Jethros Iustice of Peace*, edns. 1618, 1621, 1623, 1627.

[40] Ward, *Jethros Iustice of Peace* (1618), sig. A3, pp. 1, 27, 34. Cf. Bartimaeus Andrewes, town preacher of Yarmouth, who told the members of the corporation: 'You must know that the burthen of this people lieth upon your shoulders, and that their eyes looke at you, as those by whose example the people either perish and fall, or are preserved and staied up, for fall and upraysing of manie depended upon publique persons.' (*A very short and pithie cathechisme* (1586), Epistle.) When Andrewes was recruited out of a pastoral charge at Wenham, Suffolk, to become preacher of

Drummers' was to encourage, hearten, and put life into those that fought his battles and did his work. Jethro had instructed Moses to appoint as rulers of the people 'men of courage, fearing God, men dealing truely, hating controversies'. 'By the vertue then of this my text, I say to every good-hearted Magistrate, proceede and goe on from strength to strength.' The 'principall scope of Magistracy in God's intention' was to promote his glory, countenance the gospel and its professors and to safeguard the Church and Commonwealth. The good magistrate kept his house well but the church better: 'in frequenting whereof he with his family are presidents to all the hundreds where he dwells: And in a word, doth as much by his example, as by his authoritie'.[41]

Robert Prick of Denham enjoyed a perfect understanding with his patron Sir Edward Lewkenor, one of the most inveterate of Elizabethan parliamentarians. And Lewkenor's son and grandson were similarly supported as model Suffolk magistrates by Prick's son Timothy, so that this little village near Bury witnessed sixty years of exemplary magistracy and ministry. In *The doctrine of superioritie and subiection,* published posthumously in 1609,[42] Robert Prick expounded the fifth commandment as the sanction for 'all those estates, degrees and orders, whereby the societie or fellowship of men is as it were by certaine ioynts and sinewes ioyned and knit togither, and without which it would by a certaine pernicious confusion be cleane dissolved and utterly perish'. Among those upheld by this commandment were 'the *Aged* and *Gray-headed',* in whom could be descried 'the eternitie of God, whereby we

---

Yarmouth, Dr Richard Crick, a member of the conference to which he belonged, said: 'If I were one of that church, I had as lieve they shuldest pluck out myne eie as take from me my paster', to which the representative of the bailiffs of Yarmouth replied: 'But Sir, if you cast out your eie yow will geve me leave to take it up.' (*The Presbyterian Movement in the Reign of Queen Elizabeth,* ed. R. G. Usher, Camden 3rd ser. viii (1905), 45–6.)

[41] Ward, *Jethros Iustice of Peace,* pp. 27–8, 34, 38.

[42] *The doctrine of superioritie, and of subiection, contained in the fift commandement of the holy law of Almightie God. Which is the fundamentall ground, both of christian subiection: and also of like christian government, as well in church and common-wealth, as in every schoole and private family. A pretious memorial of the substance of manie godly sermons preached by the learned and faithfull servant of God, Mr Robert Pricke, Minister of the Word, at Denham in Suffolke* (1609). See Collinson, 'Magistracy and Ministry: A Suffolk Miniature'.

may gather that Superiors by certaine sparkes of glory which they have received from the Lord, doe shine as it were bright starres, in the middest of mankind'. There were two kinds of superiors, public and private, and two kinds of public superiors, magistrates and ministers. Among the functions of the 'sacred ordinance of magistracie', Prick put first the planting and advancement of religion, including the choice of learned and fit ministers, compelling the minister to the performance of his duty, and protecting and encouraging faithful ministers. The magistrate was to enforce the people to resort to the ministry of the word and to practise all the duties of the decalogue. 'Take away the Magistrate, and there would remaine no outward worship of God, or if it did, it would easily degenerate into Idolatrie and Superstition. Againe, take away the Magistrate, and the publicke ministerie of the word, and all other means of mans salvation do utterly cease.'[43]

The magistrate's principal civil function was the making and execution of laws for 'the good order and behaviour of the subiects one towardes another; that so they may live together sweetlie and honestlie, to the mutuall helpe and benefit one of another'. The minister possessed his own authority, which he was to commend by 'the comeliness of his bodie, in attire and gesture'. He exercised it not only by teaching and example but by executing the sentences of suspension and excommunication. The people, whose natural inclination was to 'abhorre and loath' the clergy, were instructed that their duty was to love their ministers 'not coldly nor feebly, but most fervently and aboundantly'. To the magistrate the subject owed an equally generous thankfulness and virtually unlimited obedience. He was 'patiently to beare and undergoe all such punishments and chastisements' as might be visited upon him; to 'venter and hazard himselfe and al that he hath for the benefite, comfort and reliefe of the Magistrate'; and 'to play [sic] and willingly yeeld all such taxes, customes, subsidies and other such paiements as are levied, commanded and imposed for the maintenaunce of the Magistrate, and common benefite of the land'.[44] Twenty years earlier another Suffolk preacher

---

[43] *The doctrine of superioritie* sigs. B2, B5ᵛ, C7ᵛ–D, D5ᵛ–6ᵛ.
[44] Ibid., sigs. Dᵛ, D2, E3ᵛ, E6ᵛ, F3, F, D8ᵛ, Eᵛ, E2ᵛ.

had published 'A Fardle of Christian Duties': duties of magistrates and duties to magistrates; duties of pastors and duties of the people towards their pastors.[45] And yet it is conventional to call such pastors and magistrates 'radicals'.

In Elizabethan and Jacobean Suffolk, both at the county level and in the towns of Bury St. Edmunds and Ipswich, the commonplace that magistracy and ministry were complementary functions in an orderly commonwealth exercised a strong and practical appeal. 'If magistrates and ministers agree not and the people reverence and love them both, what can come of it?' asked the town preacher of Bury, about the turn of the century, and the phraseology has a proverbial ring to it.[46] By the time this was written, the first generation to act on these principles was approaching old age: a cohort of preaching ministers who left Cambridge in the 1570s to find employment in the prosperous country around Bury, and a group of outstandingly religious gentlemen who inherited their estates and embarked on public careers as justices at about the same time. The leading preacher of this generation, the John More of Suffolk, was John Knewstub, known to history as a puritan representative at the Hampton Court Conference.[47] Knewstub was matched from the side of magistracy by Sir Robert Jermyn of Rushbrooke and Sir John Higham of Barrow, who took their turns as sheriff and then served in tandem as deputy lieutenants and in 1586 as knights of the shire. Jermyn and Higham were two of a group of 'great and hot Protestants' of Norfolk and Suffolk whose ascendancy had been assured by the events during a royal progress of East Anglia in 1578, when the anti-puritan Bishop Freke had been snubbed and the leading papists among the gentry openly disgraced. Of these events it could be said that the Privy Council had achieved at a stroke, and in despite of the bishop, what it could not allow Bishop Curteys the presumption to attempt at

---

[45] Thomas Settle, *A fardle of christian duties*, bound with his *A catechisme briefly opening the misterie of our redemption by Christ* (1587).

[46] George Estey to an unnamed correspondent, 14 April 1599; BL Add. MS 24191, fol. 41ʳ.

[47] *DNB*, art. Knewstub. For various details of Knewstub's locally important career, see Collinson, 'Puritan Classical Movement', pp. 125–6, 130, 133, 330–1, 337, 346–8, 366–7, 458–60, 506, 554, 583–4, 674, 685, 874, 993, 1016.

about the same time in Sussex. Jermyn, who with Higham received his knighthood on this occasion, reminded Sir Robert Cecil twenty-three years later of the circumstances in which the protestant gentry had received 'satisfaction'.[48]

The primary bond between the magistrates and the ministers was one of patronage. Jermyn alone presented to ten livings, Higham to four, and thirty more Suffolk benefices were in the hands of like-minded, religious patrons.[49] In exercising this patronage, the gentlemen seem to have been advised by the ministers, and especially by Knewstub.[50] They used their influence to safeguard their protégés from the unwelcome consequences of their plain preaching and non-conformity, and on occasions they petitioned and agitated on their behalf at the national level.[51] In return, the ministers showered compliments on the gentlemen in the prefaces to their published works. One of Knewstub's epistles addressed 'those gentlemen in Suffolk whom the true worship of God hath made right worshipful'.[52]

Richard Bancroft parodied this alliance in his account of a typical sermon at Bury St. Edmunds, which was punctuated by loud Amens from the weightier members of the auditory, and directed not against the notorious sins of the gentry but 'with a slaunderous invective against the present estate and government of the Churche'.

The gentlemen looke one at another with smyles and wynkes, as who should saye: This geare fadgeth: they are gyrded indeede. And when the Doctor descendeth, they rise full solemplye and embrace hym with God be thanked good Brother: The lord blesse you and

---

[48] MacCulloch, 'Power, Privilege and the County Community', pp. 144–7.

[49] Collinson, 'Puritan Classical Movement', pp. 866–71.

[50] Ibid., pp. 685, 906. The correspondence of the bailiffs of Colchester contains a testimonial from Knewstub on behalf of a candidate for the post of schoolmaster. (Essex Record Office, Essex Archaeological Society MS C.43, p. 173.) Note the rather lofty rhetoric with which this letter ends, and which it shares with the letters of John More of Norwich to his patrons and friends: 'For this tyme I take my leave, desiring the Lord more and more to blesse you with all those frutes which ar by Jesus Christ to the prayse and glory of his name.'

[51] The fullest record of this activity is in the personal and parliamentary papers of Sir Edward Lewkenor, BL Add. MS 38492; discussed in my 'Magistracy and Ministry: A Suffolk Miniature'.

[52] John Knewstub, *An aunsweare unto certayne assertions tending to maintaine the church of Rome to be the true and catholique church* (1579), Epistle.

contynewe his graces towardes you: Wee have had a worthie sermon, God make us thankfull for it. You shall goe dyne with me, saith one: Nay, I praye you lett hym be my guest todaye saith another. I omitt the like great kyndenes of the gentlewemen.[53]

Jermyn and Higham dominated the politics of Bury St. Edmunds in a working alliance with one of the earliest patrons of puritan religion in the town, Thomas Badby, who had built himself a mansion in the ruins of the great abbey church.[54] As Justices of the Peace whose petty sessions held at the Angel Inn constituted the government of a town which was as yet without a corporation, these gentlemen exercised a rule which was religiously inspired and morally censorious. A collusive act of bigamy was described by Jermyn and Higham and two of their colleagues as 'quite contrary unto the worde of God and the lawes of this realme . . . offensyve unto all good men who with sorrowful harte lament the lyke presydent in a christian commonwealth and furthermore, because the gospell of Christ with the proceeding of our gracious and godly prince be of the Enymies of them booth defamed, as brochers of lycentious lyving under christian lyberty.'[55] In 1578 the same justices drew up a severe penal code of orders and constitutions which was displayed in the two parish churches of the town. It dealt with papistry, absence from church, disturbance of prayers and sermons, railing at magistrates and preachers, blasphemy, witchcraft, gaming, usury, and sexual offences. The penalty for fornication was to be 'tyed to the poaste for that purpoase appointed (havinge hir haire cutt of if it be a woman) and so remaine tyed to the poaste for the space of one whole daie and a night, and that daie to be the Lordes daie, and after on the markett daie to be whipped, receaving thirtie strypes well layed on till the blood come, the Cunstable

[53] *Tracts Ascribed to Richard Bancroft*, ed. Albert Peel (Cambridge, 1953), pp. 71–3.

[54] MacCulloch, 'Power, Privilege and the County Community', p. 199.

[55] BL Harleian MS 286, fol. 22. The parties were a certain Henry Gibbon and the wife of William Browne of Haverhill who had obtained a decree of nullity dissolving her former marriage on the ground that she had been constrained against her will. Gibbon, who had kept the woman as his harlot for 'some years past', was the proctor who had promoted the suit of nullity. The identity of the justices is inferred from the controversy between the Suffolk gentry and Bishop Freke, in which several such cases were at issue. (BL Egerton MS 1693, fols. 89–90, 96–100ʳ; Lansdowne MS 37, no. 28, fols. 59–62.)

seeinge the execution thereof.'[56]Not far away on these bloody Mondays the preachers were engaged in the prophesying or combination lecture, a weekly event from the 1570s until the 1630s.[57] Fornicators in Rye in Sussex who at about the same time were made to wear a distinctive collar of yellow and green cloth and to spend three hours in the stocks if apprehended without it were getting off lightly by comparison.[58] And by the standards of Bury justice the white penitential sheet prescribed for sexual offenders by the church courts was an act of mere indulgence, part of what the *Admonition to the Parliament* called 'toyish censures'.[59] But there was doubtless a more magnanimous side to the puritan regime in west Suffolk. In 1583 Bury made a larger contribution than any other town in England to a fund to rebuild the Cheshire town of Nantwich after its destruction by fire.[60]

In busying themselves so earnestly with a range of social offences, the Suffolk justices were in the van of what by Jacobean times was a national groundswell of morally indignant and even Draconian magistracy. In counties as far apart as Kent, Lancashire, Somerset, and Nottinghamshire the justices regularly imposed whipping for sexual offenders, especially when bastardy was involved. In the court of the archdeacon of Canterbury in October 1588, evidence was given that Alice Whetnall had borne a child in adultery with Mr Nutbrowne 'for the which she hath beene whipped at Cranbrook by order from the iustices'.[61] In 1618 the Somerset bench ordered the reputed father and the mother of a bastard to be flogged 'till their bodies shall be bloody', and two fiddlers to play before them, 'in regard to make known their lewdness in begetting the said base child upon the Sabbath day coming from dancing'.[62] Bastardy was a matter for legitimate secular intervention, and such flogging justices

[56] BL Lansdowne MS 27, no. 70, fols. 154–5; Egerton MS 1693, fol. 97[r].

[57] See pp. 136–7 above.

[58] East Sussex Record Office, Rye MS 1/4, fol. 345[r]. The order is dated 21 January 1580/1.

[59] *Puritan Manifestoes*, ed. W. H. Frere and C. E. Douglas (1954 edn.) p. 34.

[60] I owe this information to Christopher Kitching.

[61] Cathedral Archives and Library Canterbury, X.2.4, fol. 379[v].

[62] Ronald A. Marchant, *The Church Under the Law: Justice, Administration and Discipline in the Diocese of York 1560–1640* (Cambridge, 1969), pp. 223–6.

were fully supported by an Elizabethan statute of 1576, to which the Bury orders of 1578 were a particularly prompt response.

But the Bury penal code went somewhat beyond the law of the land, citing 'the statute' against suspected papists and heretics, or those refusing to partake in the Communion, when in fact there was no such statute.[63] Bishop Freke of Norwich chose to regard the Bury ordinances as an invasion of his own jurisdiction, and complained that the justices had frequently meddled with matters 'mere ecclesiastical', many of them concerning the clergy.[64] The justices for their part were impatient with the separate jurisdiction of the bishop's commissary in Bury, Dr Day.[65] According to the bishop, Jermyn had refused to acknowledge the commissary as a magistrate, or his court as a lawful court, and Jermyn admitted to having 'often laboured the commissary to joyne authorities together to the repressing of synne and wickedness'.[66] It was said that unless Day could 'make frends to be in commission for the peace' there would be 'no dwelling for him in Bury'. When the commissary took it upon him to appoint churchwardens in the Bury parishes who were considered backward in religion, the justices called him knave and jack and bound him to his good behaviour. As for control of the Bury pulpits, there was competition between the bishop's

[63] Rose, *Cases of Conscience,* pp. 160–1.

[64] Cf. the complaint of a bishop of Exeter against the secular magistracy: 'They intermeddle in many matters of ecclesiastical concern as punishing some for disorders in church, others for incontinency, examining some upon articles and otherwise for speaking against some preachers by them misliked either for their doctrine or discipline.' (MacCaffrey, *Exeter,* p. 98 n. 39.)

[65] Compare with the situation in Yarmouth, where in 1572 Bishop Parkhurst of Norwich had freely granted to the bailiffs 'that aucthoritie I may to punishe synne', remarking: 'All that I and you with all my officers can do is to little, synne doth so much abound and punishment thereof is so slack.' But Parkhurst required the rights of his commissary to be respected. (*The Letter Book of John Parkhurst Bishop of Norwich Compiled During the Years 1571–75,* ed. Ralph Houlbrooke, Norfolk Record Society 1974 and 1975, xliii (Norwich, 1975), 213.) Compare also the situation in Rye, where under a treaty concluded between the mayor and jurats and Bishop Curteys of Chichester, the town preacher was invested with 'jurisdiction ecclesiasticall' 'for the ponishment of synne and wickednes' and the securing of 'suche a civill and vertuous order to lyvinge as the worde of God dayly taught unto us doth require'. (East Sussex Record Office, Rye MSS 47/12/5, 6; 1/4, fol. 215ᵛ; 47/12/11.)

[66] John Day to Bishop Freke, 27 July 1581, BL Lansdowne MS 33, no. 21, fol. 41; BL Egerton MS 1693, fol. 89ᵛ.

claim to appoint by collation and the alleged right of the parishioners to elect their own ministers, with some assistance from the gentry and Mr Knewstub.[67] So there were many occasions for friction between the bishop and his local representatives and the gentry. But it was the campaign of Bishop Freke and his officers to reduce the puritan preachers of Bury and its hinterland to conformity which brought matters to a head and provoked a full-scale 'country cause', bitter and prolonged.[68] The complex details can be reduced to one basic issue: was the Church in west Suffolk to be controlled by the gentry and their clerical allies or by the bishop and such political support as he could muster? The bishop was backed by elements in Bury which resented the dominance of the country gentry, and more potently by the assize judges assigned to this circuit, notably the chief justices Sir Christopher Wray and Sir Edmund Anderson.[69] But the gentry could count on the support of the Privy Council, addressed by the Bury puritans as 'the Lordes Lieutenants uppon earthe'.[70] In the summer of 1582 there was an extraordinary set piece, when the leading magnates of the county, 'fourteen of the principall men of Suffolke', seven of them knights and headed by Lord North, attended the judges at their lodging with an earnest request to deal 'more kindly' with the preachers, 'for oure sakes'.[71] Here was a tangled skein not envisaged by Calvinist divines in their textbook discourses

[67] Collinson, 'Puritan Classical Movement', pp. 892–7, 900–3, 905–7.

[68] Chapter 6 of D. N. J. MacCulloch's thesis 'Power, Privilege and the County Community', 'The Image of the Godly Gentlemen' adds fresh material to the account in Collinson, 'Puritan Classical Movement', including a previously unknown Chancery case between the two Bury townsmen of rival factions, Thomas Badby and Thomas Andrewes. (PRO C3/205/104.)

[69] Compare Anderson's reputation somewhat later in Lincolnshire. The preacher Francis Marbury wrote in 1596: 'Since my Lord Anderson hath obtayned to ryde this circuite the ministerie is growen into intollerable contempt which is universallie imputed unto him.' Marbury alleged that it was much the same at Northampton, Leicester, and Nottingham. After a particularly hostile performance at Lincoln, 'the simple people reioyced in their retorne homeward, sayeng that a ministers cause could not be so much as hard at the Assises, and gathered that all preachinge was now as it were cried downe'. On this occasion, 'manie preachers' went to the bishop to entreat him 'to labor the judge to more myldnes then his custome'. (BL Lansdowne MS 82, no. 53, fols. 110–15.)

[70] Petition of 170 townsmen of Bury St. Edmunds to the Privy Council, on behalf of their preachers, 6 August 1582; PRO S.P. 12/155/5.

[71] Lord North to Burghley, 13 February 1583; BL Harleian MS 6993, no. 33, fol. 61.

on the role of the 'inferior magistrate'. It was said that the judges responded to this *démarche* of the justices with even greater severity, so that Bury was soon 'utterly destitute' of preaching. 'We se they do study how they may gawle the justices.'[72]

The gentry were painfully aware of the paradox which is the theme of this chapter. Ten leading magnates, including seven of the fifteen muster commissioners for the shire, complained to the Council of the manner in which 'thes towers of Sion, the paynfull pastors and ministers of the worde' were brought to the bar with the worst malefactors and there indicted, arraigned, and condemned for small matters of liturgical practice. It was pitiful to see the back of the law turned towards the adversary 'and thedge with all the sharpenes layd upon the frende and trewe subiect'. The justices had been careful not to intervene publicly for fear of bringing law itself into confusion. 'And so by our silence, magistry and mynistrye brought bothe into open contempte.' 'This is our course. Wee serve her Majestie and the Countrye not accordinge to our fantasyes, as the worlde falsly beareth us in hande, but accordinge to the lawes and statutes of the realme of England. Wee reverence bothe the lawe and lawe makers. Lawe speakethe and we keepe silence. Lawe commaundethe and we obey.' As for papists, familists, anabaptists and Brownists, 'we abhorre all these, we punishe all these'. But now 'the adversary' had 'very cunninglye' christened them with the odious name of 'puritans': 'a shrewde devise' to bring them into contempt with 'every simple mane in these partes'. The nub of their complaint was the 'inversion of all order'.[73]

Worse was to come. When the Privy Council directed the judges to modify their policy, the bishop and his party appealed directly to the queen, with the consequence that the justices were called out of their own country to answer his

[72] Ibid.

[73] Collinson, 'Puritan Classical Movement', pp. 908–10; MacCulloch, 'Power, Privilege and the County Community'. Diarmaid MacCulloch notices six MS copies of the letter, apart from the printed text in *A parte of a register* (Edinburgh or Middelburg?, 1593), pp. 128–30. He follows the list of signatories in BL Harleian MS 367, fol. 24: Sir Robert Jermyn, Sir John Higham, Robert Ashfield, William Clopton, Thomas Poley, Sir Robert Wingfield, Sir Nicholas Bacon, Sir Philip Parker, Robert Forth, and Robert Wingfield.

complaints. It was said that 'everye streete doth sownde our disgrace'.[74] Wray and Anderson intensified their drive against the puritan clergy. In the summer of 1583 Bury gaol was full of preachers and Knewstub himself was among those indicted.[75] At last came the ultimate scandal, not without an element of farce: the suspension of Jermyn and Higham from the Commission of the Peace on the very eve of the Throckmorton Plot and the Bond of Association, when both were about to assume office as deputy lieutenants of the county. And for Jermyn there was the supreme indignity of service on a common jury. Both Jermyn and Higham spent much of the ensuing decade off the Commission of the Peace, although they remained in place as muster commissioners and deputy lieutenants. In 1584 they contested the two county seats in the parliamentary election. Jermyn was returned for the second seat, but Higham was defeated by the leading conservative gentleman of the shire, Sir William Drury, and had to be content with a borough seat at Ipswich. This disputed election, according to Diarmaid MacCulloch, represents the high point of political and religious polarization in Elizabethan Suffolk. In the 1587 parliamentary elections, Jermyn and Higham were both successful in the county contest, and in 1593 Jermyn became *custos rotulorum* and acknowledged president of the county bench.[76]

Long before this, Bishop Freke, 'the foolish bishop',[77] had moved on to a quieter diocese and the Suffolk preachers had emerged from under the cross. Knewstub, who was rector of Cockfield for as many years as Elizabeth was queen of England, had forty years ahead of him as the doyen of the Suffolk ministers. Samuel Ward's *Jethros Iustice of Peace* was preached at the Bury assizes in 1618, and by then there were no preachers at the bar and no angry delegations of justices outside the judges' lodgings. The Monday preaching at Bury

---

[74] BL Lansdowne MS 37, no. 28, fol. 61ᵛ. Bishop Freke's articles against Jermyn, Higham, Robert Ashfield, and Thomas Badby are in BL Egerton MS 1693, fols. 89–90 (Robert Beale's papers) and their replies in BL Lansdowne MS 37, no. 28, fols. 59–62. A second set of articles with the justices' further reply are in BL Egerton MS 1693, fols. 96–100ʳ.

[75] Oliver Pigge to Sir Francis Walsingham, 12 July 1583; PRO S.P. 12/161/33.

[76] Collinson, 'Puritan Classical Movement', pp. 926–30; MacCulloch, 'Power, Privilege and the County Community', pp. 209–27.

[77] Patrick Collinson, *The Elizabethan Puritan Movement* (1967), p. 203.

continued, and as late as 1636, more than half a century after Bancroft recorded the sonorous Amens of the gentry, the sermons were still punctuated by 'the weomens sighes and mens hauchins'.[78] After Knewstub and Jermyn and Higham and the rest of their generation were buried, the Suffolk tradition of magistracy and ministry reached its climax in the alliance of the 'eminently religious' Sir Nathaniel Barnardiston, 'one of the *Top-branches* amongst our *Suffolk-cedars*', and the preacher Samuel Fairclough, both figures of consequence in the early years of the Long Parliament. Of Barnardiston's seat of Ketton it was said that 'there was one great advantage which that Town and Corner had *above* most *other* places, and that was this: that the Magistry and Ministry *joined* both together and *concurred* in all things for the *promoting* of true Piety and Godliness', Barnardiston and Fairclough having a settled engagement to visit one another at least twice a week. 'They *heartily* also joined hand in hand to *promote* both the *force* and *power* of Godliness in that Towne and County.' Alan Everitt has written of Suffolk in the early 1640s: 'Perhaps nowhere, except in London, did the dream of the New Jerusalem seem more vivid.'[79]

III

We cross to the other side of England and the relatively stony ground of the Welsh borders to visit another little Zion in the parts of Herefordshire around the Harley family seat of Brampton Bryan. It was said of Sir Robert Harley at his funeral in 1658 that 'his *Planting* of godly Ministers, and then *Backing them* with his Authority made Religion famous in this little corner of the world'.[80] The fame was no older than the

---

[78] Patrick Collinson, 'Lectures by Combination: Structures and Characteristics of Church Life in 17th-Century England', *Bulletin of the Institute of Historical Research*, xlviii (1975), 191–5, 208.

[79] Samuel Fairclough, *The saints worthinesse* (1653), pp. 12, 17–18; Samuel Clarke, *The Lives of Sundry Eminent Persons* (1683), p. 169; Alan Everitt, *Suffolk and the Great Rebellion, 1640–1660*, Suffolk Records Society, iii (Ipswich, 1960), 12, 16. Barnardiston was addressed in one of his funeral elegies as 'Thou stately *Top-bough* of a noble Stem/One of Gods *Jewels* and thy Country's *Gem.*' (Samuel Fairclough, *Suffolkes teares* (1653), p. 13.) The fullest account of Barnardiston and Fairclough is in Kenneth W. Shipps, 'Lay Patronage of East Anglian Puritan Clerics in Pre-Revolutionary England', Yale Ph.D. Dissertation, 1971.

[80] Thomas Froysell, *The beloved disciple* (1658), p. 101.

second decade of the seventeenth century. Its roots were partly in Harley's mother's family, for his maternal grandfather was the Shropshire gentleman Sir Andrew Corbet who encouraged a godly ministry in and around Moreton Corbet in the 1580s.[81] Harley's own puritanism seems to have been nurtured at Oxford and in the godly enclave of the Blackfriars in London, where he took lodgings when in town for Parliament or the term.[82] The famous preacher William Gouge was a correspondent from 'our little state' in the Blackfriars, and probably the means of finding Harley an acceptable preacher from Oxford, the learned Thomas Peacock, and after Peacock's premature death, Thomas Pierson, an Emmanuel man and one of the editors of William Perkins's *Works,* as well as of Thomas Brightman's *Revelation of the Apocalyps.* Pierson was to be the apostle of a fervent, experiential protestantism in the Welsh Marches.[83] For twenty years, Harley and Pierson acted out a mutually supportive relationship of the kind first established in Suffolk forty years earlier. In the beginning, Harley used

[81] 'A conference betwene Mr Axton and the bishopp of Leichfild with divers others', Dr Williams's Library, MS Morrice A, fols. 3–26; calendared in *A Seconde Parte of a Register,* ed. Albert Peel (Cambridge, 1915), i. no. 40, 68–74. In my *Elizabethan Puritan Movement* (p. 479) I suggested that this conference should be dated 1573 and not, as by Peel, 1570. I am grateful to D. A. Johnson of the Victoria History of the County of Stafford for pointing out that a more likely date is 1582, in the time of Bishop Overton rather than of Bishop Bentham. A seventeenth-century life of Harley's minister Thomas Pierson (see p. 166 n. 84 below) strengthens this impression of protestantism infiltrating across the Shropshire border, since it incorporates a biographical memoir of Walter Stephens, who died in 1629 at the age of eighty-two after a ministry of fifty-three years at Bishop's Castle in south Shropshire. Stephens was 'the first Planter of Religion in those parts' and as a native of Herefordshire often came to preach in his birthplace of Lyonshall. (BL Harleian MS 7517, fol. 36.)

[82] *DNB,* art. Harley. Harley wrote to Thomas Peacock on 18 November 1611 'from my lodginge in blackfriers at one Mr Archers house a clock maker'. (BL Loan 29/202, fol. 126.) Gouge wrote to his 'very good friend' Sir Robert Harley, 24 January 1613, reporting the death of 'my sweetest child, mine only daughter'. (Ibid., fol. 135.)

[83] BL Loan 29/202, fol. 135. Letters to Harley from Peacock, ibid., fols. 120–1, 122–3, 124, and from Harley to Peacock, fols. 125–6. Letter to Harley from Pierson, after his preferment to the living, 30 March 1612, ibid., fols. 128–9. Froysell, *The beloved disciple,* p. 100. Thomas Peacock's famous death-bed struggle with the Devil and with 'desperation', in the presence of numerous notable divines, was recorded by Edward Bagshaw, preserved among Robert Bolton's papers, and printed in 1646 as *The last conflict and death of Mr Thomas Peacock.* Harley sent his man to the dying Peacock with some *aureum potabile.* Peacock responded with 'Oh if it would please God that I might live with him'—sc., Harley. (*The last conflict and death,* p. 54.)

both his weight and his affability with the bishop of Hereford to protect Pierson from the legal consequences of his very moderate and limited nonconformity. The cause of Pierson's trouble was unusual. Although Harley had acquired the advowson of his parish church as part of a marriage settlement and had used it to present Pierson, his father, Thomas Harley, was still living and it was not until 1631 that Sir Robert came into his inheritance. Harley senior was at first bitterly opposed to Pierson's ministry, so that Bishop Bennett was perplexed by letters from one Harley complaining of the preacher and from the other supporting him, another internal contradiction in the story of magistracy and ministry! But Sir Robert and Pierson and both their wives joined with other godly parishioners in prayer meetings for the father's conversion, and eventually their prayers were answered. As for Bishop Bennett, he told Pierson that he was not willing to lose his bishopric for his sake. Nevertheless, he accepted the present of a fat doe from his patron and Pierson came away from his interview a free man and with his inn charges paid by the bishop. It was all a great deal more civilized than Bury St. Edmunds in the 1580s, and Pierson continued to enjoy undisturbed peace in his ministry.[84]

After Pierson's death in 1632, a candidate for the succession was told: 'You shall find a loving patron and frend of Sir Robert . . . and beside potent in his countrey for your countenance and protection, sweet and humble in his conversation for your confort and converse, and free of his heart and purse.'[85] One of those involved, with William Gouge, in the negotiations to supply the vacancy at Brampton Bryan wrote to Harley: 'I need not commend unto you, one approved in Christ your selfe, that your house should be a church for doctrine and discipline, that ther should be morning and evening sacrifice day by day contenually, and all laid on the

---

[84] 'Divine Pierson's Life and Sermons', BL Harleian MS 7517, fols. 5ᵛ–6ʳ, 13ᵛ. Pierson's Life is a minor source for what follows. The major source is the collection of Harley Papers comprising BL Loan 29 (Portland MSS), and especially Harley Papers I 1582–1629 (Loan 29/202), Harley Papers II 1630–40 (Loan 29/172) and the loose papers in Loan 29/119. For Pierson's early troubles, see Loan 29/202, fols. 138, 145, 146–7, 148–9, 150, 151.

[85] John Stoughton to Peter Thatcher, 13 February 1633; BL Loan 29/172, fols. 79–80.

golden Alter, Christ, and kindled with fire from Heaven.'[86] Of 593 books in Harley's possession in 1637, 344 were works of divinity, mostly English writings of the puritan school, and including eleven books on the Sabbath, virtually every title on the subject by then published. (But Harley's library also contained Shakespeare's Sonnets, Spenser's *Shepheardes Kalendar* and Jonson's plays.)[87]

Harley's funeral preacher recalled that as a magistrate he was inspired with *'a most nimble Soul of Zeale against Sin'*. He was 'a Terrour to Evill works'.[88] The severity of Harley's government is implied by the presence among his papers of an order for the punishment of bastard bearers, and by a letter from his cousin, the godly Cheshire gentleman, John Bruen, expressing concern for the threat to 'the glorie of God and good of our state' if an 'impudent affront' offered to two other magistrates, 'both of them trulie religiose, fearinge God', were to go uncorrected. 'For I assure you, if a strict course be not taken for the punishment of these disorders, there will be such a gapp opened to profanes, and the devile will gett such advantage in these partes as never will be quenched in our tyme.'[89]

When Harley sat in Charles's early Parliaments, his minister and godly friends in the country synchronized their days of fasting and prayer to coincide with critical events at Westminster, much as the Suffolk puritans had done in the 1580s.[90] Pierson wrote in January 1628: 'Good sir, your letters from your lodging in Hell do bring unto us good and heavenly newes concerning your dayes of publique humiliation and the blessed resolution of your House to begin with the cause of God... The Lord enabling us, we shall ioyne with you on

---

[86] Thomas Wilson to Harley, 19 May 1636; ibid., fols 105–6.

[87] 'A catalogue of books taken the 12th day of July 1637', BL Loan 29/202, between fols. 230 and 231.

[88] Froysell, *The Beloved Disciple*, p. 105.

[89] BL Loan 29/172, fols 91–2; John Bruen to Harley, 10 September 1624, BL Loan 29/202, fols. 138–9. For Bruen, see William Hinde, *A faithfull remonstrance of the holy life and happy death of John Bruen of Bruen-Stapleford in the County of Chester Esquire* (1641). Further letters from Bruen to his 'most deare and christian cosin' Harley are in BL Loan 29/119.

[90] Collinson, *Elizabethan Puritan Movement*, pp. 280, 283; Collinson, 'Magistracy and Ministry: A Suffolk Miniature', pp. 85–6.

Wednesday next . . . Our desire is both in publique and privat by prayer to further your good desygnes.'[91] Meanwhile, in London, Harley and his religious friends were making assignations to meet at John Davenport's lectures at St. Stephen's, Coleman Street,[92] and holding their own days of humiliation in private houses. Harley's holograph notes for two of these prayer meetings contain a unique record of the pious mentality and the public and private concerns of a godly magistrate in the early years of Charles I. Matters for petition included 'the distressed state of the churches of Bohemia, the Palatinate, France, the Low Countrys, Denmarke, Rochell, Germany'; 'that God would in mercy vouchsafe a happy Parliament and blesse the meanes indevored to obtain that blessinge'; 'for strength in this duty and for the like blessing to those which join with us els where or far off'. There were matters for thanksgiving too: 'for the Lord Jesus etc. For the Gospell grace and for the meanes of it to us etc. For the manifold blessinge we do inioye by the Gospel'; and then an observation, striking for its date, 1627: 'For the life of the king and that in so many and great temptations etc. God inclines his hart still to uphold the truth.'[93]

It would be wrong to represent Sir Robert Harley as a typical country justice and parliament man of the early Stuart age. In his exemplary and exceptional dedication to religion he was one of a very small, special and self-conscious élite. In some respects, but in no means all, the religious values which he strove to promote were deviant from the norm. It is significant that in the House of Commons he hunted with Ignatius Jordan of Exeter, the promoter of a bill to impose the death penalty for adultery, for Jordan was described by his biographer as 'one of those rare examples which the Lord giveth the world now and then', whose actions 'are not to be

---

[91] Pierson to Harley, 14 January 1628; BL Loan 29/202, fol. 247.

[92] Ibid., fols. 248–9. An important role in overcoming episcopal and royal objections to Davenport's election as vicar of St. Stephen's, Coleman Street, was played by Harley's father-in-law, Secretary of State Conway. (*Letters of John Davenport Puritan Divine*, ed. I. M. Calder (New Haven, 1937), pp. 13–18, 20–3.) In all probability Harley was behind this helpful intervention.

[93] Endorsed in Harley's hand, 'Matters of Petition' and headed 'Apud Alderman Bery 30 Martii 1627 & 29 Feb. 1627'; BL Loan 29/202, fols. 238–9.

measured by an ordinary standard'.[94] Harley's cousin John Bruen (or Bryan) told him: 'I have bin longe called Bushop Brian.'[95] These were singular men, close and intimate with one another across county boundaries. By the 1630s, Brampton Bryan was a cave of Adullam, embattled against the bishops. 'Submission to the English bishops in any thing wee cannot yeeld to', the Sheffield preacher Stanley Gower was told as he prepared to take upon him Thomas Pierson's mantle. 'I beseech you, doe what you can for us, that wee be not driven to leave our native countrey and friends and, which is more, the stage of Europe, where wee are all to act our partes in the destruction of the great whore whose kingdome cannot downe among us while wee submitt to their bishops.'[96] But it would be equally false to represent Harley as part of a 'radical' opposition to the early Stuart regime. For he was an integral part of that regime. Not only did he strive to retain what proved to be a misplaced trust in Charles's 'orthodoxy', he was one of Buckingham's most faithful and consistent henchmen, right up to the year of the duke's assassination.[97] And as son-in-law of Secretary Conway and himself master of the Mint he was a beneficiary of the early Caroline Court.

One of Harley's friends assured another that Lady Brilliana, Sir Robert's third wife, 'rather transcends him' in religious qualities, a not uncommon situation in godly gentry families. And Brilliana's brother, Lord Edward Conway, wrote whimsically to his brother-in-law: 'In your howse the order of things is inverted. You write to me of cheeses and my sister writes about a good scholler.'[98] Lady Brilliana's corre-

---

[94] Patrick Collinson, '"A Magazine of Religious Patterns": an Erasmian Topic Transposed in English Protestantism', in *Renaissance and Renewal in Christian History, Studies in Church History*, xiv, ed. Derek Baker (Oxford, 1977), 239. On Harley's collaboration with Jordan, see Conrad Russell, *Parliaments and English Politics 1621-1629* (Oxford, 1979), p. 277.

[95] John Bruen to Harley, 4 March 1619; BL Loan 29/202, fols. 1–2.

[96] An undated and unsigned letter, endorsed by Harley, 'To Mr Gower from some tending to separation'. (BL Loan 29/119). Gower was not as anti-prelatical as this correspondent, for he had served as chaplain to Archbishop Ussher. (BL Harleian MS 7515, fol. 38ᵛ.) I have been helped with this point by Jacqueline Levy.

[97] Russell, *Parliaments and English Politics*, pp. 16, 26, 31.

[98] BL Loan 29/172, fol. 80; Lord Conway to Harley, 18 November 1637; ibid., fols. 172–3.

spondence with her son Edward, the father of the great earl of
Oxford, has been familiar since it was put in print in the mid-
nineteenth century.[99] One remark, of January 1641, is often
quoted: 'I beleefe that herarchy must downe, and I hope
now.'[1] Lady Brilliana's unpublished letters to her husband in
the years of her children's infancy deserve to be better known,
as a precious record of family relationships in a godly gentry
household, and indeed a practical demonstration of what her
husband's friend William Gouge called in the title of a famous
book, *Of domesticall duties.* Of the future Sir Edward, little Ned,
she wrote to Sir Robert in London that he was 'as mearry as
his littell sowle can bee, tell he is asked wheare you are, and
then he makes some monefull tune'. When another boy was
born, Brilliana sent details of the christening: 'And becaus you
saide nothinge of the name, I choos that name I love beest, it
being yours. I thanke God the childe is well, and they all say
he is as like his father as can be, and I pray God make him like
his heavenly Father . . . And now I have doune with my
nursery newes, I would faine tell you that which I can not, I
am sure not all I can not, howe much I longe to see you. It is
long sence you went . . .'[2] This admirable and spirited woman
deserved better than to die defending her house in a civil war,
while her husband sat in the Long Parliament and its
committees and the nineteen-year-old Ned fought in the
parliamentary army.

IV

But Jerusalem, after all, was a city, and the protestant ideal of
exemplary magistracy and ministry belonged most naturally
not to the deferential society of the English countryside with
its open spaces, great households, and vast social differences,
but to the more compact and homogeneous world of the
corporate town. We return to Suffolk to investigate the county
town of Ipswich as a model of the godly civic commonwealth.
The interests of religion in Elizabethan Ipswich were defended

[99] *Letters of the Lady Brilliana Harley,* ed. Thomas Taylor Lewis, Camden Society lviii
(1854).
[1] Ibid., 111.
[2] Lady Brilliana to Harley, n.d. and 21 April 1626; BL Loan 29/202, fols. 202,
204–5.

by stern sabbatarian ordinances. On Sundays the constables patrolled the inns and tippling houses and the fields around the town in search of idle persons and players of unlawful games, imprisoning the stubborn and disobedient. Paupers who stayed away from church went without poor relief.[3] These were aspects of an integrated system of social control in which, as in so many early modern towns, it would be unprofitable to distinguish between religious and secular elements. What Wallace MacCaffrey has written of Exeter may apply equally well to Ipswich: 'The oligarchy was determined to have its own way in the refashioning of the city's religious life ... Religion was to become another province in the all-embracing realm of civic control.'[4] A powerful preaching ministry was indispensable to such a regime. It was also the principal amenity and cultural resource of an affluent society aspiring to that precious attribute of 'civility' and so perhaps prepared to reverse the late medieval retreat from town to countryside. As someone remarked in a letter to the magistrates of neighbouring Colchester: 'To be seated in a healthsome place where there is an ordinary publicke sanctifyed ministry is one speciall point, and not the least to be regarded.'[5]

But as in so many English towns,[6] all twelve Ipswich parishes were impropriate and incapable of supporting such a ministry. In 1637 there was a judicial ruling that they were 'nothing or poorly endowed'.[7] By an Act of Parliament of 1571

---

[3] Orders made 23 October 25 Eliz. and 2 October 34 Eliz; Ipswich and East Suffolk Record Office, Ipswich Borough Records, Assembly Books 20–30 Eliz., 31 Eliz.—6 Jas. I. Cf. John Webb, ed., *Poor Relief in Elizabethan Ipswich*, Suffolk Records Society ix (Ipswich, 1966).

[4] MacCaffrey, *Exeter*, p. 202.

[5] Nicholas Coulte to the bailiffs 'with the rest of the worshipful brethren and senate of Colchester town', 26 April 1591; Essex Record Office, Essex Archaeological Society MS C. 46, p. 165.

[6] See the draft of 'A Bill for an Act of Parliament for the payment of tithes within cities for the maintenance of preachers', *Registrum Vagum*, i. 137–9.

[7] 'The opinion of the judges concerning presentative and impropriate parish churches within the towne of Ipswich'; The Queen's College Oxford MS 155, pp. 255–6. Compare the religious condition of seventeenth-century Colchester, where of twelve parish churches, four were said to be either demolished or otherwise rendered useless. 'The rest have during these times beane contented with two ministers, paying noe tithes, but voluntary contributions.' (Essex Record Office, Essex Archaeological Society MS C. 41, p. 275.) Four or five of the Ipswich parishes appear to have been presentative, the remainder donative cures. ('Suffolk Archdeaconry Inductions,

the corporation secured the power to levy rates to maintain the churches of the town—and to pave the streets. But while this was sufficient to provide for baptisms and burials and other routine functions,[8] the bailiffs and portmen preferred to entrust the major pastoral charge in respect of the town as a whole to a town preacher for whom they were prepared to pay, as it were, real money. As early as 1551 there is a reference in the borough records to 'the common preacher of the towne', and it is significant that the terms in use for the next eighty years were 'common', 'ordinary', 'public', 'general', or 'chief' preacher, never 'lecturer'.[9] The principal duty of this civic functionary was to preach sermons three times a week. But in 1575 it was said that he should also visit the sick and comfort 'the afflicted consciences of this towne'. In addition, he was expected to defend orthodox doctrine against 'damnable opinions' and heresies.[10] Evidently the intention

1526–1629', Transcript in Ipswich Public Library.) Until their right was challenged in the reign of Charles I, the parishioners of the donative cures nominated their own curates. See J. Wodderspoon, *A New Guide to Ipswich* (Ipswich, 1842), pp. 98–105.

[8] 13 Eliz. I cap. 24. Something more than a bare ministry was sometimes looked for, and received, from the parish curates. On 28 January 19 Eliz., George Webbe was appointed both as second preacher of the town, to assist Dr Norton, and to serve the cure of St. Mary Tower, at a total salary of £36, of which £12 was 'out of St Mary Tower parishe'. (Ipswich and East Suffolk Record Office, Ipswich Borough Records, Assembly Book 6–19 Eliz., p. 257.) In the 1590s the parish of St. Peter's was served by a preacher of some distinction, Samuel Bird, who drew a stipend of £29, and £4 a year house rent. (BL Add. MS 25344, fol. 29.) The corporation was also willing to reward the curates for 'diligence in preaching', as in 1570, when the curate of St. Mary Tower was allowed 'of the towne gyfte' 53s. 4d. to pay for a gown. (Assembly Book 6–19 Eliz., p. 114.)

[9] Ipswich and East Suffolk Record Office, Ipswich Borough Records, Great Court Book 1572–1634, Assembly Books, Treasurer's Accounts; and citations of some of this material in *The Annalls of Ipswiche . . . by Nathaniel Bacon . . . 1654,* ed. William H. Richardson (Ipswich, 1884), and in J. Wodderspoon, *Memorials of the Ancient Town of Ipswich* (Ipswich, 1850). At Colchester, too, the terms were 'common preacher' and 'general preacher'. (Essex Record Office, Essex Archaeological Society MSS C. 41, p. 115; C. 43, p. 117; C. 45, p. 81.) And see the will of two Colchester merchants, dated 1573, both providing for sermons to be preached by 'the common preacher appointed in the town', 'our common preacher'. (*Elizabethan Life: Wills of Essex Gentry and Merchants,* ed. F. G. Emmison (Chelmsford, 1978), pp. 273, 319.)

[10] Ipswich and East Suffolk Record Office, Ipswich Borough Records, Great Court Book 1572–1634, p. 53. When Dr Norton left the town's employ his testimonial stated that he had 'governed hym self, his famely and household to the good example of the inhabitants of the said town of Ipswiche'. It was also said that he had 'confuted sondrye dampnable opinions tendinge to heresye, if by his care and diligence it had not been looked into in tyme'. (Ibid., pp. 208–9.)

was that the town preacher should approximate to the *antistes* of a Swiss or South German City in the age of the Reformation: a *de facto* bishop of the souls of the inhabitants.[11]

The notion of 'lecturer', in which historians have taken much interest, is consequently something of a red herring if it diverts attention from the fundamental fact that the magistrates of corporate boroughs like Ipswich were concerned to secure the services of a learned, commanding, pastoral figure who would oversee the religious interests of the town, and whose appointment and remuneration they could control. There were many ways of providing for such a person. Financial support might be drawn from parochial tithes, or a special rate, or a semi-voluntary benevolence, or from the common chest. At Exeter, where there was an anachronistic provision of nineteen mostly small and poorly endowed parish churches, the city more than once promoted a parliamentary bill rationalizing the ecclesiastical arrangements and placing them under civic management. A bill of 1601 would have suppressed six parishes, replacing them with a single parish and a new, large church capable of accommodating two thousand people. Only after the frustration of such schemes did the city fathers take steps to appoint 'a learned person' to preach on Sundays and 'to do other godly exercises in [the cathedral] and other parish churches'.[12] At Rye, where there was but one parish church rather than twelve or nineteen, the mayor and jurats appointed the 'preacher [or 'minister'] of the word of God' and provided his maintenance not from the alienated tithes of the vicarage but partly from the public purse, partly from funds accounted for by the churchwardens. In 1575 a concordat was negotiated with the bishop of Chichester whereby the town preacher, at that time the future bishop of London, Richard Fletcher, was to exercise 'jurisdiction ecclesiastical' within the town of Rye 'for the furtherance of religion and the feare of God and the punishment of synne and wickednes'. Thereafter, Fletcher worked hand in glove with the magistrates in the operations of an effectively unitary

[11] But a town preacher might alternatively be regarded in puritan circles as exercising the office of 'doctor', more especially where he was assistant to a senior pastor.

[12] MacCaffrey, *Exeter*, pp. 196–7.

government, part spiritual, part secular, but inspired by the same principles of moral severity.[13]

At Stratford on Avon, Letters Patent of the reign of Edward VI granted the vicarage of the parish church to the town, which subsequently appointed the minister and found his annual stipend of £20.[14] At Hull in 1573 the vicar was induced to surrender his benefice into the hands of the archbishop of York, who received it for the use of the mayor and aldermen. The magistrates and townsmen on their side undertook to provide the stipends for a preacher, fixed at £40, and for a curate. The vicar, Melchior Smith, who was content to exchange his parson's freehold for the goodwill of the archbishop and of the town, was an outspoken preacher, given to the 'beating down of wicked vices reigning in these evil days amongst this sinful and adulterous generation'.[15] At King's Lynn, the salaried town preacher William Saunderson was a dominating presence from the 1560s until his death in 1590. Besides appointing to this office, the corporation controlled the parish of St. Margaret's, where in 1582 it was decided to appoint a preaching minister, 'such as Mr Saunderson our preacher like of', and to allow him £25 out of the parsonage 'if twill beare it'. Later the town sustained two preachers at St. Margaret's, allowing the senior £40 and his assistant £20. In 1619 King's Lynn tried to attract Samuel Fairclough with a salary of £50 plus a house, and 'the people' undertook to make his stipend up to £100.[16]

But in Ipswich it proved difficult to convert ambitions of this kind into achievement. The sum budgeted for the town preacher grew from £20 to £50 and then to £113, money for two preachers. But this was on paper. These large sums were

[13] Patrick Collinson, 'Cranbrook and the Fletchers: Popular and Unpopular Religion in the Kentish Weald', in *Reformation Principle and Practice: Essays in Honour of A. G. Dickens,* ed. P. N. Brooks (1980), pp. 192, 194–5.

[14] *Minutes and Accounts of the Corporation of Stratford upon Avon,* iv, 1586–1592 ed. Edgar I. Fripp, Dugdale Society, x (1929), 115, 127.

[15] Borthwick Institute of Historical Research, University of York, Chanc. AB 9, fol. 212, HC. CP 1567/8. I owe these references to Bill Sheils, Cf. G. C. F. Forster, 'Hull in the 16th and 17th Centuries', in *Victoria History of the County of York East Riding,* ed. K. J. Allison, i, *The City of Kingston upon Hull* (Oxford, 1969), 95–6.

[16] BL Add. MS 24346 (extracts from King's Lynn Corporation Records); King's Lynn Borough Records, Congregation Book 1569–91, fols. 13, 149, 253ᵛ, 269, 321ᵛ, 333, 362ᵛ, 390ᵛ, 397, 463, 466, 421; Clarke, *Lives of Sundry Eminent Persons,* p. 160.

to be made up in varying proportions from voluntary contributions, compulsory rates, and subventions from the town treasury. Many inhabitants were reluctant to pay, among them a man who after refusing his contribution in 1567 was distrained of four and a half yards of broadcloth, whereupon he took the town serjeant to court.[17] Twenty years later, the magistrates were still threatening with fines and imprisonment those who were in arrears for the preachers' wages.[18] For many years the town was equally frustrated in its efforts to place the religious establishment on a stable basis. Some of those appointed town preacher failed to fulfil the condition of residence, or were drawn away by more attractive opportunities.[19] Perhaps the large salary offered attracted the wrong kind of candidate. Other preachers were restless and transient for another reason: their extreme puritanism.[20]

But at last, in 1605, a true *antistes* was found in Samuel Ward, whom we have already encountered as the author of *Jethros Iustice of Peace*. Ward was the son of a preacher of Haverhill and the spiritual father of Haverhill's most famous son, Samuel Fairclough. For it was to one of Ward's apprentice sermons that Fairclough attributed his conversion.[21] He was also the stepson of Richard Rogers, the puritan

[17] Numerous entries in *Annalls of Ipswiche*, pp. 253–374 and Wodderspoon, *Memorials of Ipswich*, pp. 366–77; and in Ipswich and East Suffolk Record Office, Ipswich Borough Records, Great Court Book 1572–1634, Assembly Books, Treasurer's Accounts. A 'Book of Enrolments of Apprenticeship, Indentures and Rate Assessments, 1571–1651' includes a number of assessments of the governing body and the inhabitants of parishes for the preacher's wages (in addition to the assessments made to raise the wages of the parochial curates). BL Stowe MS 881 fols. 5–10 contains the accounts of Edward Cage, treasurer of Ipswich 1587–8, including detailed 'receipts of the collection for the preachers wages'.

[18] *Annalls of Ipswiche*, p. 344.

[19] Ipswich and East Suffolk Record Office, Ipswich Borough Records, Great Court Book 1572–1634, Assembly Books 6–19 Eliz., 20–30 Eliz., 31 Eliz.–6 Jas. I.

[20] Notably Robert Wright, a presbyterian who had received non-episcopal orders in Antwerp and served in Lord Rich's household before coming to Ipswich in 1586 on the recommendation of 'sondrye doctors and godly lerned prechers of the universitie of Cambridge'. Wright lasted until 1590. (Ibid., Assembly Book 20–30 Eliz., meetings held 19 July 27 Eliz., 19 March 28 Eliz., Assembly Book 31 Eliz.–6 Jas. I, meetings held 4 October 31 Eliz., 16 January 32 Eliz., 4 May 32 Eliz.) Among radical puritan parochial curates were William Negus, a member of the Dedham conference (*Presbyterian Movement in the Reign of Queen Elizabeth*) and Thomas Carew, curate briefly of St. Margaret's. (Collinson, 'Puritan Classical Movement', pp. 866–7.)

[21] Clarke, *Lives of Sundry Eminent Persons*, pp. 155, 159.

diarist of Wethersfield in Essex, and so a close kinsman of the
fiery Jacobean lecturer of Dedham, John Rogers.[22] Rogers was
said to be the Fairclough of Essex as Fairclough was the
Rogers of Suffolk. Ward's two brothers and two stepbrothers
all became preachers of some note. He himself remained in
Ipswich from his appointment as town preacher until his
death thirty-four years later. In the previous thirty-four years
ten preachers had come and gone, all claiming removal and
other incidental expenses. The corporation now provided
Ward with a house valued at £120, and increased his stipend
from a hundred marks, first to £90 and eventually to £100.[23]
At his death in 1638 this full amount was continued as a
lifelong pension to his widow and son, for by then Ward was a
local monument of great renown, 'the glory of Ipswich'.[24]

No early Stuart clergyman better personified the values of
the country, embattled against the corrupt innovations of the
Court. As a talented illustrator as well as preacher, Ward was
capable of giving graphic expression to the difference. His own
design for the title-page of his sermon *Woe to drunkards* depicts
a booted and spurred foot, an open Bible and a mailed fist
grasping a lance, captioned THIS OF OULDE, confronting a
stockinged leg with fashioned shoe, cards, dice, and a hand
holding an elaborate drinking glass, with the inverted motto
O MANNERS, O TYMES.[25] In 1621 he earned a brief spell in
prison for a caricature attacking the Spanish match. Fuller in
his *Worthies* reports that Ward 'had the superioritie of the
several parishes of Ipswich', which was no doubt effectively
the case. When Laud's chancellor Sir Nathaniel Brent offered
the town a more conformable lecturer, he was told that they
would 'have Mr Ward or none'.[26]

[22] See pp. 243–4 below.

[23] *Annalls of Ipswiche*, pp. 439–40, 445; Wodderspoon, *Memorials of Ipswich*, pp.
373–4. At Lincoln in the same period the lecturer's stipend was £35, later raised to
£40. (*HMC Report, Lincoln MSS*, p. 84.) At Worcester the salary rose from £10 in 1589
to £40 by 1628. (Alan D. Dyer, *The City of Worcester in the Sixteenth Century* (Leicester,
1973), pp. 238–9.)

[24] *Annalls of Ipswiche*, p. 374; Samuel Clarke, *A Collection of the Lives of Ten Eminent
Divines* (1662), p. 20.

[25] Editions of *Woe to drunkards* were published in 1622, 1624, 1627.

[26] *DNB*, art. Ward; *The Works of William Laud*, ed. W. Scott and J. Bliss, V. ii
(Oxford, 1853), 340.

Episcopal realists were careful not to mistake the moral ascendancy of a local patriarch for 'factious' disobedience. When Bishop Harsnet of Norwich prosecuted Ward for nonconformity, the case was referred on appeal to Bishop Williams of Lincoln, who found him 'not altogether blameless but a man to be won easily with fair dealing', and in whom he detected 'much readiness to serve the Church of England'. Williams's biographer reports that Harsnet himself subsequently acknowledged that Ward was 'as useful a man to assist him in his government, as was in all his Diocese'.[27] And his successor, the whimsical Richard Corbet, found it prudent to cultivate Ward's friendship, writing: 'Proove you a good tenant in my hart, and noe minister in my diocese hath a better landlord. Farewell! God Almightie blesse you with your whole congregation.'[28]

Wherever we look in the world of late Elizabethan and Jacobean magistracy and ministry we are likely to find a similar spectacle of Calvinist paternalism, on its own terms and within its own perspectives as factious and subversive as the Homily of Obedience:[29] an unlikely setting for what Michael Walzer calls 'the origin of radical politics'. Take as a final paradigm the religious orders imposed on Northampton in the early 1570s, which included provision for a weekly assembly of the magistrates and preachers for the correction of notorious blasphemy, whoredom, drunkenness, railing against religion or preachers, scolds, and ribalds. This tribunal was said to join together the authority of the mayor and the bishop 'tyll lief is corrected, God's glory set fourth, and the people brought in good obedience'.[30]

V

But to leave the matter there would be to miss entirely the point which Walzer and other modern students of Calvinism

[27] John Hacket, *Scrinia Reserata: A Memorial Offer'd to the Great Deservings of John Williams D.D.* (1692), i. 95.

[28] Browne, *Congregationalism in Norfolk and Suffolk*, p. 142. The original letter is in BL Harleian MS 464, fol. 12.

[29] Ronald Marchant points out (*The Church Under the Law*, p. 245) that the contents list to the Second Book of Homilies, published in 1562, ends with the two items: 'Of Repentance and true reconciliation unto God. Three Parts. An Homily against Disobedience and wilful Rebellion. Six Parts.'

[30] PRO S.P. 12/78/38.

have been at pains to make. The disposition of Calvinist magistrates and ministers to obedience carried a latent potential for disobedience. The desire to preserve the world as it was did not exclude the capacity to change it. The attempt of Matthew Wren, Bishop Corbet's successor, to terminate Samuel Ward's 'tenancy' provoked the most violent ecclesiastical disturbances of the era. When a preacher exhorted the people of Ipswich 'to fight for the puritie of the gospell and liberty of their ministers', some took his words literally and drove the bishop and his entourage out of the town, while the bailiffs and portmen looked the other way. The entire corporation was subsequently prosecuted in the Star Chamber for conspiracy to riot.[31] When Richard Baxter wrote that 'the warre was begun in our streets before the King and Parliament had any armies',[32] it might have been Ipswich and not Kidderminster which he had in mind. The lesson of the 1640s is that men do not necessarily intend the consequences of their actions, or dispositions.

Max Weber taught us to see that what Calvin may or may not have said about the ethics of political or economic action, his particular views on the right of resistance or the taking of interest, mattered less than the motives with which the major themes of Calvinist religious discourse invested all human action.[33] As Walzer suggests in *The Revolution of the Saints*, the idea that the political calling of a magistrate was a religious vocation and a conscientious duty was itself the key to a new politics.[34] The governor too was to exhibit what Richard Sibbes called *'a holy violence* in the performing of all duties'.[35] Arthur Dent observed that idleness was 'most odious' in magistrates and ministers,[36] while one of Salisbury's puritan governors reflected: 'How dreadfull will a dieing bed bee to a negligent magistrate.'[37] Walzer comments: 'The pious magis-

---

[31] 'Ecclesiastical Disturbances in Ipswich During the Reign of Charles I', MS transcript of material in Ipswich Borough Records and PRO, Ipswich Public Library.

[32] Richard Baxter, *A Holy commonwealth (1659), pp. 456–7.*

[33] Max Weber, *The Protestant Ethic and the Spirit of Capitalism,* tr. Talcott Parsons (1930).

[34] Walzer, *Revolution of the Saints,* pp. 59–60.

[35] Quoted, Seaver, *Puritan Lectureships,* p. 8.

[36] Arthur Dent, *The plaine mans path-way to Heaven* (1601), p. 195.

[37] Slack, 'Poverty and Politics in Salisbury', p. 193.

trate must be as vigilant and active as God himself . . . Though the emphasis was on orderly and disciplined behaviour, the suggestion was clearly revolutionary.'[38]

But one may recognize that the 'inner-worldly ascetic' transformed and in a manner revolutionized the motivation and quality of politics without mistaking it for a revolutionary force in the ordinary and literal sense. Walzer suggests that 'the thrust of puritan doctrine, for all its evasiveness, was clear enough: it pointed to the overthrow of the traditional order'.[39] Perhaps this was its manifest, if latent, destiny. But the conscious thrust of puritan doctrine was towards the redemption of the existing order. The Salisbury magistrates intended social amelioration, not social change in the sense of an unsettling of the existing hierarchies. Their godly commonwealth, like that of Bury St. Edmunds or Brampton Bryan, was the old world regenerated, not the world turned upside down.[40]

What must be rejected in Walzer's analysis is the connection posited between the activated Calvinist conscience and the alienation of both clergy and gentry in a society ceasing to be 'traditional', and in which they found themselves to be strangers. I find unacceptable the proposition that what is called in this context 'radicalism' was the politics of exile, of men not at home, and that Calvinism was the ideology of exiles, of men who had abandoned father and fatherland to enlist in Christ's army. According to Walzer, the Marian Exile was perpetuated in the anomy of the Elizabethan puritan ministry. They were a 'radical intelligentsia' of angry and isolated clerics, without respectable social origins or significant social connections, living in 'the margins and interstices of English society'.[41] Although it is possible that John More of Norwich grew his great beard to hide his 'unsettledness' (a favourite term with Walzer), and while many of his contemporaries must have had a worrying time making a career for themselves, I find all but a handful of Elizabethan divines

[38] Walzer, *Revolution of the Saints*, p. 62.

[39] Ibid., p. 118.

[40] Slack, 'Poverty and Politics in Salisbury' and 'Religious Protest and Urban Authority'.

[41] Walzer, *Revolution of the Saints*, pp. 115, 124.

unrecognizable in this characterization. Hugh Broughton, whom Ben Jonson pilloried, is one of a very few who would fit the bill. The equally learned but eccentric and unstable Henoch Clapham was another. By an equally unreal contrast, the Jacobean successors of these lonely outsiders are said to have enjoyed a superior pedigree and to have succeeded in cultivating more satisfactory relations with the gentry and urban upper classes. This could lead to a harmonious affinity, but more commonly to the depression of the previously rootless and masterless cleric into the dependency of chaplain or tutor. But once in this position, the puritan divine discovered what appears to have been his historical mission, transferring his own sense of alienation to a new kind of gentleman who was taught how to make his own 'internal emigration'. At the end of this lonely journey 'lay sainthood and revolution'. The gentry protégé of the preacher was disposed to become a stranger and pilgrim by his own form of 'status anxiety', even 'status panic'. The result was 'the amalgamation of sainthood and gentility . . . that reinforcement of self-esteem and confidence which made possible (and was expressed in) the diligently reforming activity of the pious magistrate'.[42]

'Model-ridden' though this analysis may appear to the historian lost in disorderly historical detail, it contains some truth as well as much brilliance. It was a helpful insight that the 'rise of the gentry' should be understood as the mental reorientation and moral reformation of an existing class rather than the birth of a new one, and that Calvinist religious experience and Calvinist seriousness was central to this transforming process. It is impossible to deny that both godly magistrates and ministers were responding to disorder. Even theologians will admit that they were alienated from sin, if from nothing else, and what is 'sin' but a name for disorder? Modern social historians are less alert to 'sin' than to the stress which was present in early modern society, and especially in urban communities, as trade declined, revenue fell, and the problem of the feckless poor raised its increasingly ugly head.

But the proposition that these ministers and magistrates

[42] Ibid., pp. 141, 247, 252.

were in any special sense themselves the victims of disorder, 'unsettled' persons, is unproven and incapable of proof, whatever Oliver Cromwell wrote to his cousin. 'You know what my manner of life hath been', wrote Oliver.[43] But how little we know, even of Cromwell. And who knows enough about the inner life of the hunting, card-playing, drinking gentry to be confident that their conduct too was not a symptom of 'unsettledness'? It is very likely that the religion of most puritans was anchored in experience, and probable that that experience related in some way to inner dissatisfaction or personal disorder. It is rather more apparent that puritan gentlemen and magistrates, having learned to apply to their condition the salves of practical, 'experimental' divinity for which they were designed, addressed themselves to a disorder which was external to themselves and to their class and calling, and which they identified with popery, or the ecclesiastical hierarchy, or the corruption of the Court, or the machinations of a contrary and evil-minded faction, or the gross sins of the rabble. Sir Nathaniel Barnardiston was the grandson of a Marian exile[44] and himself underwent 'humiliation' and conversion as a schoolboy.[45] But the mature Barnardiston was a man of great wealth and authority, as well as 'eminently religious'. It was never the intention of such men to demolish the world to which they so securely belonged, nor is there much evidence that their religion implied dissatisfaction with the positions of social dominance which they had inherited or acquired. We speak, of course, as Michael Walzer does, of mainstream Calvinism and not of the more radical religious tendencies which doubtless articulated the 'unsettledness' of the less privileged.

Prompted by evidence from non-European societies that millennial movements are as likely to be supportive of the status quo as to disintegrate it, William Lamont has asked of seventeenth-century England: 'What if millenarianism meant not alienation from the spirit of the age but a total

---

[43] *Oliver Cromwell's Letters and Speeches*, ed. Thomas Carlyle, (1930 edn.), p. 77.

[44] Or so his biographer reports: Clarke, *Lives of Sundry Eminent Persons*, p. 109. No one of his name is recorded by Christina Garrett, *The Marian Exiles* (Cambridge, 1938).

[45] Clarke, *Lives of Sundry Eminent Persons*, pp. 106–8.

involvement with it?'[46] We may well extend the question to the prevalent mentality of anti-popery, and to the fundamental calculus of salvation itself. These too were what William Lamont has called *central* doctrines, and we may well speak of 'centripetal Calvinism' as he has spoken of 'centripetal millenarianism', and with at least equal justification.

Evidently there was need in this period of history for a special kind of ideological undergirding. A society enjoying total tranquillity, not subject to change and not threatened, would have managed without the double-edged defence offered by the awakened puritan conscience and by the ethic which made all public duty a matter of religious obligation. Whether or not any such mythically 'traditional' society ever existed, we need not suppose that this was the condition of Elizabethan and Jacobean England. The energetic alliance of puritan magistracy and ministry was an index of instability. This is demonstrated by the important function which 'the adversary' served in all the argument and activity of the age, whether the adversary was identified with the pope, or the Jesuits, or witches, or 'the great rude unjust rabble', expressing what Baxter called 'malignant hatred of seriousness in religion'.[47] This society had its fair share of collective paranoia.

VI

No doubt political puritanism was an expression of vulnerability in the social fabric rather than of security. This weakness may appear especially naked in the puritan politics adopted by certain great magnates near the apex of the social and political pyramid, whose status and authority were ostensibly of the most traditional kind: the protestant earls of Elizabethan England, and especially that *dominus factotum*, Robert Dudley, earl of Leicester, 'whose excellency above

---

[46] William M. Lamont, *Godly Rule: Politics and Religion 1603– 60* (1969), p. 13. Cf. *Millennial Dreams in Actions,* ed. Sylvia Thrupp (1962), pp. 26–7.

[47] Baxter, *Holy commonwealth,* pp. 456–7. See Stuart Clark's suggestive exploration of certain 'conventions of discourse' in 'Inversion, Misrule and the Meaning of Witchcraft', *Past and Present,* no. 87 (1980), 98–127. Clark detects 'a predisposition to see things in terms of binary opposition', 'forms of argument and expression based on antithesis' and 'a preoccupation with the extreme poles of the religious and moral universe': all characteristic forms of the mentality of the age rather than of psychosis.

others is infinite, whose authority is absolute, whose commandement is dreadfull, whose dislike is dangerous and whose
favour is omnipotent'.[48] Leicester's greatness was expressed in
many traditional symbols: the retinue, the wearing of liveries,
private fortifications. Yet a significant part of his following
and 'affinity' was attached to him not by traditional bonds
but by ties of religion. After the earl had demonstrated his
religious zeal and soundness by ostentatious attendance at
sermons in the midland shires, the Northamptonshire gentleman Sir Richard Knightley assured him: 'You have thereby
gotten yow such frends as wolde be readie to venture their
lyves with your lordship in a good cause, even such as wold
not do yt so muche in respecte of your hye callinge, as for that
they espie in your lordship a zeal and care for the helpinge and
relevinge of the poore Church, which hath so manye and
myghtie enemies that fewe such as your lordship ys are frends
to yt.'[49] As a military commander Leicester put near the head
of his orders for the day this truly Cromwellian maxim: 'no
good event of any action can be expected wherein God is not
first and principally honored and served.'[50]

But were such sentiments sincere? In his manner of life
Leicester was no plain biblical Joshua, keeping his powder
dry. The Flemish tapestries on his walls were doubtless in the
sumptuous late Renaissance or Mannerist style, depicting
biblical themes, but perhaps the more theatrical and lavish of
themes. In one of his bedchambers there was a painting of
Venus and Cupid, described by the composer of an inventory,
no connoisseur, as 'a picture of a naked Lady sleeping and
Cupid menacing hir with his darte'; in 'my ladyes Chamber'
a painting of the philosopher enticed from his book by a
lady.[51] The contradictions were so obvious as to suggest to
some of the earl's contemporaries a desperate opportunism in
his cultivation of the godly. When that good puritan soldier

[48] *'Leycesters Commonwealth' 1641,* ed. F. J. Burgoyne (1904), p. 82.

[49] *Letters of Thomas Wood, Puritan, 1566–1577,* ed. Patrick Collinson, Bulletin of the
Institute of Historical Research Special Supplement v (1960), p. xxvii.

[50] Quoted, S. L. Adams, 'The Protestant Cause: Religious Alliance with the West
European Calvinist Communities as a Political Issue in England, 1585–1630', Oxford
D.Phil. thesis, 1973, pp. 57–8.

[51] C. L. Kingsford, 'Essex House, Formerly Leicester House and Exeter Inn',
Archaeologia, 2nd ser. xxiii (1923), esp. 30, 32, 36.

Thomas Wood[52] had cause to doubt his old master's sincerity he addressed him, not obsequiously as one might expect of an underling, but boldly in the language of prophetic menace: 'Loke therefore, my good Lord, against whom yow bende yourself: surely against him that hath said: "He that persecuteth yow, persecuteth me"; who no doubte is toe strong for yow, as experience by many yet fresh in memory ought to teach yow.' 'The Lord direct yow by his Holy Spiritt to do that in all your enterprises which may please him, for that is praise worthy indeed.'[53]

The preacher and schoolmaster John Stockwood in an open letter to Sir Francis Walsingham wanted to know 'what excuse' those holding 'the chiefest places of credit and countenance' would have if they failed to employ their care, travail, and labour for the benefit of the Church, furtherance of religion, and welfare of the godly.[54] Noblemen, said Laurence Humphrey, *must* be seasoned with 'the true unstayned worship of God, and sincere relygyon'. 'For they rule as wyse, not as myghtye.'[55] Praying publicly at Paul's Cross, John Foxe asked God to bless the nobility 'so as they, christianly agreeing among themselves, may submit their nobility to serve thee; or else let them feel, O Lord, what a frivolous thing is that nobility which is without thee'.[56] The Suffolk preacher Nicholas Bownd wrote that noblemen and great personages were called gods, 'carrying the image as it were of the magnificence and puissance of the Lord'. 'Yet they must remember, that as the Lord hath advanced them, so they are to advance the Lords worship: and as they be nearest to God, so God must bee nearest to them, in their houses and circuits.'[57]

---

[52] Wood had served at Newhaven in 1562–3, under Leicester's brother the earl of Warwick, as a captain and clerk to the council of war. There are numerous documents bearing his signature in State Papers Foreign, PRO S.P. 70/42–61. See my *Letters of Thomas Wood*, pp. v–vii. Simon Adams is currently engaged in a study of Thomas Wood.

[53] *Letters of Thomas Wood*, pp. 10, 23.

[54] In an Epistle 33 pp. in length, prefacing his *A right godly and learned discourse upon the booke of Ester* (1584).

[55] Laurence Humphrey, *The nobles, or, of nobilitye* (1563), sigs. 1 iv^v, x ii^v.

[56] John Foxe, 'A Sermon of Christ Crucified', in *Writings of John Fox, Bale, and Coverdale*, British Reformers, Religious Tract Society (n.d.), 94.

[57] Nicholas Bownd, *Sabbathum veteris et novi testamenti* (1606), p. 211.

Was this not a strange and perilous kind of friendship for a great nobleman to cultivate and depend upon? Lawrence Stone has made the important observation that in the correspondence between puritan peers and their godly social inferiors there was an implicit acknowledgement by both parties that questions of divine law and of the will of God transcended the normal respect due to a titular superior.[58] What was this unusual condescension if not a confession of insecurity and 'unsettledness'? Leicester's enemies jeered that he had nothing 'of his owne, either from his ancestors, or of himselfe, to stay upon, in men's hearts or conceits'.[59] There were moments—and these too were almost Cromwellian moments—when the devotion of the godly could be made to seem a substitute for the favour even of the queen herself. On one occasion, Leicester's brother, Warwick, wrote to warn him of 'our mystrys extreme radge' and 'malyce', but assuring him: 'Wherefore my good brother, repose your wholl trust in God, and he wyll deffende you in despytt of all your enemyes, and lett this be a greate confortt to you ... you warr never so honored and loved in your lyff amongest all good peopell as you ar att this daye, only for dealinge so nobly and wysely in this actione as you have done.'[60]

But what Leicester enjoyed was much more than a personal and potentially disloyal clientage of disgruntled puritans. He was no lone wolf but a central figure, the hub of a potent circle of religiously sympathetic courtiers and politicians who were his kindred, allies, and fellow-magnates, and which in its time had no equal as a political force. And beyond this charmed circle, in the country, were the 'good people' of whom Warwick wrote. Some of the roots of this grand coalition ran down into the soil of Suffolk, where we have already unearthed them. Lord North, the figure-head of gentry puritanism in the county, was one of the earl's staunchest allies, 'resolved to sinke or swimme with my lord of *Leycester*'.[61]

---

[58] Lawrence Stone, *The Crisis of the Aristocracy 1558–1641* (Oxford, 1965), p. 745.

[59] '*Leycesters Commonwealth*', p. 238.

[60] *Correspondence of Robert Dudley, Earl of Leycester, During his Government of the Low Countries in the Years 1585 and 1586*, ed. John Bruce, Camden Society xxvii (1854), 150–1.

[61] '*Leycesters Commonwealth*', p. 119.

The effective leaders of godly magistracy in Suffolk, Sir Robert Jermyn and Sir John Higham, were also Leicester's men and probably in his debt for their partial rehabilitation after the disgrace of 1584.[62] When Leicester led his expeditionary force to the Netherlands, Jermyn wrote: 'I praye God to blesse with his feare that thei maye be valiant in the Lords cause and fight his battailes with corage. The cause without contraversion is good.' The preacher Oliver Pigge in writing to Jermyn was an echo of his own voice: 'The cause which yow have in hande, I nothing doubt is the Lords, as well in respect of releving his present pore distract Churche, as allso in preventing the ruin of owers here, now in some sort florishing.'[63] Lord North joined the expedition, leading a retinue of twenty-two. Jermyn himself took over a retinue of thirty-two and then returned to Suffolk to raise more volunteers. Leicester wrote: 'He is greatly to be esteemed.'[64] When Leicester celebrated St. George's Day in Utrecht in 1586, the preacher was the captain of the Suffolk ministers, John Knewstub.[65]

In the 1570s and 1580s the spectacle of a puritan earl and viceroy was not incongruous. To those who knew of the admiration with which Calvin and other protestant theologians had written of such magistrates—'the most sacred and by far the most honourable of all stations in mortal life'[66]—and who were familiar with outstanding examples of

[62] *Rushbrook Parish Registers 1567 to 1850 with Jermyn and Davers Annals,* Suffolk Green Books vi (Woodbridge, 1906), 214; MacCulloch, 'Power, Privilege and the County Community', pp. 216–27. But Jermyn, like many other Elizabethan notables, was perhaps equally indebted to Lord Burghley, to whom he wrote on 23 November 1585: 'I cannot but reverence your lordship as *Patrem Patrie* and doe feare that when the Lord for our synnes shall take you from us, we shall to late thoughe to trulye crye oute, the horsemen and Chariot of England.' (BL Lansdowne MS 46, no. 27, fol. 53ʳ.)

[63] Sir Robert Jermyn to William Davison, 25 August 1585, Bodleian Library Tanner MS 78, fol. 73ʳ; Oliver Pigge to 'a christian knight imployet in the service of her Majestie in the Low Countries 1585', presumably Jermyn, Cambridge University Library MS Dd.11.76, fol. 21. See MacCulloch, 'Power, Privilege and the County Community', p. 225.

[64] Ibid., pp. 224–5; Adams, 'The Protestant Cause', pp. 56–8; *Leicester's Triumph,* ed. R. C. Strong and J. A. van Dorsten (Leiden, 1964), pp. 43, 54, 126, 121–2; *Correspondence of Robert Dudley,* pp. 114–15, 410–11.

[65] Ibid., p. 238n.; PRO S.P. 12/183/52; *HMC Report, Ancaster MSS,* p. 25; *Leicester's Triumph,* p. 69.

[66] John Calvin, *Institutes of the Christian Religion,* tr. Henry Beveridge (1949 edn.), ii. 654.

godly magistracy in other states, such as Coligny or Orange, Leicester seemed appropriate, timely, and providential, entirely at home in the political world which he inhabited. In measure as historians have taken account of that point of view, they have seen him as a stabilizing force in the politics of the Elizabethan age. Simon Adams suggests that for forty years after his death there was a fruitless search for his successor, for an ersatz Leicester, and that it was the final abandonment of that quest which led directly to the fatal polarization of English politics which was the precondition of civil war.[67]

In this chapter I have stood on its head some received wisdom about the value as ideology of the religion of protestants, insisting on the conservatism not only of protestantism but of the puritanism which was in continuity with it in Samuel Ward's Ipswich or Sir Robert Harley's Herefordshire. I have quarrelled with Michael Walzer's description of puritanism as 'the earliest form of political radicalism', and with Lawrence Stone's suggestion that by erecting an alternative hierarchy of spiritual grace, Calvinism and the puritan conscience sapped respect for rank and title at all levels of the social hierarchy.[68] On one page of his book *The Causes of the English Revolution* Stone writes of 'the socially disruptive idea of a hierarchy of the godly'. But on another he tells us that in the years before the Civil War 'only Puritan noblemen like the Earl of Bedford and the Earl of Warwick preserved, and possibly even increased, their prestige and political influence'.[69] The intention has not been to lose sight of the distinctiveness of godly magistracy, or to drown it in a sea of consensus conservatism, still less to argue that a majority, or anything approaching a majority, of Elizabethan and Jacobean magistrates were godly. Only that the puritanism of the minority who were resulted in a reinforcement of social values and objectives which were common to their class, not to the substitution of novel and deviant values and objectives.

---

[67] Adams, 'The Protestant Cause', p. 35.
[68] Stone, *Crisis of the Aristocracy,* pp. 743, 745.
[69] Lawrence Stone, *The Causes of the English Revolution 1529–1642* (1972), pp. 99, 84.

Christopher Hill has maintained that 'the logic of Protestantism led to an egalitarian individualism', and quotes Clarendon as complaining that 'all relations were confounded by the several sects in religion which discountenanced all forms of reverence and respect as relics and marks of superstition'.[70] Whether or not this was true of the sects, it falsifies the position of protestantism in its dominant tendency of anti-sectarian Calvinism. It was 'orthodox' Calvinists who filled their churches with seating, like that at St. Andrew's, Norwich, which placed the parishioners 'in order, in their degrees and callinges';[71] whereas it was the anti-Calvinist Arminians whose religious instincts were affronted by the massive pews or 'stalls' which, regardless of the needs of the liturgy, converted church interiors into visible representations of the social order.[72] Godly magistracy and ministry were naturally conservative forces, somewhat unnaturally and fortuitously converted into a force for revolutionary change.[73]

---

[70] Hill, *Society and Puritanism*, p. 477.

[71] I quote from an order recorded in the earliest surviving vestry minutes of Kingston upon Thames, 20 December 1585: 'It ys ordered that the seates in the churche shalbe altered and the parishioners to be placed in order in their degrees and callinges.' (Kingston Borough Archives, F.1.3, p. 103. I owe this reference to Katherine Longley.) At the time of this order, the minister of Kingston was the exceedingly 'radical' John Udall, a close associate of 'Martin Marprelate' and for a time under sentence of death. When the parish church of Myddle in Shropshire was 'uniformed' with wainscot pews in the mid-seventeenth century, the seats were allocated according to the rateable value of the property: 'A peiw or seat does not belong to a person, or to land butt to an house.' This had the effect of distributing tenants and servants throughout the church so that no strict hierarchy was preserved. Nevertheless, at the time of a dispute over a particular pew, 'it was held a thing unseemly and undecent that a company of young boyes, and of persons that paid no leawans [parish rates], should sitt . . . above those of the best of the parish'. (Richard Gough, *The History of Myddle*, ed. David Hey (1981), pp. 77, 120, 37, 96, 117.)

[72] M. E. James, *Family, Lineage and Civil Society: A Study of Society, Politics and Mentality in the Durham Region, 1500–1640* (Oxford, 1974), pp. 121–4.

[73] After this chapter went to press, an article appeared which provides an excellent example of godly magistracy and of its public values and concerns: Richard Cust and Peter G. Lake, 'Sir Richard Grosvenor and the Rhetoric of Magistracy', *Bulletin of the Institute of Historical Research*, liv (1981), 40–53.

Chapter Five

Popular and Unpopular Religion

I

'When I mention Religion,' declared Fielding's Parson Thwackum, 'I mean the Christian Religion; and not only the Christian Religion, but the Protestant Religion; and not only the Protestant Religion, but the Church of *England*.'[1] Not so today's religious historian. He is liable to mention that his subject is not what people were supposed to believe, but what they in fact believed, and still more what they did with their belief, its meaning and function. However, once we abandon arbitrary and conventional definitions of the Parson Thwackum variety, we encounter a question with which anthropologists are more familiar than historians: what is religion? That is a large matter far beyond the modest scope of this study. But it underlies a question which can scarcely be avoided. What, in the context of Elizabethan and Jacobean England, was '*popular* religion'?

Protestants and puritans of the sixteenth and seventeenth centuries sometimes used the rhetoric of populists, as if their religion was a popular cause and even a mass movement. Describing the burning of the last of the Marian martyrs in London, John Foxe reported the sympathetic presence of 'a great multitude' of 'the godly people'.[2] A puritan petition to Queen Elizabeth begged her to consider 'the miserable plight of the poore people, hungring after the foode of the word'. Another petition of the same kind was signed by 'your Grace's loving subjects . . . with infinite more in this shire of Norfolk'.[3] The puritan activist John Field thought that if the queen and Parliament failed to deliver the goods, 'the multitude and

---

[1] Henry Fielding, *The History of Tom Jones, A Foundling* (Oxford, 1974), i. 131.
[2] John Foxe, *Acts and Monuments,* ed. S. R. Cattley (1837–41), viii, 559. Cf. Bishop Bonner's report that as a group of Colchester heretics was conveyed along Cheapside, they were accompanied by about a thousand persons and received comfort '*a promiscua plebe*'. (Ibid., viii. 307.)
[3] *A Seconde Parte of a Register,* ed. Albert Peel (Cambridge, 1915), i. 229, 158.

people' would have to bring to pass the further reformation which he desired.[4] Consequently, the ecclesiastical authorities censured the puritans for following 'the folly of the people', 'calling it charity to feed their fond humour.'[5] In all these contexts, 'the people' meant not the masses but the people or *laos* of God, enlightened, responsible, dynamic, the spiritually industrious sort of people. *Vox populi, vox Dei.* As Christopher Hill has remarked: 'the ambiguity in Locke's use of the word "people" has a long preparatory history behind it.' In religious discourse, it might mean the spiritual élite, or that blind stupidity which set itself against the élite, and against the truth.[6] In the eye of the catholic polemicist Miles Huggarde, Foxe's 'godly people' were 'the simple and rude people', 'braynesicke foles'. They flocked to the burnings in Smithfield 'on heapes'. For such was the nature of Englishmen that 'if there be any vayne syghtes to be seen, or any folishe matters to be heard, Lorde howe they runne and sweate in their busines!'[7]

So we may speak in a certain sense of 'popular Protestantism'. But in their more realistic moments, protestants and puritans knew that 'the multitude', 'the great unjust rude rabble', was not of their side. If 'the poore people' were indeed starving for want of the word of God, then their potential to become the people of God had yet to be realized. The petitions

---

[4] PRO Star Chamber 5 A 49/34, deposition of Thomas Edmunds.
[5] Sir William Cecil to Archbishop Parker, 12 August 1561; *Correspondence of Matthew Parker*, ed. J. Bruce, Parker Society (Cambridge, 1853), pp. 148–9.
[6] Christopher Hill, *Society and Puritanism in Pre-Revolutionary England* (1966), p. 478. The difference between 'the people' in these two senses is well conveyed in the narrative of 'the troubles of me John Knight mynister', written in the 1580s. This described the disorderly behaviour of a drunken clergyman, Mr Stephens, in a Suffolk pulpit. At the start of these proceedings, 'the people being assembled together by the ringing of a bell' were 'sitting quietly in their seates in the churche, and being readye to singe a psalme'. When Stephens commenced his antics, it 'greved the godlie, but some laughte'. Eventually, 'the people were owt of quiet'. (Dr Williams's Library, MS Morrice A, Old Loose Papers, fols. 160–5.) In Foxe, we find adjacent accounts of two burnings in 1533. At the burning of John Frith and Andrew Hewet in London, the words of an attendant priest 'did not a little move the people unto anger'. But at the burning of Thomas Benet in Exeter, 'such was the devilish rage of the blind people, that well was he or she that could catch a stick or furze to cast into the fire'. (Foxe, *Acts and Monuments*, v. 18, 26.)
[7] Miles Huggarde, *The displaying of the protestants and sondry their practises* (1556), fol. 49.

made on their behalf were a rhetorical fiction, a mere propagandic device. An Essex vicar who had undergone the sea-change to New England encouraged his old parishioners with the good news that in Massachusetts 'the greater part' were also 'the better part'. In his experience, things had been otherwise in Old England: the greater part the worse part, the better part the lesser part. A modern study of the parish from which this man had emigrated confirms the general truth of his report. The better part in the village of Terling, 'a praying and fasting people', held private religious meetings in the house of the schoolmaster's widow, accommodation which was surely too cramped for any but a handful of the parishioners.[8] One early seventeenth-century writer thought it possible that only one part in twenty of the national population was 'christian indeed', 'the greatest part being the worst'.[9] The 'religion of protestants' in its more intense and fully internalized form was never popular in the plain and ordinary sense.

So what was 'popular religion'? 'The multitude' doubtless conformed in great numbers to the prayer-book religion of the parish church, which became part of the fabric of their lives. A Jacobean religious adventurer, who had experimented with both popery and puritanism, put a question to 'the common people', meaning it 'for no harme'. 'Is not this your religion? I meane, to say your praiers, to heare service etc., without any spetiall stirring of your heart?' And was not such a religion all one with 'that which you call the old religion'?[10] An ironical

---

[8] Thomas Weld, writing to his old parishioners in Terling, quoted, Stephen Foster, 'The Faith of a Separatist Layman: The Authorship, Context and Significance of *The Cry of a Stone*', *The William and Mary Quarterly*, 3rd ser. xxxiv (1977), 400. The full text is in *Letters from New England: the Massachusetts Bay Company, 1629–1638,* ed. Everett Emerson (Amherst, Mass., 1976), 94–8. In 1642, the governor of New Plymouth observed the increase in 'wicked persons' and wondered 'whether the greater part be not growne the worser'. (Winton U. Solberg, *Redeem the Time: the Puritan Sabbath in Early America* (Cambridge, Mass., 1977), pp. 123–3.) On Terling, see Keith Wrightson and David Levine, *Poverty and Piety in an English Village: Terling, 1525–1700,* Studies in Social Discontinuity (1979), Chapter 6; Keith Wrightson, 'Aspects of Social Differentiation in Rural England, c. 1580–1660', *The Journal of Peasant Studies,* v (1977), 42.

[9] John Darrell, *A treatise of the Church written against them of the Separation, commonly called Brownists* (1617), pp. 25–9.

[10] Richard Kilby, *Hallelu-iah. Praise ye the Lord for the unburthening of a loaden conscience* (Cambridge, 1618), pp. 29–30.

description of popular religion in this sense was recorded by the character writer, John Earle. The 'plaine countrie fellow' is not without a religion, but it is 'a part of his coppy-hold which he takes of his land-lord.' Yet if the landlord will give him leave 'he is a good Christian to his power, that is, goes to Church in his best clothes, and sitts there with his neighbours, where he is capable onely of two prayers, for Rayne or faire-weather.'[11] Like Earle, historians have often disparaged and underestimated a religion so inarticulate and undemonstrative. If, as is very possible, the parish church and its rhythmical provision of predictable, increasingly familiar rites and prayers progressively strengthened its hold on the habits and loyalties of the Elizabethan and Jacobean generations, this is a matter of indirect, inferential record. Practitioners of commonplace prayer-book religion, unlike the more strident religious minorities, do not pluck at the historian's sleeve.

If there has been an error of perspective and judgement in the neglect by ecclesiastical historians of much that was ordinary in religious life, the bias is shared by modern social historians, who are not easily convinced that the Prayer Book and the Homilies can have defined and sustained the truly popular religion of early modern England. Or, like Earle, they emphasize the affective, quasi-magical use of the Prayer Book: prayers for rain or fair weather. Having gone to school with anthropologists and folklorists, they peer beneath the surface of convention to discover a genuinely indigenous and vernacular religion in those instinctive and not necessarily Christian rituals which the religious intelligentsia all over early modern Europe were doing their best to eradicate.[12] Charles Phythian-Adams even distinguishes between 'popular' activities and 'christian' activities, while the great weight of Keith Thomas's *Religion and the Decline of Magic* has persuaded us that the content of popular religion was more magical than religious, the 'penumbra of superstition and custom' which A. L. Rowse found in Tudor Cornwall.[13] And since the repressive thrust of

---

[11] John Earle, *The Autograph Manuscript of Microcosmographie* (Leeds, 1966), p. 87.

[12] Peter Burke, *Popular Culture in Early Modern Europe* (1978), Chapter 8, 'The Triumph of Lent: the Reform of Popular Culture'.

[13] C. Phythian-Adams, *Local History and Folklore: A New Framework* (1975), p. 9; Keith Thomas, *Religion and the Decline of Magic* (1971); A. L. Rowse, *Tudor Cornwall*

Protestantism was dislodging many elements of folk catholicism, the protestant Reformation may have actually reinforced these magical alternatives to religion. As Keith Thomas confesses, magical belief, indeed belief of any kind, is not a thing which can be exactly measured. But clearly there was a lot of it about. It may not be sufficiently true to say that 'the people' lived by sub-Christian beliefs and panaceas which were surrogates for religion. But it is apparent that many people found it hard to live without them. Or so it seems towards the end of the twentieth century, when 'The Occult' is a department in many bookshops which make no provision for Theology or even Religion.

There is a further difficulty in the concept of 'popular religion'. The term implies that the sentiments of the mass of the people, or the lower ranks of society, can be differentiated from those of the ranks above them, with the implication that differences in religion are determined by economics. This is always a possibility, but it is not something to be taken for granted. When Arnaldo Momigliano was invited to lecture on 'Popular Religious Beliefs in the Late Roman Historians', he reported that according to his reading of the sources there were no such beliefs. 'In the fourth and fifth centuries there were of course plenty of beliefs which we historians of the twentieth century would gladly call popular.' But they were not so regarded in late antiquity, which did not distinguish between upper-class and lower-class religion and culture. Momigliano suspected that the irrelevance of class differences in this respect may have been a distinctive feature of Christian culture as such.[14] When did it cease to be so? It has been said that for English provincial culture, the reign of Elizabeth represented 'a major watershed'.[15] Part of that watershed was constituted by the acquisition of literacy and the worlds of experience to which literacy gave access, by large numbers of

---

(1969 edn.), p. 257. And see Imogen Luxton, 'The Reformation and Popular Culture', in *Church and Society in England: Henry VIII to James I*, ed. Felicity Heal and Rosemary O'Day (1977), pp. 57–77.

[14] Arnaldo Momigliano, 'Popular Religious Beliefs and the Late Roman Historians', in *Popular Belief and Practice: Studies in Church History*, viii, ed. Derek Baker (Cambridge, 1972), 1–18.

[15] A. G. Dickens, 'The Writers of Tudor Yorkshire', *Transactions of the Royal Historical Society*, 5th ser. xiii (1963), 74.

laymen and not a few laywomen: but still a minority of the population as a whole, and so a socially selective watershed.[16] In 1581 George Gifford could write with ironical detachment of 'the religion which is among the common sort of christians', 'the countrie divinitie'.[17] From T. S. Eliot to Peter Burke, students of culture in the seventeenth century have proposed that the full internalization of the religious changes of the preceding century introduced a profound dislocation in our civilization which was previously absent.[18] Studies on a microscopic scale, at village level, may uncover what Keith Wrightson calls 'those shifts in social relations which occurred without shattering the broader structural continuities of English rural society', including 'shifts' of a religious and cultural character.[19] But the historian requires a sensitive seismograph to detect and measure these shifts. For the first half of the seventeenth century, it may be premature to posit anything as clear-cut as a divorce between popular and élite religion. Nor is it to be taken for granted that the many religious and cultural differences which became pronounced in post-Reformation England were simply differences of wealth and status in disguise. The friction between the godly and the ungodly (to use a crude but convenient shorthand) could arise *within* and not necessarily *between* social classes.

This is not to deny that the physical arrangements at church assemblies, and especially the seating, were a deliberate demonstration of social difference. Processions were deplored by protestants as tumultuous and disorderly, the Royal Injunctions of 1559 complaining of 'challenging of places in procession'.[20] Wooden pews and stalls froze the orders of society in a static and visually edifying representa-

---

[16] David Cressy, *Literacy and the Social Order: Reading and Writing in Tudor and Stuart England* (Cambridge, 1980).

[17] George Gifford, *A briefe discourse of certaine points of the religion which is among the common sort of christians which may bee termed the countrie divinitie* (1581). See Dewey D. Wallace jun., 'George Gifford, Puritan Propaganda and Popular Religion in Elizabethan England', *The Sixteenth Century Journal*, ix (1978), 27–49.

[18] T. S. Eliot, 'The Metaphysical Poets' (1921), in *Selected Essays* (1976 edn.), pp. 287–8; Burke, *Popular Culture*.

[19] Wrightson, 'Aspects of Social Differentiation', 45.

[20] *Documentary Annals of the Reformed Church of England*, ed. Edward Cardwell (Oxford, 1844), i. 219.

tion of hierarchy. The image was familiar, not exotic, when Milton in *Samson Agonistes* depicted the Philistine assembly

> With seats where all the Lords and each degree
> Of sort, might sit in order to behold.

And when Samson pulled the temple down, it was 'The vulgar only scap'd who stood without'.[21] Common people respectfully rose from their places as their betters entered the church, which gratified the young Pepys in Restoration Cambridge-shire.[22] The 'facetious' Norfolk divine Edmund Gurney was perhaps eccentric in objecting to what he called 'the common fault of the meaner sort of people' in this respect, who, he said, were 'too prone to perform civill and outward respects upon the coming of the greater persons in the church by rising, bowing etc.' Gurney said that he preferred 'an holy-rowly-Powlinesse' in church, 'for there sure, if any where, we ought to be haile fellows well met'.[23] But the physical enactment of hierarchy, which was an important feature of sixteenth- and seventeenth-century church-going, was commonly supposed to have precisely the integrating effects which Gurney desired. Even in the nineteenth century it could be said, in defence of pews and pew rents, that 'the subordination of ranks is of divine institution and never is more beautifully or harmoni-ously exhibited than in the House of God, where rich and poor meet together to share the blessings of their common Father'.[24] That philosophy was doubtless more widely acceptable in the seventeenth century than in Sheffield (of all places) in 1840.

II

At the risk of seeming perverse, the remainder of this chapter will approach the problematical subject of popular religion by way of popular *ir*religion, or at least through the scrutiny of

---

[21] *The Works of John Milton*, I. ii (New York, 1931), 394, 396. See Richard Gough's account (1701–2) of how the church of Myddle in Shropshire was 'uniformed' with wainscot pews in the mid-seventeenth century. (Richard Gough, *The History of Myddle*, ed. David Hey (1981), pp. 77–83 and passim.)

[22] *The Diary of Samuel Pepys*, ed. R. Latham and W. Matthews, ii (1970), 147.

[23] *Anecdotes and Traditions Illustrative of Early English History and Literature*, ed. William J. Thoms, Camden Society (1839), 59; *DBN*, art. Gurney.

[24] E. R. Wickham, *Church and People in an Industrial City* (1957), p. 89.

low levels of religion commitment. Was the protestantism and puritanism of the post-Reformation Church of England as lacking in popular appeal as many contemporaries and some historians have suggested? And were the preachers and reformers as 'busy controllers' responsible for its unpopularity? Or, less heinously, did they merely perpetuate a longstanding failure of the Church to become indigenous in the hearts and minds of the populace? Was there a recalcitrant subculture of irreligion in Elizabethan and Jacobean England? And if so, what was its extent, and was it composed preponderantly of any particular social or occupational class, or age-group? It is easier to formulate such daunting questions than to provide answers. With all but a select minority, belief or 'mentality' is a matter not of certain knowledge but of inference, from external behaviour which was conditioned by habit, custom, and legal and social constraint.

Some historians have hoped to unlock the secrets of belief through study of the confessional statements with which it was conventional to preface the making of a last will and testament. If these statements were truly personal expressions of honest conviction, they would provide the only evidence we are ever likely to find of the nature and quality of the religious sentiments entertained by tens of thousands of otherwise almost anonymous and speechless men and women whose lives were bisected by the religious changes and instabilities of the sixteenth century and pursued to their conclusion in the aftermath of change.[25] From such evidence broadly-based statistical conclusions could be drawn with which to test, for example, Roland Green Usher's almost unsubstantiated suggestion, made with deceptive cartographical precision, that at the end of the Tudor epoch 'Catholic laymen' comprised from 40 per cent to as much as 85 per cent of the population in the north of England, Wales, and the extreme

[25] See the use of will evidence in A. G. Dickens, *Lollards and Protestants in the Diocese of York, 1509–1588* (Oxford, 1959), pp. 171–2, 215–17; Peter Clark, *English Provincial Society from the Reformation to the Revolution: Religion, Politics and Society in Kent, 1500–1640* (Hassocks, 1977), pp. 58–9, 74–6, 100; W. J. Sheils, *The Puritans in the Diocese of Peterborough 1558–1610,* Publications of the Northamptonshire Record Society, xxx (Northampton, 1970), 15–17, 20–4; Margaret Spufford, *Contrasting Communities: English Villagers in the Sixteenth and Seventeenth Centuries* (Cambridge, 1974), pp. 320–34.

south-west.[26] But few testators are likely to have left on public record an affirmation of beliefs which the law proscribed. And what of the mass of protestants, nominal or otherwise? Do their wills indicate the extent and the depth of their religious persuasion? Probably not. Among the minority of the population who made a will, only the wealthy and important thought it proper to put a personal stamp on what for the great majority was a matter of common form. At Cranbrook in the Weald of Kent, sometimes called 'puritan Cranbrook', only 8 out of 122 Elizabethan and Jacobean wills contain any distinctively Calvinist features, and many share a religious preamble which seems to have owed its identical wording to the parish clerk who drew up the wills, or perhaps to some formulary where the clerk found it.[27] Although most will preambles were purely formulaic, they can shed useful light on the acceptance of the new doctrines in the original age of the Reformation by indicating what the scribes, be they local clergy or notaries, or parish clerks, thought to be acceptable formulas for this purpose. But for any period earlier than the mid-seventeenth century, they are probably not good evidence of public opinion understood as the sum of many parts.

Even for the external aspects of religious practice, our evidence is incomplete and often indirect. There is no

---

[26] Roland G. Usher, *The Reconstruction of the English Church* (1910), i. 135. The Lake Counties were credited by Usher with 80 per cent Catholicism. John Bossy remarks that it would be hard to say how he arrived at this assessment from the figures of recusants which he himself printed. In Bossy's view, 'the extreme North-west displayed throughout these centuries an imperviousness to Catholicism so uniform as to indicate the lack of some essential precondition in the make-up of Cumbrian society'. (*The English Catholic Community 1570–1850* (1975), pp. 95–6.)

[27] M. L. Zell, 'The Use of Religious Preambles as a Measure of Religious Belief in the Sixteenth Century', *Bulletin of the Institute of Historical Research*, l (1977), 246–9; Margaret Spufford, 'The Scribes of Villagers' Wills in the Sixteenth and Seventeenth Centuries and their Influence', *Local Population Studies*, vii (1971), 28–43. See also the cautionary remarks of Margaret Spufford in *Contrasting Communities*, pp. 320–34; and of Dickens in *Lollards and Protestants*, pp. 171–2, 220–1. However, Susan Brigden has found that the London wills of the period 1522–47 provide a valuable index of the critical movement in belief from Catholicism to Protestantism, especially if attention is not confined to the preambles but includes benefactions and other bequests for pious and charitable uses. (S. E. Brigden, 'The Early Reformation in London, 1520–1547', Cambridge Ph.D. thesis, 1977, pp. 333–48.) For Cranbrook, see Patrick Collinson, 'Cranbrook and the Fletchers: Popular and Unpopular Religion in the Kentish Weald', in *Reformation Principle and Practice; Essays in Honour of A. G. Dickens*, ed. P. N. Brooks (1980), p. 187.

equivalent for our period of the 1851 Religious Census, or even of Bishop Compton's census of 1676, so that we cannot venture, in Delumeau's phrase, to penetrate 'the vicissitudes of belief with the dry but necessary instrument of statistics'.[28] The absence of reliable data has understandably resulted in historians finding what they have been disposed to find. On the one hand we have Peter Laslett's extraordinary statement that 'all our ancestors were literal Christian believers all of the time', which is undermined by evidence cited on almost the same page of *The World We Have Lost;*[29] and Margaret Spufford's more cautious persuasion, derived from the study of certain Cambridgeshire village communities, that 'even the humblest members, the very poor, and the women, and those living in physical isolation, thought deeply on religious matters and were often profoundly influenced by them'.[30] Whereas Keith Thomas thinks it likely that certain sections of the population, 'below a certain social level', managed without religion altogether: 'Although complete statistics will never be obtainable, it can be confidently said that not all Tudor or Stuart Englishmen went to some kind of church, that many of those who did went with considerable reluctance, and that a certain proportion remained throughout their lives utterly ignorant of the elementary tenets of Christian dogma'.[31] Peter Clark has been bold enough to put a figure on this 'certain proportion': 'Probably something like a fifth of the population of Kent stayed away from church on a regular basis in the later sixteenth century.'[32]

For the purpose of the debate about secularization, the uncertainty of early modernists is unfortunate. It is not clear where this critical period of religious change stands in the supposedly secular degeneration from a high level of religious practice in the Middle Ages to the socially circumscribed place occupied by institutionalized religion in modern society. When did traditional Christian society come to an end, or show signs of disintegration? Did it happen with industrializa-

---

[28] J. Delumeau, *Catholicism Between Luther and Voltaire* (1977), p. 132.
[29] Peter Laslett, *The World We Have Lost* (2nd edn. 1971), p. 74.
[30] Spufford, *Contrasting Communities*, p. 343.
[31] Thomas, *Religion and the Decline of Magic*, p. 159.
[32] Clark, *English Provincial Society*, p. 156.

tion and urbanization, or much earlier, as a consequence of the protestant onslaught on time-honoured rituals and the arbitrary destruction of dear and familiar images? Or conversely, did the Reformation as an episode of re-Christianization or even primary Christianization decelerate or arrest a process of secularization with much deeper roots?[33] The only thing which can relieve the embarrassment of our failure to give confident answers to such questions is the inability of medievalists to tell us whether 'traditional christian society' ever existed.[34]

Initially, we confront an apparent contradiction between two bodies of evidence: on the one hand, the pessimism of the sermons and the literature of complaint; on the other, the implied complacency of the records of ecclesiastical administration and justice, which for most of the time and most places register a statistically almost insignificant neglect of religious duties. Both sources must be used with extreme caution. The reliability of the official record is compromised by a fallible system for the detection and correction of defaulters. The evidence of literary sources is conditioned by a rhetorical convention of exaggerated moral outrage.

The pessimistic hyperbole of the Elizabethan complaint-literature was intensified by the unrealistic expectations of the writers. Judged by the rigorous sabbatarian principles which were in evidence from the 1570s, and which were supplied with a theological rationale in the 1590s,[35] it was not sufficient that the people should satisfy the bare letter of the law by attendance at church on a Sunday morning: 'thinking', wrote John Field, 'that the Sabbath is wel inough kept if they give God some little peece thereof'.[36] As Arthur Dent pointed out,

[33] On the secularization debate and the cerebral and procedural difficulties attendant upon it, see David Martin, *The Religious and the Secular: Studies in Secularization* (1969), and *A General Theory of Secularization* (Oxford, 1978).

[34] Delumeau asserts: 'The "golden age" of medieval Christianity is a legend. The religion of the mass of the people in the west has been confused with the religion of a clerical elite... On the eve of the Reformation, the average westerner was but superficially christianized.' (*Catholicism Between Luther and Voltaire*, pp. 160–1.) See the seminal local study by J. Toussaert, *Le Sentiment religieux en Flandre à la fin du moyen age*, Civilisations d'Hier et d'Aujourdhui (Paris, 1963).

[35] Patrick Collinson, 'The Beginnings of English Sabbatarianism', in *Studies in Church History*, i, ed. C. W. Dugmore and Charles Duggan (1964), 207–21.

[36] John Field, *A godly exhortation, by occasion of the late iudgement of God, shewed at Parris-garden* (1583), sig. B4ʳ.

this was not the outlook of sincere protestants but of papists, 'which thinke if they heare Masse in the morning, they may do what they list all the day after'.[37] In the puritan perspective, a merely conventional attendance upon religious duty was consistent with what was commonly called 'atheism', not a philosophical atheism but the practical godlessness of 'cold statute protestants'.[38] 'For now,' wrote Dent, 'the earth is full of ranke Atheists, and mock-gods, which scoffe at the Gospell and bleare out their tongue at all Religion.'[39] 'They be those which we call Atheists,' declared George Gifford's *Zelotes,* 'of no religion: but look, whatsoever any prince doth set forth, that they wil professe.'[40]

In puritan circles it was a commonplace that the majority had no deep attachment to the Gospel and were profoundly ignorant of its content. In 1572 it was estimated that 'not every fortieth person in England' was 'a good and devout gospeller', except perhaps in London.[41] Thirty years later a representative gathering of ministers which had been brought together by the Hampton Court Conference shared their 'common experience' that among 'our country congregations' the people were three ways affected. There were 'those effectually called by the preaching of the Gospel to the more sincere profession of religion'; those who hankered for the old ways, wishing 'that they might have again the old service' and alleging that the new faith had destroyed the old social virtues and charity; and lastly those 'either indifferent or plain neuter' who did 'greatly regard not of what religion they be'.[42] This last category of 'neuter' was considered to be particularly numerous. Thomas Cartwright wrote of the 'heapes of our

---

[37] Arthur Dent, *The plaine mans path-way to Heaven* (1601), pp. 141–2.

[38] 'Cold statute protestants' was a fairly unexceptionable expression. But William Dike, preaching at Leigh in Essex under Lord Rich's patronage in 1580, was said to have inveighed against 'statute protestants, against injunction men and against such (as he termed them) as iumpe with the queenes lawes . . .'. (Huntingdonshire Record Office, M 32/8/13.)

[39] Dent, *The plaine mans path-way,* p. 144.

[40] Gifford, *Countrie divinitie,* fol. 22; quoted by Henry Ainsworth, *Counterpoyson* (Amsterdam?, 1608), p. 206. Cf. Jeremy Corderoy, *A warning for worldlings* (1608), sig. A3ᵛ: 'But the Scripture forewarneth us of a more dangerous kind of Atheist, who wil not in words deny God, but by their deeds.'

[41] Quoted, H. N. Birt, *The Elizabethan Religious Settlement* (1907), p. 435.

[42] *HMC Report, Lord Montague of Beaulieu,* p. 37.

people' who had abandoned popery whilst remaining in 'an utter ignorance of the truth', as compared with 'the remnant of us' which had truly and faithfully believed.[43] When Arthur Dent complained of swearing as 'of all other sinnes most rife in the land', the oaths which he listed as in commonest use were the most traditional of catholic oaths: 'By my Faith', 'By my Troath', 'By our Lady', 'By St. Mary'.[44]

There is no reason to believe that an intellectually demanding and morally rigorous religion transmitted by the written and spoken word had a broad, natural appeal. In the country, the heavy, stupefied ignorance of the peasantry was a commonplace of the more sophisticated. Edward Dering wrote from his native Kent: 'We have no newes heere to write of but country things . . . every man going after his oxe and his horse, and most doe glorifie God no more than their brute beast.'[45] Fifty years later another Kentish minister told his fellow clergy: 'We dwell like men under a Frigid Zone, our parishes Friezeland, our people frozen into the mud of the world and dregges of sinne, and will you not be hissing hot in spirit?'[46] In Suffolk a preacher spoke of the people of Mildenhall as 'frosen in their dregges', 'which seeme to have made their large Fen their God'.[47] In his careful observations of 'the countrie divinitie', our Tudor anthropologist George Gifford recorded a response to the preaching ministry which could have been observed in perhaps any rural region of sixteenth-century Europe:

But let the Preacher speake never so plaine, although they sit and looke him in the face, yet if ye enquire of them so soone as they be out at the church dores, ye shall easily perceive that (as the common saying is) it went in at the one eare, and out at the other. They will say peradventure, after this manner, It was a good Sermon, I wold

---

[43] Thomas Cartwright, 'A generall confession of sinnes to be made at the exercise of fasting', appended to *A very godly and learned treatise of the exercise of fastyng* (1580), reprinted in *Cartwrightiana*, ed. Albert Peel and Leland H. Carlson, *Elizabethan Nonconformist Texts*, i (1951), 144.

[44] Dent, *The plaine mans path-way*, p. 159.

[45] Edward Dering, *Certaine godly and comfortable letters*, bound with *Workes* (1597), sig. C^v.

[46] Robert Abbot, *Davids desires* (1623), sig. *.*3.

[47] Thomas Settle, *A catechisme briefly opening the misterie of our redemption* (1587), Epistle.

we could follow it, he saide very well: hee is a perfect ready man in the Pulpet. But aske, what doctrine did he handle? Then are they at a pause, and set at a dead lift.[48]

Josias Nicholls of Kent, one of the ministers who had shared their experience at the time of Hampton Court, wrote of a parish of four hundred communicants where a policy of systematic catechizing before administering the sacrament had revealed that scarcely one in ten was familiar with the elements of protestant doctrine. Asked 'whether it were possible for a man to live so uprightlie that by well doeing he might winne heaven', there was hardly a man who failed to answer in the affirmative: 'that a man might be saved by his owne weldoing, and that he trusted he did so live that by God's grace hee shoulde obtaine everlasting life, by serving of God and good prayers etc.'[49] Gifford employed a character called 'Atheos' to express this incorrigibly Pelagian philosophy: 'I meane well: I hurte no man: nor I thinke no man anye hurte: I love God above all: and put my whole trust in him: What woulde you have more? They preache and teache, they can tell us no more but this when they have said all what they can.'[50] Such was the religion 'which is among the common sort of christians'—popular religion.

Ignorance was doubtless particularly endemic in areas deprived of a preaching ministry, Christopher Hill's 'dark corners of the land'.[51] When Samuel Crooke was 'planted' at Wrington in Somerset in 1602 he was said to have been the first in 'the whole country adjacent' who by preaching the Gospel brought religion into credit, and 'discovered to them the Heavenly *Canaan,* which before was to most of them a *Terra*

---

[48] George Gifford, *A sermon on the parable of the sower* (1582), sig. Avii. Cf. the complaint of the Lancashire preacher Simon Harward against 'idle and fruitless hearers, to let in at one ear and out at the other ear, to hear it in the church and leave it in the porch'. (*Two godly and learned sermons* (1582), quoted, Christopher Haigh, 'Puritan Evangelism in the Reign of Elizabeth I', *English Historical Review*, xcii (1977), 48.)

[49] Josias Nicholls, *The plea of the innocent* (1602), pp. 212–14.

[50] Gifford, *Countrie divinitie,* fol. 7ʳ.

[51] Christopher Hill, 'Puritans and "The Dark Corners of the Land"', *Transactions of the Royal Historical Society*, 5th ser. xiii (1963), 77–102; reprinted, *Change and Continuity in Seventeenth-Century England* (1974), pp. 3–47.

incognita, as an unknown land.'[52] But Christopher Haigh is quite right to insist that a recalcitrant population was not effectively protestantized by the mere 'planting' of a preacher.[53]

The puritans are not reliable and disinterested reporters of religious practice of an intensity below that of 'the sincere profession of religion'. Yet the historian of culture has to live with the paradox that much of his knowledge of traditional custom comes from the writings of reformers heavenbent on its destruction, just as much of our knowledge of the Elizabethan theatre is supplied by its bitterest enemies. So we may make suitably cautious use of the complaint-literature to gain a consistent and not implausible impression of religious duties in sometimes unsuccessful competition with a variety of other activities which the reformation of the Calendar had tended to concentrate on Sundays. That the churches were empty and places of entertainment full was a commonplace as early as 1560 when Bishop Pilkington wrote: 'For come into a church on the sabbath day, and ye shall see but few, though there be a sermon; but the alehouse is ever full.'[54] He was echoed by Alexander Nowell, preaching before Parliament in 1563: on the Lord's Day 'taverns, alehouses, and other unruly places be full, but the Lord's house empty'.[55] In the same Parliament Sir Nicholas Bacon asked: 'Howe commeth it to passe that the common people in the countrye universallie come so seldome to common prayer and devine service...? And yet to the helpe of this there was at the last parliamente a lawe made [sc., the Act of Uniformity of 1559], but hitherto noe man, no, noe man—or verye fewe—hath seene it executed.'[56] Forty years later, things may have been no better. Writing in the early years of James I, George Widley asked:

---

[52] Samuel Clarke, *A Collection of the Lives of Ten Eminent Divines* (1662), p. 30.

[53] Haigh, 'Puritan Evangelism'.

[54] *The Works of James Pilkington,* ed. J. Scholefield, Parker Society (Cambridge, 1842), p. 6.

[55] 'Mr Noel's Sermon at the Parliament Before the Queen's Majestie', appended to *A Catechism ... by Alexander Nowell,* ed. G. E. Corrie, Parker Society (Cambridge, 1853), p. 226.

[56] *Proceedings in the Parliaments of Elizabeth I,* i, *1558–1581,* ed. T. E. Hartley (Leicester, 1981), 82. See Patrick Collinson, 'Sir Nicholas Bacon and the Elizabethan *Via Media*', *Historical Journal,* xxiii (1980), 268–9.

'For who is it that hath not rather goe to Church, than goe to worke? but who is it (I speake of the multitude) that had not rather goe to play, than goe to church?' 'Every whistle of pleasure is sufficient to call us away.' Widley thought that people would rather 'sit at cards on the Sabbath by a hot fire, than to sit at a Sermon with God in a cold church', and we may well believe it.[57]

The world assumed in much of the Elizabethan complaint-literature was metropolitan and filled with the rival attractions of the early theatres, the bear-baiting at Paris Garden, and the gaming tables. George Whetstone, writing in 1584, noted that London had more 'ordinary tables' for dice-play than churches.[58] Richard Rawlidge estimated in 1628 that London had 122 churches, but 'I dare say above thirty hundred ale-houses, typling houses, tobacco-shops etc.', perhaps ten times as many alehouses as had existed fifty or sixty years earlier.[59] John Field, Humphrey Roberts, and John Stockwood, all writing or preaching in the early days of the London stage, complained that it was easier to fill the theatres than the churches. Field lamented that after so much preaching 'Theatres should be full, and churches be emptie'. 'I know', he added, 'that churches (thankes be to God) are frequented. But what is this in respect of the multitude?' Preaching at Paul's Cross in 1578, Stockwood asked where, apart from a few churches, 'shall you finde a reasonable company?' Whereas the theatres are full, 'so full as possible they can throng'. 'Wyll not a fylthye playe, wyth the blast of a Trumpette, sooner call thyther a thousande, than an houres tolling of a Bell bring to the Sermon an hundred?'[60] Our confidence in the value of such statements as evidence of Elizabethan social behaviour is weakened by the knowledge that all these writers were embroidering a commonplace which can be traced back at least as far as the fifth-century

---

[57] George Widley, *The doctrine of the Sabbath, handled in foure severall bookes or treatises* (1604), pp. 99, 128, 132.

[58] George Whetstone, *A mirrour for magestrates of cytties* (1584), fol. 24ᵛ.

[59] Richard Rawlidge, *A monster late found out* (1628), sig. ¶3, p. 8.

[60] Field, *A godly exhortation*, sig. aᵛ; John Stockwood, *A sermon preached at Paules Crosse on Barthelmew day being the 24 of August 1578* (1578), pp. 23–4.

writer Salvian: 'Ecclesia vacuatur, circus impletur.'[61] Yet there is no reason to doubt the testimony of the complainers when they tell us that the Act of Uniformity was not effectively in force. Field noted that the law required 'all the people of all sortes' to attend church, 'and ther is a penalty set upon it'. 'But how this is looked unto throwout the lande, I leave it to them to consider that are wise and in authoritie.'[62]

These were the complaints in London. Humphrey Roberts, minister at King's Langley in Hertfordshire, was no less exercised by the unsophisticated counter-attractions of the countryside: 'For truly, the people will not stick to go x or xii miles upon the Saboth day in the morning unto a Silver game, ther to spend the time in vanyties all the day long: so that a man may find the churches empty, savyng the minister and ii or iiii lame, and old folke: for the rest are gon to folow the Devils daunce.' Roberts was convinced that 'a great many, yea I may say a multitude, come neither at service, sermon, nor any other godly exercise in the churche. God send a redress for this, both in cities and in the country.'[63] In Lancashire, where the contest between protestant religion and 'the customs of a relaxed and traditionalist society'[64] was particularly unequal, the hyperbole of complaint was correspondingly extreme. William Harrison, one of the King's preachers in the county, thought that 'for one person which we have in the church to hear divine service, sermons and catechism, every piper (there be many in one parish) should at the same instant have many hundreds on the greens'.[65]

It was no accident that the King's Book of Sports originated in Lancashire. The county was famous for its addiction to

[61] Salvian, *De Gubernatione Dei*, vii. 37, *Corpus Scriptorum Ecclesiasticorum Latinorum,* viii, ed. F. Pauley (1933), 135. I owe this reference to Graham Anderson. Northbrooke quotes Salvian's aphorism, *A treatise,* pp. 63–4.

[62]Field, *A godly exhortation* sig. B5ʳ.

[63]Humphrey Roberts, *An earnest complaint of divers vain wicked and abused exercises practised on the Saboth day* (1572), sigs. D2, B2. The last sentence is a marginal comment. From Roberts's description, 'silver games' appear to have been fund-raising and charitable events which were publicly licensed and widely advertised, with 'banners hanged upon poles, with drommes and instrumentes played before them, proclayming this their vanities to be holden upon Sonday at such a towne'. (Sig. D3.)

[64] Haigh, 'Puritan Evangelism', p. 51.

[65] William Harrison, *The difference of hearers (1613);* quoted, Haigh, 'Puritan Evangelism', 52.

sport and communal pleasures of the most traditional kind: 'wakes, ales, greens, May games, rush-bearings, bear-baits, dove-ales, bonfires . . . gaming, piping and dancing'.[66] Elsewhere, in more 'civil' country, the wilder allegations of the moralists cannot always be tested against documentary evidence. Silver games are likely to remain one of the more inaccessible diversions of Merrie England. But something can usually be learned about dancing, both the communal village-green variety, which in the south was increasingly confined to May Day and midsummer, and the more private dancing parties organized on Sundays both in private houses and in taverns and inns, with one or two hired musicians and a liberal supply of liquid refreshment. The court books of the archdeaconry of Canterbury are particularly informative on this subject. If the host or the minstrels were prosecuted for holding dancing on the Sabbath they usually offered the less than convincing defence that the entertainment had not interfered with Evening Prayer. As the character of *Juvenis* says in a printed dialogue on dancing: 'I am sure the churchwardens . . . will suffer both the minstrels to play and us to daunce upon Sundayes, so we do not daunce in time of service.'[67] When a churchwarden of Molash in Kent had 'a great daunsinge and drinkyng of syder' in his house on Passion Sunday 1575, with 'half a hundred of youth' present, he pleaded that Evening Prayer had finished at their parish churches before the young people had set out for the dance.[68] The minstrels presented for playing in an alehouse at Bethersden on 25 August 1578, so causing the youth 'to absent themselves from evening prayer that day', alleged that they had played before and after Evening Prayer, but not during the time of the service itself. According to his own account of

[66] Bossy, *The English Catholic Community*, p. 93; Hill, *Society and Puritanism*, p. 189. See also Mark H. Curtis, 'The Trials of a Puritan in Jacobean Lancashire', in *The Dissenting Tradition: Essays for Leland H. Carlson*, ed. C. Robert Cole and Michael E. Moody (Athens, Ohio, 1975), pp. 78–99.

[67] Christopher Fetherston, *A dialogue agaynst light, lewde and lascivious dauncing* (1582), sig. C. See the information on Sunday dances collected from Essex archdeaconry records in F. G. Emmison, 'Tithes, Perambulations and Sabbath-breach in Elizabethan Essex', in *Tribute to an Antiquary: Essays Presented to Marc Fitch by Some of his Friends*, ed. Frederick Emmison and Roy Stephens (Chichester, 1976), pp. 201–2.

[68] Cathedral Archives and Library Canterbury, X.1.12, fol. 151ᵛ.

how he had spent the same Sunday, Robert Wallop of Ashford never paused for breath. He first arranged for some minstrels to play at Ashford, then rode over to Westwell (a distance of five miles) 'for certen clothes that he had there lyeng', where he took the opportunity to hear Morning Prayer. He then returned to Ashford, where he heard Evening Prayer before joining the dancing.[69] But at Cranbrook in 1606, James Rich admitted that it was in the time of divine service that he had entertained twenty persons in his house with 'a firkynge of beere', fiddling, piping, and dancing.[70] And when John Herne the minstrel played at Warden in Sheppey on a Sunday in 1576, 'both the forenoone and after noone in the servyce time', the complaint of the vicar of a neighbouring parish was poignant and suggestive: 'By reporte he had more with hym than I had at the churche.'[71] And on the nearby mainland at Eastry, in 1574, 'Mylls the minstrel' was presented for playing on his tabor and drawing the youth 'by great flocke', detaining them from church at time of divine service.[72]

III

Yet none of these dancers seems to have been prosecuted for absence from church. The Act of Uniformity required attendance on Sundays and holy days, morning and evening, of 'all and every person and persons inhabiting within this realm', not having lawful or reasonable excuse to be absent. The penalty for absence was not only the familiar twelve-penny forfeit, to be levied by the churchwardens for the use of the poor, but 'punishment by the censures of the Church'. But how was 'the Church' to know? According to the Royal Injunctions, the bishops were to appoint three or four 'discreet men' in every parish who were to see that all parishioners duly

---

[69] Ibid., X.2.2, fol. 26.
[70] Ibid., X.4.11, fol. 7ᵛ.
[71] Ibid., X.1.13, fol. 80ᵛ.
[72] Ibid., X.1.12, fol. 23ʳ. In the following year these persons were presented from the Faversham district as common minstrels: Thomas Myll, Anthony Lee, Allen Carter, Thomas Pasheley. When at the same court the churchwardens of Sheldwich presented the minstrels Thomas Mason and Syracke Mason it was said that one of the dancers 'whose name our vycar knowethe' had said and wished 'the pox on them that fynd fault with them that daunce on the sabaoth dayes'. (Ibid., X.1.12, fols. 136ᵛ–7, 139ᵛ.)

resorted to church and continued there the whole time of godly service. Those slack or negligent in attendance, 'having no great nor urgent cause of absence', were to be visited, admonished, and 'if they amend not denounced to the ordinary'. In practice this responsibility devolved upon the parochial maids of all work, the churchwardens, and seems to have been fulfilled, if at all, when the wardens and sidesmen of the parish conferred on the composition of their periodical bills of presentment. The names which came to mind on these infrequent occasions were not likely to be those of casual absentees from church. And even in the cases of habitual offenders the memory of the parish ancients was perhaps prompted by particular circumstances beyond our knowledge. They may have found it hard to remember the names of persons of wealth and consequence, but the poor and worthless may also have escaped their notice.

At Cranbrook in the Weald, the largest and most populous parish in Kent, only 14 out of a total of 717 presentments in a period of forty-seven years were for simple absence from church.[73] Ronald Marchant's analytical sampling of presentments reveals from the seventy-five parishes of the deanery of Doncaster only 31 such cases out of 286 in 1590, 8 out of 416 in 1619, and 30 out of 407 in 1633. From the forty-nine parishes of the Suffolk deanery of Sudbury there were 154 presentments in 1593, but not one of them was for absenteeism.[74] Martin Ingram's Wiltshire researches tell the same story. It is, he says, impossible to believe that the presentments represent more than a tiny fraction of the offenders.[75] The general dubiousness of the evidence is exposed by the occasional drives against irreligious behaviour mounted in particular parishes and occasioned by some passing local circumstance. From Scarborough in 1575, thirty-three persons were denounced for 'cominge slowlie to the churche, morninge praier beinge halfe doone', a churchwarden was presented for partial absence from Morning Prayer and total absence from Evening Prayer,

[73] Collinson, 'Cranbrook and the Fletchers', p. 184.

[74] Ronald A. Marchant, *The Church Under the Law: Justice, Administration and Discipline in the Diocese of York 1560–1640* (Cambridge, 1969), p. 219.

[75] M. J. Ingram, 'Ecclesiastical Justice in Wiltshire 1600–1640, with Special Reference to Cases Concerning Sex and Marriage', Oxford D.Phil. thesis, 1976, p. 85.

while twenty-six other parishioners were identified as absentees from Evening Prayer on a certain Sunday when most were said to have been engaged in shooting or card-playing.[76] From one parish near Richmond in North Yorkshire in 1633 no less than eighty-seven persons were presented for negligence in coming to the church on Sunday afternoons, which was nearly three times the total denounced for similar offences in the entire deanery of Doncaster in the same year.[77] Occasionally, circumstantial evidence will reveal how remote from reality the evidence of presentments is likely to have been. In 1570 the vicar of Kingston near Canterbury explained that it was not his custom to wear the surplice when he saw 'fewe people at churche'.[78] When Archbishop Matthew came to preach at a country church in the East Riding in 1606, he found 'neither priest nor people', although the parish had due warning of his visit.[79] It is perhaps unlikely that the congregations on holy days matched the Sunday attendances. There was little enthusiasm for saints' days among that zealous protestant element which was most concerned to secure maximum religious observance. In an admission of rare honesty, the churchwardens of the Wiltshire parish of Ogbourne St. Andrew confessed in 1628 that the entire parish was guilty of failing to observe holy days.[80] Yet the act books contain no suggestion that slackness on these days was a greater problem than on Sundays, and holy days in principle were days of equal obligation.

For some urban areas, and especially London, it is a matter

[76] *Archbishop Grindal's Visitation, 1575: Comperta et Detecta Book*, ed. W. J. Sheils, Borthwick Texts and Calendars: Records of the Northern Province iv (1977), 81–3. We should perhaps identify absence from Evening Prayer as a distinct offence. That it was an offence at all may have depended upon a rigorous glossing of the Act of Uniformity. At Black Notley in Essex, late in Elizabeth's reign, there were complaints of 'a great many of the parishioners upon the sabbath dayes absent from evening prayer, and the churchwardens and questmen sometimes themselves and not presented'. (F. G. Emmison, *Elizabethan Life: Morals and the Church Courts, Mainly from Essex Archidiaconal Records* (Chelmsford, 1973), p. 75.)

[77] Marchant, *Church Under the Law*, pp. 220, 219.

[78] Cathedral Archives and Library Canterbury, X.1.10, fol. 25. It is possible that the vicar referred to Wednesdays or Fridays which were not days of obligation according to the statute.

[79] Thomas Wilson's transcript of Archbishop Tobie Matthew's Diary, Minster Library York, p. 86.

[80] Ingram, 'Ecclesiastical Justice', p. 86.

of simple observation that there was already no room in the churches for the inflated population. In 1609 a writer asked: 'Are not the people of diverse parishes in and about London so many and their churches as places of meeting so small that it is not possible to assemble all together at one time, though they should be crowded never so much?' The churches specified were in the teeming suburbs: St. Olave's and St. Saviour's, Southwark, St. Sepulchre's, St. Giles's without Cripplegate, Stepney.[81] Late Elizabethan Exeter provided no fewer than nineteen parish churches for its population of 16,000. But in 1601 it was estimated that none of these buildings could accommodate more than two to three hundred people.[82] At Sheffield, church accommodation was already inadequate, as it would be in the days of the Industrial Revolution. But the numbers presented for non-attendance in 1619 and 1633 were one in each year.[83] In the country too it was not an utterly implausible excuse for a man to say that 'he could not get into the church by reason of the crowde of people'.[84]

The presentments for failure to receive the Communion, especially at Easter, command more respect, although it is far from clear that they provide a reliable indication of that percentage of the adult population which performed this elementary Christian duty: a matter of relatively precise knowledge in seventeenth-century France.[85] In the archdeaconry of Wiltshire in 1593 there were 126 presentments for not receiving, compared with only 19 for non-attendance.[86] Are we to believe Thomas Sperin, the London rector of St. Mary Magdalen, Milk Street, when he claimed in 1590 that he administered the sacrament to none but 'such as he knoweth faithful', but adding that he knew all his parishioners, both

[81] *M. Downames sermon preched at Lambith April 17 1608 answered and refuted* (1609), p. 62.

[82] Wallace T. MacCaffrey, *Exeter, 1540–1650: the Growth of an English Country Town* (Cambridge, Mass., 1958), pp. 176–7, 196–7.

[83] Marchant, *Church Under the Law*, p. 218; Wickham, *Church and People*.

[84] Wrightson and Levine, *Poverty and Piety in an English Village*, p. 157.

[85] Gabriel le Bras, *Études de sociologie religieuse*, 2 vols., Bibliothèque de Sociologie Contemporaine (Paris, 1956).

[86] Ingram, 'Ecclesiastical Justice', p. 91.

men and women, to be such, 'except one household?'[87] The
evidence is rarely straightforward, or conclusive. The twenty
parishioners prosecuted for not receiving at Cranbrook in
1582 may conceivably have represented all or most of the true
total of abstaining householders.[88] When ten years later a new
incumbent of the same parish complained that the churchwardens and sidesmen had failed to present to the archdeacon
the names of Easter abstainers with which he had supplied
them, it was explained that he was unfamiliar with the local
practice, which was to allow people to make their Communion at any time between Easter and Whitsun. But our
suspicions are aroused by the churchwardens' account of this
conversation. They had asked the vicar 'who were beehinde
for receaving', and he had answered that none were behind,
'and that for that matter he woulde save them harmles'.[89] How
could a newcomer to Cranbrook know for certain which
parishioners had performed their duty and which had not?
The parish contained upwards of two thousand communicants, scattered in hamlets, farms, and cottages over an area of
forty square miles, and the population was in a state of
constant flux.[90] At Easter 1585, the vicar of Redbourn in
Hertfordshire explained to the archdeacon's official why he
could not deliver to the wardens and sidesmen the names of
those who had received and of those who had not. His practice
was to minister the Communion monthly, requiring intending
communicants to give him 'some premonition' so that he
could distinguish between those who received 'so often as they
should' and those who were negligent. But the parishioners
could not be persuaded to comply with these arrangements.
'But at the verie time when I shoulde minister the said
sacramente, after divine service and sermon, the time being
then so farre spente in prayers and prechinge, that I have noe
time or leisure to take their names, they comme thronginge

---

[87] *The Writings of John Greenwood 1587–1590*, ed. Leland H. Carlson, Elizabethan
Nonconformist Texts, iv (1962), 185.

[88] Cathedral Archives and Library Canterbury, X.2.2, fol. 146ᵛ.

[89] Ibid., X.3.5, fols. 133ᵛ–4ʳ.

[90] Collinson, 'Cranbrook and the Fletchers'.

and pressinge in great numbre commonly without all good order, not giveing me any warninge or worde thereof before'.[91]

The scrupulous observance of the Canons required the incumbent and parish officers not only to detect absentees from their own parish but to repel intruders from elsewhere, for to neglect the sacraments in one's own parish and receive elsewhere was tantamount to schism. This was not easy, especially in London, where the casual crossing of parish boundaries for other purposes was common practice, officially condoned when some churches were closed for repair or otherwise put out of action. In 1630 John Davenport, vicar of St. Stephen's, Coleman Street, explained to his diocesan, Laud, that besides forbidding strangers to take Communion in his parish, which was a notorious mecca for the godly, he required his own people to give notice of their intention to communicate to the parish clerk, who thereupon issued them with Communion tokens. He would then sit in the vestry between his sermon and the Communion, while the church-wardens went through the church collecting up the tokens. But Davenport admitted that in a parish of 1,400 communicants he did not and could not know the majority of his flock. 'They are so many and...they so often change theyre dwellings.' Communion was carried to this great congregation as they knelt or often, perforce, sat, tightly packed, in their pews.[92]

Nevertheless, there seems to have been an expectation that at Easter, if not at other seasons, the majority of the population would be present in their own parish churches to receive their 'rights', non-communicants standing out as an identifiable minority. The prodigious purchases of wine often recorded in churchwardens' accounts suggest that the majority received. Many incumbents may have had a more exact knowledge of their flock than seems to have been possible at Cranbrook, or in Coleman Street. In Mr Sperin's London parish, Communion tokens were used to identify the household servants whom the vicar had previously examined to

[91] Hertfordshire Record Office, ASA 5/5/124.
[92] *Letters of John Davenport Puritan Divine*, ed. I. M. Calder (New Haven, 1937), pp. 34–5.

establish the adequacy of their knowledge.[93] It would be a serious error to suppose that even the poorest parishioners were beneath the notice of their pastor, above all at Easter, for it was then that the Easter offering was due, in some parishes twopence from every communicant, in others fourpence from every household. Even the humblest cottager would be looked to for her 'smoke penny'.[94] And the clergy kept careful account of such matters, being penny wise. In a typical Leicestershire terrier, for example, 'every man and woman maried or unmaried, householder or servant of age to receive the holy communion' was to pay twopence as an Easter offering, while every householder occupying land was to pay an additional three halfpence 'with the offering', in odd years the odd penny, in even years the even twopence.[95]

But it would be no less a mistake to construct an edifying scenario of parishioners devoutly depositing their pennies in the dish as they advanced in procession to the Communion-table, for the money was probably collected in a variety of ways and not necessarily by the incumbent in person. In 1627, Thomazine Mercy of the Wealden village of Marden confessed to her friend Alice Barrow that she had wrongly accused the vicar Mr Wood of fathering her base child, and she asked Alice to convey this confession to the vicar 'when she should carry her Easter offering' to him.[96] At the other end of England, a Westmorland preacher recorded a vivid impression of the abuses attendant upon the Lord's Supper, which he suspected were a principal provocation of the divine wrath visited upon the region in the poor harvests and ravaging epidemics of the late 1590s. At the Communion service the north-country people strove, thronged, and pressed forward to receive what they called their 'rightings', 'making no better than a common banket of it'. Meanwhile, the parson's proctor

---

[93] *Writings of John Greenwood*, 185.

[94] *Ecclesiastical Terriers of Warwickshire Parishes,* i, ed. D. M. Barratt, Dugdale Society xxii (Oxford, 1955), xlii. I have benefited from discussing the subject of Easter offerings with Dr Barratt.

[95] Geoffrey J. Cuming, 'The Life and Work of Anthony Cade B.D. Vicar of Billesdon, 1599–1639', *Transactions of the Leicestershire Archaeological and Historical Society,* xlv (1969–70), 55.

[96] Cathedral Archives and Library Canterbury, X.11.16, fol. 267ʳ. I owe this reference to Susan M. Callaway.

would be reckoning up his fees, 'in the very time of administering the Supper, and that within the Lord's house, not farre from the minister'. The attendant brawling over money matters drowned the music of the few who sang psalms. As soon as they had made their reckoning and had received the sacrament, these 'sillie, ignorant people' hastened out of the church and across to the tavern or alehouse, whence they emerged some considerable time later, with belching and beastly vomiting.[97]

Some of those missing from the throng of Easter communicants would have been marked out as unabsolved excommunicates, a class of person in which historians have taken a particular interest since F. D. Price first drew attention to the massive failure of the post-reformation spiritual courts to apply a credible and effective discipline.[98] A high proportion, sometimes even the majority of those cited to appear in court for all kinds of offence, but especially for sexual crimes, failed to present themselves.

Compliance was not easy to obtain in any system of justice in the medieval and early modern world. But in the Church courts the weapon used to obtain it, and as often as not used unsuccessfully, was the penalty of excommunication, in principle a sentence of exclusion from the Christian community. Denunciations of excommunicates must have punctuated Morning Prayer in the Elizabethan Church with the same frequency as the calling of banns of marriage. But it cannot usually be shown that more than a minority of those denounced were subsequently reconciled to the Church. At Cranbrook two-thirds of those cited in the reign of Elizabeth failed to appear in court. And of those cited for sexual and marital offences, which was 50 per cent of the total, 80 per cent were contumacious. Between 1560 and 1607 328 sentences of excommunication were pronounced against parishioners of Cranbrook and there is evidence of only forty-four of these sentences having been subsequently alleviated by the

[97] Richard Leake, *Foure sermons, preached and publikely taught, . . . at Killington within the Baronie of Kendall and Countie of Westmerland: immediatly after the great visitation of the pestilence in the fore-sayd Countie* (1599), pp. 42–7.

[98] F. D. Price, 'The Abuses of Excommunication and the Decline of Ecclesiastical Discipline Under Queen Elizabeth', *English Historical Review*, lvii (1942), 106–15.

archdeacon's court which imposed them, and this after an interval of as much as eight years.[99] These statistics suggest a rather extreme situation. Robert Marchant regards a level of compliance in court attendance of 42 to 46 per cent as 'about the national average'. But in the archdeaconry of York in 1623 it was as low as 31 per cent. Of those presented in the archdeaconry of Sudbury for sexual crimes in 1593, 67 per cent were contumacious, and in 1633 the percentage was again 67 per cent.[1] Martin Ingram's findings for early Stuart Wiltshire are more favourable. The hard core of total recalcitrance varied from 34 per cent to as little as 22 percent.[2]

By an extrapolation from the annual running totals of excommunications in the three dioceses of York, Norwich, and Chester (1,500 to 2,000 for each diocese) Marchant thought that there might have been at any one time 50,000 hardened excommunicates in these areas, or 5 per cent of their population. Adding other members of their households, Marchant arrived at a notional figure of 15 per cent of the population 'in the excommunicate class'. By means of this arithmetic, the existence was posited of 'a seam of irreligious people lying below the greater mass of nominal Christians'.[3] No wonder the separatist John Robinson complained that 'the Church of England plays with excommunications as children do with rattles'. As the Scot Robert Baylie was to remark in 1646: 'Episcopal Courts were never fitted for the reclaiming of minds.'[4]

But Marchant's notion of a subculture of 'ethical dissenters' is not without its problems. How hardened were 'hardened' excommunicates? It is not always clear whether excommunication incurred as the automatic penalty for contumacy was of the lesser order, or the heavier censure which in principle carried more drastic social disabilities.[5] Nor is it likely that the clergy invariably fulfilled their legal responsibility of regularly

[99] Collinson, 'Cranbrook and the Fletchers', pp. 183–6.
[1] Marchant, *Church Under the Law*, pp. 204–22.
[2] Ingram, 'Ecclesiastical Justice', Chapter 10.
[3] Marchant, *Church Under the Law*, p. 227.
[4] John Robinson, *A justification of separation*, in *Works*, ed. R. Ashton (1851), ii. 60; Robert Baylie, *A dissuasive from the errours of the time* (1646), p. 7.
[5] Ingram, 'Ecclesiastical Justice', p. 332.

denouncing by name those persisting in their excommunication, or of refusing them the sacraments. In 1582 the
Cranbrook churchwardens were themselves presented for
allowing 'divers' excommunicate persons to come to the
church and to communicate in the sacrament 'as others of the
parishioners doe'. They denied the charge, of course.[6] But
given the inherent failings of the system of ecclesiastical
discipline, of which the small army of excommunicate persons
was itself symptomatic, it seems likely that many 'ethical
dissenters' eventually drifted back into good standing without
making formal peace with the archdeacon, either in the course
of migrating to places where they were not known, or through
an accommodating forgetfulness on the part of the parish
authorities.

But accepting for the sake of argument the existence of a
'seam of irreligious people', what kinds of people were they?
When Marchant assumed that they belonged to 'the poorer
classes' he was in excellent company. 'Below a certain social
level', writes Keith Thomas, the efforts of the authorities to
enforce the duty of church attendance appear to have flagged.
Christopher Hill believes that the puritans discriminated
against the poor and tended to exclude them from effective
church membership. And together with Joan Thirsk and Alan
Everitt he has directed our attention to the alternative society
of the backwoodsmen and cottagers which was almost beyond
the scope of the parochial system, enjoying 'freedom from the
parson as well as from the squire'.[7] Mervyn James has written
of 'the exclusion from the churches of the poor and those who
could not pay pew rents'.[8] Peter Clark suggests that the 20 per
cent of the population of late sixteenth-century Kent which
(he believes) stayed away from church on a regular basis
corresponded to a kind of 'Third World' of the poor and
spiritually ignorant, 'with its strongholds in the woods, on the
commons, and in the urban slums outside the reach of rich

---

[6] Cathedral Archives and Library Canterbury, X.3.5, fols. 133ᵛ–4ʳ.

[7] Thomas, *Religion and the Decline of Magic*, p. 160; Christopher Hill, *Society and Puritanism*, pp. 259–97, 'William Perkins and the Poor' in *Puritanism and Revolution* (1958), pp. 215–38, and *The World Turned Upside Down* (1972), pp. 32–45.

[8] M. E. James, *Family, Lineage and Civil Society: A Study of Society, Politics and Mentality in the Durham Region, 1500–1640* (Oxford, 1974), p. 123.

and respectable society'. 'For many ordinary folk the alehouse increasingly constituted a rival pole to the respectable, establishment meeting place of the church.' But Clark also believes that in Elizabethan Kent the reform of 'non-respectable society', 'social control', became the major pre-occupation of 'radical Protestantism'.[9] There is a risk of some confusion if we take all these suggestions together. If the system was discriminatory, we must try to decide whether the poor were discriminated against by being left out of account, effectively excluded from the parish assembly, or by being hounded to the bawdy court in order to enforce their inclusion.

In any event it is still a largely untested assumption that those at odds with ecclesiastical discipline belonged predominantly to the poorer classes. In 1605 the Cranbrook churchwardens and sidesmen decided: 'Let Arthur Barnes be cited to the courte. He is but a poore man. Yet manie take offence because he commeth to noe communion.'[10] The inference may be that not many of those presented from this industrial parish for neglect of religious duty were as poor as Arthur Barnes, but that Barnes, although scarcely worth the effort, should be made an example. Both churchwardens and court officials may have regarded it as a vindictive act to present poor artisans struggling to make ends meet and sometimes working on Sundays; and a waste of time and money to prosecute paupers, except occasionally, *pour encourager les autres.*[11] The truth is that we know too little about the poorest

[9] Clark, *English Provincial Society*, pp. 152, 156. For a somewhat less committed view, compare Peter Clark's essay 'The Alehouse and the Alternative Society', in *Puritans and Revolutionaries: Essays in Seventeenth-Century History Presented to Christopher Hill*, ed. Donald Pennington and Keith Thomas (Oxford, 1978), pp. 47–72.

[10] Cathedral Archives and Library Canterbury, X.4.8, fol. 85.

[11] See, for example, a presentment of the churchwardens of Tenterden in 1589: 'We have one Roger Lewkenor whoe is a chapman and one Henry Lynseye shoemaker. Wee take them to be honest poore menne for that often uppon the sabbothe daye they are from our churches. But wee have talked with them and they have answered us that to make part of a poore lyving is the cawse of their absence.' (Ibid., X.2.4, fol. 405ᵛ.) But in Terling Wrightson and Levine have found 'a mounting initiative in the prosecution of religious offences', aimed for the most part at persons low on the social scale. In this parish, 70 per cent of those prosecuted for failing to receive Communion were drawn from the labouring poor, while a further 18 per cent were husbandmen and craftsmen. Two-thirds of those standing excommunicate came from the lowest level of village society. (Wrightson and Levine, *Piety and Poverty in an English Village*, p. 156.)

of the poor to know how they stood in relation to the Church. We may assume that they were without a voice. But vagrants and tramps aside, we cannot be sure either that they were without a place, or were conventionally assumed to be without religious obligations, although both are possibilities. In the late 1620s a young Hertfordshire tailor absented himself from church, 'not being in that trim that I would have bene in' (his clothes were dirty). For the young John Dane this was a rare occurrence which was remembered because in his absence from church an insect stung his finger with such alarming consequences that the surgeon attributed the symptoms to a divine providence.[12] But should we assume that the ragged and unsavoury poor without a change of clothes were already unwelcome in church in the seventeenth century, as they often were two centuries later?

The orders drawn up in the 1580s by the ministers and 'ancients' of the Essex clothing town of Dedham shed an interesting light on these problems, in respect of an industrial community subject to stringent puritan discipline.[13] In Dedham the obligation of church attendance was laid upon the 'governors of household', but with the intention that they should proceed to church 'accompanied orderlie and soberly with their servauntes and whole family, as many as may be spared at home for the necessary use of children etc.' The more affluent townsmen, 'so many as be of habilitie', were encouraged to invite to their houses 'one couple of such of their poore neighbors as have submitted themselves to the general orders of the Churche, and walke christianly and honestlie in their callinges'. But below the deserving poor there were lower levels of deprivation which the ministers and ancients ventured to penetrate only occasionally, and 'alwaies accompanied with one of the constables'. This was on the occasion of their quarterly visitations of 'the poore and chiefly

---

[12] 'John Dane's Narrative', *New England Historical and Genealogical Register*, vii. 149–56. I owe this reference to Susan M. Hardman of the University of Durham.

[13] *The Presbyterian Movement in the Reign of Queen Elizabeth, As Illustrated by the Minute Book of the Dedham Classis 1582–1589*, ed. R. G. Usher, Camden 3rd ser. viii (1905), 99–101. F. G. Emmison points out that among the nine ancients who signed these orders were the brothers Henry and Edmund Sherman, Dedham clothiers whose descendants emigrated to New England and founded the American family from which sprang General Sherman. ('Tithes and Perambulations', p. 209.)

the suspected places, that understandinge the miserable estate of those that wante and the naughtie disposition of disordered persons, they may provide for them accordinglie'.[14] Did these poor cottagers come regularly to church? Would it have occurred to the ancients to forward their names to the archdeacon if they stayed away? It appears unlikely. There was an interesting debate in the Dedham ministerial conference when the vicar of Dedham, Richard Parker, asked 'whether a pastor were bounde by virtue of his office to visite every particular family in his charge'. Perhaps Parker had misgivings about the 'suspected places'. Some of his brethren answered in the affirmative and thought it odd that such a question should even be put. Others considered a general admonishment of the people, presumably from the pulpit, fulfilled the minister's obligations. Others still thought that occasion should be taken for private admonition as it arose, 'though we went not to every house'.[15] At another meeting, one of the Dedham circle asked what he should do about 'some froward poore men that were every way disordered'. He was told that if they resisted correction he should 'accompt them as none of his flock'.[16]

However, it remains possible that a good proportion of those at odds with ecclesiastical authority belonged to a different category from the poor and every way disordered,

---

[14] See the 1593 will of William Button, a Dedham clothier who had been the first signatory of these orders. After a legacy to Dr Chapman, the lecturer, and another gift to the vicar, the will states: 'My executors shall take view of the poorest to go into their houses to see what lodging [i.e., bedding] they have, and [?an, i.e. if] you shall find it too bare for any Christian you shall where you see most need is and the most honestest men provided for their lodging what you shall see they have most need of and provide for them, as fare as your money will go, as to have a bed to lie in and a blanket and a coverlet of shreds or what you think good.' Pearce Butter, another signatory, left £13. 6s. 8d.' to my good friend Dr Chapman' and a generous amount to the poor. Yet another signatory, Edmund Sherman, left £6 to Chapman and £20 for a continual stock for the poor. (*Elizabethan Life: Wills of Essex Gentry and Merchants*, ed. F. G. Emmison (Chelmsford, 1978), pp. 278, 280–1, 308–9.) And cf. Foxe's account of the practice in another clothing town, Hadleigh, where in Edwardian days the vicar, Rowland Taylor, made fortnightly visits to the almshouse in company with the rich clothiers 'to see how the poor lived; what they lacked in meat, drink, clothing, bedding, as any other necessities. The like did he also to other poor men that had many children, or were sick.' (*Acts and Monuments*, vi. 698.)

[15] *Presbyterian Movement*, 72.

[16] Ibid., 71.

not necessarily drawn from 'below a certain social level'. Is there any reason to suppose that the young people of Elizabethan Kent who gadded to dances were denizens of some notional 'Third World'[17] and subject to greater deprivation than their neighbours who gadded to sermons? Their recreation, too, required money and leisure. If the sermon-goer was more respectable, that was a subjective and moral judgement. Most of those in the so-called 'excommunicate class' had been placed there by those sins of the flesh to which much of mankind is notoriously susceptible. While the ancients, the parish oligarchs, may have been beyond suspicion on this account, or at least relatively immune from detection, the majority of their neighbours were not. As the historians of crime in early modern society insist, where there were so many laws to break, lawlessness was not the prerogative of the poor, and not necessarily a shameful thing. The notion of 'non-respectable society' may be as anachronistic as the concept of a criminal class.

So we should consider the possibility that while the churchwardens may have discriminated against the poor and defenceless in making their returns to the archdeacon, their presentments will be a poor indication of the extent of religious, morally impeccable behaviour in the population at large. According to a Henrician statute, 'no maner of person' of whatever rank or occupation was to play at bowls outside his own garden or orchard, and Justices of the Peace were charged to commit those offending to ward.[18] But it would be unwise for historians of the game of bowls in this period to form their impression of its prevalence from the numbers and quality of those sent to prison for playing it. It would be no less a mistake to base an account of the social distribution of sexual misconduct on the criminal record of the ecclesiastical and civil courts.

IV

At this point in the argument it will be profitable to return to the literature of complaint, where there is little evidence of a

[17] Clark, *English Provincial Society*, Chapter 5, 'Godly Folk: The Making of Elizabethan Puritanism'.
[18] Michael Dalton, *The countrey justice* (1619), pp. 55–6.

desire to equate religious and moral reformation with social control or the correction of 'non-respectable society'. Indeed, the poor and disreputable are conspicuous by their absence from the complaints of the moralists. According to Ann Jennalie Cook, they were equally absent from the audience at the London theatres, a particular target for complaint.[19] The low-life focus seems to be exceptional in Richard Rawlidge's 1628 pamphlet denouncing alehouses. For Rawlidge was himself a 'mechanical person', no ordinary clerical complainer, and he had knowledge of the alehouse culture which the respectable clergy lacked, a world inhabited by 'those of the middle and meaner rancke, as handicraftsmen, workmen of all sorts'.[20] After the disaster at the Paris Garden bear-pit in 1583, the 'godly exhortation' of the preacher John Field drew attention to the lowly social status of the victims, who were tradesmen and servants: 'There is to be considered in the quality and condition of these persons, whome God hath thus layed a long amiddest their vanitie, to be an example unto us, howe commonly these of such sorte are affected and disposed.'[21] But the 'unto us' and the 'those of such sorte' are significant phrases. Field was addressing himself to a literate and moderately affluent class of readers, and in his pamphlet he had no direct communication or contention with 'them'. The social control demanded by such writers, if it did not overlook the poor altogether, seems to have been designed primarily for citizens of their own social level, people of a middling competence, 'us'. And since so much of the complaint-literature is concerned with the defence of the Sabbath, it touches rather lightly on the communal festivities beloved of the folklorists, dealing more faithfully with the many pleasures and pursuits of a non-traditional, non-communal kind, of which the theatre is a good example. These activities, no less than church-going itself, were adjusted to the

---

[19] Ann Jennalie Cook, 'The Audience of Shakespeare's Plays: A Reconsideration', *Shakespeare Studies*, vii (Columbia, S. Carolina, 1974). 283–305. See also her '"Bargaines of Incontinencie": Bawdy Behavior in the Playhouses', ibid., x (1977), 271–90. Both articles challenge the argument of Alfred Harbage, *Shakespeare's Audience* (New York, 1941).

[20] Rawlidge, *A monster late found out*, Preface, p. 17.

[21] Field, *A godly exhortation*, sig. B8ᵛ.

concept of a working week, and dependent on the institution of a weekly day of release from toil. This may suggest that those complained against, no less than the complainers, were denizens of the industrious world of the future.

Keith Wrightson, in his study of the puritan reformation of manners between 1640 and 1660, has noted that in many parts of England, but to a lesser extent in Lancashire, communal festivities were in decline, giving way to the 'fragmented sociability' of the alehouse and private house, representing 'a select rather than a communal neighbourliness'.[22] In the Essex village of Terling it was in about 1616 that public dancings were driven off the village green and into the alehouse.[23] According to Richard Rawlidge, the repressive action of preachers and magistrates had contributed to this development. 'When the people generally were forbidden their old and antient familiar meetings and sportings, what then followed? Why sure, ale-house haunting.' The preachers had reproved the public dalliance and dancing of maids and young men, but with the unfortunate result that they now had cause to reprove the drunkenness and whoring that went on in alehouses: 'so that the people would have their meetings, either publiquely with pastimes abroad, or else privatly in drunken Ale-houses, wasting and consuming'.[24] The interests reflected in the royal Declaration of Sports have been credited with the insight that private gatherings and private pastimes were more undesirable than public, communal festivities.[25] But whereas the Lancashire preachers were somewhat old-fashioned in their continuing fixation on the traditional pastimes, the metropolitan moralists were already contending with various forms of 'fragmented sociability', and with leisure pursuits which, like the theatre, were as modern and progressive as protestant sermon-going itself.

Sabbath-breakers and church-abstainers were acknowl-

---

[22] K. E. Wrightson, 'The Puritan Reformation of Manners with Special Reference to the Counties of Lancashire and Essex 1640–1660', Cambridge Ph.D. thesis, 1973, pp. 36–41.

[23] Wrightson and Levine, *Poverty and Piety in an English Village*, p. 157.

[24] Rawlidge, *A monster late found out*, p. 13.

[25] Wrightson, 'Puritan Reformation of Manners', p. 41; J. Tait, 'The Declaration of Sports for Lancashire', *English Historical Review*, xxxii (1917), 561–8.

edged to be of all kinds, as Field says, 'from the highest to the lowest'. In London they 'run out into the country with their bags and bottels',[26] much as Londoners have done ever since; or they go rowing on the water. They resort to summer houses or taverns and they visit the theatre, the gaming tables, and the bear-pit. In the country they attend markets and fairs, the gentry hawk and hunt, while others travel to silver games, or play bowls or stoolball or football. Marriage dinners, says Nicholas Bownd, are 'commonly kept upon this day', and people generally invite their friends to dinner on Sundays and sit at it until two or three in the afternoon.[27] (At Dedham on the Lord's Day, 'all travaylinge to ffayres, marketts, mariage dyners and dyners abroade or in the towne' was to be 'lefte off'.)[28] Young people enjoy a lie-in after the exertions of the night before, and their elders too 'give themselves and theirs over to sleepe more and longer than on other dayes besides', while others sit idle at their doors, gaping and gazing. Arthur Dent says that many 'sleepe uppon their beddes all the sermon while in the afternoone'.[29] John Knewstub has the essential point: 'For a great number, (and those not the worst of all) take that day to be ordeined only for the ease of their bodie, and to be a day of recreation after their travels and labours that have beene the six dayes before, and use it accordingly'.[30] John Angier of Denton complained that his people slept through sermons 'as if the sabbath were made only to recover that sleep they had lost in the week'.[31] A non-puritan, John Earle, observed in 1627 an ambivalent and perhaps transitional attitude in the 'plaine countrie fellowe'. Sunday he esteemed as a day to make merry in, and he thought the bagpipes 'as essential to it as Evening prayer'. Yet the same

---

[26] Field, *A godly exhortation*, sigs. B3, B4ᵛ.

[27] Nicholas Bownd, *Sabbathum veteris et novi testamenti: Or the true doctrine of the Sabbath* (1606), pp. 208–9. Again, it is interesting to observe that Bownd attacks marriage *dinners*, rather than the more popular and disorderly bride-ales: on which, see Emmison, 'Tithes and Perambulations', pp. 201–2.

[28] *Presbyterian Movement*, 99.

[29] Dent, *The plaine mans path-way*, p. 138.

[30] John Knewstub, *Lectures upon the twentieth chapter of Exodus and certeine other places of Scripture* (1577), p. 72.

[31] *Oliver Heywood's Life of John Angier of Denton*, ed. E. Axon, Chetham Society NS. xcvii (1937).

man walked back from church 'verie solemnly', with his hands
behind his back, 'and censures the dauncing of the parish'.[32]

The plain country fellow was not alone in his prejudice. If
there was one social group which exercised the moralists above
any other it was the adolescent young, and if there was one
activity which aroused their particular anxiety it was dancing,
'the vilest vice of all'.[33] 'Yet there is one above the rest', wrote
George Widley in his catalogue of unlawful pastimes, '(which
because it so much troubleth the ministerie of the word, and
because it hath gotten her a whorish forehead, so that though
we have spit 7 times in her face, yet she blusheth not, but
walketh like a daughter of Sion with a stretched out necke and
a wandring eye, mincing it, and making a tinckling with her
feete as she goeth), me thinks I have named her already (it is
wanton dancing.)'[34] John Northbrooke's *Treatise wherin dicing,
dauncing, vaine playes or enterludes . . . are reproved* takes the form of
a dialogue between 'Youth' and 'Age'.[35] Christopher Fetherston's *Dialogue against light, lewde and lascivious dauncing* is
between *'Juvenis'* and *'Minister'.*[36] Youth says of the church:
'That place is more fitte for suche olde fatherly men as you are
than for such young men as I am . . . Cannot I finde Christe as
well in a tavern as a temple?' *Juvenis* says that we must have
our 'swindge' while we are young. 'Age will come soon
enough.'[37]

In reserving their heaviest guns for dancing, the moralists
expressed hostility for a pastime in direct competition with
church-going, by which the youth was lured away from
sermons. Humphrey Roberts says that dancing 'is a meane to
drawe youth together in time of prechyng and praier, whereby

[32] Earle, *Microcosmographie,* p. 88.

[33] John Northbrooke, *Spiritus est vicarius Christi in terra. A treatise wherein dicing,
dauncing, vaine playes or enterludes with other idle pastimes etc. commonly used on the Sabboth day,
are reproved by the authoritie of the word of God and auntient writers* (?1577), p. 136.

[34] Widley, *Doctrine of the Sabbath,* pp. 102–3.

[35] The facsimile of the first edition of this tract in the Garland Series 'The English
Stage: Attack and Defense 1577–1730' (1974) is now to be preferred to J. P. Collier's
not wholly uncorrupt 1843 edition for the Shakespeare Society.

[36] See above p. 206 n. 67.

[37] Fetherston *A dialogue,* sig. B8ᵛ. See also the anonymous *A treatise of daunses, wherein
it is shewed that they are as it were accessories and dependants (or thinges annexed) to whoredom*
(1581), reprinted Garland Series 'The English Stage' (1974).

they continewe in ignorance'.[38] In Lancashire, the people were literally piped out of the churches to follow the dancers.[39] But the reformers had less to say about football, which the court records suggest could lead to mass desertion of Evening Prayer by the men of the parish. At Nottingham in 1608, thirty-five men were accused of 'beinge at the footeball' in time of divine service.[40] In 1598 at Goldhanger in Essex the teams were the married men versus the bachelors. At Great Baddow in the same year, Evening Prayer was so disturbed by the football players in the churchyard that the vicar went out and confiscated the ball.[41] This may have been a brave action, for 'camping', as it was known in East Anglia, was sometimes a vicious business. Philip Stubbes called it a 'bloody and murthering practise', 'a freendly kind of fight'.[42] Would it be wholly anachronistic to suggest that violence exercised the Elizabethan moralists less than sex?

There is no disguising the anxiety of the preachers about the irrepressible sexuality of the young and about the central place of dancing in the economy of pairing and mating. Northbrooke complains that as they dance 'maydens and matrones are groped and handled with unchast handes and kissed and dishonestly embraced'. Roberts suspects that maidens who dance 'do returne home to their friendes somtime with more than thei carried forth'.[43] It has often been observed that the hostility of the godly towards maypoles implies an obsession with the notion of an open season for carnal passion which may have existed mainly in the overheated imaginations of the moralists themselves.[44] Ac-

---

[38] Roberts, *An earnest complaint*, sig. E6ʳ.

[39] Haigh, 'Puritan Evangelism', 52–3.

[40] *Before the Bawdy Court*, ed. Paul Hair (1972), p. 36.

[41] Emmison, 'Tithes, Perambulations and Sabbath-breakers', p. 204. On the implication of football teams so composed, see Natalia Zemon Davies, 'The Reason of Misrule', in *Society and Culture in Early Modern France* (1975), pp. 97–123.

[42] Edward Moor, *Suffolk Words and Phrases* (1823), pp. 63–6; Philip Stubbes, *The anatomie of abuses* (1583), sig. Pviʳ. And not always so friendly. F. G. Emmison reports that football led to four coroner's inquests in Elizabethan Essex. (*Elizabethan Life: Disorder, from Essex Quarter Sessions and Assize Records* (Chelmsford, 1970), pp. 232–55.)

[43] Northbrooke, *A treatise*, p. 136; Roberts, *An earnest complaint*, sig. E8ʳ.

[44] Christopher Hill takes these allegations at something near face value in *Society and Puritanism*, pp. 183–4. See the more cautious comments of Thomas G. Barnes, 'County Politics and a Puritan Cause Célèbre: Somerset Churchales, 1633', *Transactions of the Royal Historical Society*, 5th ser. ix (1959), 107; and of Wrightson, 'The Puritan Reformation of Manners', pp. 31–2.

cording to Stubbes, only a third of those who go maying in the woods return undefiled. Fetherston's version is that of ten maidens who went to set may, nine came home with child.[45] *Juvenis* asks: 'I pray you sir, where shall young men and maydens meete together, if not at the dauncing place and playing oke?' 'A great many have gotten their wyves', 'and that rich wyves also', 'onely by dauncing'. But *Minister* tells him that in such company a young man will be more likely to light upon 'a wilde wanton then on a mylde matrone, which will become rather a gadding *Dina,* which will bee running abroade to see the Countrey, than a sage *Sara,* which will keepe her selfe within the doore of the tent'.[46] In Roberts's view, it is one of the evils of the pastime that girls use dances to provide 'husbandes of their owne chusynge, without the counsell and consent of their parentes and friendes'.[47] So it was, no doubt, with the young men. The elder brother of the Lancashire puritan Adam Martindale turned down the good match which his father had made for him and wed 'a young wild airy girle, beteene fifteen and sixteen yeares of age: an huge lover and frequenter of wakes, greenes and merrie-nights, where musick and dancing abounded'.[48]

If due allowance is made for rhetorical hyperbole, the burden of these complaints is consistent with some of the conclusions of Martin Ingram's investigation of ecclesiastical justice in early seventeenth-century Wiltshire, 'with special reference to cases concerning sex and marriage'.[49] Unlike some social and demographic historians, Ingram is not persuaded that the available religious and social controls were sufficient to restrain extramarital sexual activity. In this society the sexes enjoyed much freedom to meet and engage in familiarity and physical intimacy, especially at dances. But bridal pregnancy, in early seventeenth-century Wiltshire a factor in

[45] Stubbes, *The anatomie of abuses,* sig. M4ʳ; Fetherston, *A dialogue,* sig. D 7ᵛ.

[46] Fetherston, *A dialogue,* sigs. C7ʳ–8ʳ. The case of Jacob's and Leah's daughter Dina who went out to see the daughters 'of that country' sc. Canaan (Genesis xxxiv), and was ravished, was a popular topos for the moralistic condemnation of dancing. (See *A treatise of daunces,* sigs. B4ᵛ–5ʳ.)

[47] Roberts, *An earnest complaint,* sig. E8ᵛ.

[48] *The Life of Adam Martindale, Written by Himself,* ed. Richard Parkinson, Chetham Society, iv (1845), 16.

[49] See above p. 208 n. 75.

about a fifth of all marriages, was not condoned by the ecclesiastical courts; nor were the many more or less casual liaisons arising, typically, between men of a higher and women of a lower and exploitable social class, who were usually young, unmarried, and poor. Both ecclesiastical and, increasingly, civil authorities took a serious view of bastardy, particularly in the 1620s as the country moved to the edge of a subsistence crisis. Yet the very limited impact of ecclesiastical justice in matters of sexual conduct was the corollary of legal pressures which were rigorous in principle but applied to a society in which simple fornication, as one of the Homilies of the Church complained, was often counted 'no sin at all but rather a pastime, a dalliance and but a touch of youth'.[50] The uneasy balance between continence and licence in this society is implied by the great numbers of defamation suits brought and contested in the ecclesiastical courts, a high proportion of which touched the plaintiff's sexual probity. It is significant that so many parties were concerned to defend their honour in these respects. But Jim Sharpe has found that on the whole it was married women rather than the young and unattached who demonstrated this concern. And the fact that so many were willing to seek a remedy in the full light of open court proceedings is indicative that this was not the kind of 'honour and shame' society in which sexual licence was unthinkable and sexual dishonour literally worse than death.[51]

Martin Ingram's researches suggest that ecclesiastical justice was effective in measure as it answered the needs and reinforced the moral values of the parochial community. The parish needed to avoid unwanted bastards. But the courts were not capable of altering public attitudes which condoned

[50] 'A Sermon Against Whoredom and Uncleanness', *Certain Sermons or Homilies Appointed to be Read in Churches* (1840 edn.), p. 108. 'Antilogon' in Dent's *A plaine mans path-way* (p. 63) calls whoredom 'but a trick of youth'. The author of *A treatise of daunces* (sig. A2ᵛ) faced the objection that dancing (which in his view was a thing 'annexed to whoredom') was too trivial a matter for reformation, as if greater evils had been so far eradicated as to leave 'nothing els but to debate the question of leapings, skippings and daunses'.

[51] J. A. Sharpe, *Defamation and Sexual Slander in Early Modern England: the Church Courts at York*, Borthwick Papers lviii (York, 1980); see also J. A. Sharpe, 'Litigation and Human Relations in Early Modern England—Ecclesiastical Defamation Suits at York', in *Law and Human Relations*, Past and Present Society Conference Papers, 1980.

the circumstances which not infrequently led to bastardy. In effect, the archdeacon's court, the 'bawdy court', was power-less to force the youth of the parish into 'towardliness' where their parents or masters or the parish 'ancients' had already failed. An Essex alehouse keeper prosecuted for suffering dancing on the Sabbath explained that it was a wedding, and he 'could not rule the youth'.[52] A citation to appear in court might be taken seriously by someone with a stake in the community. Unless his parson was negligent, the respectable married householder could not afford to remain excommuni-cate from one Easter to the next. In spite of the shame and dishonour involved, which was greater for him than for the young and feckless, he might undergo public penance in order to recover his good standing in the community. But the young and irresponsible were more likely to treat the whole process with contempt, staying away from the bawdy court, or making a mockery of the act of penance. Hence, in part, the willingness of many civil magistrates to avail themselves of penalties under statute law that were more credible than the 'toyish censures' of the spiritual courts. At Cranbrook, about half the young husbands presented at the turn of the century for incontinence before marriage thought it in their interest to appear in court in order to clear their names by alleging a contract to marry entered into before intimacy had taken place. But single women accused of fornication in this parish were almost never seen in court.[53] In their case citation was almost equivalent to excommunication, and may have proved no great hardship. Martin Ingram concludes: 'It is hardly too much to say that there existed an adolescent culture, especially associated with servants, one of the features of which was some measure of irresponsibility'.[54]

Consequently it appears likely that at least a portion of Robert Marchant's 'excommunicate class' was made up from this age-group, on which religion and its concomitant disciplines made comparatively little impression. Many would be removed from this class not so much by 'discipline' as by

---

[52] Emmison, 'Tithes, Perambulations and Sabbath-breach', p. 201.
[53] Collinson, 'Cranbrook and the Fletchers', p. 184.
[54] Ingram, 'Ecclesiastical Justice', p. 347.

the normal process of aging and entry to the married state.[55] Christopher Fetherstone's *Juvenis* tells *Minister:* 'Age wil come soone ynough, and it will make us forsake all these sportes; and then will wee be sober and vertuous.'[56] John North-brooke's Youth says: 'The church is no wylde cat.' It will be there when he needs it. Compared with the all too brief opportunities of youth, sermons 'are not daintie but very plentie: and therefore no such great neede or haste to runne to heare sermons'.[57] Cranbrook, which recorded such a deplor-able rate of compliance with ecclesiastical discipline, was noted in 1579 as a town 'where the use or trade of good clothing doth always nowryshe a great nomber of yong people'.[58] Indeed 'a great nomber of yong people' was characteristic of this society generally, in which more than half the population may have been under twenty years of age. Moreover, given the late age of marriage which seems to have been the norm, the transition from semi-dependency to full adult status occurred for many well beyond the age of twenty.

Where the young and not yet fully responsible were apprenticed or otherwise in service in a well-ordered, godly household, they would be obliged to acquire habits of religious conformity and might even experience conversion to a religion which was more than formal and habitual. Where they escaped such formative influences the estrangement from organized religion of unmarried adolescents and young adults may itself have been habitual and deep-seated. For it is perhaps anachronistic to impose on the sixteenth and seven-teenth centuries the Victorian or post-Victorian image of children accompanying their parents to church. Charles Phythian-Adams has ventured a comment in the small print of a footnote which deserves a more general airing: 'It may be wondered whether children attended church at all before

---

[55] Ibid., p. 355. Cf. the remarks of Hair, *At the Bawdy Court*, pp. 26–8.

[56] Fetherston, *A dialogue*, sigs. B8ᵛ–Cᵛ.

[57] Northbrooke, *A treatise*, p. 4.

[58] Thomas Wotton to Sir Francis Walsingham, 3 May 1579; *Thomas Wotton's Letter-Book 1574–1586*, ed. G. Eland (1960), pp. 24–5.

confirmation.'⁵⁹ And what if the rite of confirmation was seldom or slackly administered?

V

When Fetherston's *Juvenis* defended dancing as the sovereign way to find a rich wife, *Minister* advised him to 'resort unto sermons and there marke her wel whom thou shalt see most usually to resort to weekly lectures and to behave her self most Christianlike'.⁶⁰ That was how both the diarist Ralph Josselin and the exemplary Cheshire gentleman John Bruen met their wives.⁶¹ The effect on society of the religion of protestants and its moral values was to polarize communities between those who gadded to sermons and those who gadded to dances, sports, and other pastimes; those whose speech was seasoned with godly salt and those who used the traditional oaths. For 'questionlesse', wrote Arthur Dent, the vice of swearing was the most rife of all. 'For you shall heare litle boyes and children in the streetes rappe out oathes in most fearefull manner.'⁶² The meaning of puritanism is not only doctrine, applied and internalized, but a social situation: the partly self-inflicted isolation of the godly, which contributed to a significant change in the pattern of cultural and social relations. This was far from intended, and it is a grave distortion of the Calvinist doctrine of election to suppose that the godly simply defined themselves as an élite of predestinate grace. George Widley insisted that under the Gospel, God's covenant applied indifferently and compulsively to all, even to those who defied Him. 'Every hill is Sion, every river is Jordan, every countrie Jewry, every citie Jerusalem.' 'All must be compelled unto the true religion.' 'Wee are to inforce all unto the service of the true God.'⁶³ It was quite another question, irrelevant for any public purpose, whether this or

---

⁵⁹ Charles Phythian-Adams, *Desolation of a City: Coventry and the Urban Crisis of the Late Middle Ages* (Cambridge, 1979), p. 83, n. 16.

⁶⁰ Fetherston, *A dialogue*, sig. Dᵛ.

⁶¹ *The Diary of Ralph Josselin 1616–1683*, ed. Alan Macfarlane, Records of Social and Economic History, NS iii (1976), 7; William Hinde, *A faithful remonstrance of the holy life and happy death of John Bruen of Bruen-Stapleford in the County of Chester, Esquire* (1641), p. 109.

⁶² Dent, *The plaine mans path-way*, p. 156.

⁶³ Widley, *The doctrine of the Sabbath*, pp. 190–1.

that citizen of the visible Jerusalem was elected unto eternal life and so within the Church invisible. But people would not be compelled and enforced. As a compulsory system, puritanism failed.

Perhaps it was inevitable that a century of protestant endeavour should have led not to the new Jerusalem and a new Jewry but to communities scandalously divided between those who embraced the godly way of life or had it thrust upon them and those who resisted it. In Lancashire, the darkest corner of all, it has been said, 'the puritan ministers had to fail, since their duties were too wide': as wide as the parish of Whalley with 180 square miles, forty distinct townships, ten thousand inhabitants.[64] But even in more favourable locations, a religious system so daunting in its intellectual content and ethical demands was unlikely to appeal to the masses, especially since it set its face against so much of the traditional way of life.

But some blame must attach to the evangelical protestants themselves for their failure to commend religion in genuinely popular and appealing forms. John Dod thought that 'most ministers in England usually shoot over the heads of their hearers'. Dod himself was a preacher with a genius for 'plain and familiar' communication. We are told that 'he took great care to speak to the meanest capacity', so that it was said that 'poor simple people that never knew what religion meant, when they had gone to hear him, could not choose but talk of his sermon. It mightily affected poor creatures to hear the mysteries of God (by his excellent skill that way) brought down to their own language and dialect.'[65] Another great preacher, silver-tongued Henry Smith, said that 'to preach simply is not to preach unlearnedly, nor confusedly, but plainely and perspicaciously, that the simplest which dooth heare may understand what is taught, as if he did heare his name'.[66]

But why always and only sermons? William Harrison, a Lancashire preacher, complained in 1614 that 'people hear

[64] Haigh, 'Puritan Evangelism', p. 39.
[65] Samuel Clarke, *The Lives of Thirty-Two English Divines* (1667), pp. 175–7.
[66] *The sermons of Master Henrie Smith* (1592), p. 668.

much, learn little and practise less'. But instead of being led
into a radical reappraisal of the value of preaching, Harrison
concluded: 'The fault is in the hearers, not in the teachers'.[67]
Preaching was admittedly a sacrosanct subject. To be critical
of it was to take issue with the Gospel or with Christ Himself.
But not all preachers were so complacently and repressively
uncritical as Harrison. Nor, to be fair, did protestant
evangelists and educators base the dissemination of their
religion entirely on the sermon. The religious book trade was
resourceful and some of its contributors tried to be enticing.
Summary versions of the Bible were published 'in metre', not
to say doggerel, one of them contriving the feat of sustaining
an alphabetical arrangement of initial letters of lines through
every chapter from Genesis to Revelation.[68]

Above all, this was an age of catechizing. From the quantity
of small, unofficial catechisms which survive—and little books
so ephemeral only survive as rareties—it is clear that they
existed by the score, and that the most popular of them ran
into scores of editions.[69] The earliest version of Stephen
Egerton's *A briefe method of catechizing* to survive is a single copy
of the sixteenth edition (1610). By 1644 this little book had
reached its forty-fourth edition. No student of the religious
mentality of the age, or of the dissemination of protestantism,
can afford to neglect these often skilfully composed summaries
of Christian doctrine. It has been well observed that 'those
who listened to sermons and read the Bible did so with
faculties trained by catechisms'.[70] Conversely, catechisms
addressed themselves realistically to minds and faculties
which were aphoristic and tended to store up wisdom in
proverbial forms. The intention was to replace 'ignorant'
proverbs with faithful sayings and worthy of all acceptation.

---

[67] Haigh, 'Puritan Evangelism', 47.

[68] Simon Wastel, *A true christians daily delight: Being, the summe of every chapter of the Old and New Testaments, set downe alphabetically in English verse* (1623); based on John Shaw, *Biblii summula: hoc est, argumenta singulorum capitum scripturae canonicae, utriusque Testamenti, alphabetice distichis comprehensa* (1621). See also Henoch Clapham, *A briefe of the Bible drawne first into English poesy and then illustrated by apte annotations* (Edinburgh, 1596).

[69] The best account of the unofficial catechisms is in Peter F. Jensen, 'The Life of Faith in the Teaching of Elizabethan Protestants', Oxford D.Phil. thesis, 1979.

[70] Ibid., p. 182.

To this extent catechisms were well adjusted to an oral, at best semi-literate, culture.

Advocates of the art of catechizing and competitors in such a hotly-contested market argued that only a systematic, mechanical system of rote-learning could overcome the slow mental processes of 'the ruder sort'; that there was no other way that children and especially servants could be taught. As Francis Inman wrote in his introduction to *A light unto the unlearned:*

There be many poore servants and laborers; many that are of trades and manuall sciences; many aged persons of weak and decaied memories. Of these, some never learned so much as to reade, some very little and the most of them have or will have small leisure to learne long discourses: the world, or other vanities, taking up their thoughts and cares. Yet all these have immortall soules, to remaine after a few daies in eternall ioye or in endless paines. Of these care must be had . . .[71]

Let them learn, advised Richard Bernard, 'word for word . . . Interrupt not beginners with interpretations, neither goe further with any than he can well say . . . Stay somewhat for an answer, but not too long: if one know not, aske another: if any but stammer at it, helpe him, and encourage him by commending his willingnesse.' This was 'much more profitable than to discourse and dilate upon a point sermon-wise'.[72]

It was especially profitable in that catechizing could be conducted daily, in the household, with the godly householder taking the place of the minister. The Northamptonshire preacher Eusebius Paget, whose *Short questions and answers* achieved at least thirty editions by the 1630s, claimed that household religion based on these simple principles worked. In a four-month course of indoctrination employed in a private family his 'principles and aunsweares' had been learned by 'gentlemen, yeomen, horsekeepers, shepheardes, carters, milkemaides, kitchenboyes and al in that household', with the

---

[71] Francis Inman, *A light unto the unlearned: Or, the principles of the doctrine of Christ set downe most briefly for the use of yong and ignorant persons* (1622), Epistle.

[72] Richard Bernard, *Two twinnes: Or two parts of one portion of Scripture: I is of catechizing II of the ministers maintenance* (1613), pp. 9, 11; Richard Bernard, *The faithfull shepheard amended and enlarged* (1609), p. 9. See Bernard's own catechism, *The common catechisme, with a commentarie thereupon by questions and answers,* in its eighth edition by 1635.

exception of three or four dim wits, 'and yet the simplest went not without some profite'.[73] This experience was recorded, presumably in the Isham household in Northamptonshire,[74] in the mid-1570s, and it remained in print without textual alteration until the eve of the Civil War. How many of the generations which had intervened had graduated by this method to join the ranks of what Bernard called the 'beleeving and conscionable people'? Even a captive audience had first to be captured. Many shepherds, carters, and milkmaids were beyond the catechizer's reach. And those who willy-nilly were subject to the disciplines of a religious household, or parish, were initiated through the catechism into the lower reaches of a literate, print-based culture to which their occupations and natural inclinations made them strangers. It was a more intelligent strategy to catechize than to preach over the heads of those whom Bernard called 'ignorant and indocible', a good way to bring the horse to the water. But although the method was different, the intention was the same: to implant a religion consisting of patterns of printed words in heads which had little use for words of this kind and which must have found it very difficult to convert the words into authentic and meaningful experience. In the last resort the 'rude sort' could choose not to drink.

An earlier generation of protestant reformers may have had more realistic expectations. A Henrician writer knew that 'into the common people things sooner enter by the eyes than by the ears'.[75] In the early years of the Reformation, protestant propaganda had been advanced by an alliance of the available media, including caricature and the drama. When printing a letter from Bishop Stephen Gardiner to the Protector Somerset which protested against attacks on the

---

[73] *Short questions and answeares conteyning the summe of christian religion* (1579), sig. A3. Many editions of this catechism are attributed to Robert Openshaw, but Paget's prime responsibility is established by the edition of 1586.

[74] John Isham was Paget's uncle as well as his patron in the living of Old. (W. J. Sheils, *The Puritans in the Diocese of Peterborough 1558–1610*, Publications of the Northamptonshire Record Society xxx (Northampto, 1979), 31.) That Paget was referring to his own parish and to Isham's household appears certain in the light of his reference (*Short questions and answeares*, sig. A5ᵛ) to 'the restraint of their minister'. Paget was deprived of his living in January 1574.

[75] Quoted, Burke, *Popular Culture*, p. 228.

sacraments by 'certain printers, players and preachers', Foxe allowed himself an ironical marginal comment: 'Printers, players and preachers trouble Winchester', and he added: 'He thwarteth also and wrangleth against players, printers, preachers. And no marvel why: for he seeth these three things to be set up of God, as a triple bulwark against the triple crown of the pope, to bring him down; as God praised they have done meetly well already'.[76] A late Henrician Act of Parliament specifically forbade the polemical use of the drama in plays containing 'interpretation of scripture'.[77] In 1574 a Protestant writer could still observe that 'simple souls are as well fed with seeing as hearing, so much the better as nature hath more sufficiently enabled them by outward sense to discern the one than knowledge, skill or experience to judge of the other'.[78] But this was an anti-puritan argument and already rather old-fashioned. By the 1570s the main stream of evangelical protestantism had abandoned the first of Foxe's triple defences against the papacy and was preparing its onslaught on plays and players in any shape or form. When Northbrooke's Youth reminds Age that 'many times they play histories out of the Scriptures', Age replies: 'Assuredly that is very evill so to doe, to mingle scurrilitie with Divinitie, that is, to eate meate with unwashed hands.'[79]

In spite of the profoundly iconophobic bias of protestant culture, the visual image was not so totally rejected and could still be exploited for polemical purposes. When Northbrooke's Age advised Youth to stay at home on Sunday afternoons and refresh his wits with Foxe's *Acts and Monuments*,[80] he was

[76] Foxe, *Acts and Monuments*, vi, 31, 57. And see S. R. Maitland, 'Puritan Alliance of Preachers, Printers and Players', part of 'The Ribalds', in *Essays on Subjects Connected with the Reformation in England* (1849), pp. 296–300.

[77] 34 and 35 Henry VIII c.1.

[78] (William Lambarde), *A defense of the ecclesiasticall regiment in Englande* (1574), quoted, J. S. Coolidge, *The Pauline Renaissance in England: Puritanism and the Bible* (Oxford, 1970), pp. xii–xiii.

[79] Northbrooke, *A treatise*, p. 63. Cf. William Crashawe, *The sermon preached at the Crosse Feb. xiiij 1607* (1608), p. 171: 'They grow worse and worse, for now they bring religion and holy things upon the stage.'

[80] Northbrooke, *A treatise*, pp. 142–3. There was also some light relief in the text of the *Book of Martyrs*. Introducing a farcical story of a panic about a non-existent fire in the church of St. Mary the Virgin at Oxford, Foxe remarks: 'Now I will here set before thee again a merry and comical spectacle, whereat thou mayest now laugh and refresh thyself.' (*Acts and Monuments*, v. 455.)

recommending a book which was richly illustrated with arresting and even sensational pictures, to the surprise and delight of generations of protestant children then unborn. But in spite of its title, the publishers of Thomas Beard's ever popular *Theatre of Gods judgements* resisted the temptation to alleviate the text with images of sudden death and calamity visited upon 'atheists'. And there were no pictures in the Geneva Bible, which in this important respect differed markedly from the bibles which played such a large part in moulding the religious consciousness of more recent generations. The mode of conveying a moral message visually which was most characteristic of the late Elizabethan and Jacobean age was the emblem: terse, cryptic, and allegorically bookish, certainly no part of popular culture. As for the message of the Christian Gospel, the plan of salvation, the only graphic representations available were severely diagrammatic and based on the principles of Ramist logic.[81] Ramism, to be sure, was a method of simplification in the field of logical discourse. But William Perkins's 'table' was unlikely to appeal to the likes of Northbrooke's Youth or Fetherston's *Juvenis*. Protestantism was a religion of the printed word or it was nothing. 'Well', says the ignorant man in Dent's *Plaine mans path-way*: 'I cannot read, and therefore I cannot tell what Christ or Saint *Paul* may say.'[82] Dent intended this to reflect adversely on the ignorant man. If he was willing or able to concede that the ability to read was not available in equal measure to all classes and occupations,[83] he was not inclined to follow through the implications of that restriction for popular religious education.

And what of song, so infectious a mode of conveying and giving expression to religious convictions and feeling, the

---

[81] Richard A. Muller, 'Perkins' *A Golden Chaine:* Predestinarian System or Schematized *Ordo Salutatis?*', *Sixteenth Century Journal,* ix (1978), 68–81. Perkins's diagram or 'table' is reproduced in *The Work of William Perkins,* ed. Ian Breward, Courtenay Library of Reformation Classics iii (Appleford, Abingdon, 1970). Cf. the syllogistic diagram depicting election and reprobation in *A briefe declaration of the chiefe points of christian religion set forth in a table made by Theodore Beze* (1613); and a similar device used by Richard Bernard in *Davids musicke: Or Psalmes of that royall prophet ones the sweete singer of that Israel* (1616).

[82] Dent, *The plaine mans path-way,* p. 30.

[83] Cressy, *Literacy and the Social Order,* Chapter 6, 'The Structure of Illiteracy'.

main vehicle of conversion and sanctification in the evangelical revivals of later ages? The sixteenth century was an age which sang the Psalms of David to tunes in the popular idiom. But towards the end of the century, Nicholas Bownd reported that in the shops of artificers and the cottages of poor husbandmen one would find not the Psalms but 'these new ballads, which were made only to keepe them occupied that otherwise knowe not what to doe'. Bownd remembered that when the light of the Gospel first dawned, psalm-singing had almost driven out the singing of ballads.[84] As a reader of Foxe, he would have learned that in Mary's days an apprentice musician from Colchester had been dispatched to play at a country wedding, where the company had engaged him to sing 'some songs of the Scripture'. These included a ditty called 'News out of London', which was an attack on the Mass.[85] And he would have read the correspondence between Gardiner and Somerset in which the bishop of Winchester complained that the people were paying good money for rhymes which disparaged the discipline of Lent, and the Protector conceded that people were demanding 'those foolish ballads of Jack-a-Lent' as in times past they had purchased such items as 'pardons and carols and Robin Hood's tales'.[86] When the Maidstone martyr John Denley sang a psalm in the fire at Uxbridge and was silenced by a burning brand thrown in his face, Dr Story remarked: 'Truly thou hast marred a good old song.'[87] Such psalms were the popular music of the 1550s, to which Denley's fellow townsman John Hall made significant contribution.[88] But now (1595 and in Suffolk) Bownd reported that the tide was flowing strongly in the

---

[84] Nicholas Bownd, *The doctrine of the Sabbath* (1595), pp. 241–2. See Nicholas Temperley, *The Music of the English Parish Church*, 2 vols. (Cambridge, 1979).

[85] Foxe, *Acts and Monuments*, viii. 578.

[86] Ibid., vi. 32, 35.

[87] Ibid., vii. 334.

[88] John Hall, *The proverbs of Salomon, three chapters of Ecclesiastes etc., drawen into metre* (?1549); *Certayn chapters of the Proverbes etc. translated into metre* (1550); *The courte of vertu: contayninge many holy songes sonettes, psalmes and ballattes* (1565). *The courte of vertu* was composed in response to a collection of love songs (no longer extant) called *The court of Venus*, and perhaps employed some of the same tunes. One of these moralizing songs has the refrain 'blame not my lute', an echo of Hall's fellow-Kentishman, Sir Thomas Wyatt. (*DNB*, art. Hall; John W. Bridge, 'John Hall of Maidstone: A Famous Surgeon of the Sixteenth Century', *Archaeologia Cantiana*, lxiii (1951), 119–21.)

contrary direction: 'so that in every fair and market almost
you shall have one or two singing and selling of ballads, and
they are bought up apace'. This might seem a small thing.
'Yet', said Bownd, 'I am growing afraid of it.'[89]

No wonder! What Bownd was observing was a profound
cultural change in which protestantism was losing the
popularity which it had enjoyed in the beginning as a
movement of protest, a radical, irreverent cocking of a snook
at the symbols of religious tradition and authority. Now the
Bible and the psalms were no longer exciting novelties but
symbols of order, discretion, age, and dominance in the local
community. The young John Bunyan turned up his nose at
the Scriptures. 'Alas, what is the Scriptures, give me a Ballad,
a News-book, *George* on Horseback, Bevis of Southamp-
ton . . .'.[90] Bownd assumed that psalms and ballads could
never coexist. 'They can so hardly stand together.' But he did
not suggest that a more resourceful evangelism could have
restored the popularity of the psalms by peddling them as
cheap broadsides, resembling the ballads, and sung to the
latest tunes. And he found the notion of engaging popular
musicians to sing the psalms, as Essex villagers had done in
1555, totally unacceptable. 'And indeede, many of the singing
men are so ungodly that it were better for them to have their
mouthes stopped then once to open them to pollute such holy
and sacred songs.'[91]

So Bownd was no General Booth, unable to see why the
Devil should be allowed to have all the best tunes. But the
founder of the Salvation Army, like Wesley before him, was an
evangelical Arminian. Bownd's Calvinism was ultimately
repressive, and it points towards a new élitism, presaging the
divorce of cultures which Peter Burke has sketched on a wide
canvas in his study of *Popular Culture in Early Modern Europe*,[92]
and which he believes stemmed from the efforts of the godly to

---

[89] Bownd, *The doctrine of the Sabbath,* pp. 241–2.

[90] Quoted, Spufford, *Contrasting Communities,* pp. 209–10. The Welsh preacher
Vavasor Powell was converted from similar popular tastes. (*The Life and Death of Mr
Vavasor Powell* (1671), p. 2.)

[91] Bownd added these observations to the second edition of his book, *Sabbathum
veteris et novi testamenti,* p. 424.

[92] Especially in Part 3, 'Changes in Popular Culture'.

reform and repress traditional culture, an important aspect of 'the split between the great and little traditions'.

VI

The cultural and even the social implications of a state of advancing religious and moral schism are not to be denied. As Keith Wrightson points out, the rhetorical distinction between 'godly professors' and 'the ignorant and profane multitude' is resonant of social as well as spiritual and behavioural differentiation, and he suggests that puritanism 'inserted a a cultural wedge' between 'the better part' and 'the greater part', 'the few' and 'the multitude'.[93]

But who were 'the few', 'the better part'? Max Weber's principle of 'elective affinity' may help us to appreciate how it was that godliness came to enjoy a special relationship with, and almost to presuppose, a respectable mode of existence which both depended upon but also perhaps tended to encourage the modest material competence enjoyed by Christopher Hill's 'industrious sort of people'. Abandoned by the godly, since they could 'so hardly stand together' with godly ways, the old customs and pastimes began to approximate to what Keith Wrightson calls 'a culture of poverty'.[94] The growing prevalence of 'alehouse haunting' makes the transformation of social mores somewhat concrete, for whereas the old communal festivities in principle united the whole community as effectively as attendance at mass, the alehouse was a place of segregated lowlife intercourse and entertainment, often distinct from the more respectable inn or tavern and frequented by the relatively poorly off.[95] (But this is not to say that inns and taverns were godly establishments, with the Bible chained to the counter, as in Calvin's short-lived Genevan experiment!)

In the opposite, godly camp in Keith Wrightson's Terling were many representatives of the better sort, belonging to the upper and middle ranks of village society. The godly group which coalesced in this village in the early seventeenth

---

[93] Wrightson and Levine, *Poverty and Piety in an English Village*, p. 162.
[94] Ibid., p. 182; Wrightson, 'Aspects of Social Differentiation', p. 45.
[95] Clark, 'The Alehouse and the Alternative Society'.

century was not connected by kinship or long residence in the parish but appears to have been drawn together by an affinity of common interest and outlook: the same faith, the same social ranking among the prosperous yeomen farmers, and the same resolve to reform the manners of their social inferiors, the poor whose numbers had risen so markedly as the village 'filled at the bottom'. This suggests an almost predictable and automatic response to the propositions and preoccupations of evangelical protestantism on the part of a certain class of person.[96]

Yet Keith Wrightson admits that the godly also included 'some relatively humble villagers', while later, post-Restoration evidence from the same place suggests that the puritan gospel exercised an appeal which was universal in principal, in that there was some response to it from all social levels. Historians will do well not to jump to hasty conclusions about 'the better sort', or to assume too lightly that the meaning of puritan evangelism was class war of a kind. Three recent studies of religion and society in certain villages of the Kent and Sussex Weald have all failed to discover any clear-cut difference of class between the reformed and unreformed elements. The Sussex iron village of Warbleton was very nearly evenly divided in the later years of Elizabeth between those who went along with their vicar and curate in conferring on their offspring names of 'godly signification'—Bethankful was particularly favoured, and also Sindeny—and those who were resistant to this puritan fad. One can hardly imagine a more public or scandalous demonstration of social fracture. How would it work out between these children when they began to talk, and to play? Yet the line of fraction does not appear to have been social in the commonly accepted sense of a lateral, horizontal line.[97] Even in such notoriously puritan centres as Banbury and Cranbrook there is no cause to believe

---

[96] Wrightson and Levine, *Poverty and Piety in an English Village*, Chapter 6, 'Changing Cultural Horizons: Education and Religion'.

[97] Collinson, 'Cranbrook and the Fletchers'; N. R. N. Tyacke, 'Popular Puritan Mentality in Late Elizabethan England', in *The English Commonwealth 1547–1640*, ed. Peter Clark, A. G. R. Smith, and Nicholas Tyacke (Leicester, 1979); J. J. Goring, *Church and Dissent in Warbleton c. 1500–1900*, Warbleton and District History Group Publications no. 5 (1980); and Jeremy Goring's forthcoming article which he kindly allowed me to read, 'The Reformation of the Ministry in Elizabethan Sussex'.

that a uniform godliness pervaded the middle and upper classes. Even in such places, gaming for the middle-aged, dancing for the young, drinking, and the grosser sins of the flesh were likely to have as great or greater attractive power than Bible-reading and sermons.

It might perhaps have been otherwise, if the wildest dreams of the Elizabethan puritans had come to pass, and a severe and legally enforced religious and moral discipline had been indifferently applied to all classes. But this was not the case, and as things were, in pre-revolutionary England, religion and morality of an exacting character were effectively voluntary, a matter of taste and choice. And with all due deference to 'elective affinity', we should expect a state of religious voluntarism to have promoted differences within rather than between social classes. When the protestant spokesman in a Gifford dialogue admitted that sincere Christians were 'farre the lesse number', lying like scattered corns in a great heap of chaff, the papist replied: 'Alas where is your Churche become? Where shall a man finde a companie of those rare birdes which you speake of?'[98] Since godly women were often much in evidence in the inner core of devout parishioners enjoying a special relationship with the pastor, it is as reasonable to argue for a sexual as for a social difference between the more and the less religious elements in the community: or indeed for the age differential to which attention has already been drawn. It was a schoolmaster's widow, not a person to carry much weight in parish affairs, who provided the orphaned godly of Terling with a home, after the emigration of their minister.[99]

We conclude that it is premature simply to equate the godly élite of early Stuart England with a social élite, or even with the broad band lying across the middle rungs of the social ladder. Part of the ground for this conclusion lies in the matter to be explored in the next and final chapter.

[98] George Gifford, *A dialogue betweene a papist and a protestant* (1582), fols. 35ᵛ, 37ᵛ–38ʳ.) Cf. Gifford's gloss on the parable of the sower: 'Of this great heap and rablement of people that were so zealous, and travelled so far to heare him, ther were three parts which did not profit by his doctrine but continued still damned and forlorne creatures, onely one parte of foure are true schollers.' (*A sermon on the parable of the sower,* sig. Aiiii.)

[99] Wrightson, 'Aspects of Social Differentiation', 42. Keith Wrightson has written extensively on 'Cultural Differentiation' in his *English Society 1580–1680* (1982).

Chapter Six

Voluntary Religion: Its Forms and Tendencies

I

'Let the husband say to his wife, children and servants: Come I pray you wife, let us go to the sermon. Children and servauntes, hasten and make speede, that we maye together seek after the Lord of Hostes, And let every man ad this, *I wil go with you also.* So one neighbour should say to another, I pray you neighbour, let us goe together to such and such a sermon or such a godly exercise and *I will go with you.*' These, according to a Suffolk preacher of the 1580s, were the invitations which godly and courteous Christians ought to extend as they set out for church, 'alluring and enticing' one another. Their neighbours were at liberty to accept or reject such overtures. Indeed in making them the godly man risked the 'intollerable contempt' of being regarded as a 'monster among men' or 'an owl in the day time among the birds'. 'Oh say the scorning raylers, now this holy man will goe to heaven in a hey barne, now these *Puritans* flocke together . . . But let not us be dismaid at these reproches and taunts of the wicked, so that we shoulde cease to sir up all that we can to seek Christ Jesus with us.'[1] Those who responded to the invitation of the godly and assented to the doctrine of the preacher might locate their conversion within such an experience. In the early seventeenth century it was not uncommon for a preacher to be presented with a testimonial bearing the signatures of those who owned him for their spiritual father, 'the proper means of their first conversion and their future salvation'.[2] Thereafter, like the Suffolk gentleman and future governor of Massachusetts, John Winthrop, they might develop 'an unsatiable thirst after the word of God', so that they 'could not miss a good

[1] Bartimaeus Andrewes, *Certaine verie worthie, godly and profitable sermons* (1583), pp. 185–6.
[2] Samuel Clarke, *The Lives of Sundry Eminent Persons* (1683), p. 162 (Edmund Staunton), p. 166 (Samuel Fairclough); Samuel Clarke, *A Collection of the Lives of Ten Eminent Divines* (1662), p. 4 (John Carter).

sermon, though many miles off, especially of such as did search deep the conscience'. They might even, with Winthrop, 'grow to be of some note for religion'.³

Such was a certain Devonian, referred to in a letter of 1562 as 'lately tourned to the Lord';⁴ some elderly Derbyshire miners who in the 1570s declared that they were 'ignorant and obstinate papists' until by the coming of a preaching minister they 'attayned to a comfortable feeling of their salvation in Christ';⁵ some villagers of Lawshall in Suffolk who in the 1580s were part of a 'styrrynge of manye in that place to seke the Lord in his word';⁶ and John Bruen's Chester neighbours who slipped through his back garden to prayer meetings in the early 1600s—'many converted, and many confirmed, and many convinced'.⁷ The converted and convinced would be distinguished by the bulky Geneva Bibles which they carried to sermons in order to follow the preacher from text to text. In a High Commission case of the early 1630s, the Lancashire gentleman Thomas Broughton protested that he and his family had gone to church 'without anie armes but their bibles'.⁸

In 1589, a London author imagined two neighbours meeting on their doorsteps as they hurried home from the morning service to take a hasty dinner before returning for the afternoon exercise. One of the two had spent the morning in company with his own pastor, Master Timotheus. His friend conceded that Master Timotheus was a sound preacher but declared that he was not edifying. 'His ministery was always dead and without spirit in mine eares.' So this man had been to the South Bank to hear a new and more affecting preacher. 'O sir, if you had heard this other man, you would have said there had beene a great difference. And for my parte, I desire

---

³ *Winthrop Papers*, i, *1498–1628*, Massachusetts Historical Society (Cambridge, Mass., 1929), 155–6.

⁴ BL Lansdowne MS 377, fol. 27.

⁵ *Letters of Thomas Wood, Puritan, 1566–1577*, ed. Patrick Collinson, *Bulletin of the Institute of Historical Research*, Special Supplement v (1960), 20.

⁶ BL Add. MS 38492, no. 63, fol. 107.

⁷ William Hinde, *A faithfull remonstrance of the holy life and happy death of John Bruen of Bruen-Stapleford in the County of Chester Esquire* (1641), pp. 135–6.

⁸ *Reports of Cases in the Courts of Star Chamber and High Commission*, ed. S. R. Gardiner, Camden Society, NS xxxix (1886), 142.

to heare those by whome I am most edified.'[9] Half a century later, a real rather than fictitious London sermon-taster told the High Commission that he preferred 'to hear the most powerful ministry'.[10] In the same spirit, the puritans of Ipswich and other places within riding distance made their pilgrimages to the Vale of Dedham in the days of James I, saying: 'Come, let's go to *Dedham* to get a little fire!' The fire was kindled by 'plain and powerful' Mr Rogers, a dramatic preacher of whom it was observed that 'his taking hold with both hands at one time of the supporters of the Canopy over the Pulpit, and roaring hideously, to represent the torments of the damned, had an awakening force attending it.'[11] It sounds as if 'powerful', 'edifying' preaching sometimes meant an electrifying, histrionic performance. We may distinguish it from the more winning and affectionate style of other divines, such as Richard Sibbes, the celebrated preacher of Gray's Inn. One of Sibbes's hearers testified that 'his sweet soul-melting gospel-sermons won my heart and refreshed me much.' A similar tribute is on record to another London preacher, Nathaniel Culverwell: 'He preached the love of God so sweetly that my heart melted to hear him.'[12]

We do not know how widespread such demonstrative or emotional preaching techniques may have been. An Elizabethan writer contrasts the excited gestures of the typical Italian with the immobility of a German preacher in the pulpit, as if he were 'benummed and impotent, or lame in all his members or partes of his bodie'.[13] Perhaps we should

---

[9] *Sophronistes. A dialogue, perswading the people to reverence and attend the ordinance of God, in the ministerie of their pastors* (1589), sig. A3, p. 19.

[10] *Reports of Cases*, p. 279.

[11] *Oliver Heywood's Life of John Angier of Denton*, ed. E. Axon, Chetham Society, NS xcvii (1973), 50. A similar style was affected by another Essex preacher, William Fenner, vicar of Rochford. The Fifth Monarchist John Rogers (not to be confused with the lecturer of Dedham) described him 'stirring about and thundering and beating the Pulpit; I was amazed and thought he was mad'. The matter of Fenner's 'thundering' was: 'O . . . ye knotty! rugged! proud pieces of flesh! you stony, rocky, flinty, hard heart! What wilt thou doe when thou art roaring in Hell amongst the damned?' Rogers is also a witness to Stephen Marshall's thunderous style, his 'powerful voice'. (John Rogers, *Obel or Beth-shemesh: A tabernacle for the sun: Or Irenicum Evangelicum. An idea of Church-Discipline* (1653), pp. 419–20.)

[12] *Obel or Bethshemesh*, pp. 410, 412.

[13] *A treatise of daunses, wherin it is shewed that they are as it were accessories and dependants . . . to whoredome* (1581), sig. B9.

deduce from this that the approved English pulpit manner observed a *via media,* somewhat between Mediterranean exuberance and Teutonic stolidity. Richard Bernard's popular and influential handbook on preaching, *The faithfull shepherd,* advocated 'a reverend gesture of the bodie' and condemned both nervous gestures ('hemmings, spitting, rubbing the browes, lifting up the shoulders, nodding of the head, taking often hold of the cloake or gowne, fidling with the fingers upon the breast, buttons, stroking of the beard and such like toies') and the 'phantasticall motions' of the stage. The body should be erect 'as nature hath framed; the head not wagging, the eies movable, and thy right hand onely, as occasion shall be offered, but not alway moving.' There was to be no smiting of the pulpit or throwing wide the arms, no 'lifting themselves up and againe suddenly stouping downe, very unadvisedly'.[14]

This was the advice of a 'grave' and 'reverent' minister. An aversion to 'powerful' pulpit antics, and to any style which verged on the meretricious, was likely to go with fidelity to the principle of a settled parish ministry, the hallmark of a conservative, presbyterian puritan conscience. Among the notable 'private christians' canonized by Samuel Clarke was Mrs Margaret Corbet, who 'kept close to the public Ministry where she lived ... She neither was of their opinion, nor practice, who out of I know not what kinde of singularity, separate from the Ministry of a godly Pastor and Husband.'[15] The dialogue of the two Londoners was written to correct 'partialitie and preiudice' in this respect: *'perswading the people to reverence and attend the ordinance of God in the ministerie of their owne pastors'.*[16]

---

[14] Richard Bernard, *The faithfull shepherd amended and enlarged* (1609), p. 89. See in this connection Foxe's tale of Latimer's opponent, the 'histrionical' preacher William Hubberdyne, whose 'dancings, hoppings and leapings' in a Bristol pulpit led to its collapse and a leg injury from which the preacher died. The churchwardens said that 'they had made their pulpit for preaching, and not for dancing etc.' (John Foxe, *Acts and Monuments,* ed. S. R. Cattley (1837–41), vii, 477–8.)

[15] Clarke, *Lives of Ten Eminent Divines,* p. 506.

[16] And cf. George Benson, *A sermon preached at Paules Crosse the seaventh of May MDCIX* (1609), p. 17: 'I desire you of this honorable city even in the bowells of Christ Jesus, that you will not be willing to entertaine (you care not whom) so it be not your own

But the author of this tract made no reference to the Act of Uniformity which required that every inhabitant of the realm should normally frequent his own parish church.[17] In the circles to which his argument was directed, this was considered a matter of conscience rather than of positive law. A collection of 'discourses in divinity upon divers causes of conscience' contains this chapter: 'It is questioned whether a man may goe from his own pastor to heare another.' The answer was that if there were no true profession of religion where he lived he might seek it elsewhere, although he should not ordinarily desert a constant preacher who delivered sound doctrine. But to attend sermons and lectures in neighbouring churches on days other than the Sabbath was a free and voluntary undertaking.[18] Bartimaeus Andrewes's courteous invitation ('come let us go together to such and such a sermon') suggests a religious world analogous in its voluntarism to the irreligious world of the alehouse. 'So likewise', wrote Richard Rawlidge of the drinking classes, 'they have their randevous at one anothers houses and gathering companies together they say one to another, Come let us goe to *Jack Rakars* house. Says one of the company, why will ye goe thither, let us goe to your house. No, no, saith he, wee will goe thither.' Of a scandalous Norwich minister it was reported: 'When David said he reioyced when they said unto him . . . you reioyce when your swaggering companions say: "Come, lett us go go down into the wyne seller or into the ale house." '[19]

Minister, that you will not gad (you care not whither) so it be from your own parish church.' This was to 'goe about preposterously and saucily' to break the order which God in his wisdom had set.

[17] Nor did Benson. He merely asserted that 'your owne Minister like Aaron . . . should have his parishioners neere and deare unto him'. (*A sermon preached at Paules Crosse*, p., 17.) See Injunction 46 of 1559 which required three or four discreet men in every parish diligently to see that all the parishioners duly resorted to *their* church on Sundays and holy days. (*Documentary Annals of the Reformed Church of England*, ed. E. Cardwell (Oxford, 1844), i. 228.)

[18] 'Discourses in Divinity upon Divers Cases of Conscience', Exeter College Oxford MS 165, fols. 15–16.

[19] Richard Rawlidge, *A monster late found out* (1628), pp. 18–19; *The Registrum Vagum of Anthony Harison*, ed. T. F. Barton, i, Norfolk Record Society, xxxii (Norwich, 1963), 161–2.

One may also be struck by a certain resonance between voluntary religion and what Alan Everitt has called the 'network of kinship and acquaintance' of private trading, with its 'spirit of speculation and adventure', so different from the stable traditions of the peasantry. Everitt thinks it 'not fanciful' to trace a connection between the spread of private trading and the rise of that 'mobile, virile and impatient' form of religion which was Independency, implying that a wayfaring religion was likely to be the preferred choice of wayfaring people.[20] But since not all gadders to sermons were small private traders and not all merchant men listened to sermons, the truth in this observation may be that of a metaphor, the metaphor of *Pilgrim's Progress*.

We have travelled some distance from the bloody whipping post at Bury St. Edmunds[21] and from George Widley's insistence that 'all must be compelled unto the true religion',[22] and we have entered a dimension of autonomous and voluntary religion which was the outstanding feature of the English Church in this period. Nowhere else in early modern Europe within a legally established Church was so much collective religious consciousness and behaviour conditioned not by regulation but by a more or less spontaneous consensus of private men, the religious public themselves. That was the significance and the near uniqueness of English puritanism. Not that puritan voluntarism led of necessity to a situation of anarchy or even of eclecticism. On the contrary, the consistency of puritan religion was its outstanding feature. The religious life of the Lancashire puritans as described by R. C. Richardson displays some distinctively regional features, but in most respects it resembles what we know of the ways of other puritans in East Anglia or Northamptonshire, although for Lancashire people and even for Lancashire ministers the midlands and East Anglia were foreign countries which they had rarely if ever visited.[23] Moreover the religious practice of

---

[20] *The Agrarian History of England and Wales*, iv, *1500–1640*, ed. Joan Thirsk (Cambridge, 1967), 557–8, 562.

[21] See pp. 158–61 above.

[22] See p. 230 above.

[23] R. C. Richardson, *Puritanism in North-West England: A Regional Study of the Diocese of Chester to 1642* (Manchester, 1972).

the English puritans conformed in detail to the practice of other Calvinist communities overseas. For example, the English institution of the public fast resembled in all essential respects the *deuil* of the French reformed churches. Puritan religion was certainly one of the factors which tended to transcend and redeem the insularity of provincial communities.

The important and singular fact is that we learn little about these consistent religious forms from official sources, except negatively, from articles of episcopal enquiry and other records of correction, in which they stood condemned. In 1583, for example, Archbishop Whitgift 'utterly inhibited' 'all preaching, reading, catechisme, and other such like exercise in private places and families' attended by people of more than one family, describing them as 'a manifest sign of schisme, and a cause of contention in the church'.[24] But to rely on such evidence is to derive a partly false impression of illegality and subversion. Such private meetings as Whitgift referred to were devoted to 'repetition' of the doctrine delivered in public sermons, and they were standard practice in godly circles and continued to be so, for all the archbishop's strictures. Nor were such meetings considered by those who took part in them to be expressions of dissent, still less of active disobedience. They were part of an accepted economy of religious practice which English protestants had either adopted from foreign practice or improvised and, in the course of time, institutionalized: extra-legal rather than illegal.

Whether the law inhibited either travelling to sermons in other parishes or holding religious meetings in private houses was a somewhat open question. The Elizabethan preacher and pamphleteer John Udall, noting as we have done a certain parallelism of religious and irreligious sociability, thought it unreasonable that an assembly of the godly was 'charged to be within the compasse of a conventicle', whereas twenty men could meet together in an alehouse and 'lewdly misspend their time' and this was 'but good neighbourhood, it is no conventicle'.[25] 'Conventicles and secret meetings of

---

[24] *Documentary Annals*, i. 468.
[25] John Udall, *Two sermons of obedience to the Gospell*, in *Certaine sermons* (1596), sig. Iiiiij^r.

priests and ministers' in private houses were forbidden by Canon 73 of 1604, but apparently only if they tended to the impeaching or depraving of the doctrine, liturgy, and discipline of the Church: manifestly a reference to the conferences or *'classes'* of the 1580s.[26] In 1631 a leading ecclesiastical lawyer, Dr Duck, thought that the canon gave some defence to the holding of private meetings 'if in such meetings they preach nothing against the doctrine of the Church'.[27] And in 1628, Sir Henry Marten, dean of the Arches and the wealthiest member of Doctors Commons, supported a parliamentary bill designed to ensure that no one should be molested or convented for absence from his parish church, 'so as at the same time he be at some other church or chapel and there hear the word of God'. In his speech Marten said that it was his duty to inform the Commons that if an ordinary were to trouble a man for going to another sermon when he had none at home 'it is against law and I have upon appeals given good costs against the ordinary and I will ever do it'.[28]

II

What was the significance and the tendency of voluntary religion, and in particular of 'gadding' outwards to sermons and lectures and drawing inwards upon private household meetings? In the provocative essay called 'Individuals and Communities', contained within his *Society and Puritanism in Pre-Revolutionary England,* Christopher Hill has suggested that religious voluntarism was a force assisting the disintegration of traditional local communities, a process with a certain inbuilt historical logic. Membership of the old communities had been compulsory. But now, especially in the towns, 'voluntary communities arose, independent of the parish . . . united by community of interests rather than by geographical propinquity or corporate worship.' 'Contract communities had succeeded status communities.' 'The transition from parish to

---

[26] *Synodalia,* ed. Edward Cardwell (Oxford, 1842), i. 288.

[27] *Reports of Cases,* p. 218.

[28] Quoted, B. P. Levack, *The Civil Lawyers in England, 1603–42* (Oxford, 1973), p. 191. Cf. the complaint of the people of Lawshall, Suffolk, *c.* 1584: 'Ytt were to be wysshed that people myght peaceablie goe to the word abrod tyll they may have yt better at home.' (BL Add. MS 38492, no. 63, fol. 108.)

sect is from a geographical unit which brings the members of a
community together for cultural, social and ceremonial
purposes, to a voluntary unit to which men belong in order to
hear the preacher of their choice.'[29] It was, I suppose, a
combination of my own first, appreciative reading of *Society
and Puritanism* and the effect of the sources I was then handling
which led me on an earlier occasion to express a similar point
of view. It seemed to me that left to themselves the forces
generated within popular protestantism could have had no
other end than a kind of congregationalism. 'By the mid-
seventeenth century, it was certain that they would frustrate
any attempt to conserve intact the national and parochial
church, whether episcopal or presbyterian in its constitution.'[30] I should not now want to press the argument of
historical necessity but merely to observe what cannot be
disputed: the accommodation of voluntary religious forms
within the Church of England over a period of two or three
generations or, to put it another way, within the long lifetime
of an Englishman who shared the birth and death dates of
Archbishop Tobie Matthew.

Richard Baxter tells us that it pleased God to 'instruct and
change' his father 'by the bare reading of the Scripture in
private, without either Preaching or godly Company, or any
other Books but the Bible'.[31] Historians have been prone to
agree with seventeenth-century controversialists—and with
the poet Dryden—that to read and ponder on the Bible in
such circumstances was to tamper with dynamite. Christopher
Hill derives puritan voluntarism from what he calls 'Luther's
subversive doctrines of the priesthood of all believers and of
justification by faith alone', which, by locating truth in the
heart of the believer rather than in the law and tradition of
the Church, had its logical terminus in 'individualist anarchy'.[32] But this overlooks the stress in Calvinist divinity on the

[29] Christopher Hill, *Society and Puritanism in Pre-Revolutionary England* (1966), pp. 492,
488, 483–4, 491.
[30] Patrick Collinson, 'The Godly: Aspects of Popular Protestantism in Elizabethan
England', unpublished paper circulated for the Past and Present Society Conference,
1966, on Popular Religion.
[31] *Reliquiae Baxterianae*, ed. Matthew Sylvester (1696), p. 2.
[32] Hill, *Society and Puritanism*, pp. 487–8.

total subordination of mind and will to the truth and the constraining providence of God as well as the Calvinist condemnation of 'will-worship'; and it undervalues the ecclesiastical and social disciplines which were the concomitants of intellectual and moral constraint. Within the covenant of grace, wrote William Perkins in his *Golden Chaine,* 'we do not so much offer or promise any great matter to God, as in a manner only receive'; 'for we are as clay in the hand of the potter'. The Gospel was 'as it were the conduit pipe of the Holy Ghost to fashion and derive faith into the soul; by which faith they which believe do, as with an hand, apprehend Christ's righteousness'.

But it is true that puritan theology, especially in its application to the conscience as 'practical divinity', emphasized increasingly the willing response of the individual within the covenant of grace. Perkins again: 'There is no virtue or gift of God in us, without our wills: and in every good act God's grace and man's will concur: God's grace as the principal cause, man's will renewed as the instrument of God. And in all good things, industry and labour and invocation on our parts is required.'[33] The unremitting round of puritan religiosity, the frequent journeys to the 'conduit pipe' of the sermon, the 'industry, labour, and invocation' applied both in religious 'exercises' and in a man's ordinary vocation were voluntary in this secondary and conditioned, rather than primary sense. And because it was a secondary voluntarism it was not at all eclectic but assumed predictable and consistent forms, forms which were expressive not so much of 'individualism', still less of 'anarchy', as of a stereotyped, programmed corporateness. The modern observer who comes close to the heart of the matter in the surviving puritan diaries of the period[34] discovers this religion in a thoroughly internalized form. He may think that what he is seeing is rugged individuality and inspired human will-power, for ever bracing itself and picking itself up

---

[33] *The Work of William Perkins,* ed. Ian Breward, The Courtenay Library of Reformation Classics, iii (Appleford, Abingdon, 1970), 213–14, 259, 96.

[34] *Two Elizabethan Puritan Diaries by Richard Rogers and Samuel Ward,* ed. M. M. Knappen, American Society of Church History (Chicago, 1933); *The Diary of Ralph Josselin 1616–1683,* ed. Alan Macfarlane, Records of Social and Economic History NS iii (Oxford, 1976).

after the latest fall. But however secular his own outlook he will find it hard to escape from the account of these processes supplied by the Calvinist divines themselves: for the divinity created a closed and programmatic world of language and experience. There were, of course, those who broke out of this system, declared that for them it was without authenticity, and recorded their spiritual odysseys as ranters, seekers, and quakers.[35] They went, as the quaker Mary Pennington put it, 'from the simplicity into notions' and 'from one notion to another'.[36] This was religious voluntarism of a primary sort, reviving a distinct tradition of the free will which was foreign to protestantism but never lost to sight in the undercurrents of the English Reformation. But given the unusual circumstances of the Interregnum in which these developments occurred, only a bishop Bossuet would want to argue that advanced sectarianism, 'individualist anarchy', was a natural or predictable outgrowth from the conditioned religious voluntarism which expressed itself in Calvinist and puritan piety.

III

If Calvinist divinity was the mainspring of voluntary religion, it is equally possible to account for its vitality and prevalence in the categories of religious sociology or, more simply, in terms of majorities and minorities. Early English protestants were a minority, self-consciously a remnant of 'known men', like the Lollards before them. Contemporary narratives of the Reformation, like that composed by the minor courtier and 'hot gospeller' Edward Underhill,[37] suggest that in spite of the political and legal endorsement of protestantism this was still the situation in the days of Edward VI, one which was heavily accentuated in the succeeding years by the Marian reaction and persecution. When the Marian commissions pursued their enquiries deep into the old dissenting territory of the Kentish Weald, they found evidence of a severe ethic of exclusivism

---

[35] Owen C. Watkins, *The Puritan Experience* (1972).

[36] William C. Braithwaite, *The Beginnings of Quakerism* (1923), p. 14.

[37] *Narratives of the Days of the Reformation*, ed. J. G. Nichols, Camden Society lxxvii (1859), 132–76.

and ostracism. John Fishcock of Headcorn informed his judges that he would not 'communicate with an advouterer [adulterer] nor a covetous parson that first was a brother in Christ, nether will he pray with him nether salute him'.[38]

Such principles belonged more properly to conventicles in continuity with the lollard tradition than to religious groups founded on the preaching of protestant divines and faithful to the Prayer Book and other standards of Edwardian orthodoxy.[39] Indeed, Fishcock's affirmation bears a textual resemblance to an article of doctrine confessed by the Kentish 'free will men' whose separatist conventicles were a cause of concern to the Edwardian authorities, including Archbishop Cranmer himself. Early in 1551 a special ecclesiastical commission in Cranmer's diocese had heard John Plume of Lenham testify that 'beynge emonge the congregators', he had 'herde it divers tymes affirmed as a generall doctryne that they oughte not to salute a synner or a mann whome they knowe not'.[40] Two years later a schoolmaster and cleric who had kept company with these sectaries was persuaded to change sides and to denounce them in a sermon preached at Maidstone, in which he objected particularly to the partiality with which such people called themselves brothers and sisters, dividing themselves from other Christian people. 'Whosoever therefore doth call any man or woman brother and syster otherwise then he calleth all other christian men *pecatt in unitatem ecclesiae.*'[41] These 'brethren' condemned the doctrine of predestination as the doctrine of devils. Their separatism had theological roots quite distinct from protestantism, properly so called.[42]

Yet the old lollard conventicles, or individual members of them, could be won over to those protestant doctrines which

---

[38] BL Harleian MS 421, fol. 101.

[39] J. F. Davis, 'Heresy and the Reformation in the South-East of England: 1520–1559', Oxford D.Phil. thesis, 1966; C. J. Clement, 'The English Radicals and their Theology, 1535–1565', Cambridge Ph.D. thesis, 1980. I am grateful to Dr Davis and Dr Clement for permission to consult and cite their dissertations. See also J. W. Martin, 'English Protestant Separatism at its Beginnings: Henry Hart and the Free-will Men', *Sixteenth-Century Journal*, vii (1976), 55–74.

[40] BL Harleian MS 421, fol. 134ᵛ.

[41] Thomas Cole, *A godly and frutefull sermon made at Maydstone* (1553), sigs. A1ʳ, D1ᵛ.

[42] Clement, 'The English Radicals', *passim*.

some old dissenters, such as 'Father' Henry Hart, found as unacceptable as the pretensions of the 'learned men' by whom they were taught.[43] And conversely, groups and individuals who were orthodox in their protestantism might perpetuate a severe and separating witness against 'sinners', more especially in the deeply alienating circumstances of the Marian persecution. For all his approval of social shunning, John Fishcock of Headcorn revealed to his judges a belief substantially formed by 'official' protestantism. Unlike some of his fellow heretics from the Weald, he professed to have 'a good iudgement of the Trynytie', and to think it 'yvill and ungodly' to doubt this doctrine. He expressed confidence in the royal supremacy and declared that no one might preach or teach 'onles he be sente or admytted by the rulers', a principle by which several apparently orthodox Kentish martyrs stood condemned.[44]

As an example of an Edwardian protestant of good social standing who was driven by the Marian reaction into patterns of alienated mentality and behaviour almost indistinguishable from advanced sectarianism we may cite Thomas Woodman, the Sussex ironmaster burned at Lewes in 1557, of whom it was said that all the heretics in the country did hang upon him 'as the people did in times past upon St. Augustine and St. Ambrose or such like'.[45] Woodman's episcopate was exercised from the village of Warbleton[46] over a remnant of faithful gospellers scattered over the Sussex and Kentish Weald. In one of his prison letters he asked a certain Mrs Roberts of Hawkhurst to salute 'all our brethren and sisters

[43] Hart said 'that his faithe was not growndid upon Lernyd men for all errors were broughte in by Lernyd men'. (Quoted, Clement, 'The English Radicals', p. 177.) Cf. the polemic against the 'clerkly sophistical doctrine' of learned men, 'disceivers of the people', expressed by John Champneys in *The harvest is at hand wherein the tares shall be bound and brent* (1548).

[44] BL Harleian MS 421, fol. 101.

[45] The history of the Sussex martyr Richard Woodman is in John Foxe, *Acts and Monuments,* ed. S. R. Cattley, viii, 332–77.

[46] For Warbleton's radical reputation at the end of the sixteenth century, see Nicholas Tyacke, 'Popular Puritan Mentality in Late Elizabethan England', in *The English Commonwealth 1574–1640: Essays in Politics and Society Presented to Joel Hurstfield,* ed. Peter Clark, Alan G. R. Smith, and Nicholas Tyacke (Leicester, 1979), pp. 77–92; and Jeremy Goring, *Church and Dissent in Warbleton c. 1500 to 1900,* Warbleton and District History Group Publications no. 5 (Eastbourne, 1980).

that are round about you', 'all the people of the household of God','all other of God's elect'.

O dear hearts! now is the gospel of God overwhelmed with many black and troublesome clouds of persecution, for the which cause very few go about to have their eyes made clear by the true light of the gospel, for fear of losing of the treasures of this world, which are but vain and shall perish ... Now is the Lord come with his fan in his hand, to try the wheat from the chaff ... Now I perceive, God will have a further trial to root out all dissemblers.

Bishop Christopherson of Chichester called Woodman 'neighbour Woodman' and told him that both he and 'all the worshipful men' of his country were sorry for him, for he had been 'a man of good estimation in all the country, amongst the poor and rich'. Yet it was Woodman's own father, brother, 'and certain other his acquainted friends' who had betrayed him to the authorities.

Under examination by his father's parish priest, Woodman was accused of denying the Christianity of the majority. 'You enter into judgment against the people.' 'Is the flock of Christ such a little flock as ye speak of? You may call it a great flock. How many be there of them, can you tell me?' Woodman replied that this was a pretty question. He would not make himself equal with God. Yet he read that strait was the gate and narrow the way that led to salvation and few there were that found it. So that 'the people that shall be saved is but a small company in comparison of the rest.' Whereupon the parson exclaimed that he was 'enough to trouble a whole country ... You are not meet to be in a commonwealth'.[47] In one of his letters from prison, the Marian martyr John Bradford wrote: 'I trust you be of that little flock which shall inherit the kingdom of heaven.'[48]

The social estrangement of Elizabethan protestants and even those who earned the stigma of puritans can rarely have been as pronounced as that of Woodman. And the doctrine of election was applied by Elizabethan puritanism in the public sector with an inclusive rather than exclusive force. 'Every hill

[47] Foxe, *Acts and Monuments*, viii. 374–7, 338–9, 336, 353–4, 359–60.
[48] Ibid., vii, 212.

is Sion . . . every citie Jerusalem.' But the solidarity and sense of apartness which found expression in the Marian trials and prison letters were sometimes revived by the lesser persecutions stirred up by the occasional campaigns to enforce Prayer Book uniformity. In London in 1567, when the suspension of many preachers drove the godly back into their Marian habits of meeting secretly in houses and even on ships on the river, it was said that the 'persecution grew so fast as that it brought many a hundred to know one another that never knew before':[49] another generation of 'known men'!

But a more fundamental reason for the continued social isolation of godly protestants—an isolation of which the pejorative term 'puritan' was the measure—was the elementary fact that they continued to have the status of a religious minority in a church later described by a separatist writer as 'a constreyned union of Papists and Protestants'.[50] The cloth town of Cranbrook in the Kentish Weald is sometimes called 'puritan Cranbrook'. It had a lollard past and a dissenting future. Yet after more than a generation of exposure to protestant evangelism there is no evidence that the convinced and converted comprised more than a little flock. Up to 1612 only 20 out of 138 probate inventories mention a Bible among the household effects, one of them the property of a schoolmaster who kept dancing in his house on the Sabbath and quarrelled violently with the vicar.[51] If this is thought to be less than decisive evidence, for inventories do not always mention books,[52] only 3 out of 122 Cranbrook wills of the same period make any religious or charitable bequests. In Jacobean Cranbrook the barbers and butchers plied their trade on Sunday mornings and the leading clothing families amused themselves with cards 'and such like games'. A striking material prosperity was reflected in the stock of the mercer's

[49] Peter Lorimer, *John Knox and the Church of England* (1875), p. 300.

[50] Henry Ainsworth, *Counterpoyson* (?Amsterdam, 1608), *p. 228.*

[51] Patrick Collinson, 'Cranbrook and the Fletchers: Popular and Unpopular Religion in the Kentish Weald', in *Reformation Principle and Practice: Essays in Honour of A. G. Dickens,* ed. P. N. Brooks (1980), p. 188; Cathedral Archives and Library Canterbury, X.1.10, fol. 74. I owe the latter reference to Robert Acheson, who is engaged on research into religious radicalism in seventeenth-century Kent.

[52] David Cressy, *Literacy and the Social Order: Reading and Writing in Tudor and Stuart England* (Cambridge, 1980), pp. 48–52.

shop: hundreds of pounds' worth of gloves, ribbons, silks, buttons, drinking glasses, currants, raisins, and playing cards. According to a late Elizabethan vicar, the vice of drunkenness abounded in the town.[53]

This was the condition of a parish which had enjoyed weekly sermons for forty years. What made more than nominal protestants even thinner on the ground in other places was the uneven and inadequate provision of preaching in the Elizabethan Church. In the early years, when sermons were particularly scarce, many areas seem to have depended upon itinerant preachers who enjoyed the patronage of locally influential figures. In 1629, an old minister died at Bishop's Castle in Shropshire aged eighty-two, an exact contemporary of Archbishop Matthew. This man, Walter Stephens, by then 'quite worn out with his holy labour', recalled that when he began to preach in those parts in about 1576, there was no other preacher between him and the sea. (Did he mean Cardigan Bay, to the west, or the estuary of the Dee, to the north?) When Stephens came to preach at his birthplace of Lyonshall in Herefordshire, the bell would be rung and the people ploughing in the fields would unlink their teams, crying 'away to church, Mr Stephens is come!'[54] A London citizen with Suffolk roots who died in 1581 left £10 to provide for thirty sermons to be preached in his native county in those parishes 'where the gospell hath beene leaste preached since the Queenes Maiesties reigne'.[55] It was in these circumstances that the practice arose among the godly of accompanying their favoured preachers from place to place, in a demonstrative and even provocative fashion. In the Weald of Kent in the 1560s, a blind preacher called Dawes travelled about, preaching on working days. As he came down the village street of Headcorn, 'dyvers honest men with hym', somebody cried out that it was 'a shame' that he was suffered so to go about a-preaching.[56] Dawes was treading, perhaps with deliberation, in the footsteps of such Edwardian pioneers and Marian martyrs as John Bland. The 'honest men' were

[53] Collinson, 'Cranbrook and the Fletchers', pp. 186–8.
[54] BL Harleian MS 7517, fol. 36.
[55] Will of Anthony Cage PRO PROB 11/66, fol. 33ᵛ.
[56] Cathedral Archives and Library Canterbury, X.1.9, fol. 66.

perhaps men of substance. As early as the 1530s, that precocious reformer Sir Francis Bigod maintained his own stable of preachers and 'rode all over the cuntre with theyme'.[57] The tradition of itinerating, which Wesley would revive so famously in the eighteenth century, was never dormant for long. In Jacobean Essex, it was the practice of Richard Blackerby to 'ride about from Family to Family . . .- and only alight and pray with them, and give them some heavenly exhortation, and then away to another Family'.[58] In 1661 the Weald was said to be 'a receptacle for distressed and running parsons'.[59]

But such 'posting apostles' or parsons on the run were not part of the settled economy of the Elizabethan and Jacobean Church, not only in the terms of official policy but according to Calvinist ecclesiology and emerging puritan practice. A more stable situation was achieved when a resident preaching ministry was established in enough places for sermons to be within most people's reach, but when there was still a tidal flow of the godly in and out of the neglected parishes and preaching centres, and even to receive the Communion from the hands of preaching ministers, rather than from dumb dogs and alehouse haunters.[60] At this stage, which took place in the 1570s in the midlands and the south and east of England, a generation later in the north, the godly were also coming together in force in the market towns on the days of 'prophesying' and 'combination' lecturing.[61]

At a third stage, in particularly favoured locations such as the clothing towns and villages of East Anglia in the late Elizabethan and Jacobean years, the godly in most parishes enjoyed their own preaching ministry and adhered firmly to their own pastors, but nevertheless made it their practice to go

---

[57] Foxe, *Acts and Monuments,* vii. 287–306. For Bigod's active patronage of preachers and desire to become a preacher himself, see A. G. Dickens, *Lollards and Protestants in the Diocese of York 1509–1558* (Oxford, 1959), p. 77.

[58] Clarke, *Lives of Sundry Eminent Persons,* p. 59.

[59] *Victoria County History of Kent,* ii, ed. William Page (1926), 100.

[60] This is the stage of development delineated in Part Seven of my *The Elizabethan Puritan Movement* (1967).

[61] Ibid., pp. 168–76; Patrick Collinson, 'Lectures by Combination: Structures and Characteristics of Church Life in 17th-Century England', *Bulletin of the Institute of Historical Research,* xlviii (1975), 182–213.

gadding to lectures in other churches on working days, or to combination lectures on market days. And when their own minister accepted an invitation to preach out of his own cure they kept him company. On a Sunday in 1589 the minister of Nayland crossed the county and diocesan border to preach at Boxted in Essex 'and sundrye Suffolke people' with him. This prompted the vicar of Boxted to leave off his surplice, knowing that 'some that came owt of Suffolke syde would have liked hym the worse yf he had worne it'.[62] Seven years earlier, when Edmund Chapman the lecturer of Dedham came to preach at Richard Rogers's Wethersfield, accompanied by 'sundry other godly preachers and other persons', a local farmer angrily objected: 'What make all these knaves here todaye? What, will they make a god of Rogers?'[63] John Winthrop's father contrived to hear thirty-three different preachers in a single year.[64] In the years of Samuel Fairclough's ministry at Ketton the Suffolk people travelled up to twenty miles to his lectures, arriving early in the day to make sure of a seat: 'so that ye should see the church-yard . . . barricaded with horses, tyed to the outward rayles'.[65]

Presumably such gatherings were distinguished from the more orderly parochial congregations by the indiscriminate seating arrangements, people taking their places on a first-come-first-served basis, as they did in the theatres. Sir Thomas Wroth wrote to Sir Robert Harley in March 1629: 'If you please to dine with me, then I pray let us go together to Mr Damport's [sc., John Davenport's lecture at St. Stephen's, Coleman Street] in the morning, where I will provide a seat for you, and expect you some what before 9 at my house, or meet you there if you please.'[66] In the country, the gadding must have resembled in appearance the jaunts which people took to fairs and pastimes, or the youth on their way to

---

[62] Greater London Record Office, London Division, Consistory Court of London Records, DL/C/213, depositions relating to a case against Philip Gilgate, vicar of Boxted, 3 November 1589.

[63] Essex Record Office, QSR 84/33, 43.

[64] *DNB*, art. John Winthrop.

[65] Clarke, *Lives of Sundry Eminent Persons*, p. 187.

[66] BL Loan 29/202, fols. 248–9. Wroth was a parishioner of St. Stephen's and was perhaps offering Harley accommodation in his family pew. Yet the fact remains that Harley, who was master of the Mint, was in need of a seat.

Sunday dances. Around St. Albans in the 1580s it was observed that 'many of this gadding people came from farre and went home late, both yonge men and yonge women together'.[67] 'The thing is so generall', complains the devil's advocate in a puritan dialogue. 'Doe not the people flocke after them everywhere, out of many Townes, sometimes seven miles off? . . . Is it not a factious thing, that the people are affectioned to some men, and care not for hearing other?'[68]

But what the critic represented as fanatical and factious disorder was in reality a matter of studied and demonstrative form. At Calk in Derbyshire, where people came with their victuals to spend the whole day with the preacher Julines Herring, they went away in the evening 'in companies, repeating the Sermons, and singing *Psalms* in their return home'.[69] And since notable religious exercises had their set days, these comings and goings were regulated by their own calendar. It was not quite the case, as John Bossy has suggested, that for protestants acts of religion moved in something resembling clockwork motion in which Sunday marked the hours and all Sundays were roughly equal.[70] The clock-face also accommodated 'lecture days', which were usually market days: Mondays at Bury St. Edmunds for the prophesying and later for the combination lecture; Monday too for the 'famous exercise' at Burton on Trent; but Saturday at Cranbrook.[71] And the clockwork was sometimes interrupted by the holding of extraordinary public fasts, which, to somewhat change the image, were a powerful engine of puritan religion, an action, as one preacher puts it, 'by which the faithful prepare themselves to *prayer* when they take in hand some earnest matter'.[72]

The puritan fast was in part a response to the challenge of

---

[67] BL Lansdowne MS 61, no. 24, fol. 72.

[68] *A dialogue, concerning the strife of our churche* (1584), p. 50.

[69] Samuel Clarke, *The Lives of Thirty-Two English Divines* (1677), p. 191. Cf. the practice of John Bruen, who proceeded very publicly to church with his family, attendants, and followers, singing psalms. (Hinde, *A faithfull remonstrance*, p. 210.)

[70] John Bossy, *The English Catholic Community* (1975), pp. 146–7.

[71] Collinson, 'Lectures by Combination', 191–5, 197; *Thomas Wotton's Letter-Book 1574–1586*, ed. G. Eland (1960), pp. 24–5.

[72] Eusebius Paget, *A godly sermon preached at Detford in Kent on Monday the ix of June in Anno 1572* (1586), sig. C6.

the ascetic practice of the English catholic community.[73] But among its distinctively protestant features was the sense that fasting should always be related to some particular cause of affliction; so that like the plagues which they were designed to avert, or the positive opportunities to which they were sometimes addressed, fasts interrupted the normal routine, although they might for convenience be staged on regular lecture days, or on legal holidays. Thus on Whit Sunday 1596 a minister of St. Albans, Erasmus Cooke, announced to his parishioners that on the following day, 'being holiday', 'he meant to be exercised more than ordinarily', and that they should come to church having abstained from meat. On the morrow, Cooke performed the prodigious feat of preaching three sermons which lasted for six-and-a-half hours, in the presence of many other ministers and great numbers of people from 'foreign parishes'.[74]

This was far from unusual. It was a general rule that fasts should last for a whole day at least, and should consist of a course of sermons, punctuated with prayer and psalm-singing. At Southill in Bedfordshire in 1603 the public proceedings lasted from nine to five, with four preachers.[75] At Southam in Warwickshire, a preaching centre with a formidable reputation, a fast held in 1596 was attended by 'many hundreds' from beyond the parish, who heard three sermons preached by three ministers.[76] At the end of the day there was usually a shared meal. 'They ended the farce with a plentiful supper', wrote the Jesuit William Weston of the rituals which he observed from the window of his prison in Wisbech Castle.[77]

A further indispensable part of the proceedings was the

---

[73] Bossy, *English Catholic Community*, pp. 110–16. George Gifford of Maldon answered the Catholic boast of strictness in the discipline of fasting: 'The right fast which the Scripture doeth commend is in estimation among us: wee doe not onely write and speake of it, but also have and are ready for to practise it, both publikely and privately.' (*A dialogue betweene a papist and a protestant* (1582), fol. 43ᵛ.)

[74] Hertfordshire Record Office, ASA 5/5/291.

[75] *The State of the Church in the Reigns of Elizabeth and James I as illustrated by Documents Relating to the Diocese of Lincoln*, i, ed. C. W. Foster, Lincoln Record Society, xxiii (Horncastle, 1926), cxvi.

[76] Lichfield Joint Record Office, B/C/3/3, 21. I owe this reference to Rosemary O'Day. For Southam's reputation in the 1570s, see my *Letters of Thomas Wood*.

[77] *The Troubles of our Catholic Forefathers Related by Themselves*, ed. John Morris, SJ, ii (1875), 241.

collection of money, either for the poor or for some specific charitable purpose connected with the occasion of the fast, such as the plight of foreign protestant churches.[78] In John White's Dorchester in the 1620s there was a weekly fast, held on Wednesdays. On 26 July 1625 proceedings ended with a collection for the relief of Exeter, at that time visited by the plague. The considerable sum of £23 6s. was raised, made up to a round £40 by the town, and sent to the godly and exemplary Mr Ignatius Jordan, the only magistrate to have remained in the stricken city.[79] Such practices were by then 'ancient' usage, in the settled economy of the reformed English Church. In 1584 a Norfolk minister was said to have 'appoynted solemn fastes for reformation to be had etc., and gathered money of such as came to the sermons of other townes, which he bestowed as pleased himselfe'.[80] In the opinion of a critical ecclesiastical authority, this man had no right to collect and dispose of charitable funds. But there can be no doubt that he did so with the willing consent of those who participated in the fast. In 1596 a Southwark preacher was suspended and imprisoned for holding a fast on a Thursday which the authorities had ordered to be held on a Wednesday. Moreover the Thursday in question was Twelfth Day, which should have been celebrated as a feast day. The preacher explained that since Thursday was his normal lecture day, to have complied with this order would have involved his people in two days of abstinence and two collections for the poor. When they heard that Twelfth Day was to be kept as a fast, his people had distributed to the poor the feasts which they had in readiness.[81] When the town clerk of Barnstaple witnessed a 'trental of sermons' on St. Luke's day 1586 at nearby Pilton, he was reminded of the offerings of money made in the old days by pilgrims, for Pilton had been

---

[78] It was remarked in an Elizabethan dialogue 'A brief note of the necessitie of preaching' that 'there be many collections allreadye everie Sabaoth, sometimes for one thinge and sometimes for another, and many are troubled with the monthlie payment to the poore'. (Dr Williams's Library, MS Morrice B.I, pp. 456–6.)

[79] Frances Rose-Troup, *John White the Patriarch of Dorchester (Dorset) and the Founder of Massachusetts, 1575–1648* (1930), p. 41.

[80] Norfolk and Norwich Record Office, Norfolk and Norwich Archaeological Society, MS Frere, Box K.12a. I owe this reference to Hassell Smith.

[81] BL Lansdowne MS 83, no. 34, fol. 98.

an ancient place of pilgrimage.[82] Another parallel might be drawn with such secular gatherings as ales, wakes, and silver games, for these too combined 'exercise' of a kind with an element of sociability and the raising of funds for charity. Money, like drink, was a social lubricant, for purposes religious as well as irreligious. Ralph Josselin's *Diary* records a fast held in his Essex parish in 1650: 'Wee had a very large contribucon and my wife had provided plenty of cake.'[83]

The fast as a solemn and extraordinary assembly with 'all the daie preaching and praying' was a settled institution throughout our period and beyond. In 1580 there was a fast at Stamford which received extensive publicity from a literary controversy between the Jesuit Robert Parsons and two puritan writers.[84] Fifty years later, the vicar of Stamford was accused of holding fasts on weekdays which were attended by 'a great company of the country', and which took up six or seven hours with preaching and extempore prayer.[85] Such was the social background to the political phenomenon of the fast sermons in the Long Parliament.

Sometimes, as Father Weston observed at Wisbech,[86] the religious exercises on such days concluded with an administration of the Communion. Elsewhere the Communion itself was the occasion for large and general assemblies. At Denton Chapel in Lancashire, in the 1630s, John Angier's monthly Communions attracted hundreds of godly folk, some of whom travelled distances of ten, twenty, even thirty miles to be there. The officers of the chapel moved among the visitors to ensure

---

[82] George M. Doe, 'North Devon in Elizabethan Times', *Transactions of the Devonshire Association*, lviii (Plymouth, 1927), 241.

[83] *Diary of Ralph Josselin*, pp. 223–4. Cf. Richard Gough's comment on the hospitality provided when Vavasor Powell preached at a private house in Myddle, Shropshire, *c.*1650: 'And when the people departed they had every one a quarter of a twopenny bun or cake, and everyone a glass of beere, of about halfe a pint.' (Richard Gough, *The History of Myddle*, ed. David Hey (1981), p. 160.)

[84] Documented in J. Howlet (a pseudonym for Robert Parsons), *A brief discourse why catholiques refuse to goe to church* (Douai, 1580), John Field, *A caveat for Parson Howlet* (1581), and Percival Wiburn, *A checke or reproofe of M. Howlets untimely schreeching in her maiesties eares* (1581). See Patrick Collinson, 'The Puritan Classical Movement in the Reign of Elizabeth I', London Ph.D. thesis, 1957, pp. 331–7, and W. J. Sheils, *The Puritans in the Diocese of Peterborough 1558–1610*, Publications of the Northamptonshire Record Society, xxx (Northampton, 1979), 45–7.

[85] *Reports of Cases*, 200–38.

[86] *Troubles of our Catholic Forefathers*, ii. 241.

that there were no intruders. 'For either they were known by face to them, or they had testimonials from approved Ministers or eminent Christians.'[87] These 'monthly sacraments' seem to have been an especial feature of religious life in the north-west. And all over the north, on both sides of the Pennines, the order of events on days of exercise, whether regular lectures or funeral sermons, was a sermon in the morning and another in the afternoon, with the interval occupied with a shared meal, 'repetition' and psalm-singing.[88] In the south the rule on ordinary lecture days and at funerals seems to have been a single sermon, but always followed by dinner. When William Bradshaw died at Chelsea in 1618, a large number of ministers and 'a very great multitude of private persons' came to the funeral and were entertained 'after the usuall manner in such cases and on such occasions'.[89] Samuel Crook's 'constant manner' was to invite to his table those ministers and 'friends' who came to hear his lectures.[90]

IV

All these, with the trappings, were considered 'public ordinances'. But in the Wirral in the 1620s the godly from the length of the peninsula held private 'days of conference' every three weeks in the richer men's houses. The morning was spent in a kind of catechizing, the 'younger christians' answering first, the more experienced next. Then came dinner, with 'good provision made for them by the master of the family'. And then, after a psalm, more conference.[91]

We cannot say how common the sociability of such days of conference may have been in other parts of England, outside the north-west. But evenings of conference held after sermons for the purpose of 'repetition', or as preparations before the

---

[87] *Heywood's Life of Angier*, p. 79.

[88] See especially Samuel Clarke's account of his own career, with a description of religious life in the Wirral of Cheshire, *Lives of Sundry Eminent Persons*, p. 4. Extensive evidence for the northern pattern of two sermons punctuated by dinner will be found in my two articles, 'Lectures by Combination' and '"A Magazine of Religious Patterns": An Erasmian Topic Transposed in English Protestantism', in *Renaissance and Renewal in Christian History, Studies in Church History*, xiv, ed. Derek Baker (Oxford, 1977), 223–49.

[89] Clarke, *Lives of Thirty-Two English Divines*, p. 51.

[90] Ibid., p. 206.

[91] Clarke, *Lives of Sundry Eminent Persons*, p. 4.

monthly Communion or the weekly Sabbath, were an almost
universal institution in puritan circles, and one much commended by the preachers. John Udall taught that 'after the
sermon, we ought at our comming home to meet together and
say one to another, "Come, we have all beene where wee have
heard God's woord taught. Let us conferre about it." '[92] (We
note again the insistent groundbass of 'come let us go', 'come
we have been'.) Nicholas Bownd compared 'the meetings of
the godlie' to 'a great many firebrands layde together'.
Separated, they would soon lose their heat and die. 'So though
every man hath some grace of God's spirit in himselfe, yet it is
greatly increased by conference.'[93] When John Wilson, a preacher
from the Craven district, was charged by Archbishop Sandys
with persuading people to hold private assemblies, he replied:
'My lord you now put me in mind of a dutie that I have not
yet donne but by the grace of God I will remember it
hereafter, and will exhort the people of God to meet together,
to comfort and edifie one another in these things which they
have been taught and learned.'[94] Such exercises were not easily
distinguishable from the catechizing, prayer, and psalm-
singing which was part of the daily round of every godly
houshold. The Suffolk preacher Samuel Fairclough ended the
Sabbath by examining his whole family on what they
remembered of the sermon. Then, after supper, he caused
some part of Foxe's 'Book of Martyrs' to be read and, having
prayed, concluded the day with the singing of a psalm.[95]

The office which Fairclough performed in his parsonage
laymen, 'private christians', performed for their own families.
Mrs Margaret Corbet, like so many of her contemporaries,
took notes at sermons which she then used in catechizing her
servants, especially in preparation for receiving the Communion. The servants then gave an account of their knowledge to
her husband.[96] Given the size and fluidity of larger households,
it was difficult to tell in all circumstances whether such
exercises were confined to one family, or whether they were, in
the eyes of the law, a kind of conventicle, drawn from several

[92] Udall, *Certaine sermons*, sig. Iiiiij.
[93] Nicholas Bownd, *The doctrine of the Sabbath* (1595), p. 219.
[94] Dr Williams's Library, MS Morrice II, fol. 56.
[95] Clarke, *Lives of Sundry Eminent Persons*, p. 181.
[96] Clarke, *Lives of Ten Eminent Divines*, pp. 506–7.

families. In the Essex parish of Aythrop Roding, on a Sunday in the 1580s, the godly met in the house of one of the parishioners, 'to the number of tenne persons or thereabouts, of his kindred and neighbours, being invited thether to supper'. Over the meal they conferred together about the doctrine learned earlier that day at a public catechizing. After supper, some 'attended to one that read in the Booke of Martyrs', and the rest to a minister *'in company with them'*, who was reading by the fireside *'a peece of a catechisme . . . which he had then in his hand'*.[97] Such Rembrandtesque scenes can be projected upon many hundreds of godly households. At Great Wakering in Essex the faithful met 'sometimes . . . at one neighbour's house, sometimes at another's, that are well-given'.[98] When Julines Herring preached at Shrewsbury in the 1620s and 30s, his sermons were repeated at three different houses 'by course', to avoid suspicion.[99] So many came to the exercise of repetition in John Angier's 'little house' at Ringley that it was necessary to divide into two meetings. Angier used to say: 'Better want room than good company.'[1] At Bristol in the same years, 'the chief resolved and watchful professors' met for repetition and days of fasting and prayer in the houses of a grocer, a writing master, a farrier, and a victualler and butcher.[2]

These groups were at least potentially conventicles, especially when no minister was present. It was the common practice of 'private christians' to conceive prayer on such occasions, and this capacity was perhaps the hallmark of an 'eminent' or 'noted' Christian. 'Fain would I have been a professor with them, but wanted parts', wrote Laurence Claxton, remembering his apprentice efforts to memorize a form of prayer which could then be repeated as if it were an original conception.[3] At Dedham in 1584 the question was put 'whether it were convenient a woman shuld pray, having a

---

[97] Sir Julius Caesar to Sir Francis Walsingham, 18 May 1584; BL Lansdowne MS 157, fol. 186. The underlined passage was erased by the writer.

[98] Essex Record Office, AEA/12, fol. 92ᵛ.

[99] Clarke, *Lives of Thirty-Two English Divines*, p. 162.

[1] *Heywood's Life of Angier*, 56.

[2] *The Records of a Church of Christ in Bristol, 1640–1687*, ed. Roger Hayden, Bristol Record Society Publications, xxvii (Bristol, 1974), 84.

[3] Laurence Claxton (or Clarkson), *The lost sheep found* (1660), pp. 5–6.

better gift than her husband?'[4] But private meetings were for conference, not preaching, and 'private christians' were not expected to teach and expound on the basis of their own knowledge. The conventions of repetition preserved the sovereignty of the minister in exposition and differed essentially from the inspirational 'prophecy' of the separatist and baptist congregations.

But if the transition from repetition to original exposition was critical, it might in some circumstances appear a natural transition. The Baptist William Kiffin recorded how, as a London apprentice, he joined with other young men in a regular hour of prayer and spiritual communication, 'or else to repeat some sermon which he had heard before'. After a while the little group began to read some passage of Scripture and to 'speake from it what it pleased God to enable us'. 'Wherein', remembered Kiffin, 'I found great advantage, and by degrees did arrive to some small measure of knowledge.' His next step was to join one of several independent congregations which existed in London in the 1630s.[5] According to the tradition concerning the origins of Broadmead Baptist Church in Bristol, a gathered church grew by degrees out of the practice of repetition, the godly 'repeating their notes to one another, whetting it on their hearts'. After twenty years of this activity a few, and especially the women in the circle, 'had strength to begin to goe farther'. Soon the riotous mob, 'the rude multitude and seamen', were complaining of the novelty of 'a Church with a Chimny in it'.[6] As early as 1641, a report from Norwich spoke of 'conventicles every night', 'as publickely knowne as the sermons in the day time, and thay say much more frequented'.[7] When in the 1650s the 'good men' of

[4] *The Presbyterian Movement in the Reign of Queen Elizabeth As Illustrated by the Minute Book of the Dedham Classis 1582–1589,* ed. R. G. Usher, Camden 3rd ser. viii (1905), 35.

[5] *Remarkable Passages in the Life of William Kiffin Written by Himself,* ed. William Orme (1823), pp. 11–14. On Kiffin, see Murray Tolmie, *The Triumph of the Saints: The Separate Churches of London 1616–1649* (Cambridge, 1977), Michael R. Watts, *The Dissenters, i. From the Reformation to the French Revolution* (Oxford, 1978), B. R. White, 'How Did William Kiffin Join the Baptists?', *Baptist Quarterly,* xxiii (1969–70), 201–7. Among Kiffin's fellow apprentices was John Lilburne.

[6] *Records of a Church of Christ,* 86.

[7] *The Knyvett Letters 1620–1644,* ed. Bertram Schofield, Norfolk Record Society, xx (1949), 98–9.

Royston hired a private room in an inn on market day it was to 'talk freely of the things of God'.[8]

V

The forms of religious life which have now been described, together with the social civilities and amenities connected with them, point to the existence of what John Bossy, writing of the English catholics, has defined as a 'community'.[9] The puritans who composed the godly community were mentally and emotionally separated by their radical estrangement from conventional society and its mores and recreations, and by the fervour and strength of their own exclusive fellowship. It was said of those who attended Samuel Clarke's days of conference in the Wirral that 'love by frequent society was nourished and increased, so that all the professors, though living ten or twelve miles asunder, were intimate and familiar as if they had been all of one household'.[10] John Bruen's prosperous gentry household was described as 'the common Inne, or constant harbour of the Church, and of God's children'. Bruen had a 'holy Sympathy with the godly' but 'a great antipathy against the profane'.[11] Mrs Elizabeth Wilkinson 'valued no friends like to those who were friends to her soul'.[12] Baxter and his people 'took great delight in the company of each other'.[13] Angier's flock at Ringley in Lancashire were 'kind and every way helpful'.[14] Dod and Cleaver told their readers: 'Vicinitie and neighbourhood will faile, and alliance and kindred will fail, but grace and religion will never faile.'[15] Thomas Taylor defined Christian faithfulness as drawing 'thy friends along to heaven with thee'.[16] Such transcendent and inspired human affection was an authentic note of the English protestant tradition, resounding in those letters from John Bradford's

---

[8] Margaret Spufford, *Contrasting Communities: English Villagers in the Sixteenth and Seventeenth Centuries* (Cambridge, 1974), p. 231.

[9] Bossy, *English Catholic Community*, pp. 108, 124.

[10] Clarke, *Lives of Sundry Eminent Persons*, p. 4.

[11] Hinde, *A faithfull remonstrance*, pp. 185, 192.

[12] Clarke, *Lives of Ten Eminent Divines*, p. 514.

[13] *Heywood's Life of Angier*, p. 56.

[14] *Reliquiae Baxterianae*, p. 85.

[15] John Dod and Robert Cleaver, *A plain and familiar exposition of the thirteenth and fourteenth chapters of the Proverbs of Salomon* (1609), p. 119.

[16] Thomas Taylor, *The progresse of the saint to full holiness* (1630), p. 341.

prison cell which must have been heard so often by the fireside on Sunday evenings, with their effusive salutations to 'dear hearts and dearlings in the Lord', 'my dear hearts and folks'.[17]

To what extent 'antipathy against the profane' involved social shunning is uncertain. In the 1591 Star Chamber case against a group of puritan ministers,[18] two hostile witnesses testified that the word 'brethren' had been used exclusively in such circles, and Thomas Edmunds, a London minister, alleged that 'as much as they might convenyently' 'those seekers of reformation' had 'refrayned to buy or sell or usually to eat or dryncke with any person or persons which are not of their faccion and opynions or inclyning that waye'.[19] But there is very little contemporary testimony to this effect, and the Star Chamber evidence may have been prompted by Richard Bancroft, who wrote: 'Touching the Communion, they brought their disciples to this order, that most of them will not communicate with anye, but such as are of their owne crew.'[20] The social implications of such exclusivism as may have typically prevailed in puritan circles are not easy to define. The will of Rose Austen, a Cranbrook widow, establishes by its mention of various godly preachers of the Kentish Weald that the testator was one of the gadding people, perhaps in Bancroft's book one of 'their owne crew'. Yet in the manner of widow women, Mrs Austen remembered a host of kinsfolk who shared twenty-two surnames. It seems unlikely that they were all members of the crew.[21]

Here and there, the godly added to the instinctive ties of religious affection the closer and more formal bond of a covenant. At Wethersfield in Essex, in the Armada year, such a covenant was concluded between the preacher Richard Rogers and some twenty persons, who were said to 'as farre exceed the common sort of them that professe the Gospell as the common professors do exceed them in religion which know not the Gospell', an interesting three-tiered analysis. Those subscribing acknowledged that they ought to have 'stood foorth among the rest of Gods people to give light unto others'.

---

[17] Foxe, *Acts and Monuments*, vii. 207, 213.
[18] Collinson, *Elizabethan Puritan Movement*, pp. 403–31.
[19] PRO Star Chamber 5 A 49/34, deposition of Thomas Edmunds.
[20] *Tracts Ascribed to Richard Bancroft*, ed. Albert Peel (Cambridge, 1953), p. 70.
[21] Collinson, 'Cranbrook and the Fletchers', p. 199.

But instead they had succumbed to 'worldliness', 'coldness', and 'a marvellous decay of godlinesse', and from recognizing where they stood they had fallen into 'communication, how the case stood betwixt God and themselves'. Their covenant with one another was to walk more closely with God, to avoid 'outward hindrances', such as 'unprofitable and dangerous company and acquaintance', to spend some part of every day in prayer, and to 'avoide strangenesse' with one another. These details were recorded in *Seven treatises,* a book which was kept constantly in print until the 1630s.[22] (Of Ignatius Jordan of Exeter it was said that he had read the Bible 'with special observation', and that 'the like course he took in reading over that useful Book of *Mr Rogers* his *Seven Treatises,* and other practical books'.)[23] In 1616 John Winthrop lighted on the Wethersfield covenant in the course of his own 'reading over' of *Seven treatises.* At once he resolved to renew his own 'covenant of walking with my God and watchinge my heart and wayes'. Three years earlier, on 17 September 1613, Winthrop and his 'company' had joined in a meeting with a number of Suffolk ministers and notable Christians which had some special significance. They resolved to meet on the same date in the following year, and in the mean time to be mindful of each other every Friday 'in desiring God to grante the petitions that were made to him that daye'.[24]

In old Boston in 1615, John Cotton with 'some scores of godly persons' 'entered into a covenant with the Lord to follow after him in the purity of his worship', which he later described as 'more than the old Non-conformity'.[25] And at Worksop, Richard Bernard concluded what Henry Ainsworth contemptuously dismissed as 'a pretended covenant' with about a hundred 'voluntary professors', 'to watch over one

---

[22] Richard Rogers, *Seven treatises, containing such direction as is gathered out of the holie scriptures* (1603), Treatise 5, chapter 13: 'An example of a Covenant made by certaine godly brethren, declaring what manifold lets the faithfull have in this world . . .'. Editions and imprints are listed for 1603 (two editions), 1605, 1610, 1616, 1624, 1627, 1629; and an epitome in 1618, 1619, 1623, 1629, 1635.

[23] Clarke, *Lives of Ten Eminent Divines,* p. 453.

[24] *Winthrop Papers,* i. 169, 199–201.

[25] John Cotton, *The way of the congregational churches cleared* (1648), Part II, 'Touching the Line of the Pedegree of the Independents in New-England', p. 20.

another, to admonish one another, . . . and thereupon to receive the Lord's Supper'.[26]

Like house meetings for repetition, which Archbishop Laud thought set up a church within the Church,[27] these covenanted groups may seem to resemble gathered and separated churches in embryo. But we must not discount the stand taken by these very groups against separatism, or the possibility that like the decision of Winthrop and Cotton to emigrate to America, such devices were a preferred alternative to making a schism against the Church of England which would break fellowship with the many godly dispersed throughout the Church. Mrs Wilkinson is said to have been 'a professed adversary to the withdrawing from the publick Congregations of the Saints'.[28] William Bradshaw was 'ever very averse' to separating and to 'withdrawing from the *publick places of Assembly,* or from any *part of Gods Worship* there used'.[29] Richard Rogers was at pains to insist that his covenanted people at Wethersfield were 'no Brownists', but 'diligent and ordinarie frequenters of publicke assemblies with the people of God'. 'Neither were their meetings Conventicles, for the disturbing of the state of the church and peace thereof, as many imagine that there can be no private fellowship among Christians, but it is to such ends.'[30] Bernard was said to have covenanted his Worksop flock 'in policy', to keep them from John Smyth's schism.[31] Many years later, Baxter wrote of his Kidderminster congregation that if he had not allowed them private meetings, 'such as were lawful and profitable, they would have run to such as were unlawful and hurtful'.[32]

Where exceptionally favourable conditions allowed it, forms of covenant might be imposed on entire parochial congregations, in the spirit of Widley's conviction that every country was Jewry, every city Jerusalem. This was more like involuntary religion presenting itself in voluntarist forms and

---

[26] Richard Bernard, *Plaine evidences: the Church of England is apostolicall, the seperation schismaticall* (1610), Ainsworth, *Counterpoyson,* pp. 155–6; *The Works of John Robinson,* ed. R. Ashton, ii (1851), 101.

[27] *Reports of Cases,* p. 237.

[28] Clarke, *Lives of Ten Eminent Divines,* p. 514.

[29] Clarke, *Lives of Thirty-Two English Divines,* p. 57.

[30] Rogers, *Seven treatises,* p. 477.

[31] *Works of Robinson,* ii. 101.

[32] G. F. Nuttall, *Visible Saints* (1957), p. 50.

language. In Dorchester in about 1630 that commanding patriarch John White composed a schedule of ten vows, which he made the condition of receiving the Communion. These solemn undertakings were prefaced, much like Rogers's Wethersfield covenant, by a confession, couched in the first person plural, of 'lukewarmnes', both in zeal for God's honour and truth and in love and affection towards the brethren; and of an increase in such faults as 'carnall security', pride, self-love of the world, contention, and envy. Those binding themselves by the vows which followed promised a general reform and renewal of religious conduct, and 'to watch our owne ways dayly and to call ourselves to a strict and often account for our failings'. But the semi-separatist leanings of the Wethersfield covenant, with its eschewal of 'unprofitable and dangerous company and acquaintance' and stress on the cultivation of intimacy within a godly clique, were replaced in the Dorchester covenant by a civic ethic of the common good which would not have been out of place in a South German city in the first age of the Reformation. The communicants of Dorchester resolved to submit themselves to brotherly admonition and to perform that Christian duty towards others, avoiding all groundless suspicions, slanders, and contentions 'as enemies to christian peace'. They undertook to enter into speedy reconcilation with any brethren from whom they differed, and 'to take nearer to our hearts our afflicted Brethrens' distresses'. But nowhere do the ten vows speak of avoiding the company of the ungodly. And 'brethren', so far from being used in any exclusive sense, refers more than once in this document to the people of other communities and countries, 'our neighbour churches', to whom Dorchester was to respond as a united Christian community. The impression conveyed by the Dorchester orders is of a godly people living under the salutary and mutual discipline which puritans had dreamed of for half a century and more : but their form is not that of orders but of a covenant voluntarily entered into.[33]

Nevertheless, the intention of John White in placing these vows in the mouths of his people was to refuse the

---

[33] Rose-Troup, *John White*, Appendix II, pp. 418–22, conflating versions of the covenant in Domestic State Papers (endorsed by Archbishop Laud) and in BL Add. MS 6394, fol. 159.

Communion to any who resisted the procedure of strict vetting which they implied. At Ketton in Suffolk the potent alliance of Sir Nathaniel Barnardiston and his minister Samuel Fairclough underpinned a design to exclude from the Lord's table the 'visibly prophane'. This required all desiring to communicate to first make a personal reaffirmation of their baptismal covenant, a form of confirmation to which Barnardiston first of any submitted himself, the rest of the congregation following suit. The body of communicants which had defined itself in this way promised to undergo regular admonition in case of 'the visible and apparent breach of that Covenant'.[34] Fairclough's biographer would like us to think that all who chose not to submit to the discipline—for that is what it was—were 'wholly silenced', and that profanity was forced to hide its head, so that drunkenness, swearing and bastardy were 'not practised', indeed 'scarce known'. But he stops short of claiming that all the inhabitants of the parish became willing Christians within the terms of the covenant. That desired state was never achieved in Ketton, nor in the New England churches where the churchmanship of Bernard, Cotton, White, and Fairclough received a more perfect expression. In these old English parishes, as in the churches of the New England way, the tables were fenced, but this was not a separation of the godly but a forcible separation of the ungodly: the driving of the bondswoman Hagar and her son Ishmael out of the tent and into the wilderness.

VI

In a study of Kentish society in this period, Peter Clark has conveyed an impression of widespread and endemic separatism, well before the Civil War. 'By the end of the [sixteenth] century', he writes, 'separatist or semi-separatist meetings had spread across much of the Kentish countryside.' He even speaks of 'hereditary separatism', with its roots in the lollard past.[35] It would be foolish to deny the presence of separatist sects in Jacobean England, not to speak of the radical puritan diaspora in the Low Countries and, presently, in New

---

[34] Clarke, *Lives of Sundry Eminent Persons*, p. 169.
[35] Peter Clark, *English Provincial Society from the Reformation to the Revolution: Religion, Politics and Society in Kent 1500–1640* (Hassocks, 1977), p. 177.

England. The existence of alternative churches is known, or can be inferred, in several places, including Norwich, Yarmouth, and Colchester. Some, like the congregations in London and Amsterdam deriving from the leadership of Henry Barrow round about 1590, were regarded as the 'ancient' churches of the separation. Others arose from more recent experiments, of which the most influential was the formation in Southwark in 1616 of an autonomous congregational church under the leadership of Henry Jacob. Jacob and many of his followers did not regard themselves as wholly separated from the godlier parish churches of London. Other members of Jacob's church were rigid separatists, and the internal debates over this issue and other developments gave rise to a little cluster of separated and semi-separated churches, a small but variegated religious undergound. In this underworld the groundwork of future denominations was being laid: congregationalists, more than one kind of baptist, and the seekers and other progenitors of the quakers.[36]

Nevertheless, the difference between separatism and semi-separatism, or what has been called 'quasi-separatism', ought not to be minimized, and the latter is always more probable than the former. Not every house meeting described by suspicious investigators as a 'conventicle' had the pretensions of a gathered and separated church. In 1640, Robert Abbot, vicar of Cranbrook, warned Sir Edward Dering, a knight of the shire, that the Brownists were increasing 'in many parts of the kingdom and in your deare country amongst the rest'. It was news which Dering found deeply disturbing and which influenced his allegiance in the Civil War which was soon to break out.[37] But in writing a book against 'our church-forsakers', Abbot implied that only towards the end of a quarter of a century spent in Cranbrook and as a consequence of the 'high courses of some bishops' had his ministry suffered

[36] Champlin Burrage, *The Early English Dissenters in the Light of Recent Research (1550–1641)*, 2 vols. (Cambridge, 1912); B. R. White, *The English Separatist Tradition: from the Marian Martyrs to the Pilgrim Fathers* (Oxford, 1971); Murray Tolmie, *Triumph of the Saints*; Michael R. Watts, *The Dissenters*, i.

[37] Robert Abbot to Sir Edward Dering, 15 March 1640; BL Stowe MS 184, fols. 27–30. And see further letters, 5 July, 3 October 1641; ibid., fols. 43–4, 47–8. For Dering, see Alan Everitt, *The Community of Kent and the Great Rebellion 1640–60* (Leicester, 1966), Chapter IV, 'The County Divides, 1640–2'.

rejection. 'I have loved the godly as such', he wrote, and he made it clear that he approved of what he called 'the private communion of Saints', which he did not confuse with conventicling or separatism.[38] In spite of its long exposure to lollard, protestant, and puritan evangelism, there is no reason to suppose that this large, scattered, woodland and industrial parish had witnessed any religious activity more advanced than 'private communion' before the late 1630s: not even in the late 1580s when the parish had been deprived of its more radical preachers and was often without a resident vicar, and when this clothing town experienced severe economic difficulties. An accusation of conventicling in the 1570s had brought the retort that these meetings were but 'honest and lawfull conventions'.[39]

To assume that the ultimate legacy of the protestant Reformation could only be a kind of religious anarchy is to underestimate the inhibitions and practical difficulties which stood in the way of separation, and the strength of the conventional bonds retaining many and indeed most 'forward' puritans within the formal communion and community of their parish churches. As Abbot of Cranbrook wrote in 1639: 'It is no small change to unchurch a church, to unminister a ministery, and to unworship a worship.'[40] How many English men and women of this generation were willing to deprive their children of baptism in the font of a parish church? Not many. The *Lives* gathered by Samuel Clarke, admittedly serving a post-Restoration polemical purpose, insist again and again on the antipathy expressed by the old nonconformists for divisive separatism, what Edmund Staunton called 'England's incurable wound': and these included not only presbyterians but such founding fathers of independency as William Bradshaw and William Ames.[41] The traditions of Broadmead Church at Bristol suggest how protracted and painful the birth-pangs of a gathered and fully separated church could be, even in the unusually fluid

---

[38] Collinson, 'Cranbrook and the Fletchers', pp. 201–2; Robert Abbot, *A triall of our church-forsakers* (1639), sigs. A8ᵛ, aᵛ.

[39] Collinson, 'Cranbrook and Fletchers'.

[40] Abbot, *Triall of our church-forsakers,* Sig. a2ʳ.

[41] Clarke, *Lives of Sundry Eminent Persons,* p. 170; and the various collections of Clarke's *Lives* almost *passim.*

conditions obtaining in the 1640s.[42] 'Should wee forsake the publique Assemblies and joyn together in private separated churches?' asked Allin and Shepard in 1645. And looking back on the 1630s they remarked: 'How insufferable it would then have been.' Such a strategy might have worked in great towns, but not in the countryside.[43] The London solicitor Roger Quatermayne tried to persuade Archbishop Laud that the private meetings in which he had taken part were not conventicles, and that 'godly conference' was not the same thing as preaching. 'I did always thinke that publike duties did not make voyd private, but that both might stand with a Christian.'[44] The latest historian of the separatist churches of London is in agreement. Such groups as Quatermayne's lacked 'the essential conviction that they were churches'. William Kiffin's group was at first no more than 'an ephemeral association of like-minded people'. But Murray Tolmie believes that while separation remained an unpopular alternative with the majority of puritans, the 'quasi-separatism' practised by Quatermayne contributed to a fluid and unstable religious environment in which a plurality of separatist churches was accepted as a fact of life. 'Puritan radicalism which was not in itself separatist in intent contributed in this way to the intellectual climate that permitted the separatist churches to grow.'[45]

Yet paradoxically it was voluntary and partly private religious activities which furnished the national and parochial Church with its legitimation in the eyes of many of the godly who declined to separate from it. Both separatists and non-separatists agreed that the Church of England was composed of good and bad parts. John Darrell, in a denunciation of separatism, conceded that 'the visible Church is a mixt company, compounded of christians true and false: the

---

[42] *Records of a Church of Christ*, 81–101.

[43] John Allin & Thomas Shepard, *A defence of the answere* (1648), p. 4 (Preface, dated 1645).

[44] Roger Quatermayne, *Quatermaynes conquest over Canterburies court* (1641), p. 28. See Tolmie, *Triumph of the Saints*, p. 30.

[45] Ibid., pp. 28–9. Early in the reign of James I, the lawyer Nicholas Fuller had argued along the same lines in a *cause célèbre* concerning the Sunday evening house meetings of a godly group in Yarmouth. (*The argument of Master Nicholas Fuller in the case of Thomas Lad and Richard Maunsell his clients* (1607).)

greatest part being the worst'. He thought it possible that nineteen parts out of twenty might prove to be false, 'christians only in name', but the twentieth part Christians indeed.[46] The promiscuous membership of the public assemblies had always been the nub of the separatist indictment of any churchmanship less drastically exclusive than their own. In Henry Ainsworth's words, it was a rock of offence 'that all sorts of profane and wicked men have been and are, both they and their seed, received into and nourished within the bosome of your church'.[47] 'A separation we deny not', retorted the Gloucestershire minister John Sprint in his controversy with the Amsterdam separatists. 'But the difference is, we suffer for separating in the Church, you, out of the Church.'[48] We professe separation from known evilles,' wrote John Paget, pastor of the non-separated English congregation in Amsterdam, 'but not from the churches of Christ for evilles among them.'[49] In his Chelmsford preaching, the founder of Connecticut, Thomas Hooker, distinguished between two kinds of communion, public and private. The public congregation was 'like to open pastures that are common for every man's cattle'. The public authority which gave warrant to public meetings ought to excommunicate and exclude the wicked, denying them as it were their commoners' rights. But if it failed in this duty the godly could do no more than regret it. 'I can keep a

---

[46] John Darrell, *A treatise of the church written against them of the Separation, commonly called Brownists* (1617), pp. 25, 28–9.

[47] Ainsworth, *Counterpoyson*, p. 3.

[48] John Sprint, polemic against the separatists in *Considerations touching the poynts in difference, between the godly ministers and people of the Church of England, and the seduced brethren of the separation* (?1607) and *Arguments: That the best Assemblies of the present Church of England are true visible churches* (?1607), works no longer extant and known only from Ainsworth's citations in *Counterpoyson*. This argument is cited at sig. A. Cf. the letter written by Dionis Fitzherbert to a member of Robinson's congregation at Leiden: 'Happy had yt been for yow . . . if yow had lived among our poore afflicted brethren, where the sharpe scourge of persecution would have kept yow from theis weake variances with them that love yow so well, where yow should have felt by experience how farre we are departed from Babilon, who gladly would overwhelme us all; soe truely doth she feele we are not onely gone but fly out of her.' (Quoted, Michael E. Moody, 'Puritan Versus Separatist: A New Letter', *Journal of the United Reformed Church History Society*, ii (1981), 243–5.)

[49] John Paget, *An arrow against the separation of the Brownists* (Amsterdam, 1618), p. 19. For Paget and his church, see Alice C. Carter, *The English Reformed Church in Amsterdam in the Seventeenth Century* (Amsterdam, 1964).

man out of my house, but I cannot fling him out of the open congregation: that belongs only to those that are in place and authority.' But private communion was another matter and existed on a voluntary basis. 'Hence it is the duty of all the saints of God not to close in communion and unnecessary company and inward familiarity with those that are the deniers of the power of godliness.'[50]

Separatists and non-separatists were at one in their belief that within the parishes of the Church of England were many thousands of elect and converted Christians. Non-separatists insisted that the separatists made an unjust schism against this godly leaven, consisting of what Sprint called 'the best of our assemblies' and 'the true members of our best assemblies'.[51] John Robinson complained of Richard Bernard's tactic in speaking only for 'christian professors', 'some few in the land which favour the forward preachers, frequent their sermons and advance the cause of reformation'. Whereas for Robinson the question was one of communion with the Church of England as a whole, 'the body of the land'.[52] But Robinson himself, unlike Henry Ainsworth, was not settled in the principle of a total withdrawal from the company of the unseparated godly. In Cotton's famous phrase, he 'came backe indeed the one halfe of the way' from strict separatism to argue for *the lawfulnesse of hearing ministers in the Church of England.*[53] Meanwhile, in London, Henry Jacob's gathered church was distinguished by the semi-separatism of Jacob himself and of a party within his flock whose principles allowed them to attend sermons in parish churches and, in effect, to concede the common Christianity which they shared with non-separated godly Christians.[54]

---

[50] Thomas Hooker, *The carnal hypocrite* (?1626), in *Thomas Hooker: Writings in England and Holland, 1626–1633*, ed. George H. Williams, Norman Pettit, Winfried Hergest, and Sargent Bush, jun., Harvard Theological Studies, xxviii (Cambridge, Mass., 1975), 110–13.

[51] Ainsworth, *Counterpoyson* (quoting Sprint), pp. 54, 61.

[52] John Robinson, *A justification of separation from the Church of England against Mr Richard Bernard his invective intituled the separatists schisme* (1610), in *Works*, ii. 5.

[53] Cotton, *Way of the congregational churches cleared*, p. 8; John Robinson, *A treatise on the lawfulnesse of hearing ministers in the Church of England* (1634), in *Works*, iii.

[54] Tolmie, *Triumph of the Saints*, supersedes earlier accounts. But see also John van Rohr, 'The Congregationalism of Henry Jacob', *Transactions of the Congregational*

In an exchange of pamphlets with John Robinson, an anonymous anti-separatist—perhaps William Ames, perhaps William Bradshaw—asked his opponent to consider the logic of his position. If Robinson were willing to communicate with the godly at a private level, how could he justify his separation at a public level? For the elasticity of religious conditions obtaining in England made the distinction between private and public hard to sustain. What of those many religious exercises where attendance was entirely voluntary, without any element of constraint, and where the Prayer Book was never used? The vitality of voluntary religious practice was such that a free and voluntary covenant such as Ames admitted to be necessary for the existence of a true church could be said to exist implicitly, wherever such conditions existed. What if a competent minister, 'by connivence of those that are in authoritie' should exercise a public ministry, 'not having any further warrant but the seale which God setteth to his labor in the fruight of it and the consent of the people that repare unto him for instruction'? Or what if he should take a pastoral charge, 'having the Bishop's and patron's admission', but 'cheifly and professedly grounding his calling upon the people's choice'?[55] Later in the century Richard Baxter composed catalogues of a generation of preachers who had contrived to exercise a ministry such as Ames had described, in 'privileged peculiar places':

And the Nonconformists lived according to their various opportunities: some of them conformed, some were by connivance permitted in peculiar and small impropriate places or chappells that had little maintenance in the publick ministry, which kept them from gathering secret churches. Some of them had their liberty a great part of their lives.[56]

Historical Society, xix. 107–22; and Stephen Brachlow, 'Puritan Theology and Radical Churchmen in Pre-Revolutionary England: With Special Reference to Henry Jacob and John Robinson', Oxford D.Phil. thesis, 1978.

[55] *A manuduction for Mr Robinson* (Dort, 1614) and *A second manuduction for Mr Robinson* (n.p., 1615). Robinson interposed himself in *A manumission to a manuduction* (1615). Both the *Manuduction* and *Second manuduction* are attributed to Ames. However, the *Manuduction* was appended to a larger work by William Bradshaw, *The unreasonableness of the separation* (Dort, 1614), and Peter Milward appears to lean to Bradshaw's authorship in his *Religious Controversies of the Jacobean Age* (1978), pp. 61–2.

[56] Richard Baxter, *The nonconformists plea for peace* (1679), pp. 121 ff. Among those whose ministry was preserved in this way was the celebrated divine and author John

And when one bishop silenced them the next gave them liberty (as Bishop Bridgeman did after Bishop Morton's silencing some) and when they were silenced they went off into another diocese where they rubd out a yeare or more, and then to another. And so were still in some hope of public liberty.[57]

Since Baxter was defending and illustrating the ancient and honourable tradition of 'mere nonconformity' for the instruction of the post-1662 generation, his description errs on the pessimistic side as an account of ecclesiastical life in the days of James I.

Ames (or Bradshaw) concludes: 'Now to the poynt: so many parrish assemblies of England as have any competent number of good Christians in them, united together for to worship God ordinarily in one societie, so many have essentiall and integrall forme of a visible churche: and all they have entyre right to Christ and to all the meanes of enjoying him: howsoever they are defective in the puritie of their combination, and in the complete free exercising of their power.' Such churches were 'entyre spirituall bodies, though civilly combined into a diocesan government'.[58] Robinson protested that this was an equivocation, 'pretending to prove publick communion upon private'.[59] And more recently Perry Miller accused Ames of 'glaring inconsistency' and 'adroit subterfuge'.[60] If this discussion has established anything it may have shown that Ames stood on firmer ground than Miller supposed. It was not 'labyrinthine reasoning' but some experience of a rich world of voluntary religious practice which led so many puritans to turn away from strict separation and to proceed through what Allin and Shepard called 'a wide door ... of liberty otherwise'.[61] That door

---

Dod, who was protected in Northamptonshire by the Drydens of Canons Ashby and the Knightleys of Fawsley, whence he wrote to Sir Robert Harley in December 1639: 'I thanke God I have no intermission of my peace.' (BL Loan 29/119.)

[57] Richard Baxter, *A second true defence of the meer nonconformist* (1681), pp. 33, 53, 54. I owe these Baxter references to Geoffrey Nuttall.

[58] *A second manuduction*, pp. 33–4.

[59] John Robinson, *Treatise on the lawfulnesse of hearing*, in *Works*, ii. 361; and extensively in *A manumission*.

[60] Perry Miller, *Orthodoxy in Massachusetts 1630–1650: A Genetic Study* (Cambridge, Mass., 1933), pp. 83, 84, 88, 89, 92–6.

[61] Allin and Shepard, *Defence of the answer*, p. 4.

admittedly led many to America, where in Massachusetts parish life of the English kind was left behind, the better part became the greater part, the private became the public and the ordinances of the Church were reserved to 'visible saints'.

But in England the semi- or quasi-separation of private and voluntary religion was defined along what John Bossy, writing of the catholic community, has called 'the optimum line': 'one which would provide the maximum of self-determining capacity and the minimum of destructive isolation'.[62]

Where that left the wider communion of the parish church is a question which cannot be answered without implying a judgement about the character and quality of parochial life, not only in the seventeenth century but in the sixteenth century and earlier still. If, as Christopher Hill has tended to assume, the traditional parish was all that catholic and Anglican apologists supposed it to be, conforming to Richard Hooker's model, then it may be hard to deny that puritan voluntarism, even where it stopped short of overt and formal separatism, was nevertheless a powerful solvent of traditional religious forms and of traditional society. The distinction between private and public communion, private and public duties, however important for the consciences of seventeenth-century Christians, may be an irrelevant distraction for the social historian of religion, whose proper theme in this period, according to Christopher Hill, is 'the breakdown of the parish'. But John Bossy has suggested that much late medieval religious life was characterized in its social forms not by the strength and inclusiveness of its parochial components but by bonds of kinship and alliance, of 'sib and well-willing', connecting the 'constituent cells of the christian community as a whole'. The parish may have been 'an assemblage of actually or potentially hostile entities among whom its function was to maintain a precarious peace'. The sense of genuine parochial community may have been 'an exceptional, temporary and precarious feeling'.[63]

---

[62] Bossy, *English Catholic Community*, p. 143.

[63] John Bossy, 'Blood and Baptism: Kinship, Community and Christianity in Western Europe from the Fourteenth to the Seventeenth Centuries', in *Sanctity and Secularity: The Church and the World, Studies in Church History*, x, ed. Derek Baker (Oxford, 1973), 129–43.

If this is correct, then it may be proper to interpret the voluntary and quasi-separatist religious behaviour of the English puritans as the pursuit of religious and social instincts which had always existed both within and beyond the parish: or even as a reversion to religious and affectionate relationships that were faster than those of mere 'neighbourhood and propinquity' and resembled the ties of blood relationship: 'fragmented sociability' of the godly kind, implying fragmented unsociability in all dealings with the godless. It was said of the godly of the Wirral that they were 'as intimate and familiar as if they had been all of one household'.[64] Whereas it was also said that 'many dislike that the godly should be civilly familiar with vaine and irreligious persons'.[65]

John Bossy has described the post-Reformation Church of England as 'a rather rigid institution with a limited capacity to absorb autonomous movements'.[66] This is conventional wisdom for students not only of catholicism but of methodism, evangelicalism, and tractarianism. But this investigation of some voluntary manifestations of the religion of protestants within our period has suggested almost the reverse. For all its evident imperfections, the Jacobean Church had the capacity to contain within its loose and sometimes anomalous structures vigorous forms of voluntary religious expression. Like the London citizen Roger Quatermayne and unlike Archbishop Laud it could distinguish between public and private duties and it acknowledged, in effect, that 'both might stand with a christian'.

The historian cannot tell whether a Church so constituted could itself have stood for any length of time in circumstances other than those which obtained after the York House Conference of 1626. We cannot re-run the film without Laud as a leading actor, and without the Civil War, the Interregnum, the re-establishment of the Church of England, and the banishment of Dissent. Within a traditional perspective, Jacobean church life as this book has described it was an

[64] Clarke, *Lives of Sundry Eminent Persons*, p. 4.

[65] Robert Cushman, *The cry of a stone* (1642), quoted in Stephen Foster, 'The Faith of a Separatist Layman: The Authorship, Context, and Significance of *The Cry of a Stone*', *William and Mary Quarterly*, 3rd ser. xxxiv (1977), 401.

[66] Bossy, *English Catholic Community*, p. 397.

aberration, the Church of 1662 the proper expression of the true character of Anglicanism. Yet Ian Green has shown that the Restoration Church in its origins was also a Church of moderation and latitude, as judged by its clergy if not by its more fervent cavalier sons, a Church in continuity with the Cromwellian Church in some of its personnel, and a true successor to the Jacobean Church as we have described it.[67] Among its clergy, after 1662 and until his death in 1677, was John Angier of Denton, to whom the godly had flocked in the 1630s and who had been brought up under 'plain and powerful' Mr Rogers at Dedham and Cotton at Boston. It was the Church of the next generation which, having sustained the shock of 1688, found itself in a critical impasse and (for a season) embraced a narrower constitution.

The advantage of terminating these enquiries at the death of James I has been the possibility of a relatively dispassionate view of the religious and ecclesiastical forms of the Elizabethan and more especially of the Jacobean Church and of their merits, redressing the imbalances of some earlier accounts. But there has been some risk of idealizing the pre-Laudian situation and of minimizing its tensions and potentially destructive anomalies. It was with legitimate and sombre apprehension that the 'forward' protestants who have provided the theme of this last chapter contemplated their future. John Winthrop wrote to his wife in May 1629: 'I am veryle persuaded God will bring some heavye affliction upon this land, and that speedylye.'[68] As Thomas Hooker prepared to leave his Chelmsford friends in 1631 he said that he would deal plainly with them. 'As sure as God is God, God is going from England.'[69] When people asked the Suffolk puritan seer John Carter 'shall we have popery again?' he would answer: 'You shall not need to fear fire and fagot any more: but such dreadfull divisions will be amongst God's people and Professors, as will equalize the greatest persecutions.'[70] It was a sound prediction.

---

[67] I. M. Green, *The Re-Establishment of the Church of England 1660–1663* (Oxford, 1978).

[68] *DNB*, art. Winthrop.

[69] *Thomas Hooker: Writings in England and Holland*, 244.

[70] Clarke, *Lives of Ten Eminent Divines*, p. 10. See a similar prediction attributed to Julines Herring, *Lives of Thirty-Two English Divines*, pp. 163–4.

Index

DATE DUE
